# CAMBRIDGE LATIN AMERICAN STUDIES

32

Haciendas and Ranchos
in the Mexican Bajío

LEÓN 1700–1860

# Haciendas and Ranchos in the Mexican Bajío

*León 1700–1860*

D. A. BRADING

*Lecturer in Latin American History*
*University of Cambridge, and Fellow of St Edmund's House*

CAMBRIDGE UNIVERSITY PRESS

CAMBRIDGE

LONDON · NEW YORK · MELBOURNE

Published by the Syndics of the Cambridge University Press
The Pitt Building, Trumpington Street, Cambridge CB2 1RP
Bentley House, 200 Euston Road, London NW1 2DB
32 East 57th Street, New York, NY 10022, USA
296 Beaconsfield Parade, Middle Park, Melbourne 3206, Australia

First published 1978

Printed in Great Britain by
Western Printing Services Ltd, Bristol

*Library of Congress Cataloguing in Publication Data*
Brading, D. A.
Haciendas and ranchos in the Mexican Bajío, León,
1700–1860
(Cambridge Latin American studies; 32)
Bibliography: p.
Includes index.
1. Land tenure – Mexico – León region – History.
2. Agriculture – Economic aspects – Mexico – León region –
History. 3. Haciendas – Mexico – León region – History.
I. Title. II. Series.
HD 330.L46B7    338.1'0972'4    77–90203
ISBN 0 521 22200 1

IN MEMORY OF MY FATHER

Men who love wisdom should acquaint themselves
with a great many particulars.

Heraclitus (fragment 3)

# CONTENTS

| | | | |
|---|---|---|---|
| | *Tables, figures and maps* | *page* | ix |
| | *Preface* | | xi |
| | *Measures and Money* | | xiv |
| | *Glossary* | | xv |
| 1 | Introduction: the Mexican hacienda | | 1 |
| 2 | The Bajío | | 13 |
| 3 | Population | | 39 |
| 4 | The structure of agricultural production | | 61 |
| 5 | Profits and rents: three haciendas | | 95 |
| 6 | Landlords | | 115 |
| 7 | Rancheros | | 149 |
| 8 | Agricultural prices and the demographic crises | | 174 |
| 9 | Epilogue: agrarian reform 1919–40 | | 205 |
| | APPENDICES | | |
| 1 | Select genealogy of the Marmolejo family | | 218 |
| 2 | Select genealogy of the Austri, Septién and Obregón families | | 219 |
| 3 | Archival references of inventories of estate and sales | | 221 |
| | *Archival abbreviations* | | 225 |
| | *Notes* | | 226 |
| | *Index* | | 249 |
| | *Bibliography* | | 243 |

# TABLES, FIGURES AND MAPS

## Tables

1  Approximate area of Pénjamo haciendas 1707–51  *page*  23
2  Pénjamo: arrendatarios and ranchos 1792–1833  26
3  Produce, costs and profits of La Erre estate 1700–09  32
4  Mariscal de Castilla estates: tenants and rent 1772  33
5  Juchitlán and Los Panales: production and income 1752–72  35
6  *Villa* of León: leading occupations 1719  40
7  Parish of León: census of 1781  41
8  León: intermarriage rates 1782–85, 1792–93  45
9  Age at marriage: León 1782–93 1858–60  49
10  Baptisms, burials and marriages: León 1751–1860  51
11  Baptisms of Spaniards, *castas* and Indians: León 1696–1820  52
12  Marriages of Spaniards, *castas* and Indians: León 1711–1820  53
13  Burials of Spaniards, *castas* and Indians: León 1680–1820  54
14  Variations in the ethnic composition of marriages, baptisms and burials  55
15  Proportion of infants (*párvulos*) in recorded deaths 1755–1809  57
16  Maize production in the parishes of León and Silao: tithe returns 1661–1788  70
17  Livestock production: tithe returns in the parish of León 1661–1767  71
18  Otates and Laborcita: maize production 1752–67  74
19  The expansion of cultivated area within haciendas  80
20  San Juan de los Otates: estate values 1661–1854  82
21  Inventory land values in León and Rincón 1706–1845  84
22  Inventory values of livestock in León and Rincón 1661–1849  86

ix

23  Estimated value of Church mortgages on haciendas
    in León and Rincón                                          92
24  San José de Duarte: inventory of estate 1758                96
25  Duarte: accounts rendered 1811–18                           98
26  Duarte: maize production and sales 1811–18                 100
27  San Juan de los Otates: inventory of estate 1787           105
28  Otates: accounts rendered 1814–18                          106
29  Sauz de Armenta: inventory of estate 1823                  109
30  Sauz de Armenta: accounts rendered 1827–39                 111
31  Sauz de Armenta: maize production and sales
    1827–39                                                    112
32  Changes in hacienda ownership: León and Rincón
    1711–1861                                                  116
33  Sales of estates of Miguel González del Pinal
    1705–29                                                    121
34  Purchases and inventory value of Obregón-
    Valenciana estates 1781–1860                               137
35  The formation of San Nicolás hacienda: purchases
    1742–51                                                    158
36  Estimated area of ranchero sector: León 1828               172
37  Annual prices and production of maize: tithe returns
    in the parishes of León and Silao 1660–1789                180
38  Infant mortality during smallpox epidemics and
    famine 1779–1804                                           188
39  Maize prices and burials: León and Silao 1782–88           190
40  Prices of meat, hides and tallow in municipal
    slaughterhouse; León 1616–1808                             195
41  Maize prices at León and Comanja: voluntary
    tithe returns 1833–56                                      197
42  Creation of ejidos: León 1926–64                           211

## Figures

1  Maize prices: León and Silao 1690–1788                      183
2  Baptisms and burials: León 1750–1850                        185
3  Baptisms and burials of Indians: León 1720–1820             186
4  Baptisms and burials of *castas*: León 1720–1820            187

## Maps

1  The Bajío in the mid nineteenth century                    xviii
2  León; haciendas and ranchos *c.* 1850                       120

# PREFACE

In the winter months of 1969, shortly after the completion of *Miners and Merchants in Bourbon Mexico*, I returned to the archives of Mexico. In that book I had argued that 'the Mexican hacienda was a sink through which drained without stop the surplus capital accumulated in the export economy'. But for the historian, as much as for the scientist, hypothesis often runs ahead of available evidence. It was now time to verify this proposition. Anxious to avoid a wild goose chase for random data, a procedure bound to turn up material biased in favour of my case, I chose to concentrate on haciendas in the Bajío, the region most affected by eighteenth-century expansion of silver production. In the event, only León was found to possess a continuous series of records. The scholar may propound his questions, but it is the sources which prescribe the limits of the answers. In point of fact, the very reliance on public documents, be they municipal, notarial or parochial, precluded any sustained treatment of the central issue of the original hypothesis – the rate of agricultural profit and its relation to capital investment. Only the internal accounts of individual haciendas will yield a satisfactory resolution of this problem. Similarly, without access to such papers it was difficult to obtain any sure impression of the organisation of production or the disposition of the work-force within the great estate. To turn to the positive side, concentration on one district soon uncovered an unsuspected complexity in the pattern of land tenure. The existence of a numerous body of small-holders and tenant-farmers, *rancheros* as they came to be called, was a major discovery. Then again, the sheer pace of change in the eighteenth century, the dramatic growth in population and rapid clearance of scrub-land for agriculture, came as a surprise. Finally, I experienced the pleasure of meeting old friends in new clothes: miners and merchants from Guanajuato figured as landowners in León.

A few words concerning sources may be useful to others engaged in similar study. Contrary to expectation, the section *tierras* in the national archive in Mexico City, which includes all litigation about land tried by the audiencia, proved unrewarding. By contrast, the municipal archive of León ranks among the best in Mexico, with a set of records stretching from the late sixteenth century until the present day. By far the most valuable documents here were the inventories of estate, filed by executors after the death of landowners, from which the physical anatomy of haciendas can be reconstructed. Similarly, the notary register, which covers almost three centuries of history, contains virtually all transactions in landed property and the last wills and testaments of most landowners. From about 1890 onwards, however, it is advisable to consult the public property register in which all notarised transactions were also inserted. Then again, the parochial archive, still lamentably housed in the dispensary, possesses relatively complete records of baptisms, burials and marriages from the close of the seventeenth century until 1864 when new parishes were formed. At Guanajuato, the historical archive has important materials dealing with land titles for León and the local Department of Agrarian Affairs is the relevant source for information about modern *ejidos*. Finally, at Morelia the former episcopal archive now deposited in the Casa Morelos, preserves the parochial tithe reports sent to the diocesan authorities. It was my privilege to discover the existence of these remarkable documents.

In the course of seven years of research and writing I have incurred many debts, academic and otherwise, which it is a pleasure to acknowledge. In particular, I wish to thank Richard M. Morse and the History Department at Yale University for their succour and welcome at a difficult moment in my migration from Berkeley to Cambridge. My wife, Celia Wu, collaborated with me in both the compilation and computation of the demographic data and figured as co-author of the first version of the chapter on population which was published in the *Journal of Latin American Studies*. Eric Van Young, when still a graduate student at Berkeley, assisted in gathering statistical material, both at Morelia and León; I benefited from his comments. Robson Tyrer made a helpful preliminary survey of records in León. Claude Morin kindly permitted me to read his dissertation on the diocese of Michoacán and in addition sent me valuable population estimates to which reference is drawn in the text. At León my chief debt is to José Luis Leal, whose kind hospitality lightened my way: he opened the notary records still housed in his office without reservation or time-limit. Similarly, both Eduardo Salceda López and Jesús Rodríguez Frausto, respectively the directors of the historical archives at León and Guanajuato, made valuable suggestions as to the location of certain materials. Mariano González Leal presented me with a copy of the rare Catastral Map of León compiled by Edmundo Leal. Beatriz Braniff permitted me to read the title deeds of the hacienda called Jalpa de Cánovas. Enrique Florescano, from whose wide knowledge of agrarian history I have generally benefited, helped me find the tithe returns for León in the Casa Morelos. On different occasions conversation with Ward Barrett, Jan Bazant and William Taylor proved useful. Needless to say, I alone am responsible for the arguments and conclusions put forward in this book. Finally, without the financial support provided by a years' grant from the Ford Foundation's Foreign Area Fellowship Programme and a further award for a second summer in Mexico from the Social Science Research Council of the United States, the research for this study could never have been undertaken. At Cambridge, I wish to thank Mrs Helen Clements, secretary at the Centre of Latin American Studies, for typing the manuscript.

# MEASURES AND MONEY

*Peso:* the silver peso of Mexico, sometimes referred to as the *peso fuerte* or *duro* was equal in value to the American dollar of that epoch

*Real:* there were eight silver *reales* in each Mexican peso

*Fanega:* although this unit of dry measure is usually taken to equal 1.5 English bushels, at León *fanegas* comprised 90.817 litros or about 2.5 bushels

*Varas:* all yards mentioned in the text are Mexican *varas* equal to 33 English inches or 0.838 metres

*Hectare:* equals 2.471 acres

*Fanega de sembradura:* the conventional area of land on which was sown a fanega of maize, equal to 8.813 acres or 3.5664 hectares. It formed a rectangle measuring 276 yards long and 184 yards wide. There were twelve *fanegas de sembradura* in a *caballería*

*Fanega de sembradura ranchera:* unit employed in the Bajío. There were seven in a *caballería*; it hence equalled 15.1085 acres or 6.1128 hectares

*Caballería:* equal to 105.765 acres and 42.7953 hectares. It measures 1,104 *varas* by 552 yards

*Vecindad:* in León this generally comprised 3.5 caballerías, i.e. 370 acres or 150 hectares

*Sitio de ganado menor:* grazing land for sheep and goats, 2,500 yards square, equal to 1,928.388 acres or 780.2711 hectares. There were 18.232 caballerías in a sitio

*Sitio de ganado mayor:* the large pasture grant, 5,000 Mexican yards square, equal to 4,388.867 acres or 1,755.61 hectares. There were 41.023 caballerías in each large sitio

---

*Source:* W. L. Orozco, *Legislación y jurisprudencia sobre terrenos baldíos,* II, 740–59.

# GLOSSARY

To avoid an unsightly text Spanish terms which occur frequently have not been italicised save where confusion might arise.

agostadero: seasonal or rough pasture land
agrarista: supporter of land distribution
alcabala: sales tax
alcalde mayor: district magistrate
alcaldía mayor: district, at times equal to an English county, governed by an alcalde mayor
alférez real: senior member of town council
alhóndiga: municipal grain market
alquilados: agricultural labourers, hired by the day
aparceros: sharecroppers
arrendatarios: tenant farmers
arrimados: squatters or sub-tenants
arroba: a unit of weight, equal to 25 pounds
audiencia: high court of justice
caballería: an area of land, equal to 105.8 acres. See *Measures and Money*
cabildo: town council
cacique: Indian lord or chief
cajero: apprentice merchant
capellanía: a chaplaincy or chantry fund, yielding 5% interest
carga: a load
carnero: sheep ready for slaughter
casco: administrative centre of landed estate, the main buildings
catastro: register of property, census
castas: persons of mixed ethnic ancestry, half-breeds
caudillo: military leader
censo: mortgage or loan charged on property at 5% interest
composición: fee or tax paid to the Crown for lands occupied without due title

congregación: a village, a civic unit
consulado: the merchant guild and its court
creole: Spaniard born in America
ejido: lands held under communal tenure; since the Revolution the
    communities which are endowed with communal lands
encomienda: a grant of Indian tributaries
encomendero: possessor of an encomienda
eriaza: uncleared or untilled land
estancia: grazing land, a ranch
fanega: a measure of dry weight, either 1.5 or 2.5 bushels
fanega de sembradura: area of land on which was sown a fanega of
    maize. See *Measures and Money*
fiel ejecutor: town councillor charged with the inspection of weights
    and measures
fuero: exemption from royal jurisdiction, right to trial by members
    of the same profession
gachupín: Spaniard, born in Europe, resident in Mexico
ganado mayor: cattle and horses
ganado menor: sheep and goats
gañán: agricultural labourer, a peon
hacienda: a large landed estate
hacendado: owner of an hacienda
hidalgo: a person of noble or gentle birth
huerta: a garden or orchard
inquilino: in Chile a service tenant
jornalero: a labourer hired by the day
juez de composición: an itinerant judge charged with the inspection
    of land titles
labor: a large farm
libranza: a promissory note, a bill of exchange
matlazahuatl: epidemic disease of which Indians were the chief
    victims, probably a form of typhus or typhoid fever
mayorazgo: an entail
mediero: a sharecropper
mercader: a merchant
merced: original grant of land issued by Viceroy
milpa: a maize plot
obraje: a large textile workshop
oidor: a judge of audiencia
padrón: a census, a house-count
partido: a district; also the share of ore taken by mine-workers

párvulo: an infant, usually children under seven years

peninsular: A Spaniard born in the Peninsula

peón acasillado: an agricultural labourer resident on an hacienda, usually close to *casco*

peón acomodado: peon who received a maize ration as well as wage

pósito: a municipal granary

pueblo: Indian village

pulque: alcoholic beverage made from juice of maguey plant

rancho: a small landed property, a subordinate section of an hacienda

ranchero: a farmer, usually the owner of a small agricultural property

ranchería: a hamlet, a group of ranchos

real: silver coin, one eighth of a peso

regidor: town councillor

repartimiento: system of draft labour

repartimientos de comercio: public distribution (often enforced) of merchandise and stock by district magistrate

sirviente acomodado: a peon who received a maize ration as well as wage

sitio de ganado mayor: pasture land for cattle and horses: See *Money and Measures*

sitio de ganado menor: pasture lands for sheep and goats

solicitud: application for an ejido or land grant

tierra adentro: the Northern Interior

tierra labrada: arable land

tierra templada: land falling within the temperate zone

títulos de inafectabilidad: modern land titles granted to owners of small properties to prevent annexation for agrarian reform

trapiche: small workshop, a mill

vagos: vagabonds, Indians attached to neither haciendas nor pueblos

vecino: a citizen, a house-holder

vecindad: lands given to vecinos, in León about 370 acres or 3.5 caballerías

villa: town or borough

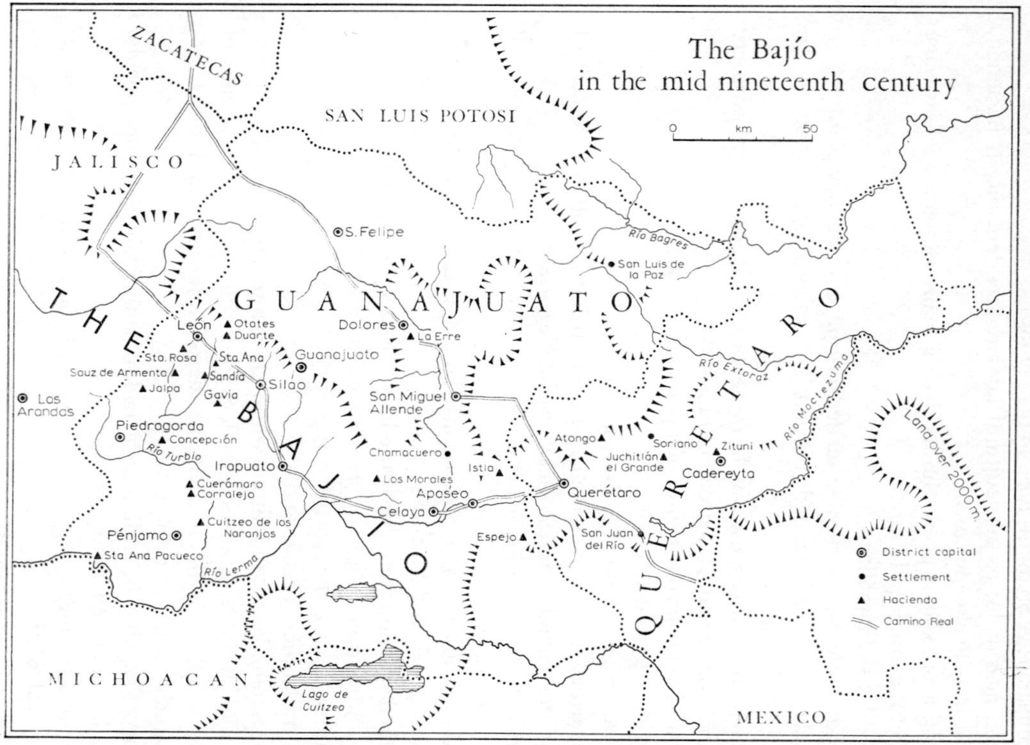

The Bajío
in the mid nineteenth century

0        50
km

○ District capital
● Settlement
▲ Hacienda
══ Camino Real

Land over 2000 m.

SAN LUIS POTOSI

ZACATECAS

JALISCO

THE GUANAJUATO BAJIO

QUERETARO

MICHOACAN

MEXICO

San Luis de la Paz

Río Bagres

S. Felipe

Dolores
La Erre

San Miguel Allende

Guanajuato

León
Otates
Duarte
Sta Ana
Sandía
Silao
Gavia
Jalpa
Sta Rosa
Souz de Armento
Piedragorda
Concepción
Río Turbio
Irapuato
Cuerámaro
Corralejo
Cuítzeo de los Naranjos
Pénjamo
Sta Ana Pacueco

Los Arandas

Chamacuero
Los Morales
Apaseo
Celaya

Atongo
Juchitlán
el Grande
Soriano Zituni
Cadereyta

Querétaro
San Juan del Río

Istla
Apaseo

Esseja

Río Extoraz
Río Moctezuma

Lago de Cuítzeo

Río León

Map I.

## CHAPTER I

# Introduction: the Mexican hacienda

In his classic account of the formation of the great estate in New Spain, François Chevalier observed with some surprise that it is not until the latter part of the eighteenth century that we encounter any contemporary description of the Mexican hacienda.[1] Moreover, it is startling to note that the first comments by travellers from abroad were almost invariably hostile. On his journey to the North in 1777–78, Juan Agustín de Morfi, a friar from the Peninsula, sharply criticised the concentration of landownership in the colony, which left the countryside vacant and uncultivated. Passing through the district of San Miguel el Grande he found that the hacienda of La Erre devoted a vast area of land to mere pasture, whereas the Indians of the neighbouring village of Dolores lacked space to plant their maize.[2] Much the same reaction was expressed by the British Minister, H. G. Ward, who in 1827 deprecated the stark contrast on Jaral between the great fortified *casco* and the squalid huts of its peons.[3]

Official opinion coincided with the views of the travellers. By the late eighteenth century belief in the economic virtues of the proprietary farmer, with the consequent condemnation of any monopoly in landownership, had become articles of faith among the enlightened administrators who served the Bourbon dynasty. The same doctrines were embraced by the Liberal politicians who fought to transform Mexican society in the decades after Independence. The authoritative text here was the *Informe. . .de ley agraria*, written in 1793 by Gaspar Melchor de Jovellanos, a Minister of the Crown and a key figure within the intellectual circles of the Spanish Enlightenment. Inspired by his reading of Adam Smith, Jovellanos attacked the mortmain of the Church and the entails of the aristocracy as the chief obstacles to the development of agriculture in the Peninsula.[4] Similarly, he advocated that the common lands of towns and villages should be distributed on an individual basis. With a free market in land thus assured, the elimination of all government regulation of the corn trade would leave the way open for an unrestricted increase in production and prosperity, based on a diffusion of ownership across the countryside.

The policies advocated by this minister of the Spanish Crown governed all future discussion of the agrarian problem in Mexico until the advent of the Revolution in the twentieth century. With the victory of the Liberal coalition in the 1850s, all Church property in land was first nationalised and then put up for sale. The common lands of the Indian communities were partitioned into family plots.[5] Entails had been abolished long since. Perhaps the only distinctive element in the Mexican political scene was a certain strain of radical *indigenismo* which condemned the great estate as an illegal institution, with title deeds vitiated by the crime of the Spanish Conquest and the subsequent seizure of Indian lands. More common, however, was the presumption that once the legal and institutional impediments to the sale and partition of landed property were removed, the pressure of market forces would automatically induce the dissolution of the haciendas.[6] It was left to Ponciano Arriaga in the Constitutional Debates of 1856 to argue that the feudal servitude which bound peons to the great estates would prevent the emergence of any broad stratum of free peasant farmers.[7]

Despite the almost universal condemnation of the hacienda by liberal intellectuals, it was not until 1895 that we encounter any juridical characterisation of the Mexican hacienda. Although the purpose of his study was a critique of recent agrarian legislation dealing with public lands, Luis Wistano Orozco concluded with a thorough-going attack upon the hacienda, defining it as a feudal institution, which, in accordance with its violent origin in the expropriations of the Spanish Conquest, continued to exercise a despotic, seigneurial power over the peons. A convinced advocate of the small property owner as the basis of political democracy, he sought to prove his case by a comparison of two districts in the state of Zacatecas. Villanueva was so dominated, not to say throttled, by six haciendas that the local town was virtually deserted owing to the absence of any market for merchandise. By contrast, its immediate neighbour, Jerez, flourished since the surrounding district was occupied by over 2,000 small proprietors, *rancheros*, among whom across the generations there operated a constant process of concentration and distribution of farmland.[8] By way of remedy, however, Orozco only called for fiscal measures to effect a partition of the great estate.

The single most influential text dealing with the Mexican hacienda was published in 1909 by an ideologue of radical positivist persuasion, who at last succeeded in providing an economic foundation for the social critique of Orozco and Jovellanos. In *Los grandes problemas nacionales*, Andrés Molina Enríquez contrasted the vast, idle terrain of the latifundia with the intensively cultivated plots of the small-holders (*rancheros*) and of the Indian villages. The great estate was not a business: it was a feudal institution, often owned by the same family for several centuries, which so tyrannised its peons that they were little better than serfs. The very reverse of entrepreneurs, these landlords sought a safe, low return upon their capital, even to the point of using fertile corn-lands for low yielding maguey plantations. Indeed, the economic survival of the hacienda depended upon the low wages of the peons and upon a policy of self-sufficiency within the estate to meet the costs of production. In the fertile cereal-growing zone of central Mexico, the great estates restricted the cultivation of wheat and maize to the limited areas of land under irrigation so that most years urban markets were supplied by rancheros and by the villages.[9] It was only after poor harvests that landowners released their stored grain to benefit from the high prices which then prevailed. Viewed from the economic standpoint, the hacienda in this zone was an artificial institution which impeded the rational exploitation of the soil by the energetic class of rancheros. Needless to say, all these points provided an ample justification for agrarian reform.

The upheaval of the Revolution prevented any further Mexican analysis of the hacienda other than in terms of polemic. Moreover, despite a certain proclivity for statistical compilation, American scholars merely extended the lines of interpretation already laid down by the Mexican jurists. For example, taking his cue from Orozco, G. M. McBride, admittedly a geographer rather than a historian, assumed that the great estate originated in the encomienda grants of Indian labour and tribute issued by the Crown to the first conquerors.[10] This view held sway for some years before Silvio Zavala demonstrated that the two institutions of encomienda and hacienda possessed quite distinct legal origins, the one being a grant of labour, and the other a grant of land.[11] They were successive rather than contemporary phenomena. Indeed, the practice of debt peonage on the great estates only slowly evolved in response to the termination, first of the encomienda, and then of the dwindling of the drafted contingents provided by the *repartimiento* system.

But the liberal critique of the great estate only obtained a persuasive, historical substantiation in the work of François Chevalier, who,
with a wealth of research material at his command, finally distinguished the feudal characteristics of the Mexican latifundium. True,
he clearly distinguished the hacienda from the encomienda, and
emphasised the importance of the export cycle based on silver-
mining, which in the years after 1570 impelled both the colonisation
of the North and the formation of the great estate. But above all
else, Chevalier stressed the spendthrift, seigneurial qualities of a
generation of settlers whose appetite for land far outstripped their
capacity to exploit its resources. Moreover, the sharp fall in silver
production which occurred during the seventeenth century provoked
an economic crisis of such intensity as to drive the great estate back
into a regime of subsistence farming in which labour was permanently retained by means of debt peonage. Reduced to a condition of rural isolation and individual self-sufficiency, haciendas in
New Spain came to resemble the latifundia of Gaul after the fall of
the Roman Empire. The Mexican peon found a counterpart in the
medieval serf.[12] In short, Chevalier emerged from the archives with
a perspective which in the last resort proved remarkably similar to
the position of Molina Enríquez. Undoubtedly, the acclaim which
greeted his book sprang from its underlying congruence with the
main critical tradition: his work will remain classic precisely because
it resumes and concludes an entire cycle of research and interpretation.

In recent years, however, a series of regional studies have raised
new questions. As is so often the case, the mass of new empirical
data has undermined long-held beliefs without as yet advancing any
general theory to explain the evidence. In his monumental survey of
the Aztecs under Spanish rule in the Valley of Mexico, Charles
Gibson described the survival of the Indian village as a free community, governed by its own elected magistrates, which frequently
retained possession of at least part of its ancestral lands until the
close of the colonial period. Turning to the haciendas, he found that
the debts of the resident peons were neither so great nor indeed so
common as to be held responsible for the reduction of an entire class
to a condition of serfdom. Indeed, to bring the harvest in, many
estates hired labourers from neighbouring Indian villages, and at
the same time were prepared to rent land to farmers from these
villages. Then again, the managers of the estates, anxious to maxi-
mise profits, kept a close watch on the movement of corn prices in

the Capital.[13] Viewed in the round, these findings offered a clear challenge to the customary perspective.

Yet more revisionist, William Taylor discovered that in the Valley of Oaxaca virtually all Indian villages remained in control of their community lands, which were more than sufficient for their needs. Equally striking, throughout the colonial period, their hereditary chieftains, the caciques, figured among the leading landowners in the area. Although debts were quite high, the peons resident on haciendas were few in number, so that most estates relied on the villages for most of their labour requirements. Profits were low, and by the eighteenth century, two thirds of the capital value of these properties was absorbed by Church mortgages and annuities, with the consequence that the turnover in ownership proved remarkably rapid.[14] The image here is of a relatively weak, unstable institution, burdened by accumulated debt and circumscribed by a recalcitrant Indian society.

A quite different pattern of land tenure and labour recruitment was to be found in the northern province of San Luis Potosí. There, Jan Bazant encountered latifundia which, in the absence of any pre-existing network of Indian settlement, dominated vast stretches of territory. By the nineteenth century debt peonage was a convenience rather than a necessity, and many workers avoided its operation. In fact, the resident peons who received a monthly wage and a weekly maize ration formed a privileged group within the work-force of the hacienda. Far more numerous and more deeply in debt were the tenants and sharecroppers who occupied an appreciable area of the estate.[15] The existence of this class of *arrendatarios* has important implications for any interpretation of the hacienda, since of course it offers comparison with the manor of medieval Europe. The similarity is heightened by the practice of hiring labourers by the day to assist with the harvest, men probably recruited from among the families of the tenants.[16] In conclusion, Bazant rejects the notion that at the close of the nineteenth century haciendas were not commercial enterprises, since they were ready to invest in new lines of production and alert to the possibilities of export markets.

Finally, it has become clear that in highland areas situated at some distance from urban markets, haciendas exercised but a loose control over their territory. In the uplands of Jalisco and Michoacán, a class of tenant farmers emerged who, in the decades after Independence, took advantage of the disintegration of several latifundia to create an entire range of small independent farms. In his *Pueblo en vilo* Luis González portrays the emergence of this class of prosperous rancheros as the constitutive social element in the district of San José de Gracia.[17] This transformation of tenants into proprietary farmers has important bearing on the nature of agricultural enterprise in Mexico. If here, why not elsewhere? No doubt, location theory will offer some clues, but at first glance the case confirms the assertions of Molina Enríquez as to the 'artificiality' of the great estate as a unit of production.

At this point let us broaden the terms of the discussion. For if the image of the hacienda as a feudal institution endured so long, it was because both positivists and marxists agreed upon the necessity for agrarian reform. The great estate presented an obstacle to their hopes for a modern system of agriculture, be it capitalist or socialist. Viewed from a historical perspective, the latifundium appeared as the bedrock of the *ancien régime* in Mexico. However, this oddly convenient alliance was disturbed by the emergence of marxist theorists, led by Andre Gunder Frank, who argued that since the Americas had been conquered under the aegis of Western capitalism, the structure of their economies was determined by their dependent condition. The hacienda was the instrument of a dependent, colonial capitalism.[18] Moreover, the enserfed condition of hacienda peons was interpreted as the consequence of this dependent relation. After all, the same regressive effects in the labour system could be observed in the tropical plantations which relied on slavery. Behind the arguments of this school, of course, was the authoritative text of Lenin on Imperialism.

For the historian, the most useful effect of these doctrines has been the encouragement to compare Latin America with Eastern Europe. For in that part of the world several scholars had already formulated certain theories about the nature of traditional agriculture which can be profitably applied elsewhere. In Russia the economist A. V. Chayanov calculated that where investment in new techniques or machinery is absent, labour forms the chief cost of agricultural production. In consequence, once the constraints of serfdom are abolished, the free peasant family, accustomed to relatively low levels of subsistence, can survive crop prices in the market which are simply uneconomic for the agriculturist dependent on hired labour. When prices fall, the peasant enterprise expands its volume of production through additional increments of labour at the very point where the landlord finds his wage-bill exceeds the market return, and hence is obliged to suspend operations.[19] In the long term, peasant farming will eliminate wage labour and the capitalist enterprise.

Chayanov's theory, elaborated to interpret the changes in Russian agriculture after the abolition of serfdom in 1861, has been deployed by Witold Kula to define the nature of feudal production in Poland during the sixteenth and seventeenth centuries. There, the great estate depended for its main income upon the export of wheat to Western Europe. Through an analysis of account papers Kula demonstrated that production was only maintained at prevailing market prices through the effective subsidy of the unremunerated labour of the enserfed peasantry. In fact, if workers had been paid wages at the going rate, the landlord enterprise could not have covered its operating costs. Moreover, when prices declined, the volume of output was expanded through greater inputs of labour.[20] Here, then, was an explanation of how the commercial relation with the capitalist West only served to strengthen the bonds of feudalism in Poland.

For Latin America, Marcello Carmagnani has applied the theories of Frank and Kula to the evolution of Chilean agrarian society in the period 1660–1830. There, it was the stimulus of Peruvian demand for wheat which impelled the transition from stockraising to cereal cultivation in the Central Valley. In the first cycle, with wheat prices high and land in abundant supply, landowners encouraged the settlement of *arrendatarios*, tenant farmers, as a source of income, and as a means to obtain more wheat. But in the latter half of the eighteenth century, when wheat prices declined, production was maintained and indeed expanded through the reduction of these *arrendatarios* to the condition of *inquilinos*, service tenants, who, in return for a plot of land for subsistence farming, provided virtually free labour for the landlord.[21] The chief profits, however, of this export economy went to the merchants of Lima and their agents in Santiago de Chile. Thus Carmagnani argues that the pressures generated by overseas trade fortified and extended a seigneurial society in Chile.

If Mexico now be viewed from the perspective of Eastern Europe, it becomes clear that the failure of the first conquerors and settlers to persuade the Spanish Crown to grant them encomiendas in perpetuity is the key to the subsequent development of colonial agriculture. In the first generation, encomenderos such as Cortés had employed the free labour of their entrusted Indians to engage in a variety of undertakings, which ranged from wheat-farming and sugar

planting to silver-mining and trade with Peru. But the application of
the New Laws of 1542, which reduced encomenderos to mere
pensioners of Indian tribute, when combined with the effects of the
catastrophic decline in Indian population, meant that Spanish landowners were now obliged to pay their workers a market wage.
True, the Crown introduced a system of draft labour, *repartimientos*,
but Indians obtained under this arrangement had to be paid a daily
wage.[22] In any case, in the vast provinces of settlement north of
Mexico City, encomiendas and communities of settled Indians were
rare, so that entrepreneurs, be they miners or stockmen, had to
attract workers from Central Mexico through generous inducements,
either in kind or in cash.

Then again, the survival of Indian villages as autonomous civic
entities, often in possession of their own land, clearly prevented the
creation of a dominant seigneurial society in central and southern
Mexico. Indeed, if these inwardly-oriented communities were ever
aroused from what Karl Marx once described as their Asiatic mode
of production, it was in part because they had to pay tribute to a
Crown more concerned with cash than with corn.[23] After the gradual
elimination of the practice of draft labour in the mid seventeenth
century, Indians were induced into the money economy through the
distribution of merchandise and credit effected, and at times enforced, by the district magistrates, the *alcaldes mayores*, acting in
partnership with merchants. In these *repartimientos de comercio*,
mules and oxen from the north were sold on credit in the south,
and the production of cochineal and cotton financed in advance by
the disbursement of cash. In these operations the merchants of
Mexico City and the leading provincial towns succeeded in hiring
the judicial authority of the Crown to safeguard their business
interests.[24] It was the system of repartimientos rather than debt
peonage which most provoked unrest and riot.

The Mexican latifundium was created during the first great
export cycle of 1570–1630 to cater for the needs of the urban,
hispanic economy. The sugar plantations, the cattle and sheep
ranches, and the cereal-growing estates all derived their income from
sales to the domestic market, since transport costs eliminated the
possibility of overseas exports for other than a few coastal properties.
In consequence, when the precipitous halving of silver production in
the years after 1630 led to a general contraction within the urban
network as overseas trade also declined, many haciendas were either
sold or simply left deserted by their bankrupt owners.[25] For without

sales whence was the money to come for wages? Vast stretches of land were abandoned for all but occasional pasture.

But what of debt peonage, that much advertised Mexican equivalent of European serfdom? For the hacendado in search of free labour, it was a remarkably poor substitute. More of an inducement than a bond, it required the advance of a considerable sum in cash or in goods to a group of labourers who might well abscond without repayment of the loan. In any case, these peons were still paid a wage at the going rate, and in addition received a weekly maize ration.[26] The contrast with Eastern Europe is all too obvious. In seventeenth-century Russia the nobility and gentry also faced financial ruin. But there the Tsars intervened to rescue them by subjecting the peasantry to the condition of serfs, charged with the obligation of supplying their masters free labour service. In later years a state bank was established to grant loans to the landowners at low rates of interest.[27] For such assistance the creole landowner pined in vain. Small wonder that the turnover in ownership was so rapid. By 1700 it was not uncommon to find landlords in debt to their workers.[28]

For Central America, Murdo Macleod has shown that the Spaniards were relatively slow to acquire land in this region, since they were more concerned to obtain Indian labour for the cultivation of cacao and for silver-mining. Moreover, when yields sharply contracted during the middle decades of the seventeenth century, the urban economy equally experienced a severe decline which led to a virtual exodus out of the towns into agriculture. But far from initiating the formation of great estates based on debt peonage, this migration marked a shift into subsistence 'dirt-farming' by mestizo and impoverished Spanish small-holders.[29] For without the income of an export economy to sustain the towns, where was the market for the produce of haciendas?

Much the same trend can be detected in Mexico. Faced with a sharp contraction in urban demand, many landowners now threw open a considerable proportion of their land to tenant farmers and mere squatters. In the vast provinces of the North, *tierra adentro*, rents were often nominal since the concern here was to provide for some occupation of great tracts of scrubland. Arrangements varied from hacienda to hacienda, and the absence of written contracts prevents any precise description of the system. Later evidence suggests that in some cases, but not in all, tenants were obliged to assist the landlord at harvest, their services being rewarded at the

standard daily rate. In effect, although rents were defined or measured in monetary terms, as so many pesos for so much land, at least
part of the cost was met by the provision of labour. Even without a
formal stipulation the presence of tenants and their families undoubtedly enabled landlords to operate their estates with a relatively
small number of 'maintained' resident peons, depending upon
workers hired by the day for the harvest and other seasonal tasks.[30]
This system became especially prevalent in the north beyond
Querétaro, where land was abundant and cheap, but labour scarce
and comparatively expensive.

In the long term, however, the decision to establish a numerous
body of tenant farmers, when taken in conjunction with the survival
of the Indian village and the emergence in some areas of an extensive
class of small-holders, threatened the economic viability of the
average hacienda, which depended for its main income upon the
sale of maize. For in the eighteenth century, when the steady increase
in both silver production and population brought a renewal of
urban demand for foodstuffs, it became profitable for tenants to sell
their produce on the open market, using the income to pay cash
rents or hire a peon to satisfy any remaining labour obligations.
Moreover, the growth of population was still more than matched by
the supply of land cleared for planting, so that corn prices, drought
years apart, remained obstinately low throughout most of the century. In short, landlord agriculture came under heavy attack from
peasant farming. It is pertinent to recall that a century later,
Molina Enríquez was convinced that most maize was produced by
villagers and small-holders.

If the great estate in Mexico during the eighteenth century in
part evaded the application of what we may call the Chayanov
principle, it was largely because the cyclical nature of colonial
agriculture periodically eliminated the competition. Through a
masterly analysis of maize prices in the Mexico City grain market,
Enrique Florescano has shown that climatic changes on the central
plateau led to such marked variations in harvests that, in addition
to sharp seasonal fluctuations, corn prices oscillated violently from
year to year. Under this regime, the key to consistent returns lay in
storage capacity. In effect, Florescano agrees with Molina Enríquez
that estate managers only sent grain to market when the supply from
the villages and small-holders was on the wane or was exhausted.
Indeed, he found that the better the harvest, the lower the volume
of sales in the official market.[31] Hacienda profits, therefore, were

essentially periodic, since they derived from intermittent sales of stored grain released when poor crop yields drove up prices.

One problem remains. Most farmers in traditional agriculture face problems over credit and the Mexican hacendado was no exception to this rule. If the sale of maize was delayed for months on end, whence came the cash to sustain production? For there were no banks or short-term credit institutions in New Spain. The answer surely must lie with the tenantry. Although many estates engaged in stockraising and other crops to supplement their main activity, the most obvious source of income was the cash rents of their tenants. It was this revenue, or in some cases, the labour services, which maintained estates in operation until the inevitable round of poor harvests brought their due reward.[32] The contrast later drawn by Molina Enríquez between the vacant spaces of the haciendas and the intensely cultivated plots of ranchos hence must be treated with great reserve. It is probable that the grain marketed in years of abundant harvests came as much from tenants and sharecroppers as from villagers and rancheros.

After the mid years of the eighteenth century, as rural population became more dense, so competition for sales outlets became more severe. In these circumstances, two paths of escape were followed by many landowners. In the first place, some hacendados abandoned all pretence of production and became simple rentiers. Clearly, for this option to be attractive an estate had to be located sufficiently close to an urban market for its rents to be high, or else so distant from these markets that tenant farming was the only practicable alternative to outright abandonment. In the second case, landlords invested in improvements or sought other lines of production. In particular, the construction of dams and reservoirs for irrigation became common, since it permitted the cultivation of wheat, a crop not exposed to small-holder competition. Similarly, with water on hand, there was little danger of livestock dying of drought. Needless to say, many estates, by reason of the variegated nature of their terrain, preserved an uneasy balance between direct administration of the 'demesne' and tenant farming, and still engaged in stockraising as well as the cultivation of cereals. Finally, it must be emphasised that these options were taken up chiefly by haciendas in Central Mexico, in the cereal zone which stretched from Puebla to Jalisco. Elsewhere, landlords turned to tropical cash crops such as sugar, cotton, coffee, and henequen, or, in some areas of the North, still concentrated on stockraising and its derivatives. The advantages of the great estate in many of these lines of production is obvious: in their evolution the plantation and the estancia differ markedly from the hacienda which grew cereals.

In the nineteenth century, a third mode of operation became common. By reason of the continued growth in population, labour now became relatively cheap when compared to the rising value of land. Certainly, all the evidence suggests that maize prices increased considerably while money wages remained constant. In consequence, many landlords adopted some form of sharecropping, since without any outlay of cash they still received at least half of the maize crop. On many haciendas the owner continued to farm wheat on the land under irrigation, leaving the remainder of the estate for maize. Moreover, since the harvests of the two crops do not coincide, it was possible to employ sharecroppers as labourers to bring in the wheat.[33] In this fashion, the landlord avoided direct competition with the peasant enterprise. Instead, he took advantage of his command over land to benefit from the exertions of the sharecroppers, but concentrated his own investment on the cultivation of more profitable crops than maize. In this context, the transition from cash rents to sharecropping should be viewed as a logical response on the part of the landowner to the changing relations of labour, land and prices.[34] It represented an advance towards a more economic exploitation of the resources of his estate, and in its division of labour formed a prelude to the system prevailing after agrarian reform.

## CHAPTER 2

# The Bajío

## I

At the close of the eighteenth century, it took from four to six days to ride on horseback from Mexico City to Querétaro, still then called 'the door to the Interior'.[1] But before entering the arid steppe-lands of the North, the traveller first came to the Bajío, an area which was 'rich and fertile and very carefully cultivated'. Indeed, Alexander von Humboldt, who visited the region in the summer months of 1803, later wrote: 'In Mexico the plains which stretch from Salamanca to Silao, Guanajuato and the town of León have the best cultivated fields in Mexico and remind one of the most attractive countryside in France.'[2] Similarly, Joel Poinsett, the first American envoy to Mexico, was surprised to find that 'the plain which extends from Apaseo to León is full of small cities, villages and farms'.[3] It is only fair to note, however, that impressions depended upon the season, since H. G. Ward, who saw the province in November 1827 after a prolonged drought, confessed his dis-appointment that 'the country wore the same dull livery of dust which gives so monotonous a character to the scenery throughout the Tableland'.[4]

Situated at the very centre of the modern Mexican republic within the states of Guanajuato and Querétaro, historically and geo-graphically the Bajío was a frontier zone, standing between the inhospitable wastelands of the north and the fertile valleys of the central plateau. During the Tertiary Age, the plains had formed a vast lake lined by volcanoes. But whereas in the central valleys such lakes continued to dominate the landscape well into the nineteenth century, by contrast in the Bajío the waters seeped away to leave a thick lacustrine sediment enriched with alluvial mud and volcanic ash.[5] The area now appears as a series of inter-connected basins which in the east begin at the valley of Querétaro and terminate in the west at the highland borders of Jalisco. To the north the out-flanks of the western Sierra Madre join the eastern Sierra Gordo to form a hilly area with soils that are thin and less productive.

Within the mountains in the district of Guanajuato were to be found lodes of silver which ranked among the richest in America. The few rivers which cross the plains drain southwards from the sierras towards the great river Lerma, which in its westward course to Lake Chapala marks the southern boundaries of the region.

With average altitudes ranging from just under 5,000 ft on the plains to about 6,500 ft in the hills, virtually all the Bajío falls within the limits of the *tierra templada*, since temperatures do not vary much beyond 14 degrees (centigrade) in January to 22 degrees in May. The upland districts are more cold and dry than their southern neighbours. About eighty per cent of all rains falls in the summer months from June to September, with another tenth in May and October. But considerable variations occur both in the intensity and incidence of these summer rains, since in over three decades of observations at Celaya (1928–48) seventeen years were described as dry, and only fourteen qualified as wet. Equal differences existed between districts, since whereas the modern annual precipitation for the state of Guanajuato is reckoned to average 22.83 inches, during much the same period Celaya experienced an average rate of 27.87 inches.[6] It was this pattern of heavy but highly variable summer rains, preceded by a relatively hot, dry spring, which determined the range of natural vegetation and the limits of colonial agriculture. For maize positively flourished in this climate and type of soil, whereas wheat required irrigation or proximity to running water if it were to survive the dry winter months. Similarly, pasture ranges were perforce extensive and livestock dependent on permanent springs, rivers or man-made waterholes and lakes.

Although geographers now include the Bajío within their maps of the central plateau – the core of modern Mexico – historically the region lay outside the zone of settled peasantry which supported the advanced societies of Meso-America. At the time of the Spanish Conquest, its fertile plains were inhabited by dispersed tribes known collectively as Chichimecas – dog Indians – who depended for their subsistence on hunting and food-gathering. Apart from a few Tarascan villages lining the banks of the Lerma, the entire Bajío thus lay untouched by the cycle of intensive cultivation which had long since transformed the landscape of the central valleys. As yet, archaeologists have failed to offer any explanation for the striking discrepancy between the agricultural potentiality of the region and the actual sequence of settlement. It is possible that its heavy soils proved intractable for the intensive hoe-farming of the pre-

Columbian peasant. Then again, modern maps of vegetation distribution show that the Bajío differs from the remainder of the central plateau in that, by reason of its lower altitude, the plains were covered by dense seasonal grass, cactus scrub and heavy thickets of mezquite trees, a type of natural growth which in less luxuriant form still characterises much of the northern steppes.[7] Whatever the reason for its tardy development, the subsequent history of the Bajío was in large measure governed by this combination of a fertile soil and the absence of fixed settlement prior to the Spanish Conquest. In contrast to Meso-America, the thriving scene viewed by Humboldt and Poinsett was entirely the work of the colony.

But if it required European intervention to clear these frontier lands of Chichimeca marauders, colonisation was a joint venture in which Indians from the South provided the bulk of the manpower. For the Conquerors were concerned with gold and silver, and in their urgent quest for El Dorado pushed as far north as Kansas in less than a generation of exploration. It was the discovery of rich silver deposits at Zacatecas which assured the permanent occupation of the open ranges of the north. Mining profits directly financed the conquest of Durango, Coahuila and New Mexico. But without any local supply of labour available, mine-owners were obliged to offer relatively high wages, together with a share in the ore cut, to attract free, migrant workers from the central valleys. At the height of its prosperity, Zacatecas was ringed by hamlets inhabited by Tarascans, Aztecs, Cholultecans and Otomies.[8] Elsewhere, the viceregal government persuaded a numerous body of Tlaxcalans to establish a series of small villages across the north, both as a source of labour, and as an example to the still unpacified Chichimecas.[9]

Nowhere was this Indian expansion beyond the limits of Meso-America more apparent than in the Bajío. Under the cover afforded by the Spaniards, Tarascans and Otomies moved northwards to occupy lands in the adjacent districts of Acámbaro, Pénjamo, Celaya and Querétaro. Relations between the two tribes were amicable, since the town of Acámbaro was divided equally between them.[10] Perhaps the most remarkable feature of this colonising venture was the role played by Otomi chieftains from Jilotepec who led expeditions to plant villages in a vast area stretching from Querétaro to San Luis Potosí.[11] These communities all received land, and at Querétaro, the pueblo of Santiago retained possession of valuable gardens and orchards situated within the city boundaries throughout the colonial period. The best known of these Otomí caciques was Diego de Tapia, son of the founder of Querétaro, who became a wealthy landowner with wheat farms, flocks of sheep and interests in silver-mining. In the next century, however, this fortune passed to the Church when his daughter, Luisa, the only heir, became prioress of the Santa Clara convent.[12]

The pattern of Spanish settlement was equally complex and hesitant. In the early years, Hernán Peréz de Bocanegra and Juan de Villaseñor respectively received encomiendas in Apaseo and Huango, and in the first case certainly employed tribute money to finance other interests. But thereafter, the encomienda disappears from view. The contrast with Chile, to cite another frontier society, is striking. Instead, the main instrument of colonisation was the town. To safeguard settlers and protect the silver trains from Chichimeca raids, the viceroys established garrison towns at San Miguel el Grande (1555), San Felipe (1562) and León (1576).[13] The discovery of silver in the sierra at Guanajuato, although at this stage much inferior to the mines at Zacatecas, undoubtedly stimulated the local economy. Moreover, although Querétaro was not formally recognised as a *villa* until the 1650s, as early as 1580 it housed over eighty Spanish residents engaged in stockraising and trade, so that the town came to serve as the chief commercial entrepot for the Bajío.[14] Finally, in the fertile lands close to the River Lerma, Celaya was founded in 1571 to encourage agricultural development, and in the same district Salamanca (1603) and Salvatierra (1644) fulfilled much the same purpose.

To attract settlers into the region, the Crown endowed each town with about six square miles of land for distribution among local householders. At Celaya, each citizen received 2½ *caballerías* – about 265 acres – measured in rectangular strips 1,104 by 552 yards. In Salvatierra these grants comprised up to 425 acres.[15] The result of this policy was that each Spanish town, with up to 20,000 acres for apportionment, became the nucleus of relatively intensive cultivation set down in a countryside which was still largely a vacant wilderness. Although the subsequent history of these farms, *labores* and *ranchos* as they were called, has yet to be traced with any precision, nevertheless, location theory suggests that where a town flourished, the survival of the small property was virtually assured. As against any dichotomy between town and country, the Spanish *villa* was the residence of a number of farmers with lands in the immediate environs.

Away from the towns and villages, all vacant land was appropriated by estancias. From the 1550s onwards, the viceroys issued titles for *sitios de estancia*, square blocks of grazing land, which measured either 4,338 or 1,928 acres, according to whether they were destined for *ganado mayor* (cattle and horses) or *ganado menor* (sheep and goats).[16] Recipients were a mixed group, ranging from local stockmen to prominent citizens of Mexico City. In general, the grants followed the line of settlement, with lands in the southwest or on the plains awarded first, so that in many instances it was not until after 1600 that great tracts of upland territory in Pénjamo, Dolores and the border hills of Jalisco passed into private ownership. Moreover, despite the terms of the deeds, which insisted on immediate exploitation of the property, many owners made little attempt to develop their holdings. In no sense should the issue of a *sitio de estancia* be regarded as synonymous with the creation of an hacienda. As elsewhere in Mexico, the great estate of the Bajío was formed through a complex process of multiple purchase, the receipt of additional *mercedes*, and the outright annexation of adjacent or encircled sections, with all titles sanctioned by *composición*, the payment of a fee during the general inspection of landed estates ordered by the Crown in the 1640s.[17] In any case, several latifundia, especially in the hilly perimeter of the region, were only created during the first three decades of the seventeenth century.

The significance of this cycle of land appropriation which was largely concentrated in the two generations from the 1570s until the 1630s was that it determined the future development of agrarian society in the Bajío. For on the plains between Celaya and León, Indians followed in the wake of the Spanish occupation, and hence were welcomed by estate-owners on an individual basis as peons and tenants. In contrast to the situation further south where the Indian village preserved its communal pattern of land tenure in the face of the expansion of the Spanish hacienda, by contrast across much of the Bajío it was the rancho, the independent small-holding, which offered the chief alternative to the great estates. But this is to anticipate the future. For although chroniclers testified to the extraordinary progress of wheat-farming in the districts of Celaya and Salamanca, which found markets as distant as Zacatecas, nevertheless in Querétaro the chief rural activity was still sheep-farming.[18] Each year vast flocks of sheep crossed the plains to winter in the meadows of Lake Chapala in Michoacán. Many estates remained mere estancias, their lands employed for rough, seasonal pasture, with security of occupation against neighbourly intrusion assisted by

the lease of land to Indians at nominal rents. In many cases exact
boundaries had yet to be determined and litigation was constant.

## II

During the eighteenth century, the Bajío emerged from its frontier
condition to become the pace-maker of the Mexican economy.
By then it had come to form a prosperous, intermediary zone, quite
distinct from either the far north with its sheep ranges and scattered
mining camps, or from the central valleys with their blend of deeply-
rooted Indian villages and haciendas.[19] Instead, the Bajío was
characterised by a degree of urbanisation unusually high for a
traditional society, matched by a complex structure of agricultural
production. The twin engines of this transformation were a remarkable increase in the output of silver and an equally remarkable
growth in population. Guanajuato now replaced Zacatecas at the
head of the mining industry, and indeed outstripped Potosí in Peru
to become the leading producer of silver in all America. Registered
output rose from an average 1,173,542 ps for the quinquennium
1716–20 to a probable peak of 5,267,284 ps in 1790–94 – figures
which comprised between a quarter and a fifth of recorded mintage
in New Spain. By 1792, the city of Guanajuato and the ring of
mining villages which formed its suburbs housed over 55,000 persons.
Since miners were the labour aristocracy of the colony, both they
and the artisans who catered to their needs constituted an ample,
prosperous market for the produce of the surrounding countryside.[20]

Domestic industry also proved a source of economic growth.
By 1790 Querétaro, with a population of nearly 30,000, had become
a leading textile city, since the industry employed at least 3,300
workers divided between 18 factories (*obrajes*) which produced fine
woollens, ponchos and blankets, and 327 workshops (*trapiches*)
which mainly wove coarse cottons.[21] Furthermore, only a day's
journey away, San Miguel el Grande was renowed for its carpets
and rugs, and Celaya and Salamanca also produced a range of cheap
cotton cloth. Clearly, the emergence of this industry in part derived
from the strategic, geographical position of the Bajío, situated close
to the sources of supply and the location of markets. Raw cotton
came from Michoacán and wool from Coahuila and New León.[22]
Markets were found, not only at Guanajuato, but throughout the
North where the resurgence of Zacatecas and the discoveries at
Bolaños and Catorce had transformed the mining industry, and

hence extended the purchasing power of the workers. No mere enclave economy, the silver mines generated employment for textile workers and urban artisans, as well as for agricultural labourers.

With land in ample supply and urban demand steadily mounting, the Bajío offered a propitious terrain for population growth. Between 1644 and 1688 the register of Indian tributaries at Querétaro rose from 600 to 2,000 and in Celaya from 2,184 to 6,419 in the years between 1657 and 1698.[23] Furthermore, according to the calculations of M. Claude Morin, the population of the entire diocese of Michoacán – in which the Bajío was included – increased fivefold during the eighteenth century. In the parishes which comprised the intendancy of Guanajuato, the annual rate of growth between 1760 and 1792 was 1.17%, which yields an overall increase of 45%.[24] Evidence from San Lius de la Paz, a largely Indian district, reveals that the pace of growth slowed almost to a halt towards the close of the century. Whereas in the period 1727–61 the annual rate of increase was 1.01, by 1781–1810 the level had dropped to 0.08.[25] However, as we shall demonstrate in the next chapter, this decline in the rate of population growth, although apparent in all districts, was most pronounced among the Indian community. Indeed, a significant feature of the 1793 census was the revelation that Indians only comprised 44.2% of the 398,029 inhabitants of the province of Guanajuato, the remainder being classified as Spaniards, mestizos and mulattoes.[26] Moreover, all the evidence suggests that the Indians of the Bajío were well advanced on the road to assimilation, and in many cases quite indistinguishable from their *casta* neighbours. Many only spoke Spanish and the majority lived scattered on haciendas or resided in towns without any attachment to particular villages. The census only listed 52 pueblos and an enquiry undertaken in 1797 found that most communities retained little land.[27] What could be more significant of their status than that two thirds of all Indian tributaries were described as *vagos*, individuals without ties to either hacienda or village?[28] Judged from the viewpoint of its social organisation, the Bajío now belonged to mestizo America.

The distribution of population between town and country is difficult to determine. But if the district and city of Querétaro be included in the calculation, then it is not unreasonable to presume that between a quarter and a third of the inhabitants of the Bajío lived in towns of over 5,000 persons. Needless to say, the balance of occupations did not square with any simple contrast of urban and rural employment, since a considerable number of farmers and agricultural workers lived in the towns. In 1793 the intendant estimated that 48.7% of the working population were engaged in agriculture as against 34.1% employed as miners, artisans, industrial workers and tradesmen. Another 15.9% were described as *jornaleros*, labourers hired by the day, without any specified line of work.[29] If these figures be accepted, then at most agriculture supported three fifths of the population, and as a full time occupation employed less than half of all workers.

The rapid increase, both in overall population and in urban demand for rural produce, transformed the face of the country. Much as in the maps of Von Thünen, the penumbra of cultivated land which encircled each town slowly expanded until the entire countryside, soil quality permitting, was cleared, drained and brought under plough. The great herds of sheep and goats, and to a lesser extent, cattle, which in the previous century had provided the basis of rural activity, dwindled in number or were driven northwards to New León and Coahuila where land was still cheap.[30] The initial emphasis on stockraising changed to a system of mixed farming, which in turn was replaced, where feasible, by a concentration on the cultivation of cereals. The value of land rose appreciably. Needless to say, the unfolding of this process was governed by the nature of the local terrain since estates adjoining sierras continued to breed cattle, sheep and mules. Then again, the high cost of transport by mule-team imposed effective limits on the extension of commercial agriculture into districts situated close to the margin of the province at the greatest distance from urban markets.

Evidence as to the dimension of these changes comes from the parochial tithe reports sent to the diocesan authorities in Valladolid (modern Morelia). At Silao, a fertile district situated on the open plains close to Guanajuato, maize production rose from 20,558 fanegas in 1689 to an annual average of 90,352 in 1751–55, to soar later to an average 166,410 fanegas in the years 1776–80. Moreover, whereas in the first year wheat farming yielded a mere 90 loads (*cargas*), in the last-mentioned quinquennium it averaged 1,910 loads.[31] Equally dramatic was the trend in San Pedro Piedragorda where the maize harvest rose from 570 fanegas in 1681 to 39,450 in 1754.[32] As might be expected, the transition from stockraising to farming was most pronounced in the northern districts. In San Miguel el Grande agricultural produce only accounted for 5% of the tithe value in the 1680s, and it was not until after 1740 that the cereals overtook other items to supply about 60% of the overall value.[33] A similar transformation occurred in San Luis de la Paz where at the beginning of the century the leading haciendas concentrated on sheep and goats to the virtual exclusion of cereal cultivation. Thereafter, maize production rose from an average 5,100 fanegas a year in the period 1732–77 to over 15,200 fanegas by 1797–1804, at which time it comprised 45% of the total tithe value.[34]

It is more difficult to obtain information about the structure of production which was responsible for this pattern of growth. Part of the problem lies in the ambiguity of the terms employed to describe the units of production. For in common usage, an hacienda simply meant a large estate, an extensive tract of contiguous land, with a *casco*, a set of buildings which generally included a residence for the owner of his manager, barns, stables, corrals and a chapel. But an hacienda could be a cattle ranch, a sugar plantation or a farm growing cereals. Equally important, it could vary in size from two thousand acres to half a million acres. Yet despite this diversity it was much easier to recognise an hacienda than to define a rancho, a term which was variously applied to prosperous farms, to hamlets of small-holders and to subordinate sections of haciendas. About the only common element here was the sense of an actual settlement with buildings. In particular, it was the presence of tenants which disrupted any simple dichotomy between the great and the small property. As far as can be ascertained, most haciendas in the Bajío rented a considerable proportion of their land in plots of varying size to tenant farmers and sharecroppers. Viewed from this perspective, a rancho might be either an independent small-holding or a farm held on lease.

A notion of the distribution of these units can be obtained from two lists compiled by the intendant in the years 1792–93. At the same time, they illustrate the difficulties of definition, especially where ranchos were concerned.[35]

|  | 1793 | 1792 |
|---|---|---|
| Estancias | 29 | – |
| Haciendas | 448 | 435 |
| Independent ranchos | 360 | } 918 |
| Subordinate ranchos | 1,046 | |
| Indian villages | 37 | 52 |

Whatever the precise nature of the terms employed, these lists certainly attest to the survival of the small property, since the tithe records show that many ranchos were in fact virtual hamlets of small-holders, i.e. what now would be called a *ranchería*. Equally important, the existence of a numerous body of tenant farmers is confirmed. Close inspection of the lists reveals that the distribution of properties varied greatly from district to district, with the south-eastern district, the former *alcaldía mayor* of Celaya, accounting for the greatest number of units with no less than 266 haciendas, 211 ranchos and 38 villages. In particular, the fertile district of Yuriria was notable for 79 ranchos and 11 villages as against only 6 haciendas. Conversely, the northern and western districts were characterised by the greatest concentration of property.

It is unfortunate that the list of 1792 which provides detailed information for each district omits to distinguish between independent and subordinate ranchos. In this respect, the findings of Cecilia Rabel Romero on San Luis de la Paz are important in that she discovered that the transition from stockraising to the cultivation of maize was largely effected by haciendas renting their land to rancheros. By 1803 some 72% of the maize harvest came from independent *labores* or from the ranchos and sitios included within the haciendas. By contrast, pastoral produce was still dominated by the great estates.[36] Thus we encounter a clear discrepancy between the formal structure of ownership and the distribution of the units of production. In general, the more concentrated the pattern of owner-ship, the greater the degree of reliance on tenants to exploit the soil. For further confirmation of this rule, let us now turn to examine in greater detail the district of Pénjamo.

## III

The most striking entry in the 1792 list of rural settlements was undoubtedly the 10 haciendas, one village and 341 ranchos of Pénjamo. Yet the military *padrón* of that year only enumerated 11 haciendas, 3 labores, 1 estancia and 24 ranchos.[37] Moreover, the circle of ownership was still further concentrated. The two Indian villages held an hacienda and three ranchos; and the Camilian fathers, a Hospital order, had acquired another hacienda. But the remaining properties were divided among no more than eleven families. Yet even this statement fails to indicate the degree of concentration since, in fact, the district was largely occupied by four great latifundia – Cuerámaro, Corralejo, Santa Ana Pacueco and the lands of the Mariscal de Castilla. As Table 1 shows, the remain-ing estates were of relatively modest dimension.

TABLE I   *Approximate extent of Pénjamo haciendas 1707–51*

| Hacienda | Sitios ganado mayor | Sitios ganado menor | Caballerías | Year | Source |
|---|---|---|---|---|---|
| Cuerámaro | 15½ | 6 | 28 | 1711 | AHML, 1711–12, 2 |
| | | | | 1751 | AGN, Vínculos, 22–3 |
| Cuitzeo | 1 | 1 | 1½ | 1707 | AHML, 1708–10, 20 |
| | | | | 1791 | ANL, 14 July 1791 |
| Peralta | 3 | – | 2 | 1743 | ANL, 18 Nov. 1743 |
| San Gregorio | 2 | – | 2 | 1718 | ANL, 31 Aug. 1718 |
| Munguía | 1 | – | – | 1743 | ANL, 18 Nov. 1743 |
| San Juan Guanimaro | 3 | – | 2 | 1711 | ANL, 16 Sept. 1711 |
| Tupataro | 2? | – | – | 1682 | AHML, 1681–84, 30 |
| Cuchiquatillo | 1 | – | – | 1751 | ANL, 23 Oct. 1751 |
| Sauz | – | – | 17½ | 1743 | ANL, 9 Dec. 1743 |
| Corralejo (half in Jalisco) | 41 | 26 | 28½ | 1707 | AGN, Vínculos, 263, 3 |
| Santa Ana Pacueco | Unknown, 40 large sitios in Jalisco | | | | Taylor, *Arandas in Jalisco* |
| La Hoya | Unknown, with other ranchos of the Mariscal de Castilla, at least 20 small sitios | | | | |

Comparatively little information has come to light about two of these 'conglomerates', the estates of the Mariscal de Castilla and the Santa Ana Pacueco. Both stretched far beyond Pénjamo, since, as we shall see below, the Mariscal owned an entire chain of haciendas which spread across the Bajío from Pénjamo to Irapuato. How much land was occupied by Santa Ana Pacueco remains similarly unknown, although in the adjacent hill district of Las Arandas it held no less than forty large *sitios de estancia*.[38] At the start of the eighteenth century the estate had been acquired by the Sánchez de Tagle family, marquises of Altamira, who owned a leading import house in Mexico City, together with a silver bank. The property remained in the family until the 1850s when it was finally partitioned and sold in small sections. These absentee landlords entrusted the management of the hacienda to general administrators. The post was evidently profitable, since one man, who had served the current Marquis for 23 years, in 1764 left his widow a fortune valued at 27,250 ps.[39] Similarly, his successor, who died in 1773, had already acquired goods worth 19,310 ps including the merchandise of a store in Piedragorda, small herds of cattle and mares, and 33 oxen for ploughing the maize fields in three ranchos rented from the owners.[40]

How much the Sánchez de Tagle benefited from the enterprise is difficult to say.

For the Corralejo, the summary inventories taken in the years 1707 and 1728 reveal that the hacienda comprised 41 large and 26 small sitios together with another 28½ caballerías, totalling 233,000 acres. Although most of this land fell within the boundaries of the *alcaldía mayor* of León, to which Pénjamo belonged, 21 large sitios and an unspecified part of a block of 22 small sitios were situated in New Galicia.[41] The number of livestock varied considerably in the two entries reflecting a change of ownership. By 1707 the owners for more than fifty years, the Alcocer family, had fallen heavily into debt. Their land, livestock and goods in the Corralejo were valued at 68,576 pesos, whereas the fixed clerical charges or *censos* amounted to 72,834 pesos. One piquant consequence of this situation was their inability to pay their employees: they owed 28 shepherds 2,768 pesos and 65 sirvientes another 8,725 pesos. At this time, the main business of the estate was sheepherding and the breeding of mules and horses, for clearly, with only 23 listed oxen, not much land was put under plough. In passing, we may note the presence of 14 mulatto slaves valued at 3,330 pesos. Under new ownership, the livestock holdings of the estate greatly increased. By 1728, Corralejo had about 24,000 sheep of all ages, some 2,700 cattle, and 2,250 brood mares. The 85 oxen, distributed in three separate farms, suggest an increased attention to agriculture. As several other examples shall prove, neither the high degree of indebtedness to ecclesiastical institutions nor the practice of what was in effect a reverse form of debt peonage were at all uncommon in New Spain. During the middle years of the eighteenth century, the general administrator of the Corralejo, Cristóbal Hidalgo y Costilla, father of the Insurgent leader, like his confrére at Santa Ana Pacueco, ran a small rancho rented from the absentee owners.[42]

The Cuerámaro, with 15½ large sitios, 6 small sitios and 28 caballerías (82,536 acres), moved into cereal production at an earlier stage than its neighbour. Already in 1711 its inventory recorded 6 caballerías under irrigation for wheat. Apparently about 200 fanegas of wheat and 50 fanegas of maize were sown each year. A reliable index of the greater area under cultivation can be found in the 171 oxen employed in four different farms.[43] At this time, largely due to the heavy fixed charges – they amounted to 30,468 pesos on an overall value of 51,676 pesos – the quantity of livestock was low. As for the labour force, the inventory mentions 51 peons who owed 1,926 pesos, and another ten owing 427 pesos had absconded. The hacienda included at least nine ranchos of tenants (arrendatarios). With a new owner, an Andalusian backed by a wealthy silver merchant of Guanajuato, the stockraising side of the enterprise was rapidly increased. Moreover, the 205 oxen, together with 3,000 fanegas of maize stored in the barn, indicated an extension in cultivation, if not in market outlets.[44]

Between 1721 and 1751 the conventional price of the land and buildings of Cuerámaro increased from 47,422 pesos to 87,465 pesos. The difference came partly from the rise in land values and also from the construction of a flour mill and a dam, between them worth over 8,000 pesos. By this time, some 125 cargas of wheat were sown, and the increase of land under cultivation is demonstrated by the employment of 437 oxen for ploughing. Livestock holdings now numbered 2,687 cattle and 1,594 brood mares. The permanent staff of the hacienda was not very large: 50 labourers, 2 shepherds, 14 cowboys, 10 millmen, 1 blacksmith and 7 muleteers were sufficient to man an enterprise valued at 136,385 pesos. These 84 workers owed the employer 1,469 pesos, or about 17 pesos a head.[45] Once the inventory was taken, after the death of the current owner, a merchant of Guanajuato, the estate was embargoed by his creditors, and soon deteriorated. In 1762 it was sold to the Camilian Fathers for 84,000 pesos. Whether this auction price included livestock was not made clear. It remained in their hands until the Reforma of the 1850s when it was expropriated, sold and divided into several ranchos.[46]

Unlike the preceding examples, Cuitzeo de los Naranjos was a modest sized hacienda comprising no more than one large and one small sitio and 1½ caballerías (6,474 acres). Yet in 1707 with 117 oxen, the land it had under plough (in direct management) exceeded that of the Corralejo. The livestock holdings were small, with herds of 436 cows and 473 brood mares. Although the clerical mortgages charged on the hacienda were low, 2,000 pesos on an overall value of 20,560 pesos, the owners, the Alcocer family, owed their peons 818 pesos for past work and a further 1,399 pesos on current account.[47] A second inventory, taken in 1791 revealed that the value of the land and buildings had risen from 7,653 pesos in 1707 to 22,485 pesos. Part of this three-fold increase derived from the construction of a dam, a flour mill, a fruit garden, stone walls and the irrigation of 210 acres for wheat growing. The number of oxen, 122, suggests that the actual area under cultivation may not have been greatly extended. In 1791 the owners rented the entire estate, with implements and stock valued at 27,081 pesos, for 1,492 pesos, an annual return, therefore, of 5.5%, from which had to be deducted 350 pesos to pay the interest on clerical mortgages.[48]

The preceding array of case studies has largely rested on the discovery of inventories of estate. The most solid conclusion to which they point is the threefold increase in hacienda value which occurred in Pénjamo during the eighteenth century. They indicate that at the beginning of the period many latifundia were heavily indebted to ecclesiastical institutions. They similarly highlight the paradox of peons 'bound' not through debt, but through fear of losing unpaid wages. An inventory, however, reveals little about the structure of production within an hacienda, nor does it describe the various sources of income. There is but passing reference to the presence of tenants. For such information other sources have to be consulted. The 1792 *padrón*, for example, listed the number of Spanish and *casta* residents and tenants (arrendatarios) housed within each hacienda. Unfortunately, it omits Indians. Alongside this data, we insert an 1833 list of ranchos.

TABLE 2  *Pénjamo: arrendatarios and ranchos 1792–1833*

|  | 1792 | | 1833 |
| --- | --- | --- | --- |
| Select haciendas | Residents | Arrendatarios | Number of ranchos |
| Corralejo | 7 | 366 | 51 |
| Santa Ana Pacueco | 29 | 66 | 63 |
| Cuerámaro | 63 | – | 2 |
| San Juan Guanimaro | 19 | 83 | 5 |
| Peralta | 6 | 74 | 13 |
| Tupataro | 9 | 18 | 2 |

*Source:* AGN, Padrones, 41; AHML 1830(3) 12.

Let us conclude this section by a brief comparison of the agricultural production of haciendas and ranchos as reported to the tithe collector. In 1779, only 6 haciendas paid direct tithes – Cuerámaro, Corralejo, Guanimaro, Peralta, Cuitzeo, and San Gregorio. The absence of Santa Ana Pacueco, signifies either that it paid tithes elsewhere, possibly in New Galicia, or that its lands were entirely occupied by tenants. The number of ranchos amounted to 84 together with the two Indian villages of Pénjamo and Numerán. The uncertain nature of a rancho is once more emphasised by the names of 164 persons living in these settlements who paid tithes.

There is no means of knowing whether this is a complete list of tenant farmers.[49] But the 1779 report demonstrates clearly the pattern of production. Whereas the haciendas dominated wheat growing with 1,385 cargas compared to the 240 cargas of the ranchos, for maize the situation was reversed, with the ranchos and villages producing 77,760 fanegas as against the 9,040 fanegas of the haciendas. Contrary to what might be expected, in stockraising both classes participated heavily, except in the cases of wool and mule-breeding – by this time, not large items – for which tithes were almost entirely paid by the haciendas.

## IV

Taken at a fixed point in time, an inventory rarely describes the history of an estate. To obtain some notion of formation and subsequent improvement, we have to turn to other source material – to lawsuits, title-deeds and account books.[50] For Pénjamo, such documents were unavailable. But these issues can be illumined by following the emergence of the hacienda later called Jalpa de Cánovas, which extended from San Pedro Piedragorda (modern Manuel Doblado) deep into the hills of Jalisco.[51] The nucleus of the estate consisted of four large sitios granted in 1544 to Juan de Villaseñor, the well-known encomendero of Huango. At that time, there were two small Chichimeca villages called Jalpa and Acámbaro. But in later years, the territory was left deserted so that in 1613 Diego Ortiz Saavedra, the current *alcalde mayor* of Lagos, acquired it in public auction for no more than 500 ps. Thereafter, Ortiz Saavedra and his widow built up a latifundium which eventually comprised over 23 large sitios or more than 100,000 acres. Among the vendors figured the grandchildren of Luis de Castilla, a leading figure in Mexico City, whose daughter, Inés de Cabrera, had obtained a grant of three large sitios in 1562.[52] It is significant that whereas the titles for valley lands date from the middle decades of the sixteenth century, most of the *mercedes* for upland sitios were issued after 1600. Equally important, the formation of the Jalpa, as distinct from the granting of mere sitios, occurred between 1604 and 1634. In all, the Ortiz Saavedra paid 3,737 ps for their acquisitions.

There is no need for a blow by blow account of the history of Jalpa. Suffice to say that when the founders' heirs became entangled in debt, the hacienda was auctioned in 1650 for 11,500 ps. A further modest rise in value was registered in 1679 when the estate was sold

to a miner from Guanajuato for 15,375 pesos. At this time, the large
sitios were appraised at 400 pesos and the additional caballerías of
arable at 50 pesos. In effect, it was not until its acquisition first in
1700 by Juan Diez de Bracamonte, owner of the great Rayas mine
at Guanajuato, and then in 1708 by Jerónimo de Monterde y
Antillón, a wealthy Aragonese merchant of Mexico City, that Jalpa
was actively developed. Between 1700 and 1712, the inventory value
rose from some 42,000 pesos to over 114,000 pesos, an increase
which, although in part based on the construction of a new residence,
with barns and stables, and for small dams for irrigation, in the main
came from the purchase of livestock backed up by the acquisitions
of fifty sitios of seasonal grazing land in New León. In the latter
year, there were listed 20,019 ewes with 6,260 *carneros* ready for
slaughter and another 11,146 lambs; 2,358 cows with 4,520 calves;
and 1,364 brood mares with an assortment of foals and young mules.
As yet, the cultivation of maize was not greatly extended, since the
estate only possessed 108 oxen; indeed, as late as 1700 only about
190 acres had been brought under plough. At this time, Church
mortgages were relatively low at 12,000 pesos, although this sum
still equalled forty per cent of the value of the buildings and land,
especially since the latter was still only assessed at 500 pesos a sitio.

In subsequent years, the area of Jalpa was augmented by the
purchase of a neighbouring hacienda which comprised over five large
sitios. Then, during the 1740s, *composición* brought official recognition of claims to another nine large sitios situated within the limits
of the hacienda for which no due title could be found. By 1760, the
owners could boast of a latifundium of over 38½ large sitios or over
158,000 acres. Far more important than this expansion in area,
however, was the new emphasis on investment in irrigation, which
obviously entailed an intensification in land use. Already in 1708, a
passing drought had obliged the owner to drive his sheep northwards
to pasture in Río Verde. And in later years, his heir, José Luis
Monterde y Antillón, complained bitterly that in the droughts of
1739 and 1746–47 he had lost thousands of head of stock. It was to
avert future disasters that he borrowed 15,000 pesos from the
Concepción Convent in Mexico City to finance the construction of
four large dams. At this time, the estate yielded only 800 pesos in
tenant rents.[53] No immediate success greeted his efforts since in 1764
his nephew, Rafael Monterde, who had married the only heir, his
cousin María Micaela, obtained a further 16,000 pesos to complete
the project. However, in 1775 he became Count of the Dam of Jalpa,

a sure sign that investment had at last brought its reward.[54] Indeed, to this very day, the approach to the village is still dominated by a series of artificial lakes. Further information about the development of Jalpa is not available other than a single statement dating from 1798, when the general manager listed average annual production. Livestock holdings were now considerably reduced, with 2,243 mares, 6,800 cows, and 5,000 sheep and goats, which respectively bred 250 mules, 500 foals, 900 calves, 900 lambs and 120 kids. Other produce included 5,000 pounds of wool, 400 loads of wheat, and a mere 50 fanegas of maize. Clearly, the owners had withdrawn from the cultivation of maize which, as in Pénjamo, occupied the numerous tenants who together paid rents amounting to 5,400 pesos a year.[55] Here, then, we encounter an integrated enterprise which combined investment in demesne agriculture with extensive tenant farming.

The entrance of mercantile capital from Mexico City was not restricted to the Monterde at Jalpa or the Sánchez de Tagle at Santa Ana Pacueco. In the first years of the century, Tomás Manuel de la Canal, the creole son of a wealthy Montañés merchant, abandoned Mexico City to take up residence in San Miguel el Grande, where he built a mansion which still dominates the main square of the town.[56] As in the case of the Monterde, he established an entail (*mayorazgo*) on his landed estates in order to preserve his descendants from 'the ruin and dissipation of funds and patrimony...which occurs all the time, causing the despair, outrage and decline of illustrious families'. At his death in 1743 he left goods worth 242,685 pesos which, apart from the house and a vineyard, consisted of an hacienda in San Miguel with 14 large sitios and no less than another 130 large sitios in New León, which pastured over 40,000 ewes and their offspring. With this support his family outlived the century.

V

By far the greatest landlords in the Bajío were the Mariscales de Castilla, who, according to the military census of 1792, then owned no less than eleven haciendas and eighteen separate ranchos stretching across several districts from San Miguel el Grande to Pénjamo.[57] Evidence concerning the formation of this vast entail is incomplete, derived as it is from a confused calendar of land titles drawn up for a lawsuit in 1723.[58] Apparently the famous hacienda of La Erre, situated in Dolores was created at much the same time as Jalpa. Between 1611 and 1617 viceregal *mercedes* for 11 large sitios, 11 small

sitios and 32 caballerías were issued to six persons, five of whom
almost at once sold their land to the remaining owner, Dr Hernán
Carrillo Altamirano, a lawyer resident in Mexico City, and active
in public defence of the creole upper class.[59] A few years before, he
had purchased two other sitios called El Gallinero, to which he
added a third obtained in *merced*. Somewhat later, in 1617–25, a
relative, possibly a brother, Juan Altamirano Saavedra, bought four
large and two small sitios to form the San Antón hacienda. All these
properties, situated in Dolores and San Miguel el Grande, passed by
inheritance to Rodrigo Mejía Altamirano, knight of the Order of
Santiago, Chief Constable of the Audiencia and possibly a miner at
Guanajuato, who thus acquired no less than 19½ large and 15 small
sitios.[60]

Equally important, in the last third of the sixteenth century,
Pedro Lorenzo de Castilla, alcalde mayor of Guanajuato, son of
Luis de Castilla, assembled a vast property of 37 sitios close to the
Río Turbio which crossed the districts of Rincón, Piedragorda and
Pénjamo. In the 1600s, his grand-daughter sold the estate to Rodrigo
Mejía Altamirano, along with the hacienda of Las Arandas in
Irapuato of 4 large sitios. To round off his acquisitions, Mejía
Altamirano purchased another 26 sitios on the area of the Río
Turbio, and in addition possibly received by inheritance a further
7 large sitios in Silao.

The heir to this vast chain of estates was the only daughter of
Mejía Altamirano, Juana, who married Carlos de Luna y Arellano,
eleventh Mariscal de Castilla, a descendant of the famous Con-
quistador Tristán de Luna.[61] Not content with their inheritance,
they bought from the Santa Clara convent of Querétaro 11 small
sitios situated in the Río Turbio area at a price of 2,125 pesos
charged as mortgage upon their estates. The original titles all date
from 1614. The Mariscala, as Juana was styled, continued her
purchases in the same area with 4 small sitios from the Jesuit College
at Valladolid for 8,640 pesos again charged upon the estate in
mortgage at five per cent in favour of the Santa Clara. The original
titles dated from the year 1613 to 1618 when some five persons had
obtained viceregal *mercedes*, only at once to cede or sell to the
Jesuits.[62] The precise dimension of these estates is difficult to determine, especially as in later years some sections were sold. But it is
worth recording that in 1800 the current Mariscal de Castilla offered
as security for a loan his haciendas of Concepción (Piedragorda)
Potrero de Río Turbio, Las Arandas (Irapuato) and San Pedro y

San Pablo (Dolores), which then comprised no less than seventy large and twenty small sitios or 324,720 acres, among which was included some of the best arable land in Mexico.[63]

Several general conclusions can be extracted from this welter of transactions. On the open plains of the Bajío, in Silao and Irapuato and parts of Piedragorda, land titles dated from the third quarter of the sixteenth century, in the years 1550–75. By contrast in the highland areas, to the north and west, in Dolores and Pénjamo, and immediately across the border in Jalisco, most land was not formally occupied until the first two decades of the seventeenth century. Moreover, the frequent recourse to lawsuit demonstrates that vice-regal *mercedes* in this still remote area often represented claims to ownership rather than actual possession. Finally, the low value of land as late as 1703 suggests that in the Río Turbio district at least, most sitios remained mere rough pasture.

But to what point these vast accumulations of land: what income did they yield their owners? Some answer to this question can be found in the summary accounts for the years 1700–09 presented during a lawsuit between the Mariscala and her son.[64] The family also owned Los Cortijos hacienda in Puebla, the Santa Caterina in Chalco, and received an annual income of 4,277 pesos from house rents in Mexico City. Another 5,157 pesos a year came from the possession of an *escribanía mayor de gobierno y guerra*, one of the two government offices through which flowed government documents for authentication. Their Guanajuato estates, simply dominated 'haciendas de La Erre', yielded a net annual income of 16,608 pesos. This term included the Río Turbio property, but it is not clear whether the Silao–Irapuato haciendas paid their profits into the same account; there is no separate mention of them.

As Table 3 indicates, these Guanajuato haciendas basically served as a vast sheep run. The overwhelming proportion of their receipts came from the sale of wool and sheep. Tallow, skins and rents complete the picture. Apparently, there was no attempt at direct cultivation, although presumably the average 4,669 pesos derived from rents came from the profits of farming; but this entry is complicated by the inclusion of the commission paid by the general manager for the lease of the hacienda store. The diversity evident in most haciendas of the region was thus replaced by an exclusive concentration upon sheep. Costs were high. Each year the Mariscal had to find over 17,000 pesos in general expenses and for wages, paid either in cash or cloth. Clearly, he required considerable cash reserves to tide him

TABLE 3 *Product and costs of Mariscal de Castilla estate denominated haciendas La Erre 1700–09*

PRODUCE AND GROSS INCOME

| | Wool | | Carneros | | Tallow | | | |
|---|---|---|---|---|---|---|---|---|
| Year | arrobas | net sale pesos* | number | net sale pesos | arrobas | net sale pesos | Rents pesos | Total product |
| 1700 | 7,977 | 22,645 | 14,493 | 25,362 | 971 | 2,922 | 3,081 | 54,263 |
| 1701–02 | 11,582 | 34,381 | 24,344 | 35,755 | 1,977 | 4,723 | 8,535 | 84,195 |
| 1703 | 6,891 | 23,339 | – | – | 1,032 | 2,011 | 3,181 | 29,532 |
| 1704 | 6,564 | 19,796 | 17,006 | 23,383 | 917 | 1,805 | 4,988 | 50,279 |
| 1705 | 5,203 | 16,322 | 14,000 | 20,125 | 854 | 2,657 | 5,325 | 46,995 |
| 1706 | 5,652 | 16,032 | 10,006 | 16,259 | 743 | 1,646 | 6,009 | 40,709 |
| 1707 | 4,666 | 12,875 | 9,276 | 16,233 | 702 | 1,550 | 4,479 | 35,292 |
| 1708 | 3,423 | 9,232 | – | – | 384 | 1,131 | 6,411 | 19,388 |
| 1709 | 2,312 | 5,815 | 16,773 | 28,371 | 313 | 1,084 | 4,686 | 40,869 |
| Average | 5,427 | 16,447 | 10,590 | 16,549 | 789 | 1,953 | 4,670 | 40,153 |

*Note:* Total includes miscellaneous items, skins, poines, etc.
\* Alcabala and freight already deducted from net sales.

COSTS AND CHARGES

| Year | Wages and shearing costs | Tithes to Valladolid | Tithes to Guadalajara | Tithe debts | Interest† | Rents, pasture, goats | Total costs | Net yield |
|---|---|---|---|---|---|---|---|---|
| 1700 | 15,506 | 4,461 | 1,104 | 1,000 | 1,343 | 480 | 23,895 | 30,378 |
| 1701 | 18,615 | 5,127 | 481 | 1,000 | 1,237 | 280 ⎫ | | 36,165 |
| 1702 | 18,571 | – | – | 1,000 | 1,237 | 480 ⎭ | 48,030 | |
| 1703 | 18,159 | 4,657 | – 190 | 1,000 | 1,087 | 280 | 27,524‡ | 2,007 |
| 1704 | 20,144 | 4,556 | – | 1,000 | 1,519 | 380 | 27,600 | 22,678 |
| 1705 | 19,082 | 4,023 | – | 1,000 | 1,519 | 80 | 25,705 | 21,290 |
| 1706 | 18,012 | 4,329 | – | 1,000 | 1,519 | 80 | 24,940 | 15,769 |
| 1707 | 17,841 | 3,873 | – | 1,000 | 1,519 | 80 | 24,314 | 10,978 |
| 1708 | 15,183 | 1,396 | – | 1,000 | 1,519 | 80 | 19,178 | 209 |
| 1709 | 11,626 | – | – | 1,000 | 1,519 | 119 | 14,265 | 16,604 |
| Average | 17,274 | 3,242 | 178 | 1,000 | 1,402 | 234 | 23,546 | 16,608 |

† 5% interest was paid on the following *censos*: 10,625 ps Hospital de San Juan de Dios; 9,000 ps San Bernardo Convent, Mexico; 2,125 ps Sta Clara Convent, Querétaro; after 1704 another 8,064 ps to Santa Clara, Querétaro.
‡ Includes 2,150 ps purchase price of 4 sitios.
*Source:* AGN, Vínculos 117.

over bad years. By contrast the interest on the ecclesiastical mortgages of 29,814 pesos only amounted to 1,518 pesos. The burden of tithes was heavy and the tendency to fall into arrears a constant. Since we have not found any inventory of these haciendas there is no way to calculate the average rate of return upon capital. All we take away is the tantalising impression of a great enterprise and a large overall profit.

At some point during the eighteenth century, the Mariscales de Castilla radically changed the manner in which they exploited their Guanajuato property. They abandoned sheepherding and became rentiers. Whether this dramatic transition applied to all their estates is not clear, but in 1772 their general manager resolutely refused to collect the tributes of Indians and mulattoes resident in the haciendas since, with the land in tenancy, he had little idea of how many persons actually inhabited the estates. His statement implied the total absence of peons to work even the casco. Furthermore he provided a statement of income.

TABLE 4  *Mariscal de Castilla estates: tenants and rent 1772*

| Haciendas | Number of tenants | Total rent |
|---|---|---|
| Las Arandas (Irapuato) | 105 | 8,040 ps |
| Concepción (Piedragorda) | 128 | 3,653 ps |
| La Rosita (San Miguel) | 361 | 10,127 ps |
| | 594 | 21,820 ps |

*Source:* AGI, México, 1370, Manager's Report, 4 February 1772.

The extent of these haciendas is uncertain. There is no mention of the Silao estates; possibly they contributed to the Las Arandas account. Similarly one suspects that La Erre was included under the rubric of La Rosita. At this time, of course, Dolores formed part of the San Miguel *alcaldía mayor*. A straw in the wind can be gleaned from the 1792 *padrón* in which La Erre, even with Indians excluded, housed some 205 Spanish and *casta* tenants.[65] For absentee landlords like the Mariscales de Castilla, the advantages of a tenancy system were manifold. Although their income was presumably lower than the yield of direct exploitation, they avoided further capital investment and eliminated entirely the risks inevitably connected with any enterprise dependent on variable rainfall. It was, of course, a logical reaction to favourable market conditions, where a rising urban demand for foodstuffs was matched by an increased supply of farmers and labourers in search of land.

## VI

Needless to say, most haciendas avoided such extreme reactions, since their owners lacked the resources for extensive capital invest-ment and needed the profits that could still be obtained from demesne farming. Moreover, the variegated nature of their terrain encouraged the persistence of stockraising alongside cereal produc-tion. To comprehend their situation at mid century, let us examine with some care the record of the Juchitlán el Grande, an estate situated to the northeast of Querétaro between the small towns of Soriano and Cadereyta and thus standing at the very edge of our region. With its subordinate ranchos of Santa Rosa, Los Panales, San José Curacupes and Zituni, it comprised at least 39 large sitios (over 170,000 acres), but since most of this land was stony or mountainous, in 1752 the entire estate with livestock was only worth 89,894 pesos.[66] Its Church mortgages had climbed to 36,540 pesos and in addition, the owners had raised another 17,332 pesos from private individuals. In 1752, with unpaid interest at 6,213 pesos, the creditors embargoed the hacienda and installed an administrator. The sketchy accounts he later submitted form the basis of our discussion.

The Juchitlán offered its owners three main sources of income: maize-growing, goat herding, and ground rents.[67] The product of the small herds of 190 cattle, 300 sheep and 100 brood mares, com-bined with occasional sales of barley and beans, complete the picture. Most of the land was used for pasture. The 30 sitios of the Panales rancho supported a herd of about 11,000 goats, which in the decade 1753–62 yielded an average income of 1,810 pesos from the annual slaughter of 1,830 animals. Some 30 flocks of sheep and goats from Huichiapán and el Mezquital pastured on these fields each year at a cost of 900 pesos a year. An unspecified income derived from maguey plants. There is reference to four and five *tlachiqueros de mescal* who periodically set up small distilleries within the hacienda. One individual moved about with 18 workers cutting firewood and milking the magueys; he paid 30 pesos a month rent.

In the two farms located at Juchitlán itself and Santa Rosa, about 2,412 fanegas were produced each year if we take the average for the period 1754–70. Actual sales amounted to just under sixty per cent

TABLE 5   *Juchitlán and Los Panales: production and income 1752–72*

| Year | Harvest fanegas | Sales fanegas | Product pesos | Goats Prime | Old |
|---|---|---|---|---|---|
| 1752 | 5,211 | | | | |
| 1753 | 3,353 | | | 746 | 263 |
| 1754 | 2,566 | 2,437 | 1,276 | 1,689 | 340 |
| 1755 | 1,211 | 1,601 | 1,601 | 1,216 | 456 |
| 1756 | 4,107 | 3,328 | 4,074 | 1,346 | 551 |
| 1757 | 1,802 | 138 | 137 | 1,400 | 451 |
| 1758 | 1,643 | 1,687 | 1,639 | 1,334 | 539 |
| 1759 | 854 | 1,145 | 1,245 | 1,444 | 624 |
| 1760 | 3,141 | 1,488 | 2,178 | 1,200 | 610 |
| 1761 | 1,932 | 2,747 | 4,157 | 1,398 | 669 |
| 1762 | 2,194 | 281 | 475 | 1,532 | 516 |
| 1763 | 1,759 | 567 | 702 | | |
| 1764 | 274* | 1,780 | 920 | Average 1,331 | 502 |
| 1765 | 3,423 | −† | − | | |
| 1766 | 6,836 | −† | − | Prices: | |
| 1767 | 3,630 | 1,169 | 380 | Chivatos at 9 reales | |
| 1768 | 3,385 | 3,132 | 1,315 | Cabras at 5 reales | |
| 1769 | 1,339 | 1,818 | 1,136 | | |
| 1770 | 910 | 890 | 1,144 | | |
| 1771 | 859 | 519 | 797 | | |
| 1772 | 77 | 210 | 341 | | |
| Average | 2,521‡ | 1,313 | 1,238 | | |

* little sown        † no sales        ‡ omitting 1772
*Note:* Maize sold derives from harvest of previous calendar year.
*Source:* AGN, Tierras, 827.

of harvests, the remainder presumably being consumed by the peons or left to rot. At an overall price of 7.4 reales a fanega, the average yield for these years came to 1,316 pesos. Marked variations occurred both in actual crop production and the prices obtained. The super-abundant harvests of the middle 1760s, a phenomenon common throughout New Spain, proved especially disastrous with little grain finding a market.

The permanent work force was not large. The mayordomo of the Juchitlán was assisted by two *caporales* to mind the horses, four cowboys for the cattle, a general help, and 18 peons (*gañanes*) for the maize farms. In Los Panales, the mayordomo had 18 shepherds and at Curacupes the slaughterhouse required a guard. In all, the wage-bill came to 1,940 pesos a year, with the two mayordomos taking 120 and 160 pesos each. The caporales, cowboys, guard and assistant were paid 4 pesos a month, and the shepherds and peons

3 pesos. In addition, they received a maize ration. The Juchitlán mayordomo took 8 pesos a month in cash, and 2 pesos in maize. But he also had free pasture for his livestock and enjoyed the customary right of milking the hacienda goats during the rainy season to make cheese which he then sold for his personal profit. There is no mention in these documents of debt peonage.

Rental of cultivated land constituted the third main source of income. The entire rancho of Zituni was leased for 500 pesos a year; whether to one or many individuals is not stated. Ground rents in Juchitlán and Panales on average yielded 1,586 pesos a year. A detailed enquiry made in 1763 listed 22 persons in Los Panales who together paid 272 pesos in rent, the sums ranging from 1 to 40 pesos. Of these entries, some 16 had held their land since at least 1752 and another 3 since 1754. The Indians of San Antonio Bernal, a small neighbouring village, rented a small rancho for 25 pesos. In Juchitlán the variations were greater, the situation more fluid. That year, 66 persons paid a combined rent of 1,245 pesos. One man paid 125 pesos for an entire sitio and another 100 pesos. Here, far fewer tenants (26) remained in their farms for the entire decade. Some 14 had only entered in the last two years. Moreover, within the hacienda itself, there was a considerable degree of movement. One Indian, Pedro Felipe, started the decade with a rent of 3 pesos and finished by paying 30 pesos. Juan Manuel Cabrera leased one rancho for 40 pesos, and then changed to another which cost him 100 pesos. These increases all sprang from the greater area taken by the tenants. In another case, however, reference is made to an individual who for two years only paid 9 pesos since he had 'opened new land'. In the third year, the rent for this same tract rose to 33 pesos. The 1752 inventory revealed that the tenants cultivated more land than the owners – 172 fanegas de sembradura compared to 44 in both Panales and Juchitlán. The average rent was 8 pesos a fanegas de sembradura.

If our calculations are correct, then in the period 1753–62, the Juchitlán yielded an average yearly gross income of 6,544, taken from the sources below.

|  |  |
|---|---|
| Maize sales | 1,748 ps |
| Goat sales | 1,810 ps |
| Ground rents | 2,086 ps |
| Pasture rents | 900 ps |
| Total | 6,544 ps |

If this annual figure be divided into the appraised estate value of 90,000 pesos, it results in a return on capital of 7.1%. However, it seems likely that the wage-bill of 1,940 pesos has to be subtracted from the gross receipts so that the net return was closer to 5.1%, a more plausible rate for such an hacienda. But since the 5% interest on the ecclesiastical mortgages and other charges amounted to 3,189 pesos a year, then in fact the owners received a mere 1,415 pesos a year. Small wonder they fell into debt, since in part they must have lived off the loans they raised as much as on income.

## VII

At first glance, the structure of agricultural production in the Bajío might appear riven by contradictions, since alongside absentee proprietors maintained by the rents of their tenants we encounter energetic entrepreneurs busily engaged in transforming their estates through extensive capital investment. In fact, both policies – withdrawal from direct cultivation and investment in dams and barns – were based on sound economic reasons. The mounting urban demand for staple foodstuffs was more than matched by an increase in rural population which provided an ample flow of potential tenants and labourers. It was this pressure on land and the competition from small-holders in local markets that led the great landlords either to lease their estates or to construct dams to irrigate land for the cultivation of wheat. Although land and estate values rose dramatically during the course of the eighteenth century, neither wages nor the price of maize followed suit. As late as 1806 the owner of the great Istla hacienda in Apaseo complained that, with current prices as low as 5 reales a fanega, it was not profitable for him to sell the several thousand fanegas of maize stored in his barns.[68] Yet his estate required 8,000 pesos a year to keep it in production and another 2,000 pesos to pay the interest charges on Church mortgages.

To turn to the labour side of the equation, the situation in the Bajío more closely resembled the system in the haciendas of San Luis Potosí, as described by Jan Bazant, than the pattern prevailing in the central valleys or the south. In place of Indian villages acting as reservoirs of rural manpower, landowners let a considerable proportion of their lands to tenants and sharecroppers. Most haciendas in the Bajío housed both resident peons and arrendatarios. In addition, they hired a third group of labourers for seasonal tasks. With an assured wage and a fixed allowance of maize, the *sirvientes acomodados*

– to give the peons their true name – enjoyed circumstances superior to the seasonal uncertainties of the day-hand or the lesser tenant. The lowest stratum in agrarian society were the *alquilados*, the labourers hired by the day for the harvest and other seasonal tasks. In 1803, the corregidor of Querétaro, Miguel Domínguez, commented on the extraordinary mobility of Indians in his district, a characteristic which rendered the collection of tribute difficult.[69] During the summer rains, large numbers of Indians entered the city seeking employment in the factories and workshops of the textile industry. Then, in the autumn, they returned to the country to hire themselves in squads for the harvest or else subrented lands as *arrimados* from regular tenants. In Querétaro, he wrote: 'one of the chief lines of business for the haciendas is the letting of small plots of land – one or two fanegas de sembradura – with the rent paid either in cash or by a share of the crop'.

Perhaps the most interesting group of men in the countryside of the Bajío were the rancheros. This class formed a broad, middle segment in agrarian society. At its head stood the small proprietors, the owners of 200 to 500 acres. Alongside them may be placed the mayordomos of the great estates and the chief tenant farmers who leased entire ranchos. Beneath these prosperous individuals were to be found the small-holders who held but ten or twenty acres and the lesser tenants. It is difficult to obtain any reliable indication of their number, all the more since conditions varied from district to district. However, the significance of this class resides not so much in numbers as in its strategic social position between the landed elite and the mass of countrydwellers. Yet despite the key role played by these men in later Mexican history, we still lack any characterisation of the ranchero other than the classic study of Luis González, which deals with but one district in Michoacán.[70] Here is a topic of social history which demands future research.

## CHAPTER 3

# Population

I

There was little in the early history of León to suggest its future prominence as a leading industrial centre. For most of the colonial period, it remained a small market town overshadowed by the booming prosperity of Guanajuato which was situated only a day's journey away in the sierra. Founded in 1576 as a military outpost to safeguard the silver trains from Chichimeca attack, the *villa* of San Sebastián de León soon benefited from its commercially advantageous position at the western border of the Bajío, straddling the trade routes which led to Zacatecas and Guadalajara.[1] The town also served as the administrative capital of an extensive *alcaldía mayor*, which included the districts of Pénjamo, San Pedro Piedragorda and Rincón. But the main purpose of the town was to serve as a place of residence for local landowners and farmers.

From the outset the small band of Spanish settlers were joined by free mulattoes and Indians. In 1591 a few Otomies set up a small village called San Miguel a few hundred yards south of the main square, and some years later another group of Indians, possibly Tarascans, built a second pueblo, called Coecillo, on the eastern outskirts of the town.[2] That Indians moved into this zone some years after the Spanish occupation is confirmed by the comparatively late foundation of San Francisco de Rincón in 1605, and still more by the viceregal recognition of its neighbour, Purísima de Rincón, in 1648.[3] An episcopal report of 1631 described the 120 Indians then living in Rincón as all *advenedizos*, new-comers, mainly of Otomí descent. The same report indicated that there were still only 75 married house-holders in León, together with a further 24 widows and bachelors. Similarly, the two Indian hamlets – *pueblecillos* – housed no more than 24 families, among whom were to be found Mexicans, Tarascans and Otomies.[4] In fact, most Indians lived on rural estates and farms, since the report listed 125 labourers. As yet, the mulatto population was small, with some 12 families in town and another five workers in the country.

39

Although the chief source of wealth and employment undoubtedly
lay in the countryside, where by the close of the eighteenth century
some 26 haciendas and 56 ranchos dominated the scene, nevertheless
the town was the chosen place of residence for most landowners and
many farmers, whose households, including family, servants and
slaves, formed an extensive market for the services and goods offered
by local artisans and merchants. Unfortunately, since the 1792
military *padrón* for León is missing, the only guide to the distribution
of urban occupations comes from a rather simple census of vecinos
compiled in 1719, which omits all reference to Coecillo and San Miguel.

TABLE 6     *Villa of León 1719: leading occupations*

| Priests | 12 | Miners | 32 | Tailors | 26 |
|---|---|---|---|---|---|
| Merchants | 21 | Weavers | 22 | Carpenters | 20 |
| Tradesmen | 36 | Muleteers | 38 | Smiths | 16 |
| Hacendados | 19 | Shoe-makers | 67 | Servants (men) | 31 |
| Farmers | 33 | Saddlers | 29 | Slaves (men) | 71 |
| Mayordomos | 10 | Charcoal-burners | 33 | Slaves (women) | 62 |
| Gardeners | 16 | | | | |

*Source:* AHML, census 1719.

In all the town was deemed to house just under 3,000 persons.
Perhaps the most surprising feature here was the comparatively large
number of slaves, who were employed as domestic servants, with
most landowners and merchants owning from three to six slaves.
No ethnic data is supplied, but to judge from contemporary inventories of estate, most slaves in León were native-born mulattoes
rather than newly-imported Africans. Otherwise, the census offers
few revelations. From the perspective of later developments, it is
perhaps significant that already by 1719 shoe-makers were the
largest trade. Similarly, the existence of weavers and muleteers
emphasises that, in addition to being the residence of agriculturists,
the town was also a centre of industry and commercial transport.
Textile and leather goods were both to experience considerable
progress in the course of the century and in 1803 the intendant
reported the existence of 107 looms for weaving cotton cloth.[5]
By then, the industrial future was already perceptible.

## II

With land in abundant supply and urban demand for rural
produce steadily mounting as silver production at Guanajuato

surged forward, León offered a propitious terrain for population growth. By the 1680s, a tribute account listed 726 mulattoes of all ages resident in the entire *alcaldía mayor* alongside 321 Indians in the district of León and another 113 in Rincón and 131 in Pénjamo.[6] Thereafter the pace of increase gathered momentum. But without a knowledge of the total population it is difficult to measure the effective rate. How many people lived in León in the eighteenth century? Here, some geographical distinctions must be made. The parish of León must be distinguished from the civil *partido* which, until the creation of a separate subdelegation of Rincón in 1787, included the parish of San Francisco de Rincón. Then again, certain haciendas, in particular Gavia and Santa Ana, fell within the limits of the parish of Silao, although they were subject to the civil jurisdiction of León. Finally, as mentioned above, the *alcaldía mayor* of León, which does not concern us, included Pénjamo and San Pedro Piedragorda.

The first reliable information about total population derives from an ecclesiastical census, requested by the bishop of Valladolid in September 1758 and finally compiled by 3 April 1761.[7] It enumerates 15,605 persons aged seven and over in the parish of León and another 3,165 in Rincón. The missing number of infants can be calculated with some degree of assurance. In the 1793 census for the entire intendency of Guanajuato, which breaks down the population by age group, children under seven comprised 23% of the total count. Moreover, in their analysis of the 1777 diocesan census of Oaxaca, Puebla, and Durango, Professors Cook and Borah arrive at similar proportions, ranging from 21 to 23%.[8] Applying this value to the 1761 census, we obtain an overall total of 19,194 persons.

The next available source is a scheme, compiled 4 April 1781 and later printed by the local antiquarian, José Guadalupe Romero. The original manuscript has not been discovered.

TABLE 7    *Parish of León: census of 1781*

|  | Spaniards | Indians | Castas | Total |
|---|---|---|---|---|
| Villa de León | 1,585 | 378 | 3,544 | 5,507 |
| Pueblo de San Miguel | – | 1,386 | – | 1,386 |
| Pueblo del Coecillo | – | 2,472 | – | 2,472 |
| Haciendas y ranchos | 1,619 | 2,109 | 5,482 | 9,210 |
| Total | 3,204 | 6,345 | 9,026 | 18,575 |

*Source:* José Guadalupe Romero, *Noticias para formar la historia y la estadística del obispado de Michoacán,* p. 190.

Both the ethnic proportions and the distribution between town and countryside appear reliable. The only difficulty lies with the final total. Did the population of León actually decline in the years between 1761 and 1781? True, in the latter year the town was recovering from the 1779–80 smallpox epidemic, but it is doubtful whether this was sufficient to negate twenty years natural increase. One explanation might be that Romero miscopied the date of the census; he was quite careless in these matters.[9] A more likely solution to the problem is to assume that, like most of its kind, the census was an enumeration of all persons aged seven and over. If this be the case, then another 23% should be added to reach a total population of 22,847.

Further problems confront us in considering the 1793 civil census totals – the manuscript house count or *padrón* does not exist or was never taken. For since all mention of Rincón is omitted, at first sight the figure of 23,711 persons might be thought to include that subordinate district.[10] However, an ecclesiastical census for the same year, recently discovered by Claude Morin, enumerated 16,819 persons aged seven and over for the parish of León and another 6,447 for Rincón.[11] It is therefore clear that the civil count applies only to León. Unfortunately, the two totals do not tally. For if we employ the value of 23% for children under seven, then the ecclesiastical total comes to 20,687. Two reasons can be advanced to explain the discrepancy. Either the proportion of infants in the 1793 population was considerably higher than usual, i.e. 29%, a not unreasonable presumption if we consider the effects of the 1785–86 famine on infant mortality and conceptions. Alternatively, the difference sprang quite simply from the district physical boundaries of the parish and the civil district. In any case, it will be noticed that on either count, the population grew quite slowly in these last decades of the eighteenth century.

For the years after Independence, contemporary estimates ranged from 50,000 to 80,000 persons. An ecclesiastical census for the period 1824–28 yields a figure of 45,952 without specifying the age groups included. The lack of reliable data is not repaired until 1882, when a state census found that the municipio or district supported 70,122 inhabitants of whom 40,742 lived in the city. The districts of Rincón had a combined total of 29,929 persons.[12] But since our count stops with the division of parishes in 1864, this census is of little assistance save to combat earlier over-estimates.

The source materials for this study are the parochial registers of baptisms, burials, marriages and marriage testimonies, all housed in the parochial dispensary.[13] The baptismal series starts in 1635, burials in 1677 and marriages in 1635, but in all three cases, materials are ill-organised, incomplete and in poor condition. The reverse is true of the eighteenth century when three separate registers were kept for Spaniards, *castas* and Indians. For all three ethnic categories, continuous entry for baptisms begins in 1693. For burials, the Indian and casta series start in 1720, but the Spanish register is lost for the years prior to 1746. The marriage records for Spaniards and *castas* begin in 1711, for Indians in 1743. With some minor exceptions, after 1746, all three series survive virtually intact until 1821. After Independence ethnic distinctions were officially abolished and a single register for all parishioners was opened. There are, however, several unfortunate breaks in the documents of these years. In 1864 the parish was divided into three, with each unit setting up its own archive. At this point our study ends.

The fourth series we employ, the marriage testimonies presented by prospective spouses, some fragments apart, only begin in 1778. Unfortunately, after 1800 lost volumes, incomplete entries and broken years, render the material discontinuous and unreliable. From the 1850s, however, at least three good volumes survive.

Two final questions require discussion before we present the data. How trustworthy are these materials for demographic analysis? How self-contained are they, i.e., what was the extent of migration in and out of the parish? In the first place, it must be emphasised that the parish priest recorded baptisms, marriages and burials, not births, procreative unions and deaths. The presumption of faithful correspondence follows a declining order. Nearly all infants born in León, with the exception of those dying soon after birth, were baptised. The sacrament acted as the indispensable entry into Christian and civil life. For marriage, the presumption is less strong. In the marriage testimonies a certain number of persons declared themselves illegitimate. Nevertheless, we may assume that most people married. There were good social, civil and religious reasons for this. By contrast there was far less incentive to pay for a church burial. We shall argue below that marked under-registration occurred. It is this probability which severely limits the utility of these records.

In the second place, there is no way to measure migration. Burial registers mention place of last residence, not of origin. A straw in the wind can be found in the marriage testimonies. In 1782–85 under

8 per cent of all informants declared birth places outside the parish borders; most of these 'foreigners' came from the adjacent districts of Silao, Rincón, Guanajuato and Lagos. This suggests that during the eighteenth century León only received a slight ripple of immigration, possibly no more in number than its emigration. On the other hand, more general sources indicate considerable physical mobility in the Bajío. In 1792 one fifth of all adult males living in the immediate district of Guanajuato originated outside the *partido*.[14] Many of these migrants came from León. The picture changes in the years following 1810. The effect of the Hidalgo rebellion was to ruin the great mines of Guanajuato, and to drive a good part of its working population into the surrounding area.[15] Since in the same years León registered an abrupt rise in the number of baptisms and burials, it seems safe to assume that a good many of these migrants settled there. No further information is available as to the physical movement of population. We therefore concentrate entirely upon the phenomenon of natural increase.

## III

Since separate registers were kept for the three ethnic categories of Spaniards, Indians and castas, it is convenient to begin our discussion with the question of intermarriage. How homogeneous were these groups? It may prove helpful to recall that both Indians and mulattoes paid tribute, the colonial capitation tax, and in common social esteem were considered inferior to mestizos and Spaniards. The term mulatto simply described anyone with some degree of African ancestry.[16] By the late eighteenth century few other ethnic designations were widely used.

Since collection of this type of data is remarkably time-consuming (each marriage requires individual entry) we chose as sample years 1782–85 inclusive and 1792–93 inclusive. The source utilised was the marriage testimonies rather than the register, as this permitted the simultaneous annotation of marital age. Unfortunately, it was only after the research was completed, that we found the testimonies did not exactly correspond with the register. For the years 1782–85, omissions ranged from 12% for Spaniards and *castas* to 22% for Indians. By contrast for 1792–93, more testimonies were presented than marriages celebrated, except for Indians where omissions persisted, albeit at 11%. Some discrepancy was expected, granted the effect of December testimonies for January marriages, but differences of such magnitude threatened to invalidate the enquiry. With some ingenuity, however, the problem was resolved. We first made the presumption that the two registers for Spaniards and Indians only recorded marriages of Spaniards with Spaniards and Indians with Indians; all other unions were entered in the *casta* register. Second, we assumed that the 12% omissions for casta marriages were evenly spread across the board. On the basis of these two premises, we then 'doctored' the initial figures by (a) increasing the numbers of Spaniards marrying Spaniards and Indians marrying Indians to the exact number recorded in the matrimonial register and (b) increasing all other unions by approximately 11%. In 1792–93, testimonies for castas exceeded marriages by 9%, for Spaniards about equalled actual marriages, and for Indians undercounted by 11%. We therefore corrected the Indian and Spanish figures to correspond to the register, thereby inserting no more than 8 individuals. Table 8 provides the corrected figures.

TABLE 8  *León intermarriage rates*
A. 1782–85

|  | Mulatas | | Españolas | | Mestizas | | Indias | | Total | | Inter-marriage rate |
|---|---|---|---|---|---|---|---|---|---|---|---|
|  | no. | % | no. | % | no. | % | no. | % | no. | % | % |
| Mulatos | 307 | 66.7 | 22 | 4.7 | 50 | 10.8 | 81 | 17.8 | 460 | 100 | 32.3 |
| Españoles | 9 | 6.7 | 102 | 75.5 | 23 | 17.0 | 1 | 0.8 | 135 | 100 | 24.5 |
| Mestizos | 24 | 31.6 | 17 | 22.4 | 29 | 38.1 | 6 | 7.9 | 76 | 100 | 61.9 |
| Indios | 114 | 32.9 | 6 | 1.8 | 18 | 5.2 | 208 | 60.1 | 346 | 100 | 39.9 |
| Total | 454 | | 147 | | 120 | | 296 | | 1,017 | | 36.4 |

B. 1792–93

|  | Mulatas | | Españolas | | Mestizas | | Indias | | Total | | Inter-marriage rate |
|---|---|---|---|---|---|---|---|---|---|---|---|
|  | no. | % | no. | % | no. | % | no. | % | no. | % | % |
| Mulatos | 220 | 67.9 | 15 | 4.6 | 35 | 10.8 | 54 | 16.7 | 324 | 100 | 32.1 |
| Españoles | 7 | 6.6 | 81 | 76.4 | 18 | 17.0 | – | – | 106 | 100 | 23.6 |
| Mestizos | 9 | 18.7 | 10 | 20.8 | 23 | 48.0 | 6 | 12.5 | 48 | 100 | 52.0 |
| Indios | 53 | 44.2 | 4 | 3.3 | 10 | 8.3 | 53 | 44.2 | 120 | 100 | 55.8 |
| Total | 289 | | 110 | | 86 | | 113 | | 598 | | 36.9 |

*Note:* In Table A, 5 informants, and in Table B, 1 informant are omitted due to insufficient data.

The column of percentages refer to the male intermarriage rate; the female rate was somewhat different.

*Source:* Informaciones y Registros Matrimoniales, Archivo Parroquial de Léon.

Despite our manipulations, the tables reveal remarkable congruence. Spanish behaviour, for example, remained consistent. In both 1782–85 and 1792–93, the male intermarriage rate was low, no more than 24%. When Spaniards chose wives from outside their category, most preferred mestizos (17%). Only a handful (under 7%) took mulattoes and almost no-one accepted Indian women. Spanish women had a somewhat higher intermarriage rate – 29.6% and, oddly enough, inclined more to marry mulattoes than mestizos. A few (4%) found Indian husbands.

The mulattoes, about half the entire sample, similarly maintained a stable pattern of preferences. About a third of all men selected wives outside their ethnic category. Their first choice was for Indians (about 17%) followed by mestizos (10.8%) and then Spaniards (4.6%). Their women had much the same overall rate of intermarriage, but far more – 24% – chose Indians. Whereas 15% of mulatto men married 'upwards', out of the tributary class, only 7% of their women followed suit.

The mestizos, the smallest group under consideration, betrayed a striking lack of homogeneity, the male intermarriage rate ranging from 61% in 1781–85 to 52% in 1792–93. As befitted their middle rank, about a fifth married 'upwards' to Spaniards, and the remainder 'downwards' to mulattoes and Indians. The ambiguous quality of mestizo status is best revealed in their women folk. In both samples there were considerably more mestizo women than men, and in each case about three quarters of them married out of their ethnic category; about two fifths chose mulattoes, and just under a fifth Spaniards. Unlike mulatto and Indian women, they were somewhat more upwardly mobile than their men. But then, granted their greater number, the suspicion exists that many may well have been mulattoes or Indians on the move.

By contrast to the other groups, the Indians experienced a considerable change in their marriage patterns between 1782–85 and 1792–93. For men overall intermarriage rose from 39.9% to no less than 55.8%. Women followed suit, their intermarriage rate rising from 29% to 53%. This transition marked a steady amalgamation with the mulattoes. In the first sample, 32.9% of Indian men found mulatto wives, but in 1792–93 as many married mulattoes as Indians (44.2%). Only a handful mated Spaniards or mestizos, 7% rising to 11%. In the case of women, their non-Indian husbands were almost exclusively mulatto. At the same time, the Indian share of total marriages fell from a third to a fifth. These changes, which are obviously linked, can be attributed to (a) a long-term trend towards fusion with the mulattoes and (b) the immediate effect of the 1785–86 famine. Whatever the cause the Indians clearly formed a declining, residual category.

Used with some caution, all these percentages throw new light into the dark corners of Mexican social history. At times, the testimonies present material for comedy. Often the informants proved mistaken as to the ethnic quality of their future spouses. Not infrequently a man declared his prospective wife to be a mulatto, only to hear her describe herself as an Indian. Some outsiders abstained from any declaration of ethnic quality, only to be revealed as mulattoes in the bride's testimony. Nevertheless, most of these errors pointed in the same direction. All the evidence presented above tends to confirm our earlier analysis of intermarriage patterns among mine-workers in Guanajuato.[17] By the close of the eighteenth century, the Indian and mulatto groups of the Bajío were on the point of coalescence. Already many individuals could not accurately describe their own ethnic status. This conclusion has an important analytic consequence. The current image of Mexican colonial society, mainly based upon the descriptions of early-nineteenth-century historians, posits a fairly sharp division between Indians and the hispanic community composed of *castas* and Spaniards. In both Guanajuato and León, however, marriage preferences suggest that the lines of social esteem were drawn upon a different axis. In this part of Mexico after two centuries of cohabitation, there still existed two separate groups in society, the one composed of Indians, mulattoes and a few mestizos, and the other of Spaniards and most mestizos. The tribute-paying categories obviously enjoyed lower social status, but in no sense can they be viewed as a lower class. The Spanish–mestizo group especially in the towns was far too numerous to constitute a mere elite group. Furthermore, needless to say, it is not helpful to interpret them as a 'middle' class in a Molina Enríquez fashion, since they scaled the entire occupational structure. The late-nineteenth-century utilisation of the term *mestizaje* proves to be little more than a convenient descriptive label; in no sense does it explain the complex social process of ethnic and cultural fusion.

## IV

The marriage testimonies provide a further class of information not available in any colonial register or census – the age of marriage.

Here the question of omissions does not arise: there is no reason to suppose that the non-informants were aged any differently from those who presented declarations. These testimonies, it must be emphasised, reveal the average age of those about to contract matrimony, not the average age of marriage. There is no information as to the number of single adults. As samples, we present the years 1782–85, 1792–93 and 1858–60.

Table 9 is largely self-explanatory. For the years 1782–85 inclusive, the median age of women about to celebrate their first marriage was 16. A full 81.5% of these informants described themselves as aged 20 and under. Certain preferences governed their statements. For some reason 18 and 20 were more favoured than 17 and 19. For the older bride 25 was attractive. At the younger limit both 15 and 16 were acceptable. Broken down by ethnic category, the pattern changes somewhat. The median age of Spaniards, mulattoes and mestizos moves to 17. That is was the Indian weight which pulled down the median is confirmed by the 1792–93 sample, where, with the decrease in the total number of Indians, the overall median rises to 17. A half century later, during the three years 1858–60, the median age had risen to 18. This increase, however, may prove illusory, since at this time the testimonies no longer distinguish between first and second marriages. It is this change which may account for the fall to 72.5% of informants declaring themselves as aged 20 and under.

The median age of men about to enter first marriage was rather later than the female equivalent. In 1782–85, it was 20. Even so, a full 84.6% described themselves as 25 and under. If we include widowers (over 13% of all informants) the median rises to 21. In 1858–60 this median rose to 22. Once again, the failure to distinguish first and second marriages probably accounts for this change. Here 73.4% gave ages of 25 or under.

The demographic effects of these low ages for the first marriage of women requires little elaboration: it bespoke a high level of fertility. Mexican women followed East European or Asian, rather than West European or Spanish patterns of behaviour.[18] The capacity of the population to recover from the effects of famine or epidemic was clearly strengthened by this short reproductive cycle.

TABLE 9 *Age at marriage León: 1782–93, 1858–60*

A. FEMALE

| Age | 1782–85 | 1786–88 | 1792–93 | 1858–60 |
|---|---|---|---|---|
| 12–13 | 11 | 1 | 15 | 16 |
| 14 | 40 | 15 | 41 | 36 |
| 15 | 157 | 61 (1) | 90 | 293 |
| 16 | 192 (1) | 90 (2) | 125 | 284 |
| 17 | 58 (2) | 34 (2) | 33 | 136 |
| 18 | 96 | 73 (4) | 73 | 312 |
| 19 | 34 (1) | 20 (3) | 44 (1) | 115 |
| 20 | 73 (5) | 53 (12) | 56 (2) | 178 |
| 21–25 | 87 (10) | 59 (24) | 62 (11) | 305 |
| 26–30 | 32 (12) | 25 (25) | 18 (5) | 159 |
| 31–39 | 18 (14) | 14 (30) | 2 (8) | 47 |
| 40– | 3 (11) | 2 (13) | 1 (8) | 35 |
| Total | 801 (56) | 447 (116) | 560 (35) | 1,916 |
| Median age of first marriage | 16 | 18 | 17 | (18) |

*Note:* Figures in brackets are remarriages and are additional. For 1858–60 remarriages are included in total.
*Source:* Archivo Parroquial, León: Informaciones Matrimoniales.

B. MALE

| Age | 1782–85 | 1786–88 | 1858–60 |
|---|---|---|---|
| 13–15 | 21 (1) | 7 | 24 |
| 16 | 58 | 29 (2) | 60 |
| 17 | 16 | 9 | 58 |
| 18 | 103 (3) | 45 (1) | 276 |
| 19 | 64 (1) | 35 | 151 |
| 20 | 144 (2) | 63 (3) | 262 |
| 21–25 | 229 (20) | 136 (18) | 565 |
| 26–30 | 68 (20) | 41 (40) | 289 |
| 31–39 | 30 (22) | 23 (47) | 101 |
| 40– | 10 (49) | 3 (72) | 116 |
| Total | 743 (118) | 391 (183) | 1,902 |
| Median age of first marriage | 20 | 21 | (22) |

*Note:* Figures in brackets refer to remarriages and are additional. The column 1858–60 includes remarriages.
*Source:* Archivo Parroquial León: Informaciones Matrimoniales.

C.
1782–85

| Women | | | | Men | | |
|---|---|---|---|---|---|---|
| Age | Total | % | Remarriages | Total | % | Remarriages |
| 12–15 | 208 | 26.0 | – | 21 | 2.8 | 1 |
| 16–20 | 453 | 56.5 | 9 | 385 | 51.8 | 6 |
| 21–25 | 87 | 10.9 | 10 | 229 | 30.8 | 20 |
| 26–30 | 32 | 4.0 | 12 | 68 | 9.2 | 20 |
| 31– | 21 | 2.6 | 25 | 40 | 5.4 | 71 |
| Total | 801 | 100.0 | 56 | 743 | 100.0 | 118 |
| Median age of marriage | 16 | | | | 20 | |

1858–60

| | Women | | Men | |
|---|---|---|---|---|
| Age | Total | % | Total | % |
| 12–15 | 345 | 18.1 | 24 | 1.2 |
| 16–20 | 1,025 | 54.4 | 807 | 42.5 |
| 21–25 | 305 | 18.1 | 565 | 29.7 |
| 26–30 | 159 | 8.3 | 289 | 15.2 |
| 31– | 82 | 3.1 | 217 | 11.4 |
| Total | 1,916 | 100.0 | 1,902 | 100.0 |
| Median age of marriage | 18 | | 22 | |

*Note:* Discrepancies in totals caused by incomplete information in individual testimonies.
*Source:* Archivo Parroquial de León, Informaciones Matrimoniales.

## V

In this section we discuss the basic series of baptisms, burials and marriages. It is convenient to examine the implications of the overall totals before breaking them down into ethnic categories. The loss of the Spanish burial register until 1746 limits the enquiry to the period 1750–1860.

The most cursory glance at Table 10 reveals its merits and default. The baptismal and marriage rates manifest a basic correspondence and coherence. Between the early 1750s and the 1830s, both experienced a threefold increase. By contrast, the burial rate not merely

TABLE 10  *Baptisms, burials and marriages: León 1751–1860*

| Years | Baptisms | Burials | Increase | Marriages |
|---|---|---|---|---|
| 1751–55 | 3,734 | 953 | 2,781 | 725 |
| 1756–60 | 4,901 | 971 | 3,930 | 866 |
| 1761–65 | 5,160 | 1,527 | 3,643 | 923 |
| 1766–70 | 5,278 | 1,491 | 3,787 | 751 |
| 1771–75 | 5,300 | 1,520 | 3,780 | 829 |
| 1776–80 | 6,360 | 3,901 | 2,459 | 1,392 |
| 1781–85 | 6,559 | 3,456 | 3,103 | 1,247 |
| 1786–90 | 4,490 | 5,532 | —1,042 | 964 |
| 1791–95 | 6,796 | 2,300 | 4,496 | 1,291 |
| 1796–1800 | (8,000) | 4,099 | (3,901) | 1,389 |
| 1801–05 | 8,873 | 4,000 | 4,873 | 1,303 |
| 1806–10 | 9,035 | 3,333 | 5,702 | 1,254 |
| 1811–15 | 9,312 | 10,644 | —1,332 | 2,092 |
| 1816–20 | 9,827 | 4,878 | 4,949 | 1,734 |
| 1823–27 | 12,556 | 9,353 | 3,203 | 2,633 |
| 1831–36 | 13,783 | 10,209 | 3,574 | 2,468 |
| 1846–50 | 13,775 | 10,835 | 2,940 | 2,726 |
| 1851–55 | 13,798 | 10,433 | 3,365 | – |
| 1856–60 | 17,942 | 14,397 | 3,545 | 3,139 |

*Note:* Casta baptisms 1797–99 are missing; the figure is an extrapolation.
*Source:* Registros de Entierros, Bautismos y Matrimonios. Archivo Parroquial de León.

oscillates wildly in reaction to famine or epidemic, it also stays at an implausibly low level until well past Independence.

To treat baptisms first, it is noticeable that the upward curve is jerky and irregular, a movement which possibly can be attributed to generational 'heaping' or to specific inroads of disease and hunger. For example, in both the twenty-year periods, 1726–55 and 1756–75, baptisms only experienced a marginal increase. Sudden leaps forward occurred in the late 1750s, the late 1770s and at the turn of the century. The extraordinary impact of the 1785–86 famine is indicated by the sharp decline in baptisms during the quinquennium 1786–90, the only example of such decline in the entire eighteenth century. After Independence, another increase occurred. Here the possible effects of internal immigration or superior registration must be taken into account. But then, between 1831–55, another plateau was attained with only marginal increase until 1856.

The marriage rate followed much the same curve. It climbed slowly between 1751–75, jumped forward in the late 1770s only to drop abruptly in repsonse to the 1785–86 famine. Unlike baptisms, it was not until after 1810 that it pushed beyond the levels of the late 1770s. After Independence, the number of marriages again increased, but then, like baptisms, reached a plateau in the quarter century after 1830.

In view of the basic correspondence between these series, it is possible to calculate fertility by simple division of marriages into baptisms.[19] Leaving to one side the quinquennium 1786–90, when famine radically distorted the usual pattern, it appears that the average number of baptisms per marriage in the period 1750–1810 was 6.6. After Independence, during the years 1830–50, this average apparently dropped to 5.7. The expectation of high fertility awakened by the low median age of marriage is here amply confirmed.

Turning to the burial rate, at once we tread treacherous ground. True, the annual fluctuations record with remarkable sensitivity the impact of each epidemic and agricultural crisis. The problem resides in the quinquennial averages. It seems unlikely, for example, that in

TABLE 11    *Baptisms of Spaniards, castas and Indians: León 1696–1820*

| Years | Spaniards no. | % | Castas no. | % | Indians no. | % | Total (= 100%) no. |
|---|---|---|---|---|---|---|---|
| 1696–1700 | 150 | 9.58 | 553 | 35.32 | 863 | 55.10 | 1,566 |
| 1701–05 | 161 | 9.70 | 474 | 28.59 | 1,023 | 61.71 | 1,658 |
| 1706–10 | 161 | 7.45 | 783 | 36.19 | 1,219 | 56.36 | 2,163 |
| 1711–15 | 186 | 8.44 | 760 | 34.47 | 1,259 | 57.09 | 2,205 |
| 1716–20 | 236 | 9.42 | 1,167 | 46.60 | 1,101 | 43.98 | 2,504 |
| 1721–25 | 164 | 5.81 | 1,417 | 50.22 | 1,241 | 43.97 | 2,822 |
| 1726–30 | 115 | 3.78 | 1,552 | 51.01 | 1,376 | 45.21 | 3,043 |
| 1731–35 | 293 | 8.11 | 1,744 | 48.23 | 1,579 | 43.66 | 3,616 |
| 1736–40 | 203 | 5.52 | 1,992 | 54.24 | 1,478 | 40.24 | 3,673 |
| 1741–45 | 280 | 7.09 | 2,090 | 52.98 | 1,576 | 39.93 | 3,946 |
| 1746–50 | 244 | 6.59 | (2,000) | 54.07 | 1,455 | 39.34 | (3,699) |
| 1751–55 | 199 | 5.33 | 1,987 | 53.21 | 1,548 | 41.46 | 3,734 |
| 1756–60 | 318 | 6.48 | 2,564 | 52.32 | 2,019 | 41.20 | 4,901 |
| 1761–65 | 559 | 10.83 | 2,417 | 46.84 | 2,184 | 42.33 | 5,160 |
| 1766–70 | 811 | 15.38 | 2,443 | 46.28 | 2,024 | 38.34 | 5,278 |
| 1771–75 | 619 | 11.68 | 2,532 | 47.78 | 2,149 | 40.54 | 5,300 |
| 1776–80 | 705 | 11.08 | 3,075 | 48.35 | 2,580 | 40.57 | 6,360 |
| 1781–85 | 592 | 9.03 | 3,222 | 49.12 | 2,745 | 41.85 | 6,559 |
| 1786–90 | 281 | 6.26 | 3,183 | 70.89 | 1,026 | 22.85 | 4,490 |
| 1791–95 | 470 | 6.92 | 4,978 | 73.24 | 1,348 | 19.84 | 6,796 |
| 1796–1800 | 1,326 | 16.61 | (4,500) | 56.35 | 2,160 | 27.04 | (7,986) |
| 1801–05 | 1,137 | 12.80 | 4,619 | 51.99 | 3,127 | 35.21 | 8,883 |
| 1806–10 | 699 | 7.73 | 6,165 | 68.24 | 2,171 | 24.03 | 9,035 |
| 1811–15 | 1,819 | 19.54 | 2,898 | 31.12 | 4,595 | 49.34 | 9,312 |
| 1816–20 | 2,176 | 22.14 | 2,655 | 27.02 | 4,996 | 50.84 | 9,827 |

*Note:* Casta baptisms for 1745–49 and 1797–99 are lost; the figures in brackets are extrapolations.
*Source:* Registro de Bautismos, Archivo Parroquial de León.

one decade 1751–60, the population of León should have experienced a natural increase of 6,711, or that burials should have amounted to less than a quarter of current baptisms. Certainly, in later years the margin grew less, so that by 1801–10, burials equalled 40% of baptisms. But it is not until the 1830s that the ratio approaches conventional expectation. There are only two possible conclusions: persistent and considerable under-registration or a truly remarkable natural increase.

Corroboration for the under-registration 'hypothesis' can be obtained by calculation of births and deaths per thousand. In 1761 León had 18,500–19,000 inhabitants. During the preceding quinquennium 1756–60, baptisms averaged 980 a year, burials 194, with hence a natural increase of 786. These averages yield rates of 51.5 baptisms and 10.2 burials per thousand, with an annual increase of 4.1%. Of these figures, only the baptismal rate is plausible, it being roughly equivalent to the estimated birth rate of all Mexico at the close of the nineteenth century.[20] The death rate, almost equal to current levels, is unacceptable.

TABLE 12    *Marriages of Spaniards, Castas and Indians: León 1711–1820*

| Years | Spaniards | | Castas | | Indians | | Total (= 100%) |
|---|---|---|---|---|---|---|---|
| | no. | % | no. | % | no. | % | |
| 1711–15 | 42 | | 129 | | | | |
| 1716–20 | 22 | | 243 | | | | |
| 1721–25 | 39 | | 252 | | | | |
| 1726–30 | 67 | | 315 | | | | |
| 1731–35 | 104 | | 377 | | | | |
| 1736–40 | 114 | | 407 | | | | |
| 1741–45 | 108 | | 380 | | | | |
| 1746–50 | 106 | 17.01 | 337 | 54.09 | 180 | 28.90 | 623 |
| 1751–55 | 100 | 13.80 | 371 | 51.17 | 254 | 35.03 | 725 |
| 1756–60 | 111 | 12.82 | 438 | 50.57 | 317 | 36.61 | 866 |
| 1761–65 | 116 | 12.57 | 485 | 52.54 | 322 | 34.89 | 923 |
| 1766–70 | 129 | 17.18 | 318 | 42.35 | 304 | 40.47 | 751 |
| 1771–75 | 98 | 11.83 | 387 | 46.68 | 344 | 41.49 | 829 |
| 1776–80 | 150 | 10.78 | 867 | 62.28 | 375 | 26.94 | 1,392 |
| 1781–85 | 121 | 9.71 | 870 | 69.77 | 256 | 20.52 | 1,247 |
| 1786–90 | 128 | 13.27 | 702 | 72.82 | 134 | 13.91 | 964 |
| 1791–95 | 160 | 12.36 | 965 | 74.57 | 169 | 13.07 | 1,294 |
| 1796–1800 | 182 | 13.19 | 865 | 62.73 | 332 | 24.08 | 1,379 |
| 1801–05 | 187 | 14.35 | 748 | 57.36 | 369 | 28.29 | 1,304 |
| 1806–10 | 153 | 12.20 | 597 | 47.61 | 504 | 40.19 | 1,254 |
| 1811–15 | 254 | 12.15 | 779 | 37.23 | 1,059 | 50.62 | 2,092 |
| 1816–20 | 298 | 17.19 | 770 | 44.41 | 666 | 38.40 | 1,734 |

*Source:* Registro de Matrimonios. Archivo Parroquial de León.

TABLE 13   *Burials of Spaniards, Castas and Indians: León 1680–1820*

| Years | Spaniards | | Castas | | Indians | | Total (= 100%) |
|---|---|---|---|---|---|---|---|
| 1689–94 | | | 87 | | 130 | | |
| 1721–25 | | | 116 | | 201 | | |
| 1726–30 | | | 153 | | 209 | | |
| 1731–35 | | | 230 | | 237 | | |
| 1736–40 | | | 290 | | 1,141 | | |
| 1741–45 | | | 223 | | 302 | | |
| 1746–50 | 273 | 17.01 | 500 | 31.18 | 831 | 51.81 | 1,604 |
| 1751–55 | 242 | 25.40 | 304 | 31.89 | 407 | 42.71 | 953 |
| 1756–60 | 176 | 18.13 | 202 | 20.80 | 593 | 61.07 | 971 |
| 1761–65 | 237 | 15.52 | 375 | 24.56 | 915 | 59.92 | 1,527 |
| 1766–70 | 268 | 17.98 | 344 | 23.07 | 879 | 58.95 | 1,491 |
| 1771–75 | 269 | 17.69 | 517 | 34.02 | 734 | 48.29 | 1,520 |
| 1776–80 | 385 | 9.87 | 1,305 | 33.45 | 2,211 | 56.68 | 3,901 |
| 1781–85 | 351 | 10.16 | 1,330 | 38.49 | 1,775 | 51.35 | 3,456 |
| 1786–90 | 339 | 6.12 | 2,855 | 51.61 | 2,338 | 42.27 | 5,532 |
| 1791–95 | 221 | 9.61 | 1,006 | 43.74 | 1,073 | 46.65 | 2,300 |
| 1796–1800 | 478 | 11.66 | 1,222 | 29.82 | 2,399 | 58.53 | 4,099 |
| 1801–05 | 480 | 12.00 | 1,280 | 32.00 | 2,240 | 56.00 | 4,000 |
| 1806–10 | 369 | 11.08 | 1,095 | 32.85 | 1,869 | 56.07 | 3,333 |
| 1811–15 | 906 | 8.51 | 2,070 | 19.45 | 7,668 | 72.04 | 10,644 |
| 1816–20 | 723 | 14.83 | 2,306 | 47.27 | 1,849 | 37.90 | 4,878 |

*Source:* Registro de Entierros. Archivo Parroquial de León.

Further complications await us in the analysis of the ethnic composition of the three basic series. Baptisms, however, tell a fairly simple story. Whereas in the first decade of the eighteenth century nearly 60% of all baptised infants were Indians, this proportion dropped to just over 40% after the famine of 1713, and then again, to under 30% in the years after the 1785–86 famine. By contrast, at the other pole of the ethnic spectrum, the Spanish share of baptisms did not greatly vary. It began the century at over 10%, fell to 6% in the decades 1721–60, and then again rose to about 12%, at which level, 1786—90 apart, it remained. The chief beneficiary of the Indian decline were the castas, whose share of baptisms roughly doubled in the course of the century.

Inside the casta category itself, a further change occurred. Samples of baptisms, taken at twenty-year intervals, showed that in 1722, 1742 and 1762, the mulatto proportion remained stable at about 44% compared to the 56% supplied by mestizos. But by 1772 the mulatto share had risen to 54% and in 1782 to 67%.[21] This change, however, may well reflect official reclassification rather than any demographic transition. During his Visitation, 1765–71, José de

Gálvez appointed a special commissioner in León, Rafael Monterde y Antillón, to revise the tribute rolls. In his drive to increase tributes, Monterde apparently classified considerable numbers of mestizos as mulattoes. For example, the tenants of the Corralejo hacienda protested to the local magistrates that Monterde had told them that 'there were not more than three categories, pure Spaniards, Indians and mulattoes'. Despite the numerous judicial appeals his methods provoked, the baptismal registers suggest that his measure in part prevailed.[22]

TABLE 14 *Variations in the ethnic composition of marriages, baptisms and burials*

### I

| | Spaniards | | Castas | | Indians | | Total (= 100%) |
|---|---|---|---|---|---|---|---|
| | no. | % | no. | % | no. | % | no. |
| Marriages | | | | | | | |
| 1751–70 | 456 | 13.9 | 1,612 | 49.4 | 1,197 | 36.7 | 3,265 |
| Baptisms | | | | | | | |
| 1761–80 | 2,694 | 12.2 | 10,467 | 47.4 | 8,937 | 40.4 | 22,098 |
| Burials | | | | | | | |
| 1761–80 | 1,159 | 13.7 | 2,541 | 30.1 | 4,739 | 56.2 | 8,439 |
| Average number of children per marriage | 5.8 | | 6.4 | | 7.4 | | 6.7 |

### II

| | Spaniards | | Castas | | Indians | | Total (= 100%) |
|---|---|---|---|---|---|---|---|
| | no. | % | no. | % | no. | % | no. |
| Marriages | | | | | | | |
| 1785–1805 | 657 | 13.4 | 3,280 | 66.3 | 1,004 | 20.3 | 4,941 |
| Baptisms | | | | | | | |
| 1790–1810 | 3,632 | 11.2 | 20,262 | 62.0 | 8,806 | 26.9 | 32,700 |
| Burials | | | | | | | |
| 1790–1810 | 1,548 | 11.3 | 4,603 | 33.5 | 7,581 | 55.2 | 13,732 |
| Average number of children per marriage | 5.5 | | 6.1 | | 8.7 | | 6.6 |

*Source:* Registros de Entierros, Bautismos y Matrimonios. Archivo Parroquial de León.

The ethnic composition of the marriage series does not call for much comment. It moved in the same direction as the baptismal series. The Indian share declined as that of the castas rose. At all times, however, the *casta* and Spanish percentages of marriages were a few points higher than their share of baptisms. By reverse, the Indian marriages always numbered 4–6% less than their proportion of baptisms. These slight variations masked a significant difference in fertility rates. In general, the Spaniards had about one child less than the average of 6.6 per marriage, whereas the Indians had about one child more. Table 14 indicates that this generalisation held good for both the years 1760–80 and 1790–1810. The peculiarly high rate for Indians in the latter period may in part be attributed to inter-marriage. It is at least possible that some Indians who married *castas* (with marriages recorded in the *casta* register) may have entered their children in the Indian baptismal roll.

As always, burials moved in a different fashion from the other two series. Whereas the Indian proportion of baptisms and marriages declined, their contribution to burials remained constant at about 55% for both the periods, 1760–80, and 1790–1810. (In absolute recorded numbers, of course, crisis years apart, baptisms always exceeded burials.) In part this high level of Indian mortality derived, as we shall demonstrate below, from a greater susceptibility to the attacks of matlazahuatl and smallpox. But samples taken from normal years show that their share of burials was at least ten per cent higher than their share in baptisms.

An explanation for this discrepancy can be found in their high level of infant mortality. Here, of course, the difficulty is to define the age of an infant. By 1840, the parish priest explicitly described a párvulo as a child aged under seven. Since both the 1761 clerical census and the 1793 intendancy census both employed the same age division, it is tempting to assume that this was a fixed definition – at least for the Bajío. But the samples taken from the 1770s, when they indicate age, generally include infants aged three and below. During the matlazahuatl epidemic of 1762–63, not a single burial was ascribed to the párvulo category. Moreover, the possibility of a moveable age category is strengthened by the lack of congruence in the samples we present in Table 15.

The variations in the overall level of infant mortality are sufficiently great as to exclude any certainty about the precise age limits of the term párvulo. The value of these samples lies in their remarkable agreement concerning ethnic differences. In each set of years

TABLE 15    *Proportion of infants (párvulos) in recorded deaths 1755–1809*

| Years | Spaniards TT | child | Castas TT | child | Indians TT | child | Total TT | child |
|---|---|---|---|---|---|---|---|---|
| 1755–57 | 166 | 26 | 144 | 38 | 335 | 193 | 597 | 257 |
| | | (22.4%) | | (26.3%) | | (57.6%) | | (43.0%) |
| 1773–75 | 176 | 27 | 309 | 53 | 481 | 175 | 966 | 255 |
| | | (15.3%) | | (17.1%) | | (36.4%) | | (26.4%) |
| 1792–94 | 104 | 35 | 648 | 325 | 604 | 359 | 1,356 | 719 |
| | | (33.6%) | | (50.1%) | | (59.6%) | | (53.0%) |
| 1807–09 | 237 | 33 | 633 | 207 | 1,171 | 616 | 2,041 | 856 |
| | | (13.9%) | | (32.8%) | | (52.6%) | | (41.9%) |
| Total | 633 | 121 | 1,734 | 623 | 2,591 | 1,343 | 4,960 | 2,087 |
| | | (19.1%) | | (35.9%) | | (51.0%) | | (46.1%) |

*Note:* TT equals total deaths; child equals total párvulos deaths.
*Source:* Registro de Entierros. Archivo Parroquial de Léon.

the proportion of infant deaths among Indians exceeded that of the *castas* or Spaniards. In broad terms, whereas about half of Indian deaths were children, only just over a third of the *castas* and about a fifth of the Spaniards belonged to the same category. At any one time, therefore, Indians had more children per marriage than the *castas* and Spaniards, but a considerably higher proportion of their children died before reaching adolescence. Excluding the abrupt, sharp incursions of epidemic and famine, there were thus two constant factors at work which in good measure explain the dwindling Indian share of baptisms: intermarriage and a high rate of infant mortality.

Finally, a note on the combined effect of the 1810 Hidalgo rebellion with its aftermath of social upheaval and the still unidentified epidemics of 1813–14. During the quinquennium 1811–15, both marriages and burials registered striking increases; by contrast baptims barely moved upwards. A marked change, however, occurred in the ethnic composition of these series. It is largely a story of the sudden termination of the *casta* preponderance. The Indian share rose to 50.6% of all marriages, 50% of baptisms and 72% of burials. The Spaniards commanded 12.1% of marriages, 8.5% of burials, and no less than 20% of baptisms. In all three basic series, the *casta* proportion fell. It is noticeable that in absolute numbers, *casta* baptisms fell by nearly a half after 1810, whereas Indian baptisms rose by much the same amount. Can this displacement be explained by an influx of Indians into the parish paralleled by a *casta* withdrawal?

Or was there, once again, an official reclassification? Whatever the cause, the change is striking, probably important, and at the moment, with evidence not forthcoming, inexplicable.

## VI

By now the various pitfalls in this line of work should be obvious. It is the death rate, the decisive element in the three vital series, which offers the greatest difficulty in interpretation. The question of an implausible excess of births over deaths was already present in Humboldt's *Ensayo político*.[23] Nearly all parochial registers in the Bajío report far more births than deaths. Yet the expectation of a rapid natural increase, proportional to the reported excess, is not confirmed by the general censuses. If to this problem we add the possibility of internal migration, then it is clear that any attempt to calculate overall rates of population growth should be treated with the greatest reserve. For León, the problem is compounded by the absence of a reliable census prior to 1761 and after Independence.

A yardstick for comparison is provided by the findings of Cecilia Rabel Romero in San Luis de la Paz, a predominantly Indian parish, where the annual rate of population increase fell from 1.01 in the period 1727–61 to 0.85% in 1762–80, only then to plummett to a mere 0.08% in 1781–1810.[24] At first glance, the figures for León corroborate this trend. For it was obviously the century prior to 1761 which witnessed the most dramatic expansion in population. Thereafter, between that year and 1793, the overall total only grew from 19,194 to either 20,687 or 23,711, according to whether we employ the civil or the parish census. Over a period of 32 years the absolute increase of either 1,522 or 4,546 yields but an annual rate of either 0.24 or 0.74. However, the trend then shifts decisively in the opposite direction. For the parish census of 1824–28 enumerated 49,952 'souls' which, if we refrain from inflating by 23% to include children under seven, still registers an overall increase in the range of 26,241–29,265 over the levels of 1793. No doubt internal migration played an important part in this surge forward, since we know that all visitors to Guanajuato after Independence commented on its ruinous aspect. Unfortunately, this explanation does not cover all the evidence. For the average number of baptisms rose markedly after 1800, well before the disturbances of 1810. Moreover, the level then remained relatively constant until the 1820s when another increase was recorded. Indeed, the upward curve of baptisms, measured between the quinquennia 1701–05, 1751–55 and 1801–05, fails to register any retardation in the second half of the century.

To ascertain the rate of increase three further exercises may be undertaken. If we accept that Romero's figures for 1781 refer to an ecclesiastical census of all persons aged seven and over, then with a total population at 22,847 rather than 18,575, division of the baptismal and burial averages for 1776–80 yields rates of 55.6 baptisms and 34.1 burials per thousand, with a natural increase of 2.1 a year. The relatively high death rate reflects the smallpox epidemic of 1779–80. Nevertheless, the rate of increase caused by the excess of registered births over deaths still appears implausibly high. Between 1761 and 1781 the total increase amounted to 3,682, which calculated on the basis of the first opening year represents an annual rate of 0.96, a far more acceptable figure.

The 1793 calculation varies according to whether we employ the extrapolated 20,687 population of the ecclesiastical census or the 23,711 of the civil count. For the quinquennium 1788–92 baptisms averaged 1,013 and burials 409, with a natural increase of 604. If these averages are divided by the census totals, they yield rates of 42.7–48.9 baptisms and 17.2–19.7 burials per thousand, with the increase at 2.54–2.9. However, if we calculate rates for the entire decade 1783–92, and hence include the effects of the great famine of 1785–86, then baptisms averaged 45.2–51.8, and burials 36.6–42.0 per thousand, with the increase at 0.85–0.97. Although the overall rate of increase is still rather high, the level of births and deaths bear the marks of verisimilitude, although undoubtedly many deaths which occurred during the famine went unrecorded.

Finally, we can attempt to calculate the average rates for the period 1831–55, when both baptisms and burials remained constant. The ecclesiastical census, if we add 23% for children under seven, gives a population of 56,520 for the years 1824–28. This figure can be corroborated by extrapolation. Both marriage and baptismal rates moved in consonance so that between the quinquennia 1756–60 and 1831–36 their common increase, expressed as a multiple, was 2.8. If this value be applied to the 1761 population of 19,194, it yields a a total of 53,662 for 1831–36, well within the range of the census. These estimates can then be divided into the average number of baptisms and burials for the same period. According to whether one takes the census or the extrapolated estimate, the calculation produces rates of 48.7 to 51.8 baptisms and 36.1 to 38.4 burials per thousand, with an annual increase of 1.26 to 1.36%. These rates appear trustworthy, since in the last decade of the nineteenth century, after some improvement in the conditions of health, the national rates ranged from 47 to 51 births and 32.5 to 35.5 deaths per thousand.[25]

The full story of population growth in Mexico will only be uncovered by the methods of family reconstitution. However, the basic congruence of the baptismal and marriage series, if corroborated elsewhere, should permit reliable estimates of average fertility. All the evidence points to a remarkably high, constant level of about 50 births per thousand inhabitants.[26] Unfortunately, it was changes in the death rate which determined the pace of overall increase, and it is on this score that the parochial registers are least reliable. Finally, whatever our conclusions concerning the precise rate of increase, it is clear that without an equally striking growth in agricultural production the population soon would have encountered a Malthusian brake on its progress. It is to this transformation of the countryside that we must now turn.

## CHAPTER 4

# The structure of agricultural production

## I

Until the first decade of the eighteenth century, the distribution of landed property in León cannot be determined with any degree of precision. For the terms of the original viceregal *mercedes* for estancias were remarkably vague, so that owners either occupied more territory than had been assigned to them, or alternatively encountered difficulties in enforcing their claims against neighbours already in possession. The title of one large sitio later called Los Sapos described its location as follows: 'three leagues from the said town (León) once past a wood of mezquites and entering some flat slopes called San Cristóbal, in a gully little more than a league from the river which runs from the meadows of the said town, which is said to be the source of the River Turbio'.[1] Fortunately, for both historian and landowner, in the years 1711–12, a royal judge, *juez de composiciones*, was despatched to León to inspect all titles and to compare them with the area of land actually occupied. From the subsequent settlement – all *de facto* possession was recognised in return for a small fee – we can establish a relatively accurate survey of land tenure in the district.[2]

The first impression is of a variegated, complex pattern of holdings characterised by extraordinary disparities in dimension. One great latifundium called Gavia and Santa Ana dominated the entire south-eastern corner of the district, reaching across the plains into the parish of Silao. Owned by an absentee landlord resident in Mexico City, most of its 53,000 acres ($13\frac{1}{4}$ large sitios) still remained under scrub serving at best for rough pasture.[3] Bordering the estate, with arable farming already under way were the large sitios of Sauces, Losa, Aguirres and another Santa Ana. Then, situated in the broad arc of hills and valleys which stretched behind the town from the northeast to the west, were another ten estancias, Duarte, Otates, Potrero, Ibarrilla, Palma, Lagunillas, Laurel, Cerrogordo, Hoya, and Santa Rosa. Finally, to the south, there were another four separate small sitios, Granjeno, Arroyohondo, San Germán, and Cerrito de

Jerez. Although virtually all these properties could point to a common origin in the viceregal *mercedes* issued before 1630, nevertheless by the beginning of the eighteenth century they displayed a considerable diversity in their mode of operation. Several haciendas, in particular Duarte, Otates and Santa Rosa – had acquired adjacent farmlands on the plains and already constituted thriving agricultural enterprises. By contrast, other sitios such as Lagunillas, Cerrito de Jerez, and Granjeno remained in much the same condition as when they were first appropriated – mere blocks of grazing land without buildings, corrals or any sign of formal occupation other than a few squatters. Indeed, apart from Gavia there were probably only another ten estates which with any justice could be described as haciendas.

By far the most distinctive feature of land tenure in León, however, was the survival of the small proprietary farm. With the original charter of the town in 1576, there went an endowment of about four or five large sitios, some 22,000 acres, assigned for distribution among settlers in the district. The two Indian villages of San Miguel and Coecillo each received 367 acres.[4] More important, all citizens, in addition to a lot in town for their house, were entitled to 3 caballerías of arable land and another half caballería for a garden or orchard. The area closest to town was farmed first, soon followed by the zone watered by the river León and its tributaries, and then an extensive tract along the highway to Silao. To the south the less fertile section known as El Monte or Tepetates remained unoccupied until the last decades of the seventeenth century, when the town council finally distributed it among a new set of applicants. It must emphasised that although several owners of estancias received or purchased council grants, there is little evidence of any concerted drive by the hacendados or their agents to engross these town lands or to absorb all small-holdings within their domain. Instead, a more subtle process occurred whereby enterprising farmers acquired or bought several *vecindades* – ranchos of 370 acres or $3\frac{1}{2}$ caballerías – and so created a series of medium-sized agricultural estates called *labores* which ranged in area from about 500 to 1,400 acres. By 1710 there were at least 29 of these commercial farms in León, which in many cases were much more valuable than mere sitios of pasture. For example, as late as 1729 the Cerrito de Jerez sold for only 750 ps, whereas a cultivated small-holding of 157 acres was valued at 950 ps, and a prosperous *labor*, with 1,417 acres went for 5,500 ps.[5]

Beneath the range of these farms, which undoubtedly depended upon hired peons for the cultivation of their fields, there were the family enterprises of 370 acres and below. Any calculation of their number is dubious, since in many cases the original grant had been already divided among the descendants of the first recipient without recourse to the notary for legal ratification. At the very least, there were 50 of these units. Needless to say, any attempt to draw sharp boundary lines between the different categories of enterprise is misconceived. Viewed in terms of value and land use, the units of agricultural property in León fell within a continuum, ranging from the latifundium of Gavia to the merest small-holding. The shibboleth of the modern sociologist – the employment of hired labour – here fails us, since unless other evidence becomes available, there is at present no practicable way of determining the degree to which different farms of much the same area employed workers either on a permanent basis or for seasonal assistance, or alternatively were operated by the family of the owner.

In the course of the eighteenth century, the application of the terms *sitio de estancia* and *labor* to denote individual estates gradually fell into disuse, and instead agricultural properties came to be called either haciendas or ranchos. This semantic shift reflected changes in the nature of production and in the pattern of tenure. For although many estates could certainly trace their origin to the estancias of the sixteenth century, they only became haciendas in the true sense of the word when their rough scrub and woodlands were cleared and converted into arable, and a start was made with the construction of barns, stables, corrals, a house for the manager and a chapel. The emergence of the hacienda as the dominant form of agricultural enterprise in León thus depended upon a complex sequence of internal colonisation.

Equally important, the predominance of the hacienda derived from a prolonged, albeit intermittent, drive to amalgamate small-holdings and large farms and absorb them into the great estate. In the case of Santa Rosa this involved little more than the continued purchase of adjacent farmlands. Elsewhere, however, profitable *labores* were united with neighbouring estancias. From such a combination came the haciendas of Losa, Cerrito de Jerez, Ibarrilla, and Pompa. A more dramatic development was the formation of four entirely new haciendas through the purchase of a numerous group of ranchos, with a *labor* serving as the nucleus. In particular, the San Nicolás, and the San Pedro del Monte, which were situated

in the heart of the former municipal endowment, effected a decisive
concentration of property ownership. Finally, in contradiction to the
preceding trends the great latifundium of Gavia was progressively
divided among different heirs to form no less than seven separate
haciendas. The result of these opposing trends was that by 1828 the
municipality counted at least 26 haciendas in the district.[6] In this
sequence, the most decisive period was the years between 1720 and
1760, a time when rural population experienced a rapid increase in
number and the mining boom at Guanajuato prompted an expansion in the urban demand for foodstuffs. Mercantile capital was the
effective agent of this wave of change.

At the other end of the scale, although the survey of 1828 reported
the existence of 56 independent ranchos, many of these properties
had been subjected to excessive partition so that areas such as Los
Hernández or Los Castillos had become dense concentrations of
minifundia within which, every generation, farms were enlarged and
divided according to the enterprise of individual owners and the
number of their children.[7] By contrast, the large commercial farms
continued to prosper, but by then there were only about 12 units in
this category, and several were owned by hacendado families. In
short, the *labor* had been attacked from both sides, with some
absorbed into haciendas and others divided into small-holdings.
By the close of our period, therefore, the contrast between the great
estate and the rancho had greatly widened.

The complexity of agrarian society in León is thrown into high
relief by the comparative simplicity of the situation in Rincón where,
apart from the lands held by the two Indian villages, most of the
countryside remained untouched by plough at the start of the
eighteenth century. Moreover, with the exception of two large sitios
which were partitioned among heirs, the remainder of the district
was owned by no more than nine families, the two most powerful
of whom were the Mariscal de Castilla and Miguel González del
Pinal, both resident in the capital. The boundaries of estates continued to be the object of extensive litigation well into the century.
Indeed, the two Solís sisters consumed their fortune in lawsuits in an
attempt to retain control over three separate haciendas. The costs
proved so high that they were obliged to cede possession of one
property to their lawyers.[8] Once this stage was past, the pace of
change in Rincón was impressive, especially in the years after 1770.
Progressive inputs of capital and labour transformed the existing
distribution of estancias into thriving agricultural estates without

much modification of their boundaries. In short, the dominant patterns here consisted of internal colonisation.

## II

In the eighteenth century agriculture in León largely consisted of the cultivation of maize. Planted at the start of the summer rains in late May or early June, and harvested in December, the size of the crop determined the subsistence of the masses and the profits of the wealthy. But in this respect, this frontier society was particularly fortunate, since the rolling plains of the Bajío offered a propitious natural environment for the rapid expansion of production. True, certain obstacles had to be overcome. Once cleared of mezquite clumps and cactus scrub, the rich soil tended to become water-logged in summer and dry-crusted and cracked in winter. Moreover, the shallow course of the river León and its tributary streams afforded small protection from the threat of seasonal drought. It was this scarcity of water which rendered wheat-growing hazardous or impracticable. More important, the considerable variations in both the volume and the incidence of the rainfall – around 1900 the average precipitation was 21.1 inches a year – led to violent oscillations from one harvest to another.[9] Nevertheless, when judged by the standards of European farming, the yields per seed sown were remarkably high. Writing after his visit to the region, Alexander von Humboldt exclaimed over reports of haciendas close to Querétaro gathering four hundred fanegas from one sown, although as a general rule he found 150 to one the common yield.[10] However, a Mexican critic, José Antonio del Raso, who had access to the accounts of these same haciendas, calculated that despite some magnificent harvests, the average return over the years was about 80 to one.[11] Similarly, at León in 1757, the owner of San Pedro del Monte declared that he generally planted 30 fanegas and obtained 3–4,000. However, he admitted that the fluctuations were considerable, since whereas in 1756 the harvest amounted to 4,000 fanegas, in the previous year it yielded a mere 700. Much the same variations occurred on Duarte where the owner reported returns ranging from 1,000 to 4,000 upon 40 fanegas sown.[12]

With land still cheap and in abundant supply, seed ratios offer the best guide to agricultural productivity. Nevertheless, it is necessary to emphasise that the yield, if measured by the acreage planted, was quite low, and indeed, was more reminiscent of medieval Europe than of the 'age of improvement'. Admittedly, calculations here are bedevilled by uncertainty as to the exact dimensions of colonial measures, especially since these varied from region to region. For our purpose, the most persuasive guide to local custom is a short statistical study of agricultural production in the State of Guanajuato published in 1903 by Pedro González.[13] To start with, the author explains that although the standard caballería of 105 acres (42.79 hectares) was legally divided into 12 fanegas de sembradura, that is to say, into 12 units of land on which a fanega of maize was sown, in the State of Guanajuato it was the practice to divide the caballería into only 7 *fanegas rancheras*, units which therefore comprised 15.1 acres (6.11 hectares). However, to complicate matters, only three quarters of a fanega of maize seed were actually sown on this *fanega ranchera*. Equally important, unlike several modern historians, González takes for his unit of measurement the large Mexican fanega of 2.497 bushels (90.8 litros) rather than the Castilian fanega of 1.55 bushels (55 litros).[14] Finally, on the question of seed ratios, he adopts 90 to one as the midpoint on a scale ranging from 30 to 150. On this basis, he then calculated that the 11.141 litros commonly sown on each hectare yielded on average a harvest of 1002.69 litros. Converted into English measures, this means that on each acre just under a gallon of maize was sown (4.5 litros) with an average yield of 11.13 bushels. Corroboration for these estimates can be found in a municipal survey of 1937 which assumed that in general the 9 kilos of maize usually sown on a hectare of unirrigated land gave a return of 576 kilos (i.e. 8 fanegas of 72 kilos), which is to say, that 8.02 pounds planted in an acre gave 513.6 pounds or 8.08 bushels.[15] These calculations referred to an ordinary harvest (*regular*) with seed ratio of 64 to one. In a good year the crop yield might well double. It will be noted that, if the seed ratio is raised to 90, their estimates coincide with those of González.

Needless to say, calculations made in this century should not be applied without careful scrutiny to an earlier age. Although weights and measures were subject of municipal inspection, in 1758 the councillor charged with the enforcement of this task, complained that landowners were selling maize in their own houses without any control over the measures employed.[16] Moreover, in respect of the fanega de sembradura, one suspects that the quality of soil often affected the conventional estimate of area, so that variations were frequent. In 1758 on one hacienda the caballería was apparently divided into eight fanegas, whereas in 1848 on Duarte the surveyors reckoned on six fanegas a caballería.[17] Any presumption of great precision in such matters is a delusion.

Whereas maize depended upon the rainfall, wheat cultivation in León was restricted to the banks of the river León or to zones irrigated from dams. Elsewhere in the district planting was a gamble. For example, in 1757 the owner of Duarte confessed that he had only harvested 30 cargas from the 11 cargas sown *aventurero* (on chance). Once again, it is Humboldt who advanced the highest estimates, since he averred that on the plains between Querétaro and León the average yield ranged from 35 to 40 cargas for one sown. In Celaya even unirrigated land still returned harvests of 15 to one.[18] But here we must remember that the rainfall in León was less abundant than in the southeastern corner of the Bajío and hence the natural obstacles to any extension in cultivation were considerable. As in the case of maize, the yields on acreage were less impressive than the seed ratios. In 1903 Pedro González noted that the weight of these wheat cargas or loads varied from 355.94 pounds (161 kilos) to 405.64 pounds (184 kilos). By this time, it was the custom to sow 53.447 litros on each hectare for an expected harvest of 801.7 litros, a return which in English measures signifies that an acre yielded 8.89 bushels on a planting of 0.59 bushels. In this calculation, however, González failed to distinguish between irrigated lands and the rest, and he adopted a low seed ratio of 15 to one. If we accept Humboldt's estimate of 40 to one – in this case Raso supports the ratio – then an acre of irrigated land gave 23.6 bushels, a level certainly equal, but hardly superior, to the best English returns of that period.[19]

The only other crops of any importance in León were barley and beans. But to judge from the tithe returns they rarely entered the market and were mainly grown for home consumption. Moreover, in comparison with maize their seed ratios were low. In 1757, the owner of Duarte stated that he generally planted 25.30 fanegas of barley and obtained a crop which ranged in two years from 100 to 200 fanegas. As for beans, he received 30 cargas from sowing 11.[20] Yet these were years in which he expected to harvest up to 4,000 fanegas of maize. Finally, on a few estates there were considerable plantations of magueyes, from which the local alcoholic drinks, mescal and pulque, could be distilled. In 1758 Duarte possessed 20,000 magueys and as late as 1844 the inventory of the hacienda still listed 9,979, with another 3,690 newly planted. Similarly, in 1807 Patiña, an estate of over 1,000 acres, had 3,500 magueyes.[21]

Whether other haciendas or farms employed their land in this fashion is uncertain, but improbable. The geography of pulque consumption in colonial Mexico has yet to be traced with any precision.

### III

To chart the progress and distribution of agricultural production in León is to navigate treacherous waters without much hope of a safe landfall. All interpretation depends upon the tithe reports, but whereas in some districts within the diocese of Michoacán these returns span the entire period from 1640 until 1800, in León documents only survive for the century between 1661 and 1767. The abrupt termination of our principal source, possibly because tithe collection was henceforth farmed for a contracted block sum, undermines any attempt to assess the long-term effects of the transformation in land tenure which occurred during the middle decades of the century. In regard to production and prices, reports from Silao, an adjacent district with much the same terrain, extend our perspective, since they cover a further twenty years up to 1789. In any case, these documents must be handled with the greatest caution.[22] Submitted by the collector, usually the local parish priest, to the diocesan court at Valladolid the reports consist of a summary chart in which all payments in kind are set out by type of produce and by contributor. Until 1751, the names of individuals were inserted, but thereafter entries are by estates. In addition to the chart, all payments were recorded in writing and, where possible, signed by the contributor. Finally, the collector provided an account of the prices he obtained for the sale of tithe produce. As a guide to the volume of agricultural production, these documents are unsurpassed. But it must be emphasised that in no sense are they a record of sales. Much grain failed to reach market, since a certain proportion was consumed on estates and farms as rations for the peons or for the subsistence of small-holders. Equally important, many estate-owners stored their corn in hopes of higher prices the next year. Then again, the prices obtained by the collector rarely register seasonal variations and hence serve only as a rough index of the returns of any individual landowner. Deposited in a granary in León, the tithe could be released on the market at the most propitious occasion, an advantage not enjoyed by all farmers and hacendados.

The most cursory examination of the tithe returns at once reveals the overwhelming predominance of cereal cultivation. Computed by value, maize accounted for 76% of the tithe for León during the quinquennium 1661–65, and a century later in 1761–65 it still comprised 65% of the total return. With some variations, wheat generally occupied second place, supplying about 12% of the overall value. Other crops, such as barley, beans and chili, were negligible, although it is of course possible that small-holders grew and consumed their own beans without reference to the tithe. The only other item of importance was livestock. Even so, the combined value of calves, lambs, kids, ponies and young mules only stood at 7% in 1661–65, although it later rose to 15% by 1761–65. Corroboration for these figures can be found in Silao where throughout the period maize accounted for over 80% of the tithe yield. These proportions sharply distinguish these districts situated on the plains of the Bajío from the upland *partidos* of San Miguel el Grande and San Luis de la Paz, where stockraising and its derivatives easily outweighed the value of cereal production until the second quarter of the eighteenth century.[23]

To turn to the curve of production set out in Table 16, the maize crop in León rose from an annual average of 26,790 fanegas in 1661–65 to a peak of 74,470 fanegas in 1751–55, a multiple of just under 2.8. However, throughout the period harvest yields doubled or halved from year to year, and it is only after 1700 that any clear indication of a permanent upward trend can be detected. The rate of increase accelerated dramatically after 1730, but then during the 1750s a plateau was reached and indeed the next decade witnessed a marginal decline in output. It is remarkable that the largest harvest recorded in the series – of 110,410 fanegas – occurred in 1751. At Silao the tithe registered a more abrupt movement. Between the 1660s and 1726–30, annual production tripled from an average 16,140 to 54,140 fanegas, but in contrast to León little further increase occurred until the quinquennium 1751–55, when the crop rose to 90,300 fanegas. In the 1760s a certain decline in output occurred so that the peak performance of 1757 – 125,780 fanegas – was not surpassed until 1774 with 192,930 fanegas. In the subsequent quinquennium of 1776–80 production once more surged forward to attain an average harvest of 166,410 fanegas, a level which represents a tenfold increase over the starting point of the series a century before. Whether León participated in the explosive growth of the late 1770s must remain unknown until new sources are discovered. A straw in the wind is offered by a municipal survey of 1826, where the maize tithe was estimated at only 6,000 fanegas; but by this period, the authority of the Church had waned so that this figure probably under-stated the true level of production.[24] In any case, the town could always draw upon Rincón and San Pedro Piedragorda for further supplies of foodstuffs.

TABLE 16 *Maize production in the parishes of León and Silao: tithe returns in fanegas 1661–1788*

| León | | | Silao | | |
|---|---|---|---|---|---|
| Years | Total | Annual average | Years | Total | Annual average |
| 1661–65 | 13,395 | 2,679 | 1661–65 | 6,213 | 1,242 |
| 1666–70 | 15,475 | 3,095 | 1666–70 | 9,988 | 1,997 |
| 1671–75 | 19,686 | 3,937 | 1671–75 | 12,410 | 2,482 |
| 1676–77, 79 | 9,068 | 3,022 | 1676–77, 79 | 5,722 | 1,907 |
| 1681–85 | 10,128 | 2,025 | 1681–83, 85 | 8,511 | 2,127 |
| 1686–7, 89–90 | 11,664 | 2,916 | 1686–87, 89–90 | 9,322 | 2,330 |
| 1691–95 | 19,511 | 3,902 | 1691–93, 95 | 12,958 | 3,239 |
| 1696–1700 | 14,412 | 2,882 | 1696–1700 | 14,339 | 2,867 |
| 1701–05 | 22,694 | 4,538 | 1702–03 | 6,781 | 3,390 |
| 1713–17 | 19,540 | 3,908 | 1715–16 | 14,172 | 7,086 |
| 1723–26 | 16,131 | 4,032 | 1723–25 | 17,829 | 5,943 |
| 1728–30 | 14,538 | 4,846 | 1726–30 | 27,074 | 5,414 |
| 1731–35 | 25,360 | 5,072 | 1731–32 | 10,279 | 5,139 |
| 1736–40 | 28,345 | 5,669 | 1738–40 | 14,807 | 4,935 |
| 1741–45 | 36,500 | 7,300 | 1741–45 | 29,434 | 5,886 |
| 1746–50 | 22,458 | 4,491 | 1746–50 | 22,126 | 4,425 |
| 1751–55 | 37,238 | 7,447 | 1751–55 | 45,151 | 9,030 |
| 1756–60 | 36,996 | 7,399 | 1757–60 | 35,500 | 8,875 |
| 1761–65 | 30,038 | 6,007 | 1761–65 | 33,415 | 6,683 |
| 1766–67 | 15,998 | 7,999 | 1766, 68–70 | 28,845 | 7,212 |
| | | | 1771–75 | 45,405 | 9,081 |
| | | | 1776–80 | 83,205 | 16,641 |
| | | | 1781–85 | 60,466 | 12,093 |
| | | | 1786–88 | 38,579 | 12,859 |

*Source:* ACM 846, 854, 857, tithe collector's reports.

Both wheat-growing and stock-raising also registered increased activity during this period. In León, the wheat harvest averaged 790 cargas a year during 1661–65, and with some variations remained at much the same level until the 1750s, when production rose rapidly to 2,210 cargas. In this instance, the increase can be positively attributed to the mercantile investment of that decade. Whether the subsequent construction of dams and irrigation channels promoted a further expansion in the area devoted to wheat must remain an open question. Once again, the municipal survey of 1826 assumed a low yield of 2,000 cargas. At Silao wheat first appears in the tithe reports during the quinquennium 1671–75, with an average crop of 116 cargas. By 1751–55, production rose to 1,050 cargas, and then after a slight decline during the 1760s, almost doubled to a yearly average of 1,910 cargas in the years 1776–80.

With mountainous terrain a considerable proportion of the district's land, stockraising continued to thrive alongside the cultivation of cereals. Indeed, the two activities cannot be separated, since in terms of preponderant value, the chief purpose of animal husbandry in León was the provision of oxen for the plough-teams, and horses and mules for transport and freight. The supply of meat, wool and tallow were secondary to the generation of draught energy. As Table 17 indicates, the breeding of most types of stock other than horses experienced a considerable increase during our period. Yet the rate of reproduction was not always very high. In 1757, the owner of Duarte and Palote reported that in the last year only five calves,

TABLE 17 *Livestock production: tithe returns in the parish of León 1661–1767*

|  | Mules | | Foals | | Calves | | Lambs | |
|---|---|---|---|---|---|---|---|---|
| Years | Total | Annual average | Total | Annual average | Total | Annual average | Total | Annual average |
| 1661–65 | 110 | 22 | 375 | 74.8 | 240 | 48 | 301 | 60.2 |
| 1666–70 | 68 | 13.6 | 295 | 59 | 280 | 56 | 254 | 50.8 |
| 1671–75 | 53 | 10.6 | 261 | 52.2 | 456 | 91.2 | 354 | 70.8 |
| 1676–77, 79 | 33 | 11 | 170 | 56.6 | 244 | 81.3 | 440 | 146.6 |
| 1681–85 | 76 | 15.2 | 387 | 77.4 | 367 | 73.4 | 1,305 | 261 |
| 1686–7, 89–90 | 105 | 26.2 | 531 | 132.7 | 291 | 58.2 | 957 | 239.2 |
| 1691–95 | 210 | 42 | 1,259 | 251.8 | 638 | 127.6 | 605 | 121 |
| 1696–98, 1700 | 85 | 21.3 | 434 | 108.6 | 447 | 111.7 | 250 | 62.5 |
| 1701–05 | 79 | 15.8 | 698 | 139.6 | 682 | 136.4 | 957 | 191.4 |
| 1713–17 | 141 | 28.2 | 240 | 48 | 273 | 54.6 | 522 | 104.4 |
| 1723–26 | 177 | 44.2 | 340 | 85 | 279 | 69.7 | 535 | 133.7 |
| 1728–30 | 147 | 49 | 422 | 140.6 | 424 | 141.3 | 643 | 214.3 |
| 1731–35 | 196 | 39.2 | 637 | 127.4 | 495 | 99 | 1,322 | 264.4 |
| 1736–40 | 204 | 40.8 | 853 | 170.6 | 567 | 113.4 | 1,322 | 264.4 |
| 1741–45 | 158 | 31.6 | 597 | 119.4 | 503 | 100.6 | 990 | 198 |
| 1746–50 | 180 | 36 | 783 | 156.6 | 432 | 86.4 | 923 | 184.6 |
| 1751–55 | 230 | 46 | 553 | 110.6 | 561 | 112.2 | 1,408 | 281.6 |
| 1756, 58–60 | 192 | 48 | 405 | 101.2 | 565 | 141.2 | 1,604 | 401 |
| 1762–67 | 330 | 55 | 393 | 65.5 | 964 | 160.6 | 1,865 | 310.8 |

*Source:* ACM 846, tithe collector's reports.

bred from a herd of 100 cows, had survived the attacks of wolves, although another herd pastured in a more protected area had calved 50 offspring. Similarly, from some 800 mares, divided into numerous strings, he obtained 153 foals and 30 young mules.[25] No doubt the efforts undertaken to construct stone boundary walls in the latter years of the century sprang in part from the necessity of a better control over livestock.

If the tithe series faithfully registered the oscillations and general trends in the volume of agricultural production, it is a less reliable guide concerning the origin of that output. True, the variegated pattern of landownership in León is clearly reflected in the multiplicity of recorded contributions. But the variations in the mode of entry are sufficiently great as to destroy any hope of exactitude. For example, whereas in 1727 some 113 persons were listed as paying tithe, two years later the number doubles to 207. Similarly, in 1732, although only 152 names are recorded, further reference is made by number alone to many other contributors, so that, in fact, at least 272 individuals paid tithe that year. Then again, after 1751, when the new collector chose to list payments by estates rather than by persons, it soon became the rule to group together several small-holders under the heading of one rancho, without any reliable indication of the number included. In short, it is not possible to ascertain from the tithe returns just how many farmers in León paid tithe in any one year.

Within the gamut of enterprise, however, there existed an obvious concentration of productive capacity. To take the year 1732, before the emergence of most new haciendas, the top thirteen contributors accounted for 52% of the tithe in maize, with the next 29 producers supplying 29%, so that the remaining 230 individuals paid only 19% of the tithe. Broken down by average output, the leading estates produced 1,745 fanegas, the intermediary group 435 fanegas, and the small-holders just over 36 fanegas each. Despite the creation of at least two new haciendas during the 1740s, which entailed a reduction in the number of independent rancheros, the tithe returns failed to register much change in the overall distribution of production. In 1760, the fourteen leading contributors still supplied nearly 50% of the maize crop. However, by this year, the different system of recording entries makes it impossible to distinguish prosperous commercial farmers from impecunious small-holders. Indeed, in the last two years of the existing series, in 1766–67, the share of the leading estates declined to 35–38% of the crop, although by this time the average production had risen to 4,115 fanegas. Unfortunately, there is no means of discovering whether this was a passing phase, caused by the superabundant harvests and low prices of preceding years, or whether it marked the opening of a new trend. It was certainly the case that in both Pénjamo and San Luis de la Paz the cultivation of maize slowly came to be dominated by rancheros.

The area in which the emergence of new haciendas decisively affected the balance of production was wheat-growing. Here the tithe returns recorded a rapid increase in output from an average 836 cargas in 1746–50 to an annual average of 2,210 cargas by 1756–60. In great measure this expansion can be attributed to the investments of Agustín de Septién, a merchant who, after creating the San Nicolás hacienda through purchase of several ranchos, utilised the waters of the river León to make the estate the chief producer of wheat in the district. By the 1760s, over half of the tithe for this crop came from his three estates.[26]

If haciendas failed to establish a monopoly in the local corn market, it was in part because several owners chose to let a considerable proportion of their land to tenant farmers. To judge from several lawsuits initiated in the first decades of the century, squatters had been welcomed at one stage as a means of assuring effective possession of a property. In later years, however, rents were increased and the original tenants evicted. Since the tithe reports unfortunately avoided any detailed assessment of minor contributors, it is often impossible to distinguish a small-holder from a tenant. Moreover, at times their payments are combined with those of the landlord. By 1767, however, at least 9,170 fanegas, some 17% of the maize crop, can be attributed to tenants. Whether this represented a genuine expansion of their production or whether it was simply the result of a different system of recording payments is difficult to say. But as Table 18 indicates, the tenants' share in maize production on the hacienda of San Juan de los Otates and the adjacent *labor* of San Miguel de los Otates rose from 16.7% in the years 1752–56 to 34% in 1762–67. In these last three years of the tithe series, the tenants accounted for 61% of production on Laborcita and 23% of output on the hacienda. It will be observed that in the latter case, the growth of tenant-farming in no way diminished the output of the demesne.

Little other systematic evidence concerning the existence of these arrendatarios is at present available. Random references, however,

TABLE 18    *Otates and Laborcita: maize production 1752–67 (in fanegas)*

| Years | Annual average production | | | |
|-------|--------|-----------|---------|-------|
|       | Otates | Laborcita | Tenants | Total |
| 1752–56 | 2,720 | 2,980 | 786   | 5,702 |
| 1757–61 | 3,894 | 494   | 1,004 | 5,392 |
| 1762–67 | 3,566 | 913   | 2,323 | 6,802 |

*Source:* Tithe reports, ACM 848.

are quite numerous. In 1733 an inventory of the Santa Rosa hacienda mentioned thirteen ranchos of tenants. Similarly, in Rincón, the owner of Sarteneja adverted to several rancherías of tenants on his estate. More surprising is their presence on quite small properties. In 1730, a standard farm of 370 acres was described as 'settled with ranchos of tenants'. In 1781 the nine tenants on a farm of the same area called Los Gómez paid a total rent of 68 ps.[27]

The significance of this stratum in the countryside as a source of income for landlords is illustrated by the hacienda called Jagüey where in 1796 an unspecified number of farmers furnished an annual rent of 1,072 ps. So also in 1822 the 58 tenants of the adjoining estate of Gavia yielded the owners an income of 1,185 ps. In this case, the rate of payment was 10 ps a fanega de sembradura (c. 15 acres).

To judge from their rents, the arrendatarios of León included within their number both enterprising farmers who employed peons to assist them and also impoverished cottagers eking out a livelihood close to the margins of subsistence. At the top of the scale there is a great similarity between the chief tenants and independent rancheros; indeed, in some cases they came from the same families. At the lower end of the scale, however, we encounter mere sharecroppers or *medieros*. Similarly, on Gavia in 1822, in addition to the 58 tenants paying cash rents, there were another 12 individuals who cultivated 21 fanegas de sembradura as sharecroppers. Then again, the manager of San Cristóbal explicitly distinguished the three fanegas he had planted on his own account, presumably with peons, and the other six fanegas sown *a medias*. Finally, when Los Sapos hacienda was leased in 1858, a clause in the contract stipulated that 'all lands already distributed among sharecroppers [*medieros*] and which are now cultivated, shall be left to the persons who have them'.[28] If this did not prove convenient, then an indemnity had to be paid. The transition from cash tenancy to the full-blown system of sharecropping which characterised the district at the opening of the twentieth century is a theme which still awaits its historian. As always, the problem is to discover the appropriate type of evidence.

More precise data can be found in an inventory of Losa, a prosperous hacienda situated on the plains, where in 1809 about a third of all arable land within the estate was leased to some 109 arrendatarios for a total rent of 1418 ps. Individual charges varied greatly since, although twelve men paid over 30 ps, with the highest rent standing at 160 ps, another 38 persons paid only 2 ps or under.[29] If the going rate of 10 ps a fanega de sembradura was applied on this hacienda, then many tenants rented areas ranging from one to three acres, from which in a good year they could expect to reap between 11 to 33 bushels of maize.

Further confirmation of the prevalence of this system comes from a leasehold account for the San Nicolás, an estate situated on the outskirts of León, which had been created through the purchase of numerous small-holdings during the 1740s. A century later, in 1844, a list of tenants included 42 persons renting plots of irrigated *huertas* or gardens, and another 34 with ordinary arable land. Another 104 individuals are mentioned as owing rent on the *huertas*.[30] The areas leased ranged from a quarter to three fanegas de sembradura, (c. from 4 to 45 acres) with the average rate charged varying between 12 to 15 ps a fanega. There is the strong presumption that most of the estate was, in fact, cultivated by tenants, since the area under the direct management in that year had only 16 plough oxen and but 12 fanegas of maize sown.

Finally, on many haciendas, the mayordomos were granted a small field to grow their own maize. In 1747 the mayordomo of Sauces recorded that in addition to a yearly salary of 150 ps and weekly expenses of 4 reales and a quarter fanega of maize, he also received the use of a fanega de sembradura within the estate. Much the same terms prevailed in Palote, where in 1802 the mayordomo was paid 100 ps a year, along with weekly expenses of 4 reales and one fanega of maize, but with only a half fanega de sembradura. Then again, in 1838 the manager of San Cristóbal, a prosperous hacienda in Rincón, declared in his will that he had three fanegas of maize sown on the estate, and that in addition he leased an entire rancho on the neighbouring hacienda of Sandía, where he maintained a variety of livestock, including 24 plough oxen.[31]

The discovery of an extensive stratum of tenant farmers in León corroborates the evidence already presented when dealing with other districts in the Bajío. In this case, however, there existed a certain 'overlap' between the emergence of tenants and the survival of a numerous class of small-holders. For example, in 1750 an Indian who sold his farm to an enterprising ranchero remained on the land as a tenant.[32] It is a testimony to the random nature of the sources for this subject that we lack any index of the changes in the rental value of land. For how long was 10 ps the standard rate for a fanega de sembradura?

## IV

The absence of private account books vitiates any attempt to define the nature of the internal economy of haciendas in León. Without this sort of document it is virtually impossible to describe the organisation of production within a particular estate. All that survives in this line are a few summary returns for properties held in ward which we shall discuss in the next chapter. Otherwise, the chief source material for any further consideration of haciendas are the inventories of estate filed by heirs after the death of a landowner. These legal instruments appraised the value of land, building, implements and livestock. The work-force is mentioned only in regard to debts and allusion to tenants is infrequent. There is no assessment of profits or income. Needless to say, the appraised value should not be confused with the market price, since at subsequent auctions haciendas rarely fetched more than two thirds of their 'true' worth. Then again, the municipal archives lack any record of several estates, and only in a few cases are there several inventories of the same hacienda. Yet these documents are most useful when encountered in series, since they then constitute an index of economic change. In short, the selection is arbitrary, possibly misleading, but sufficiently generous as to yield some significant conclusions.

To start with the least satisfactory and incomplete strand of data, the available evidence suggests that peons employed by haciendas were commonly in debt to the owner, but it also indicates that flight to evade payment was frequent. In many instances the inventories simply list the total sum of debts without specifying the number of workers concerned. In Rincón, for example, in 1757 on San Angel Pedregal debts amounted to 971 ps, and on Cañada de Negros in 1767 to 976 ps. On occasion the evidence is more precise. In 1770 the 41 'servants' of Palote and Palma on average owed 21 ps, although it should be noted that the hacienda itself owed 12 workers a total 208 ps. A later inventory for the same estates taken in 1798 found that the debts of 58 workers came to 906 ps, which yields an average of 15½ ps. The same document also mentions another 20 peons who had fled, leaving on average unpaid debts of about 13 ps.[33] If these figures were at all typical, then with wages for resident peons standing at 4 ps a month, most workers in this category received advances of between three and six months salary.

Where our sources undoubtedly score, however, is in their demonstration of the extent to which agriculture in the Bajío depended on livestock for draught power, transport and freight. No discussion of an hacienda can afford to neglect this indispensable basis of its operation, which formed the equivalent of modern machinery. The number of plough oxen maintained on an estate provides the best measure of its productive capacity. It also offers the best clue as to whether a property was under direct management or operated through tenants. Livestock were capital assets which could be readily converted into cash, and hence their number and value indicate the level of investment within a given estate.

The provision of draught power for ploughing represented a costly item for all haciendas. The price of an ox for most of the century was about 10 ps, the equivalent in value of forty days of peon labour. In 1787, for example, Otates required no less than 196 oxen to sustain its operations. The inventory value here was 1,666 ps. Similarly, in 1809 Losa maintained 258 oxen worth 2,580 ps.[34] Replenishment of this stock was expensive, hence most landowners possessed small herds of cattle, anywhere between 100 and 400 head, from which to breed their own plough teams. Much the same observation applies further down the scale, since it was common for small-holders to own a yoke of oxen and a cow or two. Indeed, if we compare acreage with stock, many farms of 370 acres were more heavily capitalised than the great haciendas.

The other great necessity for a profitable enterprise was a mule-team to carry produce to market. Freight was expensive. By the close of the eighteenth century, when prices ranged from eight to twelve reales a fanega, it cost most haciendas in the district one real to shift a fanega of maize to León, and 2½ reales if they chose to sell at Guanajuato. In the crisis year of 1787 charges on grain coming from Pénjamo were 3–4 reales. Further afield, transport costs comprised the greater part of the price. For example, when in 1793 the owner of Palote sold 2,000 fanegas of maize to the municipal granary at Zacatecas, freight absorbed 21 reales out of a final price of 32 reales per fanega. In these circumstances, it was obviously desirable to possess the means of transport. As a contemporary declared: 'whatever the harvest, the hacienda which plants grain must have a mule-team to carry it, since if prices are low, the costs will be covered and if they are high, then the profits will be all the greater'.[35] Yet mules were not cheap. In an inventory of Palote taken in 1758, the price of a mule rose sharply from 4 ps for a one-year old to 11 ps for animals between two and five years. A mature mule broken in for transport was valued at 15 ps and if fully equipped for freight cost from 25 to 30 ps. A team of 30 head with reserves saddled for the drivers was worth anywhere between 800 and 1,000 ps.[36]

Whether some hacendados took advantage of the strategic position of León straddling the trade routes both north and west to engage in commercial freight is difficult to say. In only one inventory is a prosperous ranchero specifically described as the owner of teams employed in the carriage of silver to Mexico City.[37] But in 1758 the owner of Palote and Duarte maintained no less than four teams with a total of 152 head, all newly fitted out, together with another 79 beasts as replacements, the entire force valued at 5,745 ps. His source of supply was a herd of 300 mares devoted exclusively to mule-breeding, and on his two haciendas there were another 486 animals, aged between two and five years, ready either for sale or for entrance into his teams.[38] The advantage here was that the hacendado could release his grain from the granary whenever and wherever prices moved upwards. In 1763, for example, the owner of Los Sapos sent his mayordomo to Sierra de Pinos in the province of Zacatecas because rumour claimed that prices there were unusually high.[39] In the event, the news proved false, so that his man had to sell the grain in small quantities at different haciendas and villages on his journey home.

The third type of stock employed on haciendas were, of course, the horses or ponies used for personal transport. For most of the century these were far less valuable than either oxen or mules, with prices ranging from 3–5 ps. Most estates possessed several strings of mares to supply them, and it was equally common for smallholders to own a mare or two. It is striking to reflect that with daily wages at two reales, some twelve days labour could buy one a horse.

Any examination of the precise role of livestock within the hacienda economy is complicated by the dual function of the breeding stock, since mules, ponies and oxen could be as easily sold as employed by the estate. Moreover, the inventories show that the quantity and composition of stock varied greatly from hacienda to hacienda and from decade to decade. The advance of arable farming certainly did not displace animal husbandry, since the tithe reports record an increase in the number of mules, cattle and sheep bred in the years up to 1767. Obviously the hilly terrain of much of the district favoured the continuance of stockraising. About the only clue as to markets comes from a notarised contract of October 1745, where the owner of Cañada de Negros in Rincón agreed to raise 162 mules at the cost of one peso a head, with ten per cent discount against losses. The animals were to be ready for the July Fair held in July 1747 at Puebla.[40]

The second great advantage of the inventories is that, if read with care, they reveal the slow advance of internal colonisation throughout the eighteenth century. What can be more striking than to discover that as late as 1750 only 18 caballerías, some 1,890 acres, were under plough in the vast latifundium of Gavia and Santa Ana? Much of the 58,500 acres consisted of 'high stony hills' and 'swampy gullies'. Owing to the lack of drainage and irrigation, the flat lands were described as 'swampy during rains, but utterly without water in the dry season'. Yet the land in question ranks among the most fertile in Mexico, and later was to provide the basis of several of the richest haciendas in León. Only a generation later, Jagüey, just one estate carved out of the latifundium, had 46 caballerías (4,830 acres) under cultivation.[41]

As a rule, inventories distinguished clearly between *tierra labrada*, arable land, and *eriaza*, uncleared or waste land, and furthermore described hillside pasture as *agostadero*. Comparison of inventories taken at different years almost invariably reveals an expansion in the area of arable. In Rincón the process is especially clear. In 1745 the Cañada de Negros had but 11 caballerías under plough; by 1771 the cultivated area had risen to 30 caballerías, and later in 1791 most of the 94 caballerías which comprised the estate were described as fit for planting.[42] The sequence, although less dramatic, is equally apparent in León. Between 1731 and 1809, the area in Losa under plough almost doubled. Table 19 sets out the available data.

TABLE 19 *The expansion of cultivated area within haciendas*

### LEON

*Otates*
15 caballerías in 1688
19 ,, ,, 1787
$27\frac{1}{2}$ ,, ,, 1837
*Cerrogordo*
9 caballerías in 1787
$12\frac{1}{2}$ ,, ,, 1833
*Palote*
11 caballerías in 1758
$13\frac{1}{2}$ ,, ,, 1770
$16\frac{1}{2}$ ,, ,, 1793
$18\frac{1}{2}$ ,, ,, 1798
*Gavia and Santa Ana*
18 caballerías in 1750

*Duarte*
21 caballerías in 1758
$32\frac{1}{2}$ ,, ,, 1809
*Lagunillas*
2 caballerías in 1745
4 ,, ,, 1755
11 ,, ,, 1784
*Losa*
45 caballerías in 1731
$87\frac{3}{4}$ ,, ,, 1809
*Cerrito de Jerez*
14 caballerías in 1742
24 ,, ,, 1784

### RINCON

*Sarteneja*
c. $4\frac{1}{2}$ caballerías in 1708
10 ,, ,, 1749
22 ,, ,, 1792
*Pedregal*
$14\frac{1}{2}$ caballerías in 1757
34 ,, ,, 1770
*San Cristóbal*
$7\frac{1}{2}$ caballerías in 1734

*Cañada de Negros*
11 caballerías in 1746
30 ,, ,, 1771
$94\frac{1}{4}$ ,, ,, 1790
*Fuentes de Medina*
12 caballerías in 1761
14 ,, ,, 1793

*Sources:* see appendix 3.

The evidence suggests that the movement of colonisation extended quite slowly since, whereas the lands closest to León had already been cleared by the start of the century, in Rincón and on the Gavia latifundium it was only after 1750 that the process gathered momentum. However, it is equally significant that on well-established estates such as Cerrogordo and Otates, a considerable expansion in the area of arable land occurred after the 1780s. The example of Palote indicates an almost constant process of marginal reclamation of hilly terrain.

Along with land clearance, there went a considerable range of investment in land improvement. During the last decades of the eighteenth century there was a concerted drive to construct dams and reservoirs for irrigation, walls to enclose estates, and stone barns for the storage of grain. The story has to be pieced together from scattered entries in different inventories. By far the most satisfactory illustration of this trend is afforded by Palote and Palma where between the inventories of 1770 and 1798 the owners constructed two large barns worth 3,386 ps, a dam valued at 3,145, and extended the stone walls from 10,800 yds to nearly 60,000 yds. The effect of the dam was to irrigate two caballerías or 210 acres of wheat, the fields surrounded by walls.[43] On Cerrogordo it was between the two inventories of 1787 and 1821 that five reservoir *cajas* were built for the watering of 2½ caballerías. Similarly, on Otates, it was after 1787 that a substantial dam was constructed. By contrast, on Lagunillas a dam 12 yds high and 350 yds long had been built at a cost of 6,000 ps in the years before 1755. In Rincón the story is much the same. If Cañada de Negros tripled in value between 1771 and 1790, it was owing to the erection of a dam and walls as well as to the clearance of land. In 1782 the San Cristóbal was leased on the express condition that the tenant build a dam 4 yds high and 1,200 yds long, at an estimated cost of 2,000 ps.[44] Finally, we may note that in 1806–07 the general manager of the second Count of Valenciana, the current owner of Santa Rosa and Santa Ana, obtained the agreement of the respective owners of Duarte and Pompa estates to construct extensive canals through their property to channel the water of the rivers León and Tigre towards the dams situated on his haciendas. In sum, during this period, not merely was the area of arable land extended, but in addition the quality of an appreciable section was greatly improved. By the twentieth century the Sandía estate, once part of Gavia latifundium, had over 662 acres under water in the great artificial lakes shaped by its system of dams and irrigation channels.[45]

In the last resort, the most telling measure of the transformation wrought in the countryside is the dramatic increase in the value of rural property. Once again, the arbitrary nature of the evidence, in terms of coverage and the actual variations in the quality of land on different estates, prevents any sure calculation of the overall rate of increase, especially since the calculation depends upon the initial value. In Rincón, where in several instances cultivation only began in the eighteenth century, the rise in value was quite extraordinary. For example, Sarteneja, which comprised one large sitio, sold for 800 ps in 1693, was already worth 3,012 ps in 1708, but by 1792 was valued at 11,855 ps. The rate of increase here is either threefold or more than tenfold according to which initial year is chosen. Perhaps the most extreme case is afforded by Talayote, an estate acquired for 400 ps in 1729, which was appraised at 27,481 ps in 1792.[46]

Obviously these figures only serve to demonstrate that it was during the eighteenth century that haciendas, as distinct from blocks of mere pasture, were created in Rincón.

In León, the pattern of settlement had already driven up the value of *labores* and haciendas by the start of the century. It cost 26,792 ps to purchase the lands which comprised the San Nicolás, an hacienda situated to the immediate south of the town and only created during the 1740s. Perhaps the best guide to the overall pattern is offered by the series of inventories of San Juan de los Otates, an estate of about 20,000 acres, most of it in the hills.

TABLE 20    *San Juan de los Otates: estate values 1661–1854*

| Source | Year | Value in pesos | Index | Index |
|---|---|---|---|---|
| AHML 1660/63–16 | 1661 | 7,782 | 100 | – |
| AHML 1708/10–18 | 1706 | 12,452 | 160 | 100 |
| AGN, Civil 286–3 | 1787 | 26,901 | 345 | 216 |
| AHML 1815(1)–6 | 1810 | 41,886 | 538 | 336 |
| AHML 1837(1)–6 | 1835 | 35,947 | 462 | 288 |
| ANL, 8 November 1854 | 1854 | 48,667 | 625 | 390 |

In general, the indication of a threefold increase in estate values during the eighteenth century appears to agree with other items of evidence. What is perhaps more startling is the evidence of a rise in property value in the decades after Independence, and in particular after 1840. For the Cerrogordo, a small hacienda situated in the hills behind León, rose in appraised worth from 10,334 ps in 1734 to 24,974 ps in 1823, but then sold for 54,000 ps in 1863.[47] Clearly, all depended on the starting point. The San Nicolás was leased in 1836 for 2,000 ps, a rent which, at the contemporary assessment ratio of 5% on the principal, yields a value of 40,000 ps, an increase of only 49% on the initial cost some 85 years before. Then again, Potrero, a hillside hacienda, after an auction of 7,000 ps in 1742 rose to a value of 21,549 ps in 1783, only in 1840 to be auctioned for 8,000 ps, a sum exactly corresponding to the Church mortgages it bore.[48]

The most spectacular change in assessment occurred on the lati-fundium called Gavia and Santa Ana. Purchased in 1726–27 for 29,366 ps and in later years divided into at least seven haciendas, by the years 1840–55 the combined value of the properties was about 500,000 ps.[49] Obviously, as in the case of Rincón, conversion of pasture and scrub into arable accounted for a good part of the initial increase in value. But the subsequent history of the different haciendas carved out of the latifundium, suggests that capital investment in improvements also played an important role in the later period. For example, in 1787 Jagüey was valued at 27,915 ps and some sixty years later sold for only 27,900 ps, the sum of all the mortgages and debts charged on it. Yet by contrast the Sandía, although purchased by the Count of Valenciana for 20,000 ps in 1788, eventually sold for 120,000 ps in 1864, an increase which surely sprang from investment in improvements.[50]

To record the mere fact of an increase in the monetary assessment of an hacienda does not tell us a great deal. Simple inflation in the value of land or of livestock could easily account for the phenomenon. Alternatively, the conversion of rough pasture into arable might well serve as a comprehensive explanation. In reality, over a period of a century and a half, several distinct elements entered into the reckoning. To interpret this complex sequence, it is first necessary to examine the shifts in value of the components of any hacienda, that is to say, the changes in the price of land and livestock.

It was the practice in those days, as it is now, to appraise land according to its quality and use, assigning different values for irrigated sections, arable dependent on rainfall, uncleared but potentially fertile land (*eriaza*) and barren or hillside pasture (*agostadero*). As can be observed in Table 21, for most of the eighteenth century a caballería of arable, *tierra labrada*, was worth 300 ps, with occasional entries of 200 ps for land of inferior quality. This means that an acre cost about three pesos, and a fanega de sembradura just over 40 pesos. But then in the years around 1800 – the evidence does not permit greater precision – the price of a caballería rose to 400 ps. At the same time surveyors now tended to distinguish more exactly between lands of different quality, so that the best arable could sell for as much as 600 ps. Finally, by the 1830s most *tierra labrada* was appraised at 500–600 ps. For irrigated soil, valuations are less frequent and hence the evidence as to trends less reliable. But in most cases a caballería *de riego* was assessed at 400 ps until after 1800 when its price rose to 600 ps, and after 1821 to no less than 800 ps. Then again, the distinction between eriaza and agostadero was not always observed in the early eighteenth century, when the prevailing rate was about 50 ps a caballería. But by the 1740s the value of good quality uncleared land rose to 100–200 ps, a range at which it apparently remained. Quotations for mere pasture are less common, but with some exceptions there was an increase from 50 ps to 150 ps by the nineteenth century. If sold in entire sitios, then at the start of the period uncleared land went for 400 ps a small sitio of 1,928 acres and 800 ps for a large sitio of 4,388 acres. As late as 1750 the large sitios of Gavia were assessed at 1,300 ps. In short, all land, no matter what its quality, increased in value, but viewed from the perspective of assessment, the greatest rise in value came from clearance and irrigation.

TABLE 21     *Inventory land values in León and Rincón 1706–1845*

| | | PESOS A CABALLERIA | | | |
|---|---|---|---|---|---|
| Years | Irrigated land | Arable land | Uncleared | Pasture | Estates |
| 1706 | | 300 | 50 | | Otates |
| 1714 | | 200 | 20 | | Sauces |
| 1718 | | 300 | 75 | | Fuentes de Medina* |
| 1722 | | 300 | | | S. Nicolás |
| 1726 | | 300 | | 40 | Palma |
| 1729 | | 300 | | 50 | Sardaneta |
| 1730 | | 300 | 100 | | Losa |
| 1731 | | 300 | | 50 | Alfaro |
| 1733 | | 300 | 150 | | S. Pedro del Monte |
| 1734 | | 300 | 200 | | Los Castillos |
| 1738 | | 300 | 50 | | Los Hinojosa |
| 1742 | | 200 | 100 | | Granjeno |
| 1743 | | 300 | 100 | | Laborcita |
| 1745 | | 200 | | 100 | Lagunillas |
| 1748 | | 250 | 150 | 75 | San Lorenzo* |
| 1749 | | 300 | 100 | | Sarteneja* |
| 1750 | | 300 | 150 | 75 | S. Nicolás Arriba |
| 1752 | | 300 | 150 | | Guadalupe |
| 1753 | | 300 | 50 | | Campoverde |
| 1754 | | 300 | | 80 | S. Gerónimo* |
| 1757 | 800 | 350 | 175 | | Pedregal* |
| 1757 | | 350 | 100 | | Ibarrilla-Herrera |
| 1758 | | 200–300 | 250 | 120 | Palote, Duarte |
| 1759 | | 250 | 150 | | Saucillo |
| 1760 | | 300 | 200 | | Sarteneja* |
| 1761 | | 350 | 100 | | Ibarrilla-Herrera |
| 1763 | | 300 | 200 | | Sauces |
| 1768 | | 250 | 200 | 100 | Potrero |
| 1769 | 700 | 400 | 300 | 150 | Pedregal* |
| 1770 | 500 | 200–300 | 200 | 120 | Palote, Sauces |
| 1771 | 700 | 400 | | | Cañada de Negros* |
| 1774 | | 200 | 125 | | Los Tanques* |
| 1778 | | 300 | | 120 | Potrero |
| 1781 | | 300 | 100 | | S. Rosalía |
| 1784 | 400 | 250 | 100 | | Lagunillas |
| 1785 | | 300 | 150 | | Cerrito de Jerez |
| 1786 | 350 | 200 | | | Cerrogordo |
| 1786 | | 450 | 300 | | Los Sapos* |
| 1787 | 400 | 300 | | 50 | Otates |
| 1790 | | 200 | | 100 | Campoverde |

| Years | Irrigated land | Arable land | Uncleared | Pasture | Estates |
|---|---|---|---|---|---|
| 1792 | | 300 | | | Sarteneja* |
| 1793 | | 300 | 250 | 125 | Fuentes de Medina* |
| 1793 | | 300 | 175 | | Talayote |
| 1798 | 500 | 300 | 200 | 100 | Palote; Ocotes |
| 1799 | | 400 | 200 | | Los Aguileras |
| 1802 | | 400 | | | Talayote* |
| 1804 | | 400 | 120 | | Laborcita |
| 1806 | | 600 | | | S. Rosalía |
| 1807 | 600 | 300–500 | | | Patiña, Guadalupe |
| 1807 | | 600 | | 150 | S. Cayetano |
| 1809 | 800 | 400–600 | 200 | 150 | Losa, Hoya |
| 1810 | | 600 | | 150 | Potrero |
| 1812 | 400 | 300 | 150 | | Los Tanques* |
| 1816 | | 300–600 | | 150 | Echeveste |
| 1817 | | 600 | | | Los Gómez |
| 1820 | | 300–400 | | | Guadalupe |
| 1821 | | 300 | | 200 | Fuentes de Medina* |
| 1823 | 800 | 600 | 150 | | Cerrogordo |
| 1823 | | 400–600 | 100 | 50 | Sauz de Armenta* |
| 1824 | | 300 | 200 | | Talayote* |
| 1831 | | 300–450 | | | Ocotes |
| 1833 | 800 | 600 | | 150 | Cerrogordo |
| 1833 | | 500 | | | Concepción |
| 1835 | | 600 | | 125 | Potrero; S. Cayetano |
| 1836 | | 500–600 | 200 | | Capellania |
| 1837 | | 500 | | 50 | Otates |
| 1842 | | 600 | | 150 | S. Nicolás Arriba |
| 1843 | 900 | 500 | | 100 | Duarte |
| 1843 | | 400 | 125 | | Mesa de Reyes |
| 1845 | | 500 | 150 | | Talayote* |
| 1849 | | 600 | | | S. Juan Zitaquaro |
| 1851 | | 500–600 | | | S. Vicente Tuna–Agria |

\* indicates estates in Rincón.
*Source:* see Appendix 3.

For livestock, the evidence of the inventories (presented in Table 22) is less trustworthy, since unrecorded variations in the age and quality of the animals obviously influenced the appraisals. On average the price of plough oxen started the century at 8 ps, fell to 6 or 7 ps until the 1780s when it rose to 8–10 ps. After the depredations of the Insurgency the value of oxen climbed to 15–16 ps, although by the 1840s a handful of entries suggest that the price had begun to fall towards 10 ps. In the case of horses broken in for riding, the price varied between 3–5 ps until the 1780s when appraisals moved upwards towards 12 ps, with a standard range of 8–10 ps common after 1821. At much the same time, the value of

TABLE 22   *Inventory values of livestock in León and Rincón 1661–1849 (in pesos)*

| Years | Saddle horses | Brood mares | | Equipped freight mules | Saddle mules | Plough oxen | Branded cattle | Cows (*paridas*) |
| | | For foals | For mules | | | | | |
|---|---|---|---|---|---|---|---|---|
| 1661 | – | $1\frac{1}{2}$ | 2 | 20 | 11 | 8 | 4 | 6 |
| 1688 | 3 | 3 | 5 | 30 | 15 | 5 | $2\frac{3}{4}$ | 3 |
| 1705 | $2\frac{1}{2}$ | 2 | $3\frac{1}{2}$ | 20 | 12 | 8 | $5\frac{1}{2}$ | $5\frac{1}{2}$ |
| 1706 | – | $2\frac{1}{2}$ | 3 | 20 | 10 | 8 | – | $5\frac{1}{2}$ |
| 1708 | – | $1\frac{1}{2}$ | 2 | – | – | 8 | – | $5\frac{1}{2}$ |
| 1711 | 2 | 2 | 4 | 25 | $12\frac{1}{2}$ | 8 | $3\frac{1}{2}$ | – |
| 1713 | – | – | $2\frac{1}{2}$ | – | – | 8 | – | – |
| 1714 | $2\frac{1}{2}$ | $2\frac{1}{2}$ | | | | | | |
| 1717 | 3 | 2 | $3\frac{1}{2}$ | 20 | 10 | 7 | | |
| 1726 | 3 | 2 | 3 | 30 | 15 | 6 | | |
| 1728 | 8 | 2 | 3 | 25 | 12 | | | |
| 1729 | 5 | $2\frac{1}{4}$ | 4 | 22 | 13 | 6 | 4 | 4 |
| 1729 | 3 | – | – | 25 | 15 | 6 | | |
| 1730 | – | – | 4 | 28 | 14 | 6 | 4 | – |
| 1733 | 5 | 2 | – | 25 | $12\frac{1}{2}$ | 6 | 5 | 4 |
| 1734 | 4 | 2 | 3 | 24 | 12 | 6 | 4 | – |
| 1736 | 6 | 3 | | 26 | 15 | 7 | 4 | – |
| 1738 | – | 2 | | – | – | 6 | 4 | |
| 1741 | 4 | – | – | 20 | 10 | 6 | – | 4 |
| 1742 | – | – | $2\frac{1}{2}$ | 26 | 13 | – | 6 | 5 |
| 1743 | 3 | 2 | – | 21 | 12 | 6 | – | 5 |
| 1749 | – | – | 3 | – | – | 8 | | |
| 1750 | 4 | $1\frac{3}{4}$ | $2\frac{1}{4}$ | 22 | 13 | 6 | $3\frac{1}{2}$ | – |
| 1751 | 3 | 2 | – | 23 | $11\frac{1}{2}$ | 8 | | |
| 1752 | 5 | 2 | – | 20 | 10 | 7 | 4 | 6 |
| 1752 | 5 | 2 | $3\frac{1}{2}$ | 23 | 14 | 8 | – | 7 |
| 1753 | 5 | – | – | 35 | 15 | 8 | 4 | – |
| 1757 | – | 2 | $3\frac{1}{2}$ | 25 | 15 | 6 | 2 | – |
| 1757 | 5 | 2 | – | – | – | 8 | 4 | 5–7 |
| 1758 | 5 | 2 | $3\frac{1}{2}$ | 30 | 17 | 7 | $4\frac{1}{2}$ | – |
| 1758 | – | 2 | 3 | 25 | 15 | 7 | 5 | 5 |
| 1759 | $2\frac{1}{4}$ | – | $3\frac{1}{2}$ | 25 | 12 | 7 | 4 | – |
| 1759 | 5 | 2 | 3 | 20 | 10 | 7 | 6 | 6 |
| 1759 | 4 | $2\frac{1}{2}$ | – | 20 | 10 | 7 | – | 5 |
| 1763 | 4 | $1\frac{3}{4}$ | 3 | 20 | 8 | 6 | 5 | 6 |
| 1764 | 5 | $2\frac{1}{2}$ | $2\frac{1}{2}$ | – | – | 6 | – | 6 |
| 1767 | 5 | – | $3\frac{1}{2}$ | 25 | 13 | 6 | $3\frac{1}{2}$ | – |
| 1770 | 4 | 2 | | 16 | 11 | 6 | $2\frac{1}{2}$ | – |
| 1774 | 6 | 2 | – | – | – | $5\frac{1}{2}$ | 5 | – |
| 1776 | 5 | – | 2 | – | – | 5 | – | $5\frac{1}{2}$ |
| 1781 | 5 | – | – | – | – | $6\frac{1}{2}$ | – | 5 |
| 1784 | 6 | $2\frac{1}{2}$ | – | – | – | 8 | 5 | – |
| 1785 | 7 | – | $3\frac{1}{2}$ | 20 | 8 | 10 | 5 | – |
| 1786 | 5 | $2\frac{1}{4}$ | $3\frac{1}{2}$ | 30 | 15 | 8 | 6 | – |
| 1786 | 7 | – | 3 | 25 | 12 | 9 | 6 | – |
| 1787 | $4\frac{1}{2}$ | $2\frac{3}{4}$ | – | 30 | $14\frac{1}{2}$ | $8\frac{1}{2}$ | $4\frac{1}{2}$ | – |

TABLE 22—*continued*

| Years | Saddle horses | Brood mares For foals | For mules | Equipped freight mules | Saddle mules | Plough oxen | Branded cattle | Cows (*paridas*) |
|---|---|---|---|---|---|---|---|---|
| 1787 | 5 | 3 | 3 | 25 | – | 10 | – | 7 |
| 1790 | 7 | – | 4 | – | – | 10 | 8 | 8 |
| 1793 | 9 | 3 | 5 | 35 | 22 | 9 | 6 | – |
| 1794 | – | – | 2½ | – | – | 11 | 7 | 9 |
| 1794 | 5–7 | 3 | 4 | 28 | 16 | 9½ | 7½ | – |
| 1796 | – | – | – | – | – | 10 | – | 10 |
| 1798 | 10 | 4½ | 8 | 40 | 22 | 10 | 6 | 7 |
| 1798 | 9 | – | 7 | 26 | 18 | 9 | – | 7½ |
| 1799 | 6 | 3½ | 5 | 35 | 22 | 8 | 6 | – |
| 1800 | – | – | 8 | 30 | 22 | 9 | – | – |
| 1802 | 9 | – | 6 | 28 | 12–20 | 9 | – | 9 |
| 1803 | 6 | 3¼ | | 35 | 22 | 10 | 6 | – |
| 1804 | 8 | 6 | | 28 | 14 | 8 (old) | 5 | |
| 1807 | 12 | – | | – | – | 11 | – | 10 |
| 1808 | 8 | 7 | | 22 (old) | | 9–12 | | 10 |
| 1809 | 12 | | 7 | 28 | 15 | 10 | 6–7 | – |
| 1813 | 12 | 6 | | 28 | 18 | 15 | – | 10 |
| 1823 | 10 | 5 | | 30 | 15 | 15 | 12 | 13 |
| 1823 | 10 | 6 | | 30 | 14 | 16 | – | 14 |
| 1824 | 8 | 5 | | – | – | 15–18 | – | 14–16 |
| 1831 | – | – | | – | – | – | – | 13 |
| 1833 | 10 | 5 | 8 | 35 | 11 | 14 | – | 10 |
| 1837 | – | – | – | – | – | 13 | 8 | 10 |
| 1843 | 8 | 3–6 | | – | 15 | 10 | 8 | 10 |
| 1844 | – | – | | – | – | 10 | 7½ | – |
| 1844 | – | | 6 | 35 | 15 | 8 | – | 9 |
| 1849 | – | 4 | | – | 23 | – | 12 | 10–12 |
| 1849 | – | 6 | | – | – | 16 | 14 | 14 |
| 1849 | 8 | 5 | | – | – | 9 | 7 | 8 |

*Source:* see Appendix 3.

brood mares, hitherto reckoned at 2 or 3 ps, according to whether they bred foals or mules, rose to 5–6 ps. The variations in the price of mules are more difficult to establish. In general the price of a mule broken in for transport rose from a range of 10–15 ps to 18–22 ps, the decade of change once more being the 1780s. Mules equipped for freight probably rose in price from 20–25 ps to a range of 28–35 ps during the 1780s. In both cases, assessments after Independence were not much higher than before 1810, and indeed on occasion somewhat lower. Finally, sheep were also affected by this upward trend in prices since appraisals rose from ½ ps a head to ¾ ps.

It is the shift in the estimated worth of both land and livestock which casts doubt on any attempt to calculate the proportionate value of the constituent elements of the typical hacienda. In any case, agricultural estates in the cereal zone were often little more than units of ownership put together in haphazard fashion. Not only was the balance eventually struck between arable farming and stock-raising largely governed by the quite variable distribution of good soil and hillside terrain present on each estate; in addition the financial resources available to particular owners often determined the choice taken at any stage either to invest in irrigation or to rely on rents for an income. Then again, some owners used their estates as a base of operations for their activities in mining or in commercial transport. However, despite these qualifications, one generalisation appears to hold good. To judge from the  haciendas for which we possess several inventories taken at distant intervals, the proportion-ate value of land, as contrasted to the share supplied by livestock, steadily grew throughout our period. To take two examples, on Otates, whereas in 1688 land only comprised 34.6% of the overall assessed value, by 1787 its share rose to 51.5%, and by 1837 amounted to no less than 61.3%.[51] By contrast, the share of stock fell from 49% to 25.5% before the disturbances of the Insurgency eliminated all breeding other than for replacements of the plough teams, so that by 1837 the animals only represented 10.9% of the inventory value. The same trend can be found on Palote, an estate which in 1758, despite an appreciable maize production (there were 242 plough oxen), was used for mule-breeding and possibly for com-mercial freight, with the result that livestock accounted for 68.9% of the inventory value as against only 18.5% represented by land. But forty years later, with the hacienda greatly enlarged by the acquisition of the adjacent mountainous sitio of Palma, although land still only accounted for 25.9% of the total assessment, the construction of walls, barns and a dam drove up the share in value supplied by fixed plant to 33.4%, whereas livestock, despite the entry of a herd of 1,722 cattle, now only represented 40% of the inventory value.[52] Any number of other examples could be adduced to demon-strate the great variations which existed between estates, and where inventories are found in series, the marked rise in the proportionate value of land and constructions.[53] At the same time, any sharp distinction between land and the capital embodied in barns, dams and walls should be avoided, since the rise in land values obviously depended on considerable inputs of labour and capital, and in the case of irrigation, was directly attributable to the investment in dams.

To return to our initial query, it is clear that the prime cause of the increase in estate values lies in the clearance and cultivation of land hitherto covered by scrub. Arable simply carried a higher price than waste-land. Moreover, the greater the area under plough, the more numerous the oxen and mules required to service the estate. However, this explanation only holds good for the first phase of internal colonisation, a process which varied from estate to estate, but which had probably exhausted its momentum by the 1780s. Thereafter, in the last decades of the eighteenth century there was a perceptible drive to construct dams and reservoirs for irrigation, boundary walls to control livestock and protect cereals, and barns for storing grain. In some cases, this investment greatly improved the quality of considerable tracts of land, a change soon registered in inventory assessments. At much the same time, during the 1780s, the price of livestock experienced a marked increase. More important, about 1800 the value of all types of land also shifted upwards. Now, although many estates were left in ruins or in debt as a result of the depredations wrought by both royalists and patriots during the civil wars of the Insurgency, land values did not decline and, indeed, after Independence edged forward to a new plateau at about double the level prevailing before 1800. By contrast, although for a decade or more scarcity forced up the price of livestock to unprecedented heights, by the 1840s, as former losses were repaired, the overall level tended to decline. In general, despite the political unrest of these years, most estates experienced a pronounced increase in their monetary assessment in the two decades after 1840. Whether this rise sprang from continued improvements or simply registered a general inflation in prices remains uncertain. Finally, throughout the period, the major element responsible for the transformation of the countryside was the sustained increase in population, both urban and rural, without which the transition to arable farming could not have occurred.

## V

Although the failure to discover any private account books prevents any reliable calculation of profit or even income, there is one strand of evidence which can be employed to provide some notion of what was deemed to constitute an acceptable return on agricultural capital. From the 1780s onwards, several haciendas were leased for periods which varied from three to seven years. By far the most notable example here was the San Nicolás, situated due south of the town, where the owners entirely abandoned direct cultivation. Although the rent slowly climbed from 1,400 ps a year in 1792 to 2,000 ps by 1836, the return of 6.2% on an estimated value of 32,000 ps in the latter year was not overly high, if we consider the favourable position of the estate.[54] But then in 1806 even the Santa Rosa, a much larger hacienda with fertile wheat fields, only yielded 3,200 ps.[55] It was after Independence that the custom of letting an entire hacienda became common so that by the 1850s at least eleven of the 26 estates in León were on lease. In particular, the absentee heirs of the second Count of Valenciana, the greatest landlord in the district chose to let most of their property. But since we lack contemporary valuations, it is quite difficult to calculate the actual return on capital, other than for a few examples. The Otates was sold for 48,617 ps and let for 2,000 ps, an annual yield of 4.1%.[56] More significant, the Sandía, which in the 1780s had been let for 1,600 ps a few years before being sold for 20,000 ps, in 1856 was leased for 6,000 ps, and then four years later sold for 120,000 ps, a valuation surely calculated on the conventional ratio of 5% income on capital. Indeed, at times the rent offers a more reliable guide to the value of an estate than some assessments, since in the case of Santa Ana, although the appraisal of 1840 fixed its inventory at 216,132 ps in 1861 the estate was let for but 6,400 ps.[57]

The evidence offered by these notarised contracts is too heterogeneous to permit any more than the general conclusion that owners could rarely obtain more than 6% return on their capital through leasehold, and in several instances had to be content with the lower rate of 4%. The advantage of the system was that it threw the weight of risk on the shoulders of the tenants who, despite the great variations in annual maize prices, had to pay a fixed rent. At the same time, the practice offered an opportunity for profit to the ambitious ranchero. On estates such as San Nicolás or Santa Rosa, most land was sublet to a large number of farmers and sharecroppers, so that the tenant simply cultivated a portion of the hacienda and for the remainder collected rents. Viewed from this angle, the lease-holder in effect acted as a general manager who voluntarily accepted the task of paying the owner a fixed income. Alternatively, in the case of hillside haciendas, such as Lagunillas, the tenant often possessed a wide range of livestock which were obviously not tied to that particular estate.[58] Finally, we may note that the outbreak of the 1810 Insurgency ruined several men who had recently leased haciendas, since in subsequent years few were able to meet their contractual obligations.[59] On the other hand, the ranchero who rented the Sandía in 1856 later purchased the entire estate.

It would be quite false to presume that most landowners received a 5% return on the inventory value of their property. For by the close of the eighteenth century a considerable proportion of the assessed value on most estates was absorbed by mortgages and annuities charged in favour of ecclesiastical institutions and individuals. The annual interest was invariably 5%. The sources of the often bewildering array of charges were diverse. In the first place, many hacendados created *capellanías* – chantry funds – for sons who entered the priesthood, with the rights of succession usually restricted to other members of the family. In these cases, no money actually changed hands; instead, the estate henceforth became liable to interest on the sum stipulated in the endowment, which usually ranged anywhere from 1,000 ps to 4,000 ps. In much the same way, small charges in favour of local confraternities or other parish funds were quite common. More important, in a few cases priests who either inherited or who acquired haciendas bequeathed the entire value of their property to a variety of clerical funds. For example, in 1778 one vicar of Silao assigned no less than 26,500 ps to confraternities in his parish, all imposed on the San Cristóbal, an hacienda he had purchased in Rincón. Similarly, his successor burdened Peñuelas, another hacienda in Rincón, with no less than 52,000 ps in *capellanías* and other charges, some charitable, some devotional.[60]

In addition to these transfers in value, there were also many loans. Impecunious landowners could apply to any number of clerical institutions, ranging from local confraternities and pious funds to the *juzgado de capellanías y obras pías* in the diocesan capital of Valladolid which reinvested all capital that had been redeemed, or finally to wealthy convents such as Santa Clara at Querétaro or Santa Caterina in Valladolid. Although the possibility of paying off these loans was ever present, the tendency was for such charges to occupy an increasing proportion of the capital value on most estates. For when an owner defaulted on interest payments, clerical creditors frequently secured an embargo and auction, so that the mortgages were simply transferred to the new proprietor. However, it is only fair to observe that the rising value of haciendas steadily reduced the proportionate share of clerical mortgages in the total inventory assessment. But this trend, where it existed, was sharply reversed by the Insurgency of 1810 which plunged most landowners still further into debt to the Church, since few were able to meet their interest obligations. In the decades after Independence, most estates were burdened by a massive sum of unpaid interest dating back to these years, debts for which clerical institutions still pressed for redemption as late as the 1840s.

TABLE 23  *Estimated value of Church mortgages on haciendas in León and Rincón*

### A. LEON

| Haciendas | Estate values | Church mortgages | Year |
|---|---|---|---|
| | pesos | pesos | |
| Cerrito de Jerez | 17,831 | 8,136 | 1784 |
| Cerrogordo | 12,000 | 1,600 | 1786 |
| Duarte | 36,000 | 10,300 | 1778 |
| Gavia | 27,000 | 5,250 | 1777 |
| Ibarrilla | 27,500 | 15,625 | 1783 |
| Jagüey | 30,000 | 16,500 | 1806 |
| Lagunillas | 9,700 | 3,000 | 1777 |
| Losa and Hoya | 154,000 | 66,444 | 1809 |
| Ocotes | 15,500 | 1,000 | 1805 |
| Otates | 24,063 | 9,500 | 1788 |
| Palote | 51,819 | 22,000 | 1804 |
| Pompa | 18,000 | 16,800 | 1801 |
| Potrero | 15,500 | 9,000 | 1782 |
| Sauces | 35,314 | 12,500 | 1763 |
| Sandía | 20,000 | 10,242 | 1788 |
| San Nicolás | 30,000 | 14,000 | 1787 |
| San Nicolás de Arriba y Abajo | 17,831 | 12,673 | 1786 |
| San Pedro del Monte | 16,294 | 2,650 | 1781–83 |
| Santa Rosa | – | – | – |
| Santa Ana | 27,272 | 5,000 | 1780 |
| Sardaneta | 10,887 | 6,000 | 1798 |
| Sardina | 16,877 | 5,250 | 1788 |
| Tuna Agria | 14,000 | 7,500 | 1796 |
| Total | 624,835 | 249,870 | |
| | 100 per cent | 39.9 per cent | |

### B. RINCÓN

| Haciendas | Estate values | Church mortgages | Year |
|---|---|---|---|
| | pesos | pesos | |
| Cañada de Negros | 61,000 | 26,900 | 1790 |
| Fuentes de Medina | 11,505 | 5,400 | 1793 |

TABLE 23—*continued*

| Haciendas | Estate values | Church morgages | Year |
|---|---|---|---|
| | pesos | pesos | |
| Pedregal | 40,366 | 6,470 | 1795 |
| Peñuelas | 64,000 | 52,000 | 1799 |
| Sauz de Armenta | 30,156 | 8,000 | 1823 |
| San Cristóbal | 32,000 | 26,500 | 1782 |
| San Isidro | 8,150 | 2,000 | 1799 |
| San Lorenzo | 16,000 | 4,600 | 1801 |
| Sapos | 15,816 | 6,000 | 1789 |
| Sarteneja | 11,855 | 3,100 | 1792 |
| Talayote | 33,269 | 1,400 | 1793 |
| Tanques | 9,300 | 3,500 | 1791 |
| Terrero | 8,270 | – | 1782 |
| Total | 341,687 | 145,870 | |
| | 100 per cent | 42.6 per cent | |

*Sources:* see Appendix 3.

Any attempt to calculate the share of Church capital in the overall capital value of agricultural property is vitiated by the absence of any central registry, so that information has to be gathered from inventories and notary entries scattered across a period of years. Direct clerical ownership was rare. True, in 1732 the Jesuits were bequeathed Hoya and Losa, but with their expulsion in 1767 these estates passed into the hands of the Crown, and in 1792 reverted to private ownership. Then again, although in 1836 Palote and Palma were donated to the Oratory by two priests whose families ranked among the leading landlords in the district, these haciendas were soon lost to the Church through the application of the desamortisation laws of the Liberal Reforma.[61] Nevertheless, if we accept the evidence presented in Table 23, then by the close of the eighteenth century, the Church owned about 40% of the assessed value of agricultural property in León and Rincón. Needless to say, the level varied greatly from estate to estate. Moreover, the largest sums held by the Church were the result of specific donations rather than a gradual accumulation of debt. For example, the heavy burden of charges assigned to Losa and Hoya derived from the transfer of funds from the Jesuits to the college administered by the Oratory in Guanajuato. Similarly, the 22,000 ps on Palote was the inheritance of the owner's daughter who had entered the Santa Clara convent and, as we mentioned above, the charges on San Cristóbal and Peñuelas came from the endowments assigned by their outgoing clerical owners. In conclusion, although the overall level of debt was high, nevertheless it was significantly lower than in Oaxaca where the Church controlled two thirds of the total value of the hacienda sector.[62] Nevertheless, after Independence there can be little doubt that the burden became more onerous. Apart from the initial upset, the laws of the Reforma, therefore, brought little but improvement to the finances of the average Mexican hacienda.

## CHAPTER 5

# Profits and rents: three haciendas

How many workers were employed on haciendas in León? What was the ratio of resident peons to the number of seasonal jornaleros? How many tenants were there and how much of the hacienda did they farm? What proportion of the harvest was actually sold each year? What was the rate of profit? As we argued above, answers to such questions can only come from an analysis of the accounts of particular haciendas. Unfortunately, there were no legal reasons why anyone should deposit his private papers in a public archive. Indeed, only in cases of judicial embargo or when an estate was managed by a guardian was there any call for a public comprobation of accounts. In León summary returns were filed with the municipal magistrates for only three states – Duarte, Otates and Sauz de Armenta – which at the time were respectively managed by a legal executor or guardian on behalf of an elderly infirm spinster, a lunatic and a child. Clearly, the reasons which dictated the survival of these documents also biased their direction against any high yield of profit. The selection is also distorted, although the interest greatly heightened, by the coincidence of our first two examples with the Insurgency of 1810–21. Despite these obvious defects, the records provide invaluable evidence about the internal organisation of agricultural production which cannot be found in any other type of source material of this period.

I

Located about ten miles due east of León, San José de Duarte encompassed 103 caballerías or about 10,800 acres, of which only a third was arable, the remainder of the land being hill-side terrain only suitable for light pasture. Its titles dated back to a 1566 vice-regal *merced* for a small sitio and two caballerías of arable, to which was subsequently added two standard council grants of $3\frac{1}{2}$ cab. each. It was only in 1711 that *composición* was paid on the remainder of the land which had been quietly appropriated during the preceding century.[1] At that time only 12 caballerías or 1,260 acres were cleared for ploughing. The only detailed inventory we possess, which was taken in 1758, provides an impression of later development.

TABLE 24  *San José de Duarte: inventory of estate, January 1758*

| | pesos | % |
|---|---|---|
| **LAND** | | |
| Pasture: 82 caballerías | 5,000 | |
| Arable: 21 caballerías at 275 ps | 5,775 | |
| | 10,775 ps | 33.90 |
| **BUILDINGS** | | |
| House and chapel | 2,010 | |
| 2 barns | 3,000 | |
| Walls: 9,800 yards | 2,109 | |
| Other buildings | 1,080 | |
| | 8,199 ps | 25.79 |
| **EQUIPMENT** | 249 ps | 0.78 |
| **WORKSTOCK** | | |
| 173 oxen at 7 ps | 1,211 | |
| 37 young oxen at 5 ps | 185 | |
| 16 equipped freight mules at 25 ps | 400 | |
| 59 saddle mules at 16 ps, 3 at 12 ps | 980 | |
| 75 horses at 5 ps | 375 | |
| | 3,151 ps | 9.92 |
| **LIVESTOCK** | | |
| 52 cattle at 5 ps | 260 | |
| 12 calves at 1 ps | 12 | |
| 340 brood mares at 2–3½ ps | 764 | |
| 53 foals at 1 ps | 53 | |
| 166 mules, 3–5 years, at 11 ps | 1,826 | |
| 23 mules, 1–2 years, at 6 ps | 138 | |
| 23 mules, new-branded, at 4 ps | 92 | |
| 36 donkeys at 1–12 ps | 213 | |
| 2,412 sheep and lambs at 2–12 rls | 1,746 | |
| 145 goats at 2–8 reales | 73 | |
| 223 pigs at 1–6 reales | 154 | |
| | 5,414 ps | 17.03 |
| **MAGUEY** | | |
| 20,000 plants | 4,000 ps | 12.58 |
| **TOTAL** | 31,856 ps | 100.00 |
| **PRODUCE** | | |
| Soap | 567 | |
| Maize: 2,432 fanegas (previous harvest) | | |
| 3,862 fanegas (just harvested) both at | | |
| ½ ps | 3,147 | |
| Other produce | 353 | |
| | 4,067 ps | |
| **INVENTORY TOTAL** | 35,856 ps | |

*Source:* AHML 1758/59–31, taken 26 January 1758.

In accordance with its terrain, the Duarte concentrated upon maize-growing and stockraising; major irrigation for wheat was apparently not feasible. Despite common assertions to the contrary, this type of hacienda obviously required a considerable outlay of capital if it was to yield a profit. Its financial success depended upon a numerous herd of oxen for ploughing, ample dry storage in stone-built barns so as to await the best season or year for sale, and an expensive mule-team to carry grain to market when and where prices were the most inviting. The volume of production was high and the yield upon the quantity sown remarkable. In response to an official inquiry, the owner declared that he generally sowed 40 fanegas of maize from which in good years he expected to reap 4,000 fanegas, and in poor years, 1,000.[2] The inventory shows that the barns still held 3,432 fanegas from 1756 alongside 3,816 unthreshed fanegas from the December harvest of 1757. Tithe records report that the hacienda produced an average 2,141 fanegas for the years 1761–67. Its tenants (of whom the inventory makes no mention) produced 393 fanegas, just under a fifth of the landlord's output.[3] At this time the hacienda employed 39 workers whose debts amounted to 496 pesos, an average of 13 pesos each, the equivalent of three to four months wages.[4]

For the years 1811–18 relaitvely detailed accounts of Duarte's operations were deposited in the municipal archive, by the trustee for the current owner, an elderly, infirm spinster.[5] Their value is enhanced by their coincidence with the period of Insurgency and the invasion of Javier Mina. The estate suffered considerable depletion of its livestock but managed to maintain maize production at a time when many haciendas were obliged to suspend operations. In consequence, the high prices obtained from the sale of maize offset the losses incurred in capital value. Tables 25 and 26 present a reconstruction of these accounts. Unfortunately, damp destroyed the summaries for 1815 and 1816 so that although most entries can be calculated from itemised records, certain key strands of information are missing. Figures in brackets are extrapolated estimates.

In these years the chief business of Duarte was the cultivation of maize, from which it drew over sixty per cent of its gross receipts, with an average production of 2,514 fanegas, a figure influenced by the renewal of the Insurgency after 1813. Just under sixty per cent of the harvest was actually sold, of which 2,990 fanegas, i.e. 14% of the total, was purchased by the hacienda peons at prices somewhat lower than the market rate. These workers, the *sirvientes*

TABLE 25  *Duarte, accounts rendered 1811–1818 (pesos)*

| | 1811 | 1812 | 1813 | 1814 | 1815 | 1816 | 1817 | 1818 | Total |
|---|---|---|---|---|---|---|---|---|---|
| INCOME | | | | | | | | | |
| Maize | 5,767 | 1,376 | 1,998 | 1,141 | 4,443 | 2,028 | 6,884 | 2,167 | 25,804 |
| Cane | 1,003 | 572 | 145 | 216 | 200 | 96 | 48 | 92 | 2,372 |
| Minor crops | 407 | 249 | 11 | 298 | 13 | 36 | 73 | 54 | 1,141 |
| Livestock | 535 | 516 | 255 | – | 23 | 33 | – | 126 | 1,488 |
| Pulque | 203 | 43 | – | 195 | 113 | 147 | 231 | 61 | 993 |
| Rents | 1,474 | 1,440 | 1,461 | 1,260 | 1,086 | 911 | 1,145 | 904 | 9,681 |
| Miscellaneous | 162 | 17 | 19 | – | 18 | – | – | – | 216 |
| Total | 9,551 | 4,213 | 3,889 | 3,110 | 5,896 | 3,251 | 8,381 | 3,404 | 41,695 |
| Debts paid | 285 | 66 | 47 | 57 | – | – | 113 | 168 | 736 |
| Peons' debts | 541 | 789 | 627 | 474 | (500) | (500) | 693 | 526 | 4,650 |
| León interest | 175 | 177 | 28 | 36 | 29 | 29 | 186 | 188 | 848 |
| Cash in hand | 1,880 | 1,999 | 1,270 | – | – | (470) | – | – | 4,819 |
| Grand total | 12,432 | 6,444 | 5,861 | 3,677 | (6,425) | (4,250) | 9,373 | 4,286 | 52,748 |

| EXPENSES | | | | | | | | | Total |
|---|---|---|---|---|---|---|---|---|---|
| Annual wages | 4,408 | 3,114 | 2,874 | 2,657 | (2,400) | (2,400) | 2,219 | 2,550 | 22,622 |
| Seasonal wages | 306 | 70 | 162 | 257 | 87 | 72 | 112 | 196 | 1,262 |
| Costs | 657 | 851 | 829 | 464 | 884 | 1,367 | 1,728 | 2,586* | 9,366 |
| Chapel | 94 | 85 | 83 | — | — | — | — | — | 262 |
| Debts | 296 | 94 | 151 | 271 | (100) | (102) | 332 | 34 | 1,380 |
| Balance to mayordomo | — | — | — | 386 | 1,472 | — | 1,223 | 22 | 3,103 |
| Total | 5,761 | 4,214 | 4,099 | 4,035 | 4,943 | 3,941 | 5,614 | 5,388 | 37,995 |
| To owner | 5,472 | 960 | 2,148 | 1,114 | 1,012 | 1,532 | 3,781 | 499 | 16,518 |
| Grand total | 11,233 | 5,174 | 6,247 | 5,149 | 5,955 | 5,473 | 9,395 | 5,887 | 54,513 |
| Balance | +1,199 | +1,270 | −386 | −1,472 | (+470) | −1,223 | −22 | −1,601 | – |
| Annual profit | 4,791 | 1,031 | 492 | 28 | 2,954 | −161 | 4,982 | −1,080 | 13,037 |

Figures in brackets are extrapolations.

* 1,150 ps purchase of bulls.

*Note*: Annual profits are calculated on the basis of income less expenses, with cash in hand deducted from income and the mayordomo's commission and share of profit deducted from expenses.

*Sources*: AHML 1811(4)–28; 1814–32; 1815(1)–5; 1818(1)–1.

*acomodados*, took as their free rations twenty per cent of the crop. The remainder went to pay the tithe, to feed the owner, to be sown, for livestock feed, or was stolen. The owner took about 74 fanegas a year for household consumption. The amount set aside for sowing was remarkably small and implies yields ranging from 82 to one in 1812 to 68 to one in 1817. The volume and value of sales varied markedly from year to year. Half of all revenue came from the high returns of the two years 1811 and 1817. It is noticeable that between 1812 and 1815 large stocks of grain – over 2,000 fanegas – had to be stored. With the confiscation of its mule-team, the hacienda either sold its produce on the estate or sent it to León. The one day journey to town cost no less than one real a fanega. Possession of a town barn in León permitted the owner to await the most favourable moment to sell her grain. In 1815, for example, all maize from Duarte was sold in León during the summer weeks between 17 June and 31 August.

TABLE 26    *Duarte: maize production and sales 1811–18*

| Years | Stock | Harvest | Sales | Income | León price |
|---|---|---|---|---|---|
| | fanegas | fanegas | fanegas | pesos | average in reales |
| 1811 | 240 | 3,706 | 2,179 | 5,767 | 20.3 |
| 1812 | 404 | 3,720 | 609 | 1,375 | 17 |
| 1813 | 2,380 | 3,213 | 1,077 | 1,997 | 14.2 |
| 1814 | 2,250 | 2,100 | 1,206 | 1,141 | 8 |
| 1815 | 2,271 | 1,970 | 2,333 | 4,443 | 16 |
| 1816 | 770 | 1,977 | 951 | 2,028 | 18 |
| 1817 | 937 | 1,759 | 2,125 | 6,883 | 27.7 |
| 1818 | – | 2,173 | 1,010 | 2,167 | 18 |
| | 1,155 | 2,577 | 1,499 | 3,226 | |

*Note:* Sales include all grain issued on account to peons.

*Consumption of maize* (fanegas)

| | |
|---|---|
| Sown | 184 |
| To owner | 675 |
| Peon rations | 4,049 |
| Sold on account to peons | 2,990 |
| Sold in hacienda | 2,113 |
| Sold in León | 6,892 |
| Church tithes | 1,739 |
| Miscellaneous | 255 |
| Stolen | 1,961 |
| | 20,858 |

*Source:* AHML 1811(4)–28; 1814–32; 1815(1)–5; 1818(1)–1.

The hacienda also regularly planted small quantities of barley and beans but the object here was internal consumption, both for workers and stock, with only occasional sales. Despite the large plantation of magueys, the return on pulque was low, ranging from 100 to 200 pesos a year. An unexpectedly high income derived from the sale of *caña* or cane, although here the disparity between 1811 and subsequent years reduces the overall value of this entry. In addition, the huerta or garden produced green chili which was sent to both León and Guanajuato, although after 1812 production seems to have dwindled. In sum, these minor crops supplied a tenth of the gross receipts. In the two years 1811–12, however, this proportion rose to 18%, so that here we possibly encounter some measure of the effects of the Insurgency.

The livestock accounts require careful examination. In 1811 Duarte possessed 185 oxen, 201 mules, 80 saddle horses and herds of 378 cattle and 264 brood mares. Apart from the elimination of sheep and goats, these numbers were remarkably similar to those recorded in the 1758 inventory. The documents reveal an intimate relation between the working stock and the breeding herds. In 1811, 21 young bulls were converted into plough oxen, enabling the discard of an equal number of presumably aging beasts. In the two succeeding years another 13 and 16 animals were respectively transferred. Thus the herd of cattle served a twofold purpose. Apart from the sales which provided an additional, albeit minor, source of income, it replenished and maintained the plough oxen at small cost to the owner. The brood mares likewise fulfilled a dual function. In 1811 they provided 7 additions to the mules and 32 to the saddle horses; no doubt in other years a proportion would also have been sold. In 1812 this balance between work stock and breeders was broken. The Insurgents stole 249 head of cattle; another 40 were sold; and with only 55 left, the yield of calves was barely sufficient to replace minor thefts. By 1818 through natural wastage, the number of oxen had dropped to 102, so that the owner was then obliged to invest no less than 1,150 pesos in the purchase of 100 fresh oxen. By then, the cattle herd amounted to 48 head. During the same year the hacienda lost most of its saddle horses and mules. In 1812–13, 87 mules were stolen by the insurgents and another 65 appropriated by the royal army. By 1818 further thefts left the hacienda with no more than 16 mules. At the same time, the insurgents took 71 horses and the royalists 25; after 1814 no saddle horses were listed. By contrast, however, the herd of brood mares survived. Over the years 1814–17,

149 were stolen, but these losses were offset by natural increase, so that in 1818 they still numbered 274 head. These severe losses prevent any reliable estimate of the relative importance of income derived from the sale of livestock. In both 1811 and 1812 it amounted to over 500 pesos, or 7.6% of the combined income of these two years. The prime importance of the herds lay in the replenishment of the working stock.

The success of Duarte in maintaining production throughout these years can be attributed to the large number of workers who were employed on a permanent basis. In 1812 maize rations were issued to 34 men. The cost of this labour force was high since over a period of eight years the wage bill averaged 2,850 pesos a year in addition to 506 fanegas of maize. The role of debt in binding men to the estate is difficult to estimate. In 1812, the 34 *sirvientes acomodados* owed their employer 765 pesos, an average of 22 pesos each, about equal to half a year's wage. Part of this debt, however, probably came from the additional maize purchased by the peons. For the harvest and other seasonal tasks labourers were hired at a daily rate of 2 reales. In 1812 about 30 men were employed for short periods of time, most of them recruited from the tenants or their families.

About a quarter of gross revenue over the eight years came from rents, at an annual average of 1,212 pesos. Three distinct types of land were held in tenancy. In 1811, 19 persons paid 246 pesos for an unspecified area of irrigated land suitable for the cultivation of green chili and other vegetables. Another 48 men rented just over 75 fanegas de sembradura, which at the current rate of 10 pesos a fanega yielded the owner 756 pesos. Finally, another 54 persons described as *moradores* paid 471 pesos for their *asientos* or dwellings and for ranchos or pasturage. One individual in this last group paid 200 pesos for what was obviously an entire rancho. It should be noted that persons in the first two categories paid on average 13 and 15 pesos a head; the plots of land they rented were thus rarely larger than two fanegas.

Some indication as to the extension of land held in tenancy can be obtained from a later inventory drawn up in 1843. At that time the total area of arable land in Duarte was estimated at 195 fanegas, of which 12 fanegas were irrigated, and hence was described as the huerta.[6] According to this measure six fanegas de sembradura were reckoned as the equivalent of a caballería, that is to say, each comprised about 17½ acres. In 1843 the rent for ordinary land was still assessed at 10 pesos a fanega. The area under irrigation, however, was let in plots 50 paces square, at the rate of 60 pesos a fanega. If these measures be applied to the hacienda of 1811, we find that, with 76 fanegas let out of 183 fanegas suitable for maize and 4 out of 12 irrigated fanegas, Duarte leased just over a third of its arable land.

Little can be said about this class of tenant farmers, arrendatarios as they were invariably called. As far as can be ascertained, all tenure was customary, based upon verbal or informal agreement; contracts were not notarised and apparently did not carry any guarantee of renewal beyond the year in question. No doubt, however, some farmers remained on one hacienda for a lifetime; others came and went quite rapidly. In these years, the area in Duarte under tenancy varied remarkably, the consequence, we may presume, of the turmoil of the invasion of Javier Mina. The extension let for maize growing reached a peak of 89 fanegas in 1813; fell to 13 in 1816 and rose again to 56 by 1818. We may note that in 1817 the mayordomo himself rented 4 fanegas for maize, and another one and a half of the huerta. Whether other permanent employees of the hacienda also rented land cannot be discovered. Finally, there is no indication that these tenant farmers acted as sharecroppers, save for one reference in 1816 to the medieros of the huerta; but these men were apparently distinct from the tenants of that year.

To calculate the actual profit of Duarte in these eight years, we first have to subtract the cash in hand carried over from 1810 (1,880 pesos) and the final debit balance of 1818 (1,601 pesos). Thus the true profit was 13,037 pesos or an average of 1,629 pesos a year, the equivalent of a four or five per cent return upon the capital value of the estate. The true source of this profit makes a nice question. It is startling to note that for the three years 1812–14 the fixed wage bill (8,635 pesos) exceeded the value of all sales of produce (7,053 pesos). Only the high yields of 1811, 1815 and 1817 justified the continuance of maize cultivation. Judged from this perspective, we can say that the function of rents was to provide a steady flow of cash sufficient to cover the wage bill and to offset the fluctuations of the corn market. The practice also permitted the landlord to share in the benefits of good harvests. One last query remains: would it not have been more profitable to have rented the entire hacienda? At a uniform rate of 10 pesos a fanega de sembradura receipts upon arable land would have amounted to 1,950 pesos, a greater sum than the net return of 1,629 pesos. But these years of turmoil were sufficiently exceptional as to invalidate the value of our evidence when pushed to such extreme conclusions. At the very least, however, our calculations demonstrate that for haciendas like Duarte the margin between profit and loss was both narrow and uncertain.

## II

Our second estate, San Juan de los Otates, bordered Duarte to the west and north, stretching deep into the sierra. Although the accounts arising from the years 1814–19 are summary, nevertheless they offer valuable corroboration on several key issues. Apparently formed during the seventeenth century without any procurable viceregal title, Otates was deemed to encompass nearly 20,000 acres at the 1711 *composición*.[7] An anatomy of the hacienda can be obtained from the inventory taken in February 1787 in which only 15 caballerías, or 1,575 acres, were described as arable as against some 15,870 acres of mountainous pasture, still valued at 2,050 ps a large sitio. The herds of livestock were relatively small and, as in the case of Duarte, served mainly to replenish the work-stock. Comparison with a previous inventory drawn up a century before in 1688 shows that the estate had reduced its stockraising in favour of cereal cultivation.[8] The number of plough oxen doubled from 107 to 196 whereas the herd of brood mares fell from 320 head to 89. The number of cattle and transport mules remained much the same and the less valuable flock of sheep and goats dropped in number from 700 to 302. In consequence of this shift in activity, land and building accounted for 73% of the total inventory value as against 50.6% in the first year, whereas stock fell from 49% to 25.6% of the overall assessment. Equally important, as we mentioned above, after 1751 the tithe returns consistently report the existence of tenant farmers on Otates, and by the years 1762–67 they accounted for 23% of the maize production of the hacienda.[9]

Throughout the eighteenth century, Otates was owned by three successive generations of the Quijas family. Unfortunately, the daughter of the last owner, the sole surviving heir, proved mentally deficient, so that her affairs were managed by a guardian. In 1804 the hacienda was leased for a period of nine years to Pablo Pompa (whose family owned an hacienda in León) for an annual rent of 1,850 ps.[10] With the estate went 208 oxen, 102 mules, 329 cattle and 31 mares. Pompa also inherited the 502 ps in debts owed by the resident peons. Since in June 1810 a summary appraisal of Otates assessed its worth at 41,886 ps (including livestock), then this rent represented a 4.5% return on capital.[11]

After the expiry of Pompa's tenancy in 1813, Otates was managed

TABLE 27   *San Juan de los Otates: inventory of estate 22 February 1787*

|  | pesos | % |
|---|---|---|
| LAND |  |  |
| 2 large sitios and 29 cab. in mountains at 50 ps a cab. | 5,550 |  |
| 36 cab. at 50 ps | 1,800 |  |
| 2 cab. in peaks at 25 ps | 50 |  |
| 14 cab. for maize at 300 ps | 4,200 |  |
| 1 cab. irrigated at | 400 |  |
| 4 cab. scattered at 100 ps | 400 |  |
|  | 12,400 ps | 51.54 |
| BUILDINGS |  |  |
| House and chapel | 1,676 |  |
| 2 barns | 1,138 |  |
| Stone walls, 7,211 yds | 1,370 |  |
| Other buildings | 1,001 |  |
|  | 5,185 ps | 21.55 |
| EQUIPMENT | 310 | 310 ps | 1.28 |
| WORKSTOCK |  |  |
| 196 oxen at $8\frac{1}{2}$ ps | 1,666 |  |
| 33 equipped mules at 30 ps | 990 |  |
| 44 mules, for saddle, some old, from $13\frac{1}{2}$ to $15\frac{1}{2}$ ps | 617 |  |
| 5 mules at 10 ps, 2 at 6 ps | 62 |  |
| 4 mules for carriage | 130 |  |
| 6 horses (*mansos*) $12\frac{1}{2}$ ps | 74 |  |
| 9 mares at 3 ps | 27 |  |
|  | 3,566 ps | 14.81 |
| BREEDING-STOCK |  |  |
| 89 brood mares at $2-2\frac{3}{4}$ ps | 223 |  |
| 63 horses at $4\frac{1}{2}$ ps | 283 |  |
| A donkey | 12 |  |
| 404 cattle at $4\frac{1}{2}$ ps | 1,818 |  |
| 302 sheep at $\frac{3}{4}$ ps | 226 |  |
| 8 fat pigs at 5 ps | 40 |  |
|  | 2,602 ps | 10.82 |
| TOTAL | 24,063 ps | 100.00 |
| PRODUCE |  |  |
| 1,172 fanegas of maize at 2 ps | 2,344 |  |
| 29 fanegas of barley at $1\frac{1}{4}$ ps | 44 |  |
| 13 fanegas, chile at 4 ps | 52 |  |
| 19 loads of straw $\frac{1}{2}$ ps | 9 |  |
| $22\frac{3}{4}$ fanegas, beans, at 4 ps | 91 |  |
|  | 2,540 ps |  |
| INVENTORY TOTAL | 26,603 ps |  |

*Source:* AGN, Civil 286–3.

by a mayordomo for Julián de Obregón, who had been charged with the direction of the financial interests of the heiress.[12] Later, he deposited in the municipal archive a summary of his administration to which he added some itemised accounts of the hacienda. The results are decidedly incomplete, however, since after 1815 the depredations of the Insurgents caused harvests yields to plummet so that direct cultivation was virtually suspended. Indeed, in February 1820, when the estate was once more put on lease, it went for a mere 700 ps rent.[13]

TABLE 28   *Otates: accounts rendered 1814–18 (pesos)*

|  | 1814 | 1815 | 1816 | 1817 | 1818 | Total |
|---|---|---|---|---|---|---|
| INCOME |  |  |  |  |  |  |
| Maize* | 5,761 | 2,062 | 999 | 1,505 | 1,059 | 11,386 |
| Other crops | 20 | – | – | 113 | – | 133 |
| Livestock | 372 | 171 | – | 8 | – | 551 |
| Rents | 407 | 247 | 230 | 400 | 313 | 1,597 |
| Total | 6,560 | 2,480 | 1,229 | 2,026 | 1,372 | 13,667 |
| COSTS |  |  |  |  |  |  |
| Fixed wages | 1,088 | 886 | 284 | 122 | 126 | 2,506 |
| Hired labour | 1,476 | 1,488 | 257 | 1,319 | 1,409 | 5,949 |
| Costs | 779 | 665 | 248 | 617 | 358 | 2,667 |
| Total | 3,343 | 3,039 | 789 | 2,058 | 1,893 | 11,122 |
| Profit | 3,217 | -559 | 440 | -32 | -521 | 2,545 |
| MAIZE |  |  |  |  |  |  |
| Harvest (fanegas) | 5,375 | 2,888 | 737 | 885 | ? |  |
| Sales (fanegas) | 4,268 | 1,628 | 668 | 865 | 993 |  |
| Average price in reales | 14.2 | 12.5 | 16.1 | 18.6 | 12.2 |  |

* Taxes and transport costs already deducted.
*Source:* AHML 1828(4)–2.

Still more than Duarte, Otates depended upon the sale of maize for its income. In the years 1814 and 1815 receipts under this heading amounted to 86% of all revenue. One revelation to be gleaned from these accounts is that an hacienda might well have a good year precisely when its neighbour failed to find a market for its grain. In 1814, when Duarte sold 1,206 fanegas for about eight reales each, Otates contrived to sell 4,268 fanegas in León for no less than 7,595 pesos, that is to say, at an average price of 14.2 reales. From this sum were deducted 1,318 pesos in sales tax, alhóndiga charges, etc., the equivalent of 2.8 reales a fanega. Transport charges came to another real a fanega. The net income from maize of 5,761 pesos far exceeded all other sources of revenue. Rents yielded 407 pesos and other produce 392, so that even with charges subtracted, maize still amounted to 87% of the total. Needless to say, this proportion was not maintained in the years after 1815.

As regards its organisation of labour, Otates differed from Duarte in that it kept fewer permanent workers relying instead upon hired hands for harvests and other seasonal jobs. In consequence both its maize rations and fixed wage bill were much lower than the corresponding items for Duarte. In 1814 only eleven men were employed all through the year with annual salaries of 48 pesos. These men cared for the stock, whereas the field hands were hired when required. It may be of interest to note that the hacienda employed a schoolmaster paid at the same rate of 48 pesos. In the years after 1816 only the mayordomo was retained upon a permanent basis with maize ration and a salary of 117 pesos; all other workers were hired by the day. As it was, the costs of harvests in the years after 1815 just about equalled the income derived from the exiguous yield.

Although tenants were less numerous in Otates than in Duarte, they appear to have belonged to much the same class of individual. In 1814, some 26 persons paid 311 pesos at the general rate of 10 pesos a fanega de sembradura; another 8 paid 27 pesos for dwelling places; and a further 69 pesos came from the rent of oxen and the huerta. Probably less than a quarter of all arable land was let. In 1817 after the hacienda had lost its oxen through insurgent raids, the number of tenants rose to 53 persons, but since the rates of rent now declined to 5 and $7\frac{1}{2}$ pesos a fanega, the total income only came to 342 pesos. As late as 1826 most tenants on Otates only paid 8 pesos a fanega, although by then total revenue from both huerta and other land had risen to 745 pesos.

Few other points of interest can be found in these accounts. Their value lies chiefly in their reminder of the differences which existed between enterprises of the same general type. Duarte and Otates shared many characteristics, yet they differed markedly in the amount of land under lease and the number of peons retained on a permanent basis. Each hacienda was unique with its own history, and its own disposition of production.[14] Otates steadily recovered its value after Independence, but as late as 1837 it still possessed only 155 plough oxen. In the 1850s the hacienda was leased for annual rent of 2,000 ps, a rate which suggests that by that decade the destruction wrought by the Insurgency had been made good. It then sold for 48,600 ps.[15]

### III

Further insight into the complex economic evolution of the hacienda in the Bajío can be secured from the accounts of Sauz de Armenta, an estate which lay about 20 miles to the south of León. In 1708 the entire hacienda, then comprising 105 caballerías or about 14,000 acres, was sold for 6,000 pesos, its 24 plough oxen, 64 cattle and 165 remaining beasts being included in the price. In fact, since the estate carried two Church mortgages worth 3,900 pesos, the purchaser only had to find 2,100 pesos.[16] Half a century later, the tithe records indicate a thriving enterprise which in the three years 1756–58 on average produced 2,913 fanegas of maize, 137 ponies, 80 mules, 103 calves and 940 lambs. In the years which followed, the stockraising side of its activities declined, to be replaced by a greater concentration on maize-growing. By 1793 the hacienda maintained no less than 172 plough oxen.[17] But then a disputed inheritance resulted in the division of the estate, so that when an inventory was taken in 1823, the remaining nucleus consisted of 59 caballerías or about 6,220 acres.

Following the declaration of this inventory, much of the livestock was sold to satisfy the claims of several heirs.[18] Since the actual owner was a young child, the mayordomo appointed by the guardian was ordered to submit regular accounts which were then deposited in the municipal archive to avoid future litigation. When in 1827 the new manager entered his duties, he found only 25 plough oxen, 24 other cattle, 102 brood mares and 11 mules. Testamentary division had thus entailed a severe undercapitalisation of the estate. The small herd of cattle could not maintain, still less expand, the existing stock of oxen. Similarly, the handful of mules could not meet the seasonal transport requirements. Moreover the low number of plough oxen suggests that the area of land under cultivation was probably far less than the 10 caballerías listed in 1823.

By 1827 it is evident that Sauz de Armenta diverged markedly from the usual stereotype of the Mexican hacienda. Whereas according to our calculations about a third of the arable land in Duarte was let to tenant farmers, in Sauz that proportion in all likelihood approached three quarters. During the twelve years 1827–38, no less than 69% of its gross income derived from rents. Moreover, if we are

TABLE 29 *Sauz de Armenta: inventory of estate, June 1823*

|  | pesos | % |
|---|---|---|
| **LAND** |  |  |
| Pasture: 32 caballerías (20 at 100 ps, 12 at 50 ps) | 2,600 |  |
| Arable: 10 caballerías at 600 ps | 6,000 |  |
| Rented: 17 caballerías at 400 ps | 6,800 |  |
|  | 15,400 ps | 57.82 |
| **BUILDINGS** |  |  |
| House | 1,492 |  |
| Chapel | 902 |  |
| Barns | 348 |  |
| Dam | 2,751 |  |
| Other buildings | 829 |  |
|  | 6,322 ps | 23.75 |
| **EQUIPMENT** | 208 ps | 0.78 |
| **LIVESTOCK** |  |  |
| 46 cattle at 12–14 ps | 582 |  |
| 25 calves at 4 ps | 100 |  |
| 131 brood mares at 6 ps | 786 |  |
| 92 foals at 2–8 ps | 349 |  |
| 10 donkeys at 6–7 ps | 62 |  |
| 549 goats at 5–14 reales | 582 |  |
| 86 sheep at 4–12 reales | 120 |  |
| 46 pigs at 1–2 reales | 62 |  |
|  | 2,643 ps | 9.92 |
| **WORKSTOCK** |  |  |
| 72 oxen at 16 ps | 1,152 |  |
| 19 mules, most at 30 ps | 520 |  |
| 37 horses at 10 ps, 3 horses at 6 ps | 388 |  |
|  | 2,060 ps | 7.73 |
| **TOTAL** | 26,633 ps | 100.00 |
| **PRODUCE** |  |  |
| 300 fanegas of maize at 2 ps | 600 |  |
| 12 fanegas of beans at 5 ps | 60 |  |
|  | 660 ps |  |
| **INVENTORY TOTAL** | 27,293 ps |  |

*Source:* AHML 1827(3)–26. Inventory taken 2 June 1823.

to trust the accounts presented by the mayordomo, the home-farm, the demesne so to speak, failed to cover its costs of operation, so that in effect its continued operation was subsidised from rents. Clearly, with the estate under wardship, Sauz suffered from weak management, so that we should be cautious in using this case for any general interpretation. At the very least, however, it indicates that when

absentee ownership was combined with insufficient capital investment, direct cultivation of maize was exposed to considerable risks,
not to say losses.

The majority of the arrendatarios were probably substantial
farmers rather than mere squatters. In 1831 some 40 men paid a
total rent of 1,136 pesos. Of these, the six who paid under 8 pesos
(charged at the rate of 10 pesos a fanega de sembradura) were called
*terrasgueros*. At the other end of the scale, the brother-in-law of the
owner was assessed at 116 pesos. Excluding these extremes, there
remain 33 men with an average rent of 30 pesos each, the mayordomo himself paying 32 pesos. The more prosperous farmers obviously enjoyed the assistance of hired hands. In 1822 a local census
enumerated 525 persons or 115 families as resident in Sauz de
Armenta. Now since the owner at most maintained 9 permanent
workers as *sirvientes acomodados*, then it is clear that about half the
heads of families were labourers employed by the ranchos.[19] Thus
the hacienda housed two distinct classes of men – tenant farmers
and mere labourers – even if at the lower end of the scale considerable overlap occurred. The so-called debt peons were probably better
off than either the poorer tenants or the hired hands.

Upon turning to the accounts rendered by the mayordomo, we
encounter a dismal story of failure, the result either of managerial
ineptitude or adverse market conditions. Part of the trouble, however, can be attributed to the insufficient quantity of livestock left
from the testamentary apportionment. In 1827 the estate owned 25
oxen and a herd of 24 cattle; twelve years later numbers had risen
to 44 oxen and 38 cattle. During this period the mayordomo sold
18 aging oxen for 192 pesos, recruited 22 young bulls from the
increase of the herd, but was furthermore obliged to purchase
another 49 oxen at a cost of 583 pesos to replenish the plough teams.
Much the same pattern applied to the mules, with the number
increasing from 11 beasts in 1827 to 29 in 1839. Over the years 46
young mules were obtained from the brood mares; 21 were sold for
366 pesos, but in 1836 an entire team of 17 head was acquired for
405 pesos. About the only positive entry in the livestock account was
the herd of brood mares, where in addition to the young mules
already mentioned, sporadic sales of ponies brought in another 277
pesos. In all, over a twelve-year period, purchase of stock cost 1,311
pesos as against 903 pesos realised from sales. These figures explain
the maintenance of relatively large herds of cattle and mares on
haciendas such as Duarte and Otates. Granted an abundance of

TABLE 30  *Sauz de Armenta: accounts rendered 1827–39 (pesos)*

| | 1827 | 1828 | 1829 | 1830 | 1831 | 1832 | 1833 | 1834 | 1835 | 1836 | 1837 | 1838–9 | Average |
|---|---|---|---|---|---|---|---|---|---|---|---|---|---|
| **INCOME** | | | | | | | | | | | | | |
| Maize | 912 | 14 | 17 | – | 811 | 407 | – | 577 | 1,294 | 753 | 176 | 165 | 427 |
| Minor produce | 45 | 51 | 12 | 10 | 60 | – | 29 | 20 | 18 | 10 | – | – | 21 |
| Livestock | 100 | 21 | 76 | 281 | 9 | 57 | 18 | 122 | 27 | 89 | 32 | 71 | 75 |
| Rents | 991 | 1,073 | 1,153 | 1,149 | 1,101 | 1,210 | 1,153 | 1,224 | 1,290 | 1,464 | 1,347 | 1,429 | 1,215 |
| Miscellaneous | – | 6 | 27 | 16 | 57 | 50 | 4 | 16 | 23 | 3 | 10 | – | 18 |
| Peon debts | 81 | 89 | 188 | – | – | – | – | – | – | – | – | – | 30 |
| Total | 2,129 | 1,254 | 1,473 | 1,456 | 2,038 | 1,724 | 1,204 | 1,959 | 2,652 | 2,319 | 1,565 | 1,665 | 1,786 |
| Carried forward | 1,039 | 1,318 | 1,200 | 475 | 459 | 719 | 1,033 | 703 | 981 | 708 | 920 | 518 | – |
| Total income | 3,168 | 2,572 | 2,673 | 1,931 | 2,497 | 2,443 | 2,237 | 2,263 | 3,633 | 3,027 | 2,485 | 2,183 | – |
| **COSTS** | | | | | | | | | | | | | |
| Annual wages | 364 | 521 | 688 | 509 | 340 | 382 | 346 | 343 | 324 | 362 | 326 | 334 | 404 |
| Seasonal wages | 177 | 90 | 135 | 167 | 275 | 112 | 93 | 64 | 45 | 115 | 7 | 202 | 123 |
| Costs | 136 | 87 | 183 | 78 | 304 | 205 | 88 | 287 | 104 | 268 | 180 | 127 | 170 |
| Livestock purchase | 80 | 138 | 51 | 4 | – | – | 163 | 96 | 113 | 542 | 104 | 20 | 109 |
| Management | 595 | – | 589 | 146 | 204 | 172 | 120 | 196 | 265 | 233 | 157 | 167 | 237 |
| Total | 1,352 | 836 | 1,646 | 904 | 1,123 | 871 | 810 | 986 | 851 | 1,520 | 774 | 850 | 1,043 |
| **EXPENDITURE** | | | | | | | | | | | | | |
| To owner | 228 | 266 | 218 | 208 | 208 | 268 | 454 | 358 | 258 | 311 | 977 | 655 | 367 |
| Interest payments | 270 | 270 | 270 | 270 | 270 | 270 | 270 | 270 | 270 | 170 | 170 | 120 | 242 |
| Litigation, guardian | – | – | – | – | 177 | – | – | 68 | 46 | 106 | 46 | 60 | 49 |
| Capital redemption | – | – | – | – | – | – | – | – | 1,500 | – | – | 500 | 166 |
| Total | 498 | 536 | 488 | 569 | 655 | 538 | 724 | 696 | 2,074 | 587 | 1,193 | 1,335 | 824 |
| Grand total | 1,850 | 1,372 | 2,134 | 1,473 | 1,778 | 1,409 | 1,534 | 1,682 | 2,925 | 2,107 | 1,967 | 2,185 | 1,868 |
| Carried forward | 1,318 | 1,200 | 539* | 458 | 719 | 1,033 | 703 | 981 | 708 | 920 | 518 | – | – |

\* 64 peso not carried, unaccounted.

*Sources*: AHML 1830(1)–2; 1831(1)–7; 1832(2)–4; 1835(1)–2; 1836(1)–2; 1837(2)–26; 1838(2)–23; 1839(1)–13.

pasture, it was surely cheaper to breed working stock and to sell the surplus rather than to purchase replacements.

The major cause of the hacienda's problems, however, came from the failure to find a market for its maize, the only product of importance. Each year the estate harvested maize – on average 425 fanegas – but in only eight out of twelve years did it sell appreciable quantities. Situated twenty miles or more from León, the nearest urban market, with transport costs at $1\frac{1}{2}$ reales a fanega, Sauz de Armenta was apparently unable to compete with haciendas like Duarte which, in addition to their greater proximity, possessed greater storage capacity. Tables 30 and 31 summarise the results.

In all the hacienda sold 58% of maize produced between 1827 and 1838, with the overall price averaging 13 reales a fanega. The rations of kept peons consumed just over a fifth of output, a propor-

TABLE 31    *Sauz de Armenta: maize production and sales 1827–39*

| Years | Stock (fanegas) | Harvest (fanegas) | Sales (fanegas) | Income (pesos) | Prices in León (average in reales) |
|---|---|---|---|---|---|
| 1827 | 408 | 154 | 430 | 912 | 17.2 |
| 1828 | 11 | 249 | 5 | 14 | – |
| 1829 | 135 | 227 | 11 | 17 | – |
| 1830 | 211 | 931 | – | – | – |
| 1831 | 1,000 | 733 | 774 | 811 | 8.7 |
| 1832 | 796 | 501 | 336 | 407 | 10 |
| 1833 | 831 | 446 | – | – | – |
| 1834 | 1,083 | 452 | 393 | 577 | 11 |
| 1835 | 994 | 144 | 546 | 1,294 | 19.2 |
| 1836 | 134 | 464 | 409 | 753 | 14.8 |
| 1837 | 42 | 162 | 71 | 176 | 20 |
| 1838 | 21 | 454 | 113 | 165 | 10 |
| Average | 472 | 410 | 257 | 427 | – |

*Note:* Tithes already deducted from harvest; taxes already deducted from income.

*Maize consumption* (fanegas)

| | |
|---|---|
| To owner | 42 |
| Sown | 157 |
| For livestock | 170 |
| Peon rations | 1,109 |
| Sold to peons | 116 |
| Sales in León | 2,972 |
| Lost or unaccounted | 759 |
| Total | 5,325 |

*Source:* See Table 30.

tion similar to that of Duarte. Broken down by year, the performance appears yet more damning. After a reasonable year in 1827, the hacienda did not sell any noticeable quantity of maize until 1831, and then it only obtained an average 8.7 reales per fanega. Indeed it was not until 1835 that the estate did well, selling over 550 fanegas at an average price of 19 reales. In both 1831 and 1834 Sauz had to carry stocks of over 1,000 fanegas. It was presumably this failure which drove the mayordomo to reduce the wage-bill by sowing all maize *a medias*, that is to say, on some unspecified sharecropping basis. After 1829 only six to nine men were retained as permanent workers, entitled to maize rations and paid a monthly wage of 4 pesos. Their principal task was the care of livestock. The harvest and other seasonal jobs were undertaken with labour hired by the day. Even so, the home farm of Sauz showed a consistent loss. Spread over the twelve year period, the sale of all produce yielded an annual average of 541 pesos, whereas wages and annual costs equalled 526 pesos. When, however, we add the costs of transport, taxes, the repair of equipment and the replacement of livestock, the total operating cost rises to an annual 785 pesos, a sum well in excess of income. In effect, therefore, the operation of the farm was subsidised from rents. As Table 30 demonstrates, rents provided 69% of the gross income, whereas maintenance of the hacienda as a productive unit absorbed nearly 45% of all income.

In general, Sauz de Armenta yielded a remarkably low return upon invested capital. The young owner received a derisory 367 pesos a year from an estate still worth about 25,000 pesos. However, to this sum must be added the annual 270 pesos paid in interest upon the 5,400 pesos of Church mortgages charged on the estate. If in addition we add the fees of the guardian, litigation costs, capital redemption, and more important, the salary of the mayordomo, then the potential yield of the estate rises to 14,318 pesos or an annual 1,193 pesos, the equivalent of a 4.4% return upon capital value. Even so, this sum is still lower than the 1,219 pesos obtained from rents. Clearly, the attempt at direct cultivation had proved a miserable failure; the owner would have been better served if his guardian had leased the entire hacienda.

## IV

By way of conclusion, let us reiterate the reservations expressed at the outset. The reasons which determined the survival of these records biased the eventual balance of profit. Moreover, whereas the richest haciendas in León – Santa Rosa, Sandía and Santa Ana – all possessed extensive irrigation dams which permitted the cultivation of wheat, the three estates discussed above all depended on maize for their main crop. Similarly, their holdings of livestock were comparatively meagre. Yet there is a sense in which the very limitations of our sample constitutes its chief value. For these accounts surely support the hypothesis that by the opening of the nineteenth century haciendas which still farmed maize derived but a marginal return on their capital. By then cash-tenancy or sharecropping probably offered a more reliable source of income than direct cultivation by the landlord. In any case, the severe losses in working stock experienced by haciendas during the Insurgency could only serve to hasten the abandonment of demesne farming.

## CHAPTER 6

# Landlords

In a frontier society such as eighteenth century León, where the development of haciendas depended on the financial resources of their owners, it was only to be expected that merchants and miners would play an important role in the transformation of the countryside. In a few cases hacendado families contrived to improve their estates over the course of the century. But in the years prior to 1760 it was mainly merchants who were responsible for the formation of new haciendas, either by financing the conversion of scrubland into arable, or through the purchase of entire series of ranchos and *labores*. Only in the last decades of the century did wealthy miners from Guanajuato and Catorce emerge as the leading landowners in the district. Obviously, these distinctions in period and occupation should not be pressed too hard, since from the start several merchants derived their profits from mining operations and they certainly did not disappear from the scene after 1780. Indeed, at all times, many proprietors were described as 'merchants and landowners'. It is surely significant that in a group of ten leading merchants who contracted to farm the royal excise or *alcabala*, no less than six owned or were about to own haciendas.[1] Then again, apart from a few absentee landlords, virtually all the hacendados in the district lived in León, so that it would be quite false to present any radical dichotomy between the rural gentry and urban traders. Similarly, although most merchants were immigrants from the Peninsula, nevertheless some creoles offered a successful challenge to this dominance, even if in general terms it is true that most immigrants tended to start their careers in trade, whereas creoles turned more readily to mining or agriculture. In 1770 the town council had six members equally divided between the two sections of the Spanish nation. But although all three peninsulars were merchants, two were shortly to purchase haciendas. Similarly, whereas the creoles all owned haciendas, one was also operating a thriving trading house.[2] In short, it is difficult to prove that in this part of Mexico there was a class of landowners

TABLE 32  Changes in hacienda ownership: León and Rincón 1711–1861

| Haciendas | c.1712 | c.1760 | c.1810 | c.1860 | Sales |
|---|---|---|---|---|---|
| Cerrito de Jerez | M. González del Pinal | F. A. González de Castañeda | J. A. Rocha | M. A. Arismendi* | 1729, 1748, 1766, 1784, 1790, 1834 |
| Cerrogordo | S. Herrera Arcocha | J. Herrera Arcocha | J. Herrera Arcocha | Aranda Brothers (1863) | 1711, 1863 |
| Duarte | C. Moreno Avalos | T. Menchaca | I. Urruchua | L. Samano | 1716, 1731, 1737, 1828, 1844 |
| Garbancillo | M. González del Pinal | N. Austri | C. of Valenciana | A. Obregón | 1728, 1782 |
| Gavia | M. González del Pinal | B. Austri | J. F. Villamor* | Liceagas | 1728, 1790?, later divided |
| Santa Ana | P. Aguilera | L. Austri | C. of Valenciana | A. Obregón | 1718, 1727–29, 1781 |
| Sandía | M. González del Pinal | P. Septién | C. of Valenciana | L. Guerrero | 1728, 1788, 1852, 1860 |
| Jagüey | M. González del Pinal | M. Austri | M. I. Austri | J. López de Lara | 1728, 1849 |
| S. Nicolás Arriba | ranchos | N. Austri | P. González | González heirs | 1719, 1786, 1796, 1821 divided |
| S. Juan Abajo | ranchos | N. Austri | F. Palacios | I. González | 1731, 1786, 1796, 1806, 1834, 1859 |
| S. Vicente | M. González del Pinal | J. T. Austri | M. Austri | Hernández heirs | 1728, 1795?, divided |
| Sardina | M. González del Pinal | J. T. Austri | M. de la Riva | J. Sánchez | 1728, 1820, 1844 |
| S. Ramón Ocotes | M. González del Pinal | J. T. Austri | Hoyos brothers | Hoyos heirs | 1728, later divided |
| Hoya | N. Aguilar Ventosillo | Jesuits | J. Diez Quijano | M. Quijano | 1731, 1790s? |
| Losa | M. González del Pinal | Jesuits | J. Diez Quijano | M. Doblado | 1729, 1731, 1790s?, 1838, 1847, 1861, 1864 |
| Lagunillas | M. González del Pinal | G. Losa | C. of Valenciana | A. Obregón | 1725, 158–53, 1771, 1784 |
| Ibarrilla | labores | A. Septién | P. Domínguez | F. Pastor | 1752–61, 1783, 1793, 1826, 1845, 1851, 1860 |
| Palma | N. Busto y Moya | F. C. Marmolejo | J. C. Somera | The Oratory | 1759, 1780s?, 1795, 1802, 1850 |
| Palote | ranchos | F. C. Marmolejo | J. C. Somera | J. M. Ruiz | 1780s?, 1795, 1802, 1860? |
| Pompa | M. González del Pinal | A. Pompa | Pompa heirs | J. Tejada | 1729–33, 1750, 1810–20?, 1848 |

| Potrero | *P. Martínez Zavala* | *M. Septién* | *I. A. Sánchez* | *I. Septién* | |
| --- | --- | --- | --- | --- | --- |
| S. Juan Otates | D. Quijas | *D. A. Quijas* | M. Quijas | *G. Torres* | 1732, 1742, 1778, 1787, 1829, 1840, 1861 |
| S. Nicolás | ranchos | *A. Septién* | J. I. Septién | *M. Urteaga* | 1710, 1827, 1854, 1859 |
| S. Pedro del Monte | ranchos | *F. de la Fuente* | C. of Valenciana | *A. Obregón* | in same family c. 1770, 1781 |
| S. Rosa | A. Sánchez Caballero | *S. E. Arroyo* | C. of Valenciana | *C. Otero* | 1734, 1807, 1852 |
| Sauces | ? | *I. Pérez* | Pérez heirs | ? | ½ in 1713, 1743, 1752, ? |
| Cañada de Negros | D. Reynoso | *Reynoso Brothers* | I. Obregón | *J. G. Ibargüengoitia* | 1763, 1790, 1856 |
| Fuentes de Medina | F. Navarrete | *G. Peredo* | Guerrero heirs | Divided | 1772, 1793 |
| Pedregal | M. González del Pinal | *M. García Alvarez* | I. Obregón | *J. G. Ibargüengoitia* | 1725, 1729, 1765, 1792, 1856 |
| Peñuelas | Mariscal de Castilla | *J. Martínez d. l. Concha* | R. S. Septién* | *J. Septién* | 1746, 1784, 1799 |
| San Cristóbal | G. Fernández d. l. Concha | *A. J. Vásquez Victoria* | C. of Valenciana | *F. Echeverría* | 1734, 1770, 1782, c. 1790, 1850, 1854 |
| San Germán | P. Sardaneta | *S. E. Arroyo* | C. of Valenciana | *C. Otero* | 1715, 1740, 1807, 1852 |
| San Isidro | Solís sisters | *F. Barrio Lorenzot* | G. Palomino | Divided | 1741, 1781, 1836 |
| San Lorenzo | Solís sisters | *E. Aguirre* | Aguirre heirs | *I. Camarena* | 1740, 18??, 1849 |
| Los Sapos | M. González del Pinal | *P. de la Fuente* | J. López de Lara | *J. Obregón* | 1725, 1774, 1795, 1834, 1845, 1855 |
| Sarteneja | J. Ponce de León | *S. Pérez d. l. Fuente* | S. Buso | *M. Guerrero* | 1728, 1751, 1771, 1791, 1842 |
| Sauz de Armenta | P. Sardaneta | *Sardaneta brothers* | *J. Frausto* | Frausto heirs | 1806 |
| Talayote | M. González del Pinal | *F. Guerrero* | Guerrero heirs | Divided | 1729 |
| Los Tanques | M. González del Pinal | *J. Palomino* | M. Ibarra | *J. Septién* | 1713, 1735, 1742, 1780, 1790, 1828 |
| Terrero | Solís sisters | *F. Barrio Lorenzot* | C. of Valenciana | *A. Echeverría* | 1748, 1782, 1852 |
| Santiago | - | - | - | - | - |

* indicates widows or heirs of stated owner.

Names in italics indicate that the owner acquired estate by sale during previous sixty years.

*Source:* see Appendix 3.

distinct from the miners and merchants who invested in land. Instead, the wealthy in León formed a relatively unified entrepreneurial elite. From the start, land was a marketable commodity.

The most striking feature of landownership in León was its volatility. On average, as Table 32 shows, between 1710 and 1865 estates changed hands by sale just under four times, that is to say, virtually every generation. Only two estates remained in the same family throughout the period. Obviously, the turnover was not as regular or predictable as the overall average might suggest. During the 1720s, the decision of the greatest landowner in the district, a resident of Mexico City, to sell all his holdings led to an overall reshuffling of ownership. Then again, the influx of mining capital during the 1790s provoked a second flurry of transactions in which some 15 out of 27 estates changed hands. Finally, the 1850s and early 1860s witnessed another concentration of sales in which about half of all haciendas in León were sold.

Why haciendas should have entered the land market so often is by no means clear. At times, natural causes intervened to break the continuity of ownership as when in at least two cases the surviving heiress remained a childless spinster. Similarly, if an estate passed to a priest, it was usually sold after his death. Then, in several instances young men who inherited haciendas displayed a quite startling lack of business sense, entering into commitments which were bound to bankrupt them. But it is the overall trend which requires explanation, all the more, since in an epoch of rapid economic expansion, agriculture surely offered ample opportunity for the cautious farmer to prosper. True, as we have seen, the rate of profit was not overly high and it varied greatly from year to year, but the success of some hacendados indicates that most estates could certainly support their owners in comfort. More important by far was the burden of ecclesiastical mortgages which in good years and bad alike exacted a 5% return on capital. Several estates were embargoed by clerical creditors for the failure to satisfy interest charges. Moreover, since new owners often acquired an embargoed hacienda by simply accepting the existing set of mortgages, the same properties were prone to re-enter the market at comparatively short intervals. This cycle of inherited or transferred debt was not terminated until the desamortisation laws of the Reforma.

The most important single cause of the turnover in property, however, was the Spanish testamentary system.[3] There is no record of any entail established on any estate in León. In consequence, the laws of inheritance prescribed that in each generation all possessions of the deceased should be divided equally between the children or other heirs. Only two exceptions mitigated the effect of this rule. The surviving spouse was entitled to retain half of all increments to the joint estate which had occurred since marriage. Then, a *mejora* or betterment of a third of the estate of either spouse could be allotted to a favoured heir. Similarly, a fifth could be freely willed to anyone, heir or third party. Elsewhere, we have emphasised the dissolution of mercantile fortunes which the application of these laws effected.[4] The same was true in agriculture. Unless a family was exceptionally wise or united, the danger always existed that the death of a landowner would lead to the sale of his estate in order to satisfy the claims of every heir. Moreover, even where this step was not taken, the brother who emerged as the sole owner often found himself a virtual caretaker, since the portions of the other heirs remained charged on the estate. This was as much true of children who became priests or who took the veil as of lay heirs. Indeed, from the point of view of the owner, the best co-heir was a sister who remained a spinster. In short, a prolific wife was almost a guarantee that a family would lose its estate.

One caveat should be advanced. The circulation of property should not be equated with the decline of families. Social mobility was not always downward. Although the rapid turnover in estate ownership might suggest a constant replenishment of the hacendado class, in fact on several occasions the sons of former landowners succeeded in recouping their fortunes through mining, in trade or by marriage. Individuals of the same family might own different haciendas at different periods. In the exercises which follow, we shall trace the fortunes of the leading families of landowners in León, and to a lesser extent in Rincón. The method is descriptive but the sample generous. The nature of the documents, however, is to register effects rather than to explain causes.

# I

Although the existence of the municipal endowment and the nucleus of Spanish settlers resident in the *villa* prevented any radical monopoly of land being established within the immediate district of León, nevertheless, the opening decades of the seventeenth century witnessed a significant concentration of landed property. Fortunately for the town's future development, the Mariscal de Castilla

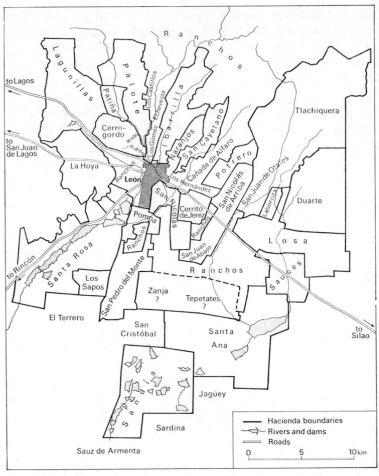

Map 2   León: haciendas and ranchos *c.* 1850

*Note*: This map is based on the *Carta Catastral* of 1920 compiled and drawn
by Ing. Edmundo Leal. The boundaries are approximate and in some cases
extrapolated back to the presumed areas of 1850.

did not inherit any lands close to León and only possessed seven large
sitios in Rincón. Instead, the threat came from a peninsular immigrant, Andrés López de Lara, a vecino of the neighbouring town of
Santa María de Lagos, who through purchase and additional viceregal *mercedes* succeeded in creating a vast estancia stretching across
the district. After his death in 1636, his heirs sold to a treasury
official from the capital no less than 22½ sitios in Rincón and León,

and another 30½ sitios in San Miguel el Grande. The sale-price of 30,439 ps included flocks of over 20,000 sheep.[5] Thereafter, this patrimony passed to the González del Pinal family, who proved to be absentee landlords, resident in Mexico City, without either the interest or resources to exploit their holdings in the Bajío. In 1711, when the itinerant land judge, *juez de composiciones*, compared the original titles with the actual area under occupation, he found that the González del Pinal certainly possessed authentic *mercedes* for 12½ large and 8 small sitios, but that in addition, they held over 5 large sitios on the hacienda called Gavia *en demasía*, without legal right. However, for a mere 50 pesos a sitio, he granted the appropriate documents so that Gavia without question now dominated the entire southeastern corner of the district, occupying an area of nearly 55,000 acres. By contrast, however, the remaining sitios of the González del Pinal were scattered across the two parishes without any unity of operation, or evidence of exploitation.

TABLE 33 *Sale of estates of Miguel González del Pinal 1705–29*

IN LEON

Gavia: 3 March 1728, to José de Austri 12 large sitios and 10 caballerías for 24,300 ps, of which 13,300 ps in *censos*.

Bolas Blancas: 14 May 1729, to José de Austri, one large sitio and one cab. for 500 ps.

Lagunillas: 20 February 1725, to Rafael López de Lara, one small sitio and one cab. (price unstated, entered ANL, 12 January 1746).

Cerrito de Jerez: 13 May 1729, to Alfonso de Obregón y Arce, one small sitio and one cab. for 750 ps.

Granjeno: 11 May 1729, to Manuel de Urbieta, one small sitio and one cab. for 750 ps.

Losa: 16 May 1729, to Manuel de Aguilar Ventosillo, one large sitio and 29½ cab. called Los Albarradones and Cieneguilla, for 9,000 ps of which 1,500 ps in *censos*.

IN RINCON

Los Tanques: 14 December 1713, to Diego de Reynoso, 13 cab. for 3,000 ps of which 2,000 ps in *censos*.

Los Sapos: 13 February 1725, to Pedro Carranza, one large sitio for 1,200 ps.

Pedregal: 12 February 1725, to Juan de Herrera Quintana, one large sitio and 10 cab. for 8,100 ps of which only 2,500 ps paid (entered ANL, 5 May 1728).

Fuentes de Medina: 23 May 1704, to Francisco de Navarrete, one large sitio for 900 ps charged as *censo*.

Talayote: 17 May 1729, to Juan Guerrero, one small sitio for 400 ps in *censo* (reference in AGN, Tierras 1081–1).

Unless stated otherwise, the dates of sale refer to entries in ANL register.

During the 1720s, at a time when Mexico City families such as the Canal and the Monterde purchased estates in the Bajío, Miguel González del Pinal decided to dispose of his holdings in León and

Rincón. As Table 33 indicates, the value was still remarkably low. It was out of this vast patrimony that in the next thirty years came sixteen separate haciendas. For the most part, the agents of this dramatic development were merchants or men with interests in mining, especially at Comanja, a small camp across the border in New Galicia.

To take a clear example, Alfonso de Obregón y Arce, the creole son of an immigrant from the village of Llerana in the mountains of Santander, inherited a thriving rancho of 735 acres, situated along the road to Silao. But not content with a modest comfort, he obtained a mortgage of 2,600 pesos in 1720, purchased an adjacent small sitio from González del Pinal for a mere 750 pesos, and invested the remainder in the mining industry at Comanja. At his death in 1748, his hacienda, called San José del Cerrito de Jerez, comprised 3,000 acres.[6] But his mining ventures apparently failed to yield their desired profit, since his property, although valued at 14,700 was encumbered with no less than 8,100 pesos in clerical charges. A much married man, his sons by the third wife were obliged to sell the hacienda and employ their talents and capital in trade or mining. It is a startling commentary on the uncertainty of economic life at this period that all four sons, despite business commitments extending over several decades, lived to see their property embargoed for debt.[7] The hacienda was later taken up by a series of merchants, but always remained oppressed by the transferred burden of mortgages.

Mining profits also financed other estates. In the years 1745–53 two brothers, Gaspar and Gerónimo de Losa, who had a refining mill at Comanja, succeeded in purchasing the two small sitios called Laurel and Lagunillas, the first in dispersed lots from Gómez family, mestizo rancheros, and the latter from Rafael López de Lara, who had bought it from González del Pinal. These hillside estancias had little value until the new owners invested some 6,000 pesos to construct a dam which irrigated about 260 acres for wheat growing. In the upshot, this varied range of activity failed to yield the expected return, and the heirs of the brothers were obliged to sell the hacienda to a local merchant since they lacked the resources to finance further operations.[8]

Another family with mining interests at Comanja who benefited from the withdrawal of the Mexico City landlord were the Aguilar Ventosillo brothers, creole sons of a peninsular immigrant, who formed the prosperous Losa hacienda through successive purchases, first of a small sitio, then of a thriving *labor* of 14 caballerías, which in its turn derived from the aggregation of four separate vecindades of 3½ caballerías. Another rancho was added, and finally the estate was completed by the acquisition in 1729 of one large and one small sitio (called Los Albarradones) from González del Pinal.[9] By 1730, the Losa encompassed nearly 11,000 acres and with its livestock was valued at over 32,000 pesos. However, the family lacked direct issue, and their only nephew, Alfonso de Obregón, still prospered, so the surviving brother, the priest Bachiller Nicolás, bequeathed Losa and another hacienda, Hoya, which had been left by his mother, to the Jesuits to establish a college in León.[10] This was to be the only significant example of haciendas in the district owned directly by ecclesiastical institutions until the foundation of the Oratory in the next century.

Merchants as much as miners were active in the creation of haciendas in the first decades of the eighteenth century. José de Austri, an immigrant from Miranda de Ebro in Castile, in one document described as 'a merchant, farmer and stockman', was also the financial backer of Los Remedios mine and a refining mill at Comanja. Already worth 20,000 pesos by 1711, and soon to become *regidor alférez real* of León, Austri then married Estefanía de Obregón, the niece of the Aguilar Ventosillo brothers with whom he was associated in business.[11] Determined to assure the future for his growing family, he now set about building up a great landed estate. As a start he bid for a farm of 1,470 acres, a *labor* formed before 1631 from four original vecindades. Of the auction price of 5,500 pesos, no less than 3,920 pesos consisted of transferred mortgages. Thereafter, between 1701 and 1734 in eight separate purchases, Austri created an estate called San Nicolás de Arriba y Abajo which covered 4,725 acres (45 caballerías).[12] Here, then, was the first example in León of an hacienda entirely assembled from small-holdings.

It was in the 1720s, however, that Austri scored his major coup. First, he purchased the large sitio called Santa Ana from the Marquis of San Clemente, a wealthy silver miner from Guanajuato, the price of 4,565 pesos including a considerable range of livestock. Then, the next year, in 1728, he took over the entire Gavia latifundium from González del Pinal for 24,300 pesos, of which no less than 13,000 pesos were transferred Church mortgages, mainly held by the Dominicans of Mexico City. As before, the sale brought stock, with over 1,000 brood mares.[13] A shrewd merchant rather than a speculator, Austri passed the remainder of his life slowly reducing the burden of debt that the latifundium carried. By 1749, he had redeemed the chief mortgages of 12,000 pesos. However, examination of the inventory taken the next year after his death, shows that the chief purpose of this vast latifundium, which comprised so much potentially fertile soil, was still stockraising, since only 18 caballerías, some 1,890 acres, were assessed as *labrada*, or cleared for ploughing. The remainder of the $14\frac{1}{2}$ large sitios – over 56,600 acres, was employed as pasture for a varied range of livestock which included 2,063 brood mares with their offspring – 787 foals and 744 young mules – 460 cattle, 4,750 sheep and 1,160 goats. The importance of this inventory is that it clearly demonstrates that at the heart of the Bajío, in part of the district now known as Romita, agricultural development was still about to begin.[14] A hundred years later, the same area was renowned for its rich haciendas. It is significant that on San Nicolás, Austri's other estate, which lay on both sides of the road to Silao, over half the land, some 27 caballerías, was described as arable. The value of Gavia was estimated at 46,453 pesos, divided almost equally between the assessment of land and the value of livestock with the fabric, including corrals and water-wheels appraised at no more than 2,184 pesos.

The practice of acquiring estates for a relatively small outlay of cash through the transfer of existing mortgages was a dangerous procedure which could easily lead to personal bankruptcy and the impoverishment of the hacienda. In 1751–52 the regidor Antonio de la Pompa purchased the small hacienda called Granjeno, which comprised a small sitio sold in the 1720s by González del Pinal for 750 pesos and a labor composed of several vecindades. The price of 11,500 pesos included 6,800 pesos in transferred mortgages. To judge from subsequent inventories, it was Pompa and his sons who were responsible for converting the greater part of the estate into arable. But over the years, the burden of Church debt rose rather than fell, so that at the turn of the century, the grand-children, by then faced with the task of paying interest on over 16,000 pesos of mortgages, were obliged to sell the hacienda.[15] Thereafter, we find different members of the family gaining a livelihood by leasing entire estates, in one case Otates and later, in the 1830s, Lagunillas.

An example of failure is afforded by the peninsular merchant Manuel de Septién y Montero, who in 1742 bought Potrero, an hacienda situated alongside San Nicolás de Arriba, with a large sitio of barren hillside and another 13 caballerías of possible arable. The estate, however, was never very prosperous. Already in 1731 it had been embargoed by clerical creditors because the current owner had failed to pay interest on the 6,300 *censos* imposed by a previous proprietor in order to establish chairs of theology and philosophy at the San Nicolás College in Valladolid. Now Septién accepted 5,000 ps in mortgages, paid 2,000 pesos cash down and promised to put up another 5,000 pesos in the coming months. In fact, he raised a series of loans from relatives, fellow merchants and ecclesiastical institutions, with the result that he was unable to redeem the principal. In 1768 his entire belongings were embargoed and the hacienda was then managed on behalf of his creditors.[16] The practical lessons of this episode were neglected (perhaps because they were commonplace), and in 1778 the hacienda was auctioned in favour of another merchant who at once applied to the Santa Clara convent in Querétaro for 9,000 pesos to finance the renovation of the property, a mortgage which haunted all future owners of the estate until the Liberal Reforma of the 1850s.[17]

That personal acumen rather than general economic trends governed these matters is demonstrated by the financial success of Agustín de Septién y Montero, the brother of the bankrupted owner of Potrero, who by the time he died had accumulated a fortune of over 200,000 pesos. An immigrant from the village of Llerana in the mountains of Santander, Septién dealt in silver and owned a store in Guanajuato, where he became *regidor fiel ejecutor*.[18] He also married the only daughter of José de Austri and invested his commercial profit in the acquisition and creation of haciendas in León. But, whereas his father-in-law had taken over a vast deserted latifundium, Septién concentrated his purchases on a series of small farms and estates all situated relatively close to León. His most notable venture was the creation of the San Nicolás hacienda just south of town. The nucleus here consisted of two farms which grew wheat on lands irrigated by the river León. The initial cost was high: 18,500 pesos for some 885 acres ($8\frac{1}{2}$ caballerías). Thereafter, in the brief span of nine years, between 1742 and 1751, Septién added another 2,415 acres in 14 separate purchases. Several of the vendors were Indians, other were mestizos or Spanish small-holders.[19] Here, then, is a classic example of commercial profits generated in the export economy associated with silver mining employed to replace peasant farming by one great landlord enterprise. In the next chapter, we shall discuss the reasons why so many rancheros chose to sell their land. In all Septién paid 26,792 ps, with only 7,200 ps in transferred mortgages, for some 3,540 acres of prime, well-situated agricultural land.

Not content with just one estate, in 1752 Septién acquired
Ibarrilla, a *labor* of 945 acres north of town to which former owners
had added a half sitio of hillside pasture. Ten years later, he purchased the adjacent hacienda called Herrera, some 27½ caballerías in
area, which itself had been formed out of two *labores*. Thus, Ibarrilla
sprang from two distinct phases in the concentration of landownership. In the early seventeenth century several standard ranchos or
vecindades of 370 acres were grouped together to form *labores*.
Now, in the mid eighteenth century, these large farms were in turn
amalgamated to create a single hacienda. In the 1790s another *labor*
was to be annexed. By reason of this long history of cultivation, the
cost to Septién was comparatively high – 19,000 pesos.[20] To round
off the story, we may note that in 1762 Septién also acquired another
large rancho called Patiña, situated to the northwest of León, which
comprised 12 caballerías. In this case the cost was low, since of the
5,251 pesos sale price 3,251 consisted of transferred charges, capellanías held by the descendants of a former owner.[21]

In much the same years as Septién put together the San Nicolás,
another immigrant, Francisco de la Fuente, a native of the valley of
Camargo in Santander, succeeded in creating another hacienda in
the southern zone known as Tepetates or El Monte. Unlike Austri or
Septién, he was not a merchant, although to judge from the 54 mules
equipped for freight that he owned in the 1730s, he may well have
engaged in commercial transport. The basis of his operations was a
farm of 682 acres, which he acquired in 1728 for 1,600 ps. Then in
five transactions spread over the years 1738–52, he purchased another
1,200 acres from neighbouring small-holders, most of whose titles
only dated from the late seventeenth century. Meanwhile, he enlarged the estate still further by payment of *composición* to the town
council for a further 1,470 acres of barren hillside, which he had
surreptitiously occupied.[22] In all, he paid 4,305 pesos for some 3,380
acres. Equally important, in the same key decade of the 1740s, the
town notary put together another large property of 900 acres buying
land from much the same group of mestizo and mulatto small-
holders.[23] But the profits on the investments were obviously not very
high, since much of the soil in this zone was infertile or covered in
wooded thickets. As late as 1757 Fuente declared that he only had
840 acres under plough. Indeed, once he died his widow soon fell
into debt and eventually was obliged to sell the estate.[24] In this case,
the cycle of consolidation was completed in the 1780s when the
Count of Valenciana purchased another three *labores* (including the

property of the notary) to create an hacienda called San Pedro del Monte which comprised over 6,000 acres.[25]

By now the manner in which new haciendas were formed in León during the middle decades of the eighteenth century should be clear: the decisive element was the investment of mercantile and mining capital in the purchase of estancias and ranchos. At the same time, the willingness of some entrepreneurs to accept intolerably high levels of debt often led to subsequent foreclosure. Equally important, creole sons frequently lacked the business sense of their immigrant fathers. This observation of course echoes a colonial commonplace, but it is a commonplace which finds ample confirmation in the history of the Austri family. After their father's death the laboriously assembled patrimony was divided into six separate haciendas. The partition was not notarised until 1777, however, when each heir – five brothers and a sister – each received about 2½ large sitios or 11,000 acres. Only a year later, the eldest son, the *regidor alférez real*, José Tomás de Austri, died and in turn his children divided the hacienda of Sardina into three independent estates.[26] It will be noticed that, whereas the original Gavia was a latifundium more reminiscent of Pénjamo or Jalpa than of León, by contrast the haciendas into which it was divided conformed to the size of estates such as Duarte or Losa.

Despite this breakdown of the family inheritance into manageable units, few of Austri's descendants retained possession of their land. The immediate cause of their ruin was the contract by which Luis de Austri became the recognised tithe collector for León, Rincón and San Pedro Piedragorda, with the obligation to pay the diocesan court at Valladolid 13,500 pesos a year. His brothers Nicolás and Manuel acted as his guarantors. In the upshot this sum proved grossly in excess of actual yields, so that by 1781 the brothers owed no less than 30,540 pesos. At this juncture, the diocesan authorities first embargoed and then auctioned the Santa Ana hacienda, the property of Luis, and Garbancillo, a sitio belonging to Nicolás.[27] Moreover, in order to meet costs, Nicolás had raised fresh loans, so that in 1786 he had to sell San Nicolás de Arriba y Abajo for 17,800 pesos, since he could no longer meet the interest on the 12,670 pesos mortgages.[28] The third brother involved in this debacle, who owned Jagüey, died the next year, leaving his widow an estate encumbered with a debt of 19,500 pesos, a sum equivalent to two thirds of its estimated value. His son-in-law, a merchant of no great acumen, contrived to retain control of the hacienda for another generation.[29]

Oddly enough, the one brother who escaped ruin, the priest Bachiller
Bernardino, left his hacienda (called Gavia) to Francisco de Villamor,
a peninsular merchant who had acted as the business manager for
the Countess of Valenciana. Behind this mysterious decision, which
was contested by other members of the family, was probably a secret
agreement by which Villamor promised to transfer funds to various
illegitimate children of the priest.[30] Finally, to turn to the three heirs
of the eldest Austri heir, José Tomás, the two properties managed by
sons-in-law stayed in the family for at least another generation,
whereas the lawyer, Bernardino de Austri, lost his hacienda when a
merchant relative, José María de Obregón, (the son of Alfonso), for
whom he had acted as guarantor, went bankrupt.[31] Little further is
known about the descendants of these spendthrift creoles. In the
notary register of 1859, we find mention of one Cándida Austri, the
owner of three houses and a small shop, who had to support a
penniless brother.[32] Were these the last issue of José de Austri?
The records of the period rarely permit us to trace families once they
ceased to be property holders.

   Not all the sons of the wealthy were doomed to lose their estates.
After the death of Agustín de Septién, his son, Pedro Antonio, moved
to Querétaro, where he found a bride with a rich dowry and became
*regidor alférez real*. During the 1790s he figured as subdelegate of
Celaya. By reason of this change in residence, together with a certain
degree of indebtednes, in the 1780s he disposed of his estates in León,
selling Ibarrilla for 41,200 pesos and Sandía, the hacienda inherited
from his Austri mother, for 20,000 pesos, sums from which had to be
subtracted 25,267 pesos in Church mortgages.[33] However, his half
brother, José Ildefonso de Septién, remained quietly in León, letting
the San Nicolás to a series of tenants. With rents of 1,500 pesos and
interest payments at 700 pesos on the 14,000 pesos mortgages, the
available income was modest. Nevertheless, with the assistance of his
wife's 26,000 peso dowry, Septién succeeded in bequeathing the
estate to his son-in-law, whose son in turn retained possession until
his death in the 1880s.[34] By then, the expansion of the city had
greatly increased the value of the land, although by reason of the
continued reliance on leasing the estate, the overall growth in inventory value was much below haciendas directly exploited by their
owners.

## II

Emphasis upon the emergence of new haciendas may well confer an undue prominence upon the peninsular merchants largely responsible for their formation. Several long-established creole families multiplied the output and wealth of their estates simply by amplifying the acreage of arable or by acquisition of adjoining farms. Not, however, that these families proffer any image of rural hebetude, since, to judge from the case of the Marmolejos, the owners at diverse periods of Otates, Duarte, Palote, and Cañada de Negros, their economic survival was always precarious and decidedly dependent on entrepreneurial flair or a 'good' marriage. The first notice of their existence comes from the 1661 testament of Pedro Marmolejo *el viejo*, a native of San Felipe just across the sierra, who declared that at the time of his marriage to an heiress of Santa María de Lagos he did not possess 'any goods of worth other than the clothes I wore'. Presumably, it was with his wife's money that he acquired a *labor de maíz* called Cañada de los Otates for 2,000 pesos. Since subsequent owners failed to discover any original viceregal titles, it is probable that the hacienda started off as a small farm at the foot of the valley and that successive occupants simply pushed deeper into the mountainous hinterland. This process of expansion was completed by Marmolejo's son Nicolás, who purchased three large sitios in the high sierra for 150 ps, so that with other minor transactions, San Juan de los Otates finally encompassed over 18,000 acres, of which only about 1,500 was arable.[35]

After the death of Nicolás Marmolejo, his widow failed to maintain the property and in 1709 her numerous children sold Otates to their brother-in-law, Diego Clemente de Quijas, a wealthy landowner resident in Sierra de Pinos, a mining town in the province of Zacatecas.[36] Henceforward until 1821, the hacienda remained in the possession of the Quijas family. The original purchaser left but one heir whose four sons in turn chose not to divide their inheritance until 1783, when they ceded Otates to the eldest of their number. In this third generation some genetic deficiency haunted the family, since of the four brothers one went mad, another died without issue, a third entered the priesthood, and the eldest was survived but by one mentally defective daughter.[37] Under this stable administration, the area of the hacienda did not increase; its value, however, rose from some 11,000 pesos in 1711 to 26,901 pesos in 1787.

The quiet, continuous prosperity enjoyed by the Quijas family was shared by comparatively few of their relatives in León. Of the eleven children of Nicolás Marmolejo, one daughter married a wealthy silver miner at Guanajuato, who became the Marquis of San Clemente and another became the wife of his cousin.[38] But of the four sons only one achieved more than a modest income, despite an inheritance of about 2,000 pesos. Indeed, at the time of his death in 1742, Pedro Marmolejo had no other goods than an old house and a couple of slaves; in his will, he explicitly asked for a modest funeral, as befitted his circumstances.[39] Another brother entered the priesthood. Antonio acquired a *labor* of 9 caballerías called Los Naranjos, situated close to the village of Coecillo. By his death in 1733, he had converted it into a thriving miniature hacienda with a wide range of livestock, including 41 mules equipped for transport. The value of his entire estate was reckoned at 5,000 pesos.[40]

But it was the youngest son, Cristóbal Marmolejo, who restored the family to a leading place in León. A man of some discipline, he once notarised his oath that, subject to a penalty of 6,000 pesos, he would not gamble at cards for the next nine years.[41] It is difficult to ascertain the precise means of his rise to wealth, but without doubt his successive marriages to two heiresses proved of great assistance. For example, in 1713 it was his first wife who purchased a *labor* called Palote – 13½ caballerías for 5,500 pesos – already assembled from four council grants issued before 1636. Subsequently, Marmolejo added a farm of 5½ caballerías, so that, together with other fractions and holdings, by 1758 Palote formed an hacienda of 27½ cab. or 2,900 acres. Long before this, however, he had married Teresa de Menchaca, the daughter of a rich merchant of San Miguel el Grande, who brought him in dowry and by inheritance over 33,000 pesos. It was this money, so his wife later commented, which in 1737 permitted the acquisition of Duarte, a prosperous hacienda of about 10,800 acres, for the sum of 20,000 pesos.[42] Over the years prior to his death in 1758, Marmolejo built up a fortune worth 138,660 pesos, an estate considerably greater than that left by José de Austri only a decade before. The inventory reveals that he was a merchant as well as a landowner, with a shop in town supplied by the leading trading houses of the Capital, to which a wide range of local residents, including several landowners, owed considerable sums for goods advanced on credit. Moreover, if the chief produce of his estates was undoubtedly maize, he also engaged in mule and horse breeding on a large scale, maintaining a herd of 1,043 brood mares.

Equally important, he operated no less than four mule-teams all equipped for transport, which in all numbered 171 head, together with an equivalent number of replacements and saddle mules for the teamsters, the combined value here being 9,675 pesos. Since Duarte and especially Palote were not distant from León, Marmolejo lived in town, where he owned a large house served by 12 slaves, his shop, and a stone barn for storing grain.[43] That his entire estate was only charged with 2,000 pesos in Church mortgages offers perhaps the best measure of his financial acumen and standing.

If in his career Cristóbal Marmolejo belied the old peninsular prejudice that creoles were unfit for business, by contrast his only son, Captain Francisco Cristóbal, provided impressive proof for the conventional position. Aged only twenty in 1759 when he received Palote as his inheritance – his mother retained Duarte – he at once moved to expand his holdings with the purchase of Palma, an hacienda situated in the sierra just beyond Palote with only about 160 acres cultivated out of an area of over 6,000 acres. However, not content with the comfortable profits of a relatively small hacienda, in 1764 Francisco Cristóbal foolishly sold Palote and Palma, without livestock, to a local merchant for 9,750 pesos, with payment to be completed in annual instalments of 1,000 pesos. In the same year he acquired two prosperous haciendas in the adjoining jurisdiction of Silao for 26,000 pesos, of which half consisted of transferred mortgages and the remaining half of a deposit on the estate held by the outgoing owner. Thus Marmolejo now had to pay 1,300 pesos annual interest, as well as meet operating costs, with only the 1,000 pesos from Palote to help him. Unfortunately, the mid sixties were years of abundant harvests and low profits for landowners, and in the upshot Palote was soon returned to him, since the new proprietor failed to pay the yearly instalments. The result of these manoeuvres was that by 1767 Marmolejo had to meet interest charges on a total sum of 57,000 pesos, including further loans, his wife's dowry of 8,000 pesos and certain monies owed to his mother.[44] In the subsequent settlement – the affair dragged on for several years – he lost all his haciendas, and as late as 1790 we find a notary entry dealing with some still outstanding minor debts in which he is described as insolvent, sustained only by employment as an accountant in the royal customs house at León.[45] His wife had long since fled his company to take up residence in Mexico City.

In contrast to this prodigal waste of an inheritance, the widow of Cristóbal Marmolejo retained possession of Duarte and succeeded into bequeathing it to her one surviving grand-daughter, Isabel Urruchúa, a life-long spinster, who held the estate until her death in 1832. Thus, Duarte, like its neighbour Otates, was occupied by one family through three generations for a period of a century. Similarly, no further increments in area were made, although it too experienced a considerable rise in value in part arising from an expansion in the acreage of arable land.[46]

In the next generation of the Marmolejo family, it was Francisco Javier, the son of Antonio and hence the nephew of Cristóbal, who made his mark in León. The initial basis of his enterprise was presumably the small *labor*, Los Naranjos, inherited from his father, to which he added another large farm called Coecillo. But he was also a merchant, and a stockman. In 1745 he rented Duarte from his uncle for a period of eight years at an annual rent of 1,500 pesos. The inventory of his estate taken in 1753 shows that the stock he pastured in Duarte – mainly brood mares, young mules and sheep – were far more valuable than his two farms.[47] Equally important, the merchandise and credits of his shop accounted for about half of his total assets of 44,701 pesos. Already *regidor alcalde provincial*, Francisco Javier Marmolejo now took steps to become a major land-owner. In 1756, he acquired an hacienda in the hills of Lagos for 5,300 pesos (2,000 pesos in transferred mortgages) and then the next year took over Comedero, a large estate in the same district for 1,500 pesos. To finance these acquisitions he raised a 16,000 pesos loan from Martín de Septién, a wealthy silver merchant at Guana-juato, and it was only in 1763 that he formally agreed to redeem the debt in annual instalments of 2,000 pesos.[48] But it was in this last year that he scored a major coup when, at a public auction held at the insistence of clerical creditors, he obtained control of Cañada de Negros, an hacienda of 2½ large sitios or 9,900 acres for a mere 10,000 pesos. In this case, he simply accepted 7,000 pesos in trans-ferred mortgages and raised another 2,000 pesos loan from a neigh-bouring landowner. Additional cash came from the subsequent sale of Los Naranjos and Coecillo. Despite this reliance on loans to finance his enterprise, Marmolejo succeeded where his cousin failed. Cañada de Negros, situated in Rincón next to Jalpa, became a thriving estate, its value greatly augmented by the construction of a dam, walls and an expansion in arable acreage. By the time of his death in 1777, Marmolejo left possessions estimated at 107,248 pesos.[49]

Of the six children of Francisco Javier Marmolejo, one son entered trade and died young, another became a priest and a daughter took the veil at Santa Clara in Querétaro. The remaining heirs each took an hacienda. The Cañada de Negros went to José Francisco and, in tribute to the improvements undertaken in 1790, he was able to sell the estate for 61,000 pesos, a sixfold increase in less than thirty years. No less than 18,700 pesos of the 26,900 pesos mortgages belonged to the sister who had become a nun.[50] With cash in hand, Marmolejo bought the Noria hacienda in Lagos, but then in 1795 for some unexplained reason took over Palote and Palma. These estates had been developed over the previous fifteen years by a leading merchant of León, Ignacio Gómez Poleo, an immigrant from Seville. His three children, all girls, decided that 'for a convenient division and distribution between heirs, it is necessary to hold a public auction of Palma and Palote'. In fact, Marmolejo simply accepted the greater part of the estimated value of their inheritance as a charge upon his combined property, including here 26,000 pesos belonging to his niece, a grand-daughter of Gómez Poleo, who had followed her aunt into the Santa Clara. The result of these added responsibilities was that when death surprised José Francisco in 1798, the mortgages and debts secured upon his haciendas amounted to some 86,000 pesos, as against an inventory value of about 130,000 pesos.[51] In these circumstances his widow and children had no alternative other than to sell Palote. Henceforth, after a conspicuous presence for a period covering one and a half centuries, the name of Marmolejo no longer figured among the landowners of León.

Despite the wealth of inventory material, few sure conclusions can be deduced from our discussion of this family. Certainly, the disastrous impact of the inheritance laws is only too clear, but the precise means by which individuals of enterprise accumulated capital eludes our grasp. Without doubt, trade and transport were of key significance. Equally important, was the combination of agriculture with stockraising, and in particular, with mule-breeding. The survival of the Marmolejos demonstrates the ability of creole landowners to profit from the expansion in the colonial economy of the Bajío. It also disposes of any facile insistence on either mining wealth or on the peninsular immigration as the only sources of economic innovation and enterprise. Finally, on the social side, it must be confessed that, although our documents usually register cases of material success, they have little to say about the men without property. In each generation at least one son entered the priesthood. But what of the other sons? It is of interest to note that in 1770 both

the mayordomos of Palote and Palma were called Marmolejo,
although it is not clear whether they belonged to an impoverished
or an illegitimate line of the family.[52] The theme of downward social
mobility in Mexico awaits its historian.

## III

Mining capital from Guanajuato was never absent from León.
In the first decades of the century, the Marquis of San Clemente
bought and sold Duarte and the sitio of Santa Ana before investing
his great fortune in the distant Villachuato hacienda.[53] Moreover,
the heirs of his brother, Nicolás de Busto y Moya, continued to own
the hill estancia of Palma until the 1760s. Similarly, Pedro de
Sardaneta, who leased the great Rayas mine for a few years, acquired
Sauz de Armenta in Rincón, an estate which remained in the
possession of two sons, who entered the priesthood, until the 1790s.
His brother, Manuel, purchased a small *labor* in the hills, soon
named Sardaneta, which was finally absorbed into Ibarrilla at the
close of the century.[54] For many years, however, the only direct
investment by an active mine-owner was confined to Santa Rosa, a
prosperous hacienda situated to the southwest of town, which in
1711 comprised a large and a small sitio dating back to sixteenth
century *mercedes*, together with another 19½ caballerías derived
from council grants issued in the years 1592–1603. Here, then, was
a long-established agricultural estate which enjoyed the advantage
of direct access to the waters of the river León, and hence possessed
a considerable range of land suitable for wheat. In 1734 the hacienda
was sold for 15,500 pesos to Simón Francisco de Arroyo, who through
his marriage to Clara Joaquina de Sardaneta had become a leading
share-holder in the Rayas.[55] Thereafter, he and his only son and heir,
Simón Eugenio, consistently endeavoured to purchase neighbouring
farmlands. Already by 1740 they had acquired the two *labores*,
San José and Santa Rita, which had been patiently put together in
various transactions by a peninsular merchant who had married into
the Marmolejo family. The sale price of 7,500 pesos, included 110
oxen and other stock. At much the same time cousins who owned
the large sitio of San Germán ceded it to Arroyo for an unspecified
sum.[56] The next round of expansion occurred during the 1770s, a
decade of high profit for Rayas, when, in four separate purchases,
Simón Eugenio acquired some 16 caballerías at a total cost of 5,300
pesos. In one case, the Hinojosa family had occupied their rancho

for four generations, since the issue of the original council award in 1659.[57] Taking into account some further transfers of land, Santa Rosa eventually extended over four large sitios, about 17,870 acres, forming an estate equal in area to Otates, but by reason of its fertile, irrigated fields far superior in value. The hacienda passed from Arroyo, who died childless, to his cousin, José Mariano de Sardaneta, the second Marquis of San Juan de Rayas. But then in 1806 the estate was embargoed and auctioned by the diocesan Consolidation junta in order to pay off some part of the vast debts assumed by the Marquis in a last attempt to renovate the family mine of Rayas.[58] As we shall see, the Santa Rosa was destined always to be leased or managed on behalf of absentee landlords.

It was only after 1780 that miners from Guanajuato replaced merchants as the leading landowners in León. For the discovery of Valenciana in 1767, assisted by certain official measures designed to increase the rate of profit in the industry, led to the creation of huge private fortunes; and once the first stage of reinvestment and consolidation was past, this capital sought traditional outlets in the Mexican countryside. In León a new cycle now began, a phase characterised by investment rather than by the formation of new haciendas. However, although the ownership of landed property became more concentrated than before, much of the change consisted of a circulation of estates within the existing elite. For if some new figures appeared on the scene, mainly peninsular managers and merchants from Guanajuato, the man who emerged as the greatest landlord in the district was no other than Antonio de Obregón y Alcocer, son of the former owner of Cerrito de Jerez, and hence a nephew of José de Austri. Moreover, his mother's family, the Alcocer, had been the dominant hacendados in Pénjamo during the previous century. What we here encounter is the return of the prodigal, and in this case, a prodigal accompanied by his bastard son. For Obregón had been educated for the priesthood, and indeed in his will, Austri had set aside 500 pesos for a capellanía, to support him. Instead, like his father before him, the young man chose to follow the uncertain career of a miner, but unlike most prospectors, finally discovered his El Dorado in a rich stratum of ore along the Veta Madre at Guanajuato.[59] As Count of Valenciana he ranks among the most successful of Mexican miners.

Whereas in later years his two sons-in-law, the Counts of Pérez Gálvez and Casa Rul, looked northwards, to Zacatecas and San Luis Potosí, for latifundia to sustain their nobiliary pretensions, Obregón, and his widow and son after him, concentrated their search for estates in León and Rincón. As Table 34 indicates, for a silver millionaire the costs were not exorbitant. Only in the case of San Pedro del Monte was there any attempt to emulate Austri and Septién through the amalgamation of small properties. Elsewhere, Obregón was the chief beneficiary of the bankruptcy of the Austri brothers. For 63,000 pesos, he acquired Sandía, Santa Ana and Garbancillo, about seven large sitios, which comprised about half of the original Austri latifundium of Gavia. Indeed, with the acquisition of Santa Rosa in 1807, the second Count owned a chain of haciendas which extended across seventeen large sitios or 74,550 acres, all of which, apart from Lagunillas, formed a compact mass of continuous territory. Moreover, mining revenue was soon employed to boost the productivity of this domain. In 1806–07 we find two notarised agreements in which the owners of Pompa (alias Granjeno) and Duarte permitted the Count to construct irrigation channels and dams to control the waters running through their lands.[60] Although they were granted first call, the bulk of the supply obviously went to irrigate the lands of Santa Rosa, Santa Ana and Sandía.

This second cycle of estate-building was brought to an abrupt end by the outbreak of the 1810 Insurgency. The Valenciana flooded and although after Independence the Anglo-Mexican Mining Company attempted to renovate the mine, income barely covered costs and the venture was soon abandoned. The mining industry at Guanajuato was not to attain former levels of output until the late 1840s, when the discovery of a rich new lode at La Luz restored the town to its former prosperity.[61] One consequence of this chronic depression was that several of the great fortunes created in the boom of the late eighteenth century now slowly sank under the weight of their accumulated liabilities. When the second Count of Valenciana died in 1833, his total assets were appraised at 1,114,526 pesos. The shares in mines were not formally valued, although they were encumbered with debts of 123,786 pesos in favour of British investors.[62] The inventory value of the haciendas was calculated at 918,136 pesos, from which had to be subtracted no less than 253,436 pesos in mortgages and other charges, together with 64,313 pesos in deferred interest. Partition of this extended patrimony proved difficult, so that it was not until 1840 that the two heirs received their property. María Antonia Obregón de Camacho, presumably the Count's daughter, took Sandía, Santa Ana with Garbancillo, San Pedro del Monte, and Lagunillas, whereas Dr José Francisco

TABLE 34   *Purchases and inventory value of Obregón–Valenciana estates 1781–1860*

### A. PURCHASES BY THE COUNTS OF VALENCIANA

San Pedro del Monte

| | |
|---|---|
| San Pedro | 28 June 1781, from María Teresa Marmolejo, 32⅛ caballerías for 9,314 pesos. |
| San Judas | 18 January 1783, from José Ignacio de Olaez, 6½ caballerías for 2,950 ps, of which 1,350 ps in *censos*. |
| San Miguel | 6 May 1782, from Pedro Sánchez, 3¼ caballerías for 1,830 ps. |
| San Miguel | 2 May 1794, from María Teresa Marmolejo, 3½ caballerías for 900 ps. |
| Cerrito de Mateos | 26 February 1782, from Mateo Ramírez de Coy, 8½ caballerías for 2,200 ps. |
| Lagunillas | 15 May 1784, from widow of Luis de Carmona, 61¼ caballerías for 14,350 ps. |
| Santa Ana | 29 August 1781, auction from Luis de Austri, 100 caballerías for 25,100 ps. |
| Sandía | 23 August 1788 (AHGP) from Pedro Antonio de Septién, 93½ caballerías for 20,000 ps, of which 10,242 ps in *censos*. |
| Garbancillo | 6 March 1782, from Nicolás de Austri, 88 caballerías for 21,300 ps, of which 8,000 ps in *censos*. |
| San Cristóbal | in 1790s, from Félix Gutiérrez de la Concha, 82 caballerías, price unknown (price in 1782, 32,000 ps). |
| Terrero | 5 January 1782 (AHGP) from Lic. Juan del Barrio Lorenzot, 53 caballerías for 8,270 ps. |
| Santa Rosa | 13 February 1806 auction (ref. 2 August 1852) from the Marquis of San Juan de Rayas, 167 caballerías, price not stated. |
| *Total* | 698 caballerías i.e. 73,824 acres. The cost of estates, apart from Santa Rosa, and San Cristóbal, was 106,214 ps. |

Unless stated otherwise, the dates of sale refer to entries in ANL, register.

### B. INVENTORY VALUE OF VALENCIANA ESTATES 1839–40

| | Estate value | Livestock and seed |
|---|---|---|
| | pesos | pesos |
| Santa Ana–Garbancillo | 216,132 | 35,057 |
| Sandía | 77,050 | 17,649 |
| Santa Rosa | 143,666 | 19,438 |
| San Cristóbal | 133,785 | 11,782 |
| San Pedro del Monte–San Judas | 48,964 | – |
| Lagunillas | 41,362 | – |
| Terrero | 71,271 | – |

*Source:* AHGP, 18 December 1839, 15 September 1840.

### C. SALES AND RENTS OF VALENCIANA ESTATES

Santa Ana–Garbancillo  19 November 1861, rented for 6,400 ps a year (ANL).
23 September 1889, sold to Juan Velasco, *c.* 180 caballerías for 220,000 ps (RPPL).

TABLE 34—*continued*

| | |
|---|---|
| Sandía | 22 December 1860, sold to Lucas Guerrero, 123½ caballerías for 120,000 ps, of which 64,900 ps in *censos* (ANL). |
| Santa Rosa | 2 August 1852, sold to Concepción Otero, 167 caballerías for 127,000 ps, of which 59,598 ps, in *censos* (ANL). |
| San Cristóbal | 28 December 1850, sold to Ignacio Alcocer, 82 caballerías for 75,000 ps, of which 57,498 ps in *censos* (AHGP). |
| Sa Pedro del Monte–San Judas | 12 April, 7 May 1861, rented in two sections for 2,250 ps (ANL). |
| Lagunillas | 28 September 1857, rented for 1,600 ps. |
| Terrero | 19 August 1852, sold to Trinidad and Arcadio Echeverría, 53 caballerías for 30,000 ps, of which 8,000 ps in *censos* (AHGP). |

D. ESTATES OF IGNACIO DE OBREGÓN

| | |
|---|---|
| Cañada de Negros | 23 July 1790, bought from José Francisco Marmolejo, 94½ caballerías for 61,000 ps, of which 26,900 ps in *censos* (ANL) |
| Pedregal | 30 October 1795, bought from Br. Antonio López Portillo, 52½ caballerías for 40,366 ps, of which 6,470 ps in *censos* (ANL). |
| Cañada–Pedregal | 17 October 1856 (AHGP) sold to José Guadalupe Ibargüengoitia for 256,861 ps, of which 117,169 ps in *censos*. |

Contreras, a cousin of the deceased, was granted Santa Rosa, San Cristóbal, and Terreros. This division was but the prelude to the sale of several of these haciendas. In 1850–52 first Contreras and then his executors disposed of all his estates, with the Santa Rosa being sold for 127,000 pesos (59,600 pesos in transferred mortgages) to Concepción de Otero, the grand-daughter of the chief partner of the first Count of Valenciana.[63] Similarly, the heirs of Antonia de Obregón first sold Sandía in 1852, and then Santa Ana in 1871. Perhaps the most striking feature of these sales was the extraordinary increase in estate values which they registered. The Sandía experienced no less than a sixfold rise in market price between 1788 and 1860, from 20,000 pesos to 120,000 pesos.[64] That improved productivity was the cause of this remarkable increment can be demonstrated by a comparison with Jagüey, a former part of the Austri latifundium, which assessed in 1787 at 25,895 pesos, sixty years later in 1849 was auctioned for 23,915 pesos, the precise sum of its accumulated debts.[65] Throughout the period its hard-pressed owners had simply let most of the estate to tenant farmers. Here, then, is a measure of the impact of mining investment.

Along with the Count of Valenciana went his illegitimate son, Ignacio de Obregón, who became a successful miner at Catorce, a new camp discovered during the 1770s in the province of San Luis Potosí. No doubt anxious to fortify his dubious social position, Obregón purchased a colonelcy in the militia, and eventually obtained election as Deputy-General in the Mining Court at Mexico City. Previously he had occupied a series of municipal offices in León, and it was here that he chose to establish his base of operations. In León he found a wife, and it was here that he set up his house, together with a trading store and a refining mill.[66] More important for our purpose, in 1790 Obregón acquired Cañada de Negros from José Francisco de Marmolejo, and two years later added to it the adjacent estate called San Angel del Pedregal. In this fashion he formed an hacienda of 147 caballerías or 15,440 acres at a cost of 104,366 pesos, of which 36,370 pesos consisted of transferred charges.[67] Complementary to this investment, he bought a flour mill and its pond in the town of Lagos, the price here being 63,000 pesos with no less than 43,000 pesos in mortgages.[68] Since the bonanza at his mine at Catorce was barely under way at the time of these purchases, Obregón borrowed 20,000 pesos from the dowager Countess of Valenciana, and apparently persuaded her general manager, Juan Francisco de Villamor, to grant him further monies without notarising the loan, since a subsequent inquiry, carried out in 1793, revealed that he owed over 63,000 pesos on this account.[69]

Too intent on cutting a figure in the society of Mexico City – he acquired a house in the fashionable resort of San Agustín de las Cuevas – Ignacio de Obregón neglected to reduce the massive ecclesiastical debts charged on his estates. In consequence, when the decline in silver production during the years of British naval blockade after 1797 was followed in 1805 by the implementation of the Amortisation decree by which all Church capital had to be paid into the royal treasury, he was driven to misappropriate 80,000 pesos from the investment funds of the Mining Court. Thereafter, with the halting of production from 1810, debts piled on debts.[70] His sons were to devote the remainder of their lives to a heroic attempt both to renovate the flooded mines at Catorce and to liberate the haciendas in Rincón from their burden of debt.

To disentangle the financial affairs of the Obregón family in the years after Independence, however, would be a Herculean task, and indeed a task only possible if their private papers were to be discovered. Of the eight brothers, three became lawyers and one a priest; the other four, Julián, Lorenzo, José María and Isidro apparently never married. During the 1820s, they welcomed the

Anglo-Mexican Mining Company to Catorce, but despite the costly installation of a steam engine to drain the mines called Concepción and Purísima, the flow of water underground proved too great an obstacle. In the upshot the brothers were left saddled with another 157,000 pesos in debts to the British Company. One last attempt to restore the mines was launched in 1846, but met with scant success.[71] Yet without the promised income of their Catorce holdings, the family had little hope of meeting their obligations.

Not deterred by the weight of their Church debt, in fact the Obregón brothers extended both their possessions and their accumulated mortgages. Already since 1799 they had rented Cuitzeo de los Naranjos, a prosperous hacienda in Pénjamo, but in 1835 Julián inherited the property from distant aunts.[72] A few years before, in 1828, he was left Duarte and the neighbouring estate of Comanjillas by Isabel de Urruchúa. True, she was a childless spinster who had once entertained hopes of employing her capital to establish a Dominican house in León, but why she should have made Obregón her heir remains something of a mystery.[73] Then again, in 1827, another brother, Colonel José María, obtained Otates by the simple but ruinous expedient of accepting the liability of 25,737 pesos in transferred mortgages, a sum the equivalent of two thirds of the estate's inventory value.[74]

By the 1840s, creditors such as the Santa Mónica and Santa María de Gracia convents of Guadalajara were pressing the brothers for redemption of the original loans charged on Cañada de Negros and the mill at Lagos, together with a steadily rising quantity of unpaid interest. The heirs of José María de Fagoaga, a former business associate, also demanded return of their monies. In consequence, in 1844 Duarte and Comanjillas were put up for auction, and then during the same decade Cuitzeo de los Naranjos was divided into small plots and sold to former tenants and workers.[75] In 1854 Otates was also released, with the sale price largely covered by the mortgages. In the same year, after the death of the surviving brother, Lorenzo de Obregón, Cañada de Negros was sold for 256,861 pesos, with no less than 117,169 pesos in accumulated mortgages.[76] The increase in value over the cost price of 1790–92, although not as dramatic as in the case of Sandía or Santa Ana, was nevertheless substantial, since it represented a multiple of 2.6.

In conclusion, one is impressed by the comparative rapidity with which the great fortunes created during the mining boom of the late eighteenth century dissolved in the decades after 1810. The economic crisis, so suddenly provoked by the onset of the Insurgency, probably did not lift until the 1840s. But the revival came too late to save the Obregón from their inherited burden of debt. The result was that within a period of no more than seventy years there was an almost complete turnover of property within both branches of the family. The ruin of the mining industry brought in its wake the ruin of an important section of the landowning class.

## IV

With the Obregón came a number of other men associated with the mining boom at Guanajuato and the commercial upswing it produced. As much as their grand exemplars, they were at times tempted to acquire estates through the acceptance of transferred mortgages. The combined blows of amortisation and the Insurgency proved equally disastrous. Thus, for example, in 1793 Pedro Antonio Domínguez, the owner of a thriving refining mill at Guanajuato, purchased Ibarrilla for 41,201 pesos, of which 19,000 consisted of mortgages, with the remainder of the sale price held in deposit on the estate at the usual interest rate. Some five years later, Sardaneta, a *labor* of 16½ cab. situated in the hills behind Ibarrilla, was obtained for 10,887, a sum which again was simply added to the debts of the enterprise. Needless to say, by 1810 Domínguez had failed to redeem these charges and indeed was in debt to his aviador in Guanajuato on the account of his refining mill.[77] It comes as no surprise, therefore, to learn that in 1826 his heirs ceded Ibarrilla to Lieutenant-Colonel Genaro de la Garza, who took over liabilities of 20,400 pesos. As might be expected in an estate situated so close to León and hence under cultivation since the seventeenth century, the increase in value was much less than in more distant areas. As late as 1860 Ibarrilla sold for no more than 45,000 pesos.[78]

Not all our case-studies end in foreclosure. The pattern of patient enterprise typified by Austri or Septién was not entirely broken by the hegemony of the Obregón; peninsular entrepreneurs still made fortunes in León. In 1792 José Manuel Diez Quijano, an immigrant from Vallecarriedo in the mountains of Santander, took over the former Jesuit haciendas of Hoya, Losa and El Sitio. For a few months, he had acted as general manager of the great Valenciana mine and in recognition of his services the dowager Countess lent him 10,000 pesos. The precise cost of the haciendas was not specified, although Diez Quijano was certainly obliged to recognise a 40,000 pesos charge in favour of the College at Guanajuato. Despite the difficulties of the next few years, at his death in 1809 Diez Quijano left assets worth 198,667 pesos as against debts and mortgages of 100,356 pesos. In addition to the three haciendas, he possessed a large house in León and a thriving store run by a nephew brought from Spain for this purpose.[79] It was to require all the latter's devoted management to prevent foreclosure during the period of the Insurgency when the rural properties, by reason of their owner's background, were an especial target for patriot forces. It was not until 1836 that the two heirs, a daughter and Bachiller José Manuel, divided their patrimony, each taking an hacienda. By this time most debts had been repaid other than 50,000 pesos which were now held in favour of State education funds.[80]

Much the same sequence occurred in the case of José Cristóbal de Somera, a native of Aymonte in Castile, who also owned a store in León, together with some interests in Comanja where he acquired two small haciendas. In 1802 he took over Palote and Palma from the heirs of José Francisco de Marmolejo at a cost of 51,819 pesos, of which 27,000 pesos were in mortgages. Here also the Insurgency ambushed the plans of an ambitious man of business and Somera left his children haciendas heavily indebted without the means to satisfy interest charges. Indeed, if we are to believe legal testimony, it was not until the 1830s that the estates showed a clear profit. But even then, with mortgages of 45,000 pesos on assets generously assessed at 97,000 pesos, it proved difficult to effect a partition between the four heirs. In the upshot, one son took the estate in Comanja, another received the large house in town, so that Palote and Palma were retained by Bachiller José Manuel and a devout sister.[81]

At this juncture our story reaches an unexpected, albeit traditional, conclusion. In April 1836 the two priests, creole sons of peninsular fathers, Br. José Manuel Diez Quijano and Br. José Manuel Somera, formally agreed to pool their resources in order to provide the necessary funds for the establishment of a house of the Oratory in León.[82] The exact details of the subsequent transactions are not clear. But in 1838 Diez Quijano sold Losa for 68,000 pesos, and it is possible that part of this sum went to the new foundation. Later, in 1863, this valuable hacienda passed into the hands of Manuel Doblado, the famous Liberal governor of Guanajuato, whose peninsular grandfather had once served as regidor in León.[83] Whatever the case, Somera, assisted by his sister, was able to pay off the charges on Palote assigned to other heirs and donate the hacienda to the Oratory. Unfortunately, this initiative, so similar to the gift of Losa and Hoya to the Jesuits a century before, was defeated by the Liberal Reform laws of the 1850s which nationalised all Church property.[84] The incident, however, demonstrates both the revival of the Mexican Church in the 1840s and the traditional nature of that revival.

Where great fortunes foundered, lesser enterprises broke asunder. In the early nineteenth century at least four haciendas in León were partitioned. It is only fair to note, however, that these partitions formed the second stage in the dismemberment of the great latifundia put together by José de Austri. In the first place, San Nicolás de Arriba y Abajo was purchased in 1798 by Pedro González, a merchant from Guanajuato, who accepted over 14,000 pesos in mortgages. But then in 1806, unable to meet the demands of the amortisation junta, he ceded over half the estate, some $27\frac{1}{2}$ cab. to Francisco Aniceto Palacios, at that time the general manager of the second Count of Valenciana, on condition that he pay 9,500 pesos to the junta.[85] Finally, in 1820 the heirs of González divided the remaining lands of San Nicolás into three equal ranchos which each comprised just over $7\frac{1}{2}$ cab. or about 800 acres. It will be remembered that Austri had pieced together this estate out of a series of small farms, so that the hacienda had only lasted for about a century. The other section, however, now called San Juan de Abajo, still counted as an hacienda in a list drawn up in 1846.[86]

In the area of the former latifundium of Gavia, the descendants of Austri's eldest son, José Tomás, after dividing Sardina into three equal parts in 1777, proved unable to retain any unity of direction. The San Ramón de Ocotes was partitioned into two large ranchos of about 15 cab. each by José Ramón and Juan de Hoyos at some point between 1798 and 1821.[87] Similarly, María Ana de Austri proved unable to pay the interest on mortgages of 5,600 pesos owing to the depredations of the Insurgents and in consequence in 1820 was obliged to auction her hacienda, San Vicente Tuna Agria. The beneficiaries in this case were the Castro family, which since 1791 had leased the entire hacienda, save for a small farm reserved for the needs of the owner.[88] However, in their turn the Castros fell into debt and had to cede the estate to creditors. Finally, in 1851 Tuna Agria, then worth some 14,000 pesos, with an area of 31 cab. or 3,255 acres, was divided into four equal sections by the children of the last owner, one Mariano Hernández.[89]

By far the largest hacienda to be partitioned in León was Gavia, an estate of 121 cab. or 12,700 acres, which had been acquired by Juan Francisco de Villamor in such curious circumstances from Bachiller Bernardino de Austri. By 1807 the property was valued at 50,000 pesos with charges of only 10,280 pesos. But then, by reason of its exposed position on the plains of the Bajío, it was devastated, and the livestock stolen, so that the owners simply let the land to such tenants as dared continue cultivation. Part of the problem derived from the highly political role played by the owners. For Gavia had passed to Villamor's widow, María Josefa Reina and to the children of her first marriage, the four sons of Manuel de Liceaga. The family was bitterly divided during the Insurgency, since whereas José María de Liceaga, assisted by his brother Ignacio, emerged as a rebel general, Mariano was killed fighting for the Crown and Juan became a royalist officer.[90] After Independence was achieved, the two surviving brothers engaged in litigation concerning the disposition of the hacienda, which by then bore a heavy burden of debt in favour of the Count of Valenciana. Unfortunately, little further information is available, save for a few scattered entries in the notary register which indicate that Gavia was in fact split into four sections by the heirs of the four brothers, and that in at least one case by the 1860s further subdivision had already occurred.[91] In these examples we find confirmation in León of the trend towards the fragmentation of haciendas already observed in Pénjamo and the uplands of Jalisco.

## V

The emphasis on mercantile and mining capital should not be thought to exclude the possibility of survival in agriculture without this type of assistance. It would be quite false to suggest that an hacienda could not support a family of the provincial elite in sufficient comfort. Church debts were not the inevitable accoutrement of every Mexican landowner. To weather the vicissitudes of the century, all that was required was a relatively modest style of life. More important, a family had to devise agreements between heirs so as to prevent sale, partition or imposition of Church mortgages. In León the Herrera Arcocha family present us with an unfamiliar example of such stability. The story starts in 1711 when Sebastián Herrera Arcocha, an immigrant from the mountains of Santander, bought out his brother-in-law to become the sole owner of Cerrogordo, an hacienda of 54 cab. or 5,670 acres, situated in the hills immediately behind the town. In the next generation, one son succeeded in paying off his fellow heirs and, in turn, his son José Francisco Arcocha benefited from the entry of two brothers into the priesthood and the spinstershood of his two sisters. For most of the century, Cerrogordo remained backward, and with most of the land barren pasture, as late as 1787, the overall inventory only amounted to 13,244 ps.[92] But then José Francisco, obviously a more enterprising man than his father, succeeded in constructing five small reservoirs or *cajas* which provided irrigation for over 260 acres of wheat-growing. A flour mill was built in town. With such measures, the enterprise prospered and by reason of the proximity of Cerrogordo to the town, no doubt escaped relatively unharmed from the devastation of the civil wars after 1810. Whatever the reason, Arcocha was able to purchase an entire series of small properties surrounding Cerrogordo. These ranged from the ranchos called Los Gómez to the *labor* of San José del Cerrito which comprised nearly 10 cab. or over 1,000 acres. By the time of his death in 1823, Arcocha possessed assets valued at 45,685 pesos from which only 11,268 pesos in Church mortgages had to be deducted. His widow refused to divide the estate, and indeed added the valuable *labor* of Patiña, which once had belonged to Agustín de Septién.[93] After her death in 1833, the ten children divided the range of small properties between them, but left Cerrogordo to be managed by Felipe Arcocha, who over the years contrived to pay off the various sums assigned to his co-heirs. This cycle, which had lasted a century and a half, was brought to an end by his sons, who in 1863 chose to sell the hacienda for 63,000 pesos.[94] In this fashion they avoided the problem of dividing the inheritance. Few families in Mexico ever succeeded in outwitting the combined effects of the testamentary system and the fertility of their womenfolk.

The chief alternative to selling an hacienda was to divide it among the heirs. If the great estate survived for so long in the Bajío, in large measure it was because landowners rarely wished to become mere farmers. That this was a practical alternative can be demonstrated from the example of the Guerreros of Rincón. In 1729 Juan Guerrero, a mayordomo of Miguel González del Pinal, bought from his employer a deserted small sitio in Rincón called Talayote. The terms were favourable, since the cost – some 400 pesos – was charged in deposit on the property. Moreover, although Guerrero made no attempt to pay the 25 pesos annual interest, the González del Pinal, who by this time had sold all their lands in the district, did not threaten foreclosure. In fact, since Guerrero had already lost one sitio some years before through his inability to find the interest, we may presume that the waiving of this charge was implicit in the contract. In the upshot, in 1738 Guerrero's daughter-in-law borrowed and saved sufficient monies as to redeem the principal and obtain full title of ownership.[95]

During the 1780s, a lawsuit initiated by disgruntled heirs for once illumines this neglected stratum of Mexican rural society.[96] It is interesting to learn that although all the sons of this Creole landowner went to school, not all of them learnt to read or write and in later years some could barely sign their names. Moreover, in 1747 when the widow of Guerrero's son handed over the management of the estate to her son Diego Francisco, the only livestock he found were three yoke of oxen which had been hired for the season. In fact, most of the sitio still consisted of scrubland, since only three fanegas de sembradura – about 36 acres – were under plough, apart from a few plots let to Indians. Most of the brothers had little desire to work on the land, so, after their mother effected a formal partition of the estate in 1757, they chose to sell their sections to Diego Francisco for about 120 pesos apiece. In this fashion, apart from the four caballerías retained by José Antonio Guerrero, he obtained control over the entire hacienda for about 1,000 pesos. At least three brothers now migrated to Durango to seek their fortunes in the mining camps of that province. But in the search for wealth, it was to be the farmers rather than the miners who met with success. Patience and toil brought their reward. According to later testimony presented in court, Diego Francisco 'driving the plough with his own hands. . .through his own sweat and labour, rendered fruitful the greater part of the lands of Talayote'. Obviously, this dramatic description referred to the first years, since the area in question was far too extensive as to be farmed by one man and his family. There can be little doubt that Guerrero soon was able to employ labourers. Nevertheless, the emphasis on close personal management was not misplaced: here is the very image of the Mexican ranchero.

By the time of his death in 1793, Diego Francisco Guerrero left assets worth 44,774 pesos, balanced by only 6,800 pesos of Church mortgages, which were mainly charged on Fuentes de Medina, a neighbouring hacienda he had acquired earlier in the year. Talayote now comprised just under 40 cab. (4,150 acres) of which 28 cab. were cultivated. Since the original purchase had referred to a small sitio, it is clear that the Guerreros had filched over 2,000 acres from their neighbours. Small wonder that during the 1770s there had been a series of lawsuits. In particular the two Sardaneta brothers, the priests who owned Sauz de Armenta, complained of land seizures.[97] Moreover, in addition there was another large sitio, mainly barren, called Tolimán. By contrast, Fuentes de Medina, which encompassed 38 cab., had been ceded to Guerrero by a son-in-law to whom he had lent 5,000 pesos.[98]

To judge from the inventory, the main business of Talayote was the production of maize. For this purpose, Guerrero maintained 184 plough oxen and kept four mule teams each of 26 head. But in addition, he had an extensive herd of 514 cattle, including calves; about 195 brood mares, with both foals and young mules; 360 sheep and 930 goats. It is instructive to compare this inventory with the listed assets of Guerrero's brother, José Antonio, who died in 1802 leaving a farm of $3\frac{1}{2}$ cab. worth 5,635 pesos. For it is clear that the rancho and the hacienda operated in identical fashion. The range of livestock on the rancho was simply less numerous, with 55 oxen and 33 mules, and smaller herds for breeding.[99] The only difference, therefore, was the size of the enterprise. In this context, it is surely significant that both brothers had built their homes in Talayote; neither owned a town house.

True to their type, the children of the two brothers decided to partition the property rather than sell out. Admittedly, the eleven surviving children of José Antonio soon found that their plots were not sufficient, so that most chose to transfer their land to an energetic brother who slowly re-created the original rancho.[100] But in the case of the hacienda, the twelve heirs of Diego Francisco each obtained a farm ranging in size from 210 to 420 acres, in accordance with the quality of the land. That these properties could yield a comfortable livelihood can be shown by an inventory taken in 1824, which lists assets of 4,590 pesos on a farm of 472 acres. The same document, however, states that the children planned to divide the farm between them. It was not to be long before fields measured by the yard rather than by the caballería were to come on to the market. For some reason, possibly a result of its mortgages, Fuentes de Medina was only partitioned in 1822, and then only among four brothers.[101]

Here, then, in the history of one family and their estate, we encounter another Mexico. Where many an overly ambitious young Austri or Marmolejo soon plunged into debt and ultimate ruin, the Guerreros prospered. Practical farmers rather than gentry, they were equally far from being peasants, since they obviously relied on hired labour to operate their enterprise. Nevertheless, their economic success suggests that the Liberal proposals for a yeoman farmer solution to the ills of the Mexican countryside were not so far removed from reality as has been commonly supposed. However, the contrasts here should not be over-drawn, the more especially as with time the differences grew less pronounced. At the close of our period, in 1856 Lucas Guerrero, owner of a quarter of the former Fuentes de Medina hacienda, together with some fields in Talayote, backed Francisco Guerrero to lease Sandía for 6,000 pesos. Four years later, he purchased the hacienda for 120,000 pesos, putting up no less than 59,000 pesos in cash and accepting the remainder of the sale-price in transferred mortgages. Somewhat later he acquired Sardina in Rincón. This cycle of upward social mobility reached a thoroughly traditional conclusion when his daughter, María Guerrero, sole heiress of Sandía, married an immigrant Basque merchant.[102] In more ways than one, Mexican society under the regime of Porfirio Díaz maintained patterns of behaviour reminiscent of the Colony.

## CHAPTER 7

# Rancheros

Although both foreign travellers and native novelists of the last century commented extensively on the manners and life of the rancheros, it was left to the American geographer, G. M. McBride, to provide the first systematic survey of this neglected stratum of society in the Mexican countryside.[1] From a brief study of the census returns, he found that the number of small properties in the Republic had risen from 15,085 in 1854 to no less than 47,939 in 1910. By this latter year, about a third of all ranchos were located in the adjoining states of Guanajuato, Jalisco and Michoacán. Strongly influenced by the theories of Luis Wistano Orozco and Andrés Molina Enríquez, he ascribed this surprising increase to the Liberal Reform Laws of the 1850s which had effected the auction of corporate property in land and enforced the distribution in separate lots of the communal holdings of the Indian villages. Equally important, he identified the rancheros as an embryonic, rural middle class of predominantly mestizo origin.[2] Confirmation for these hypotheses came from a study of Las Arandas, a district situated among the hills of Jalisco, where in the middle years of the nineteenth century the great estates which hitherto had dominated the zone were broken into small units and sold to a numerous group of local farmers.[3] More recently, in his classic *Pueblo en vilo* Luis González traced the sequence whereby a deserted upland hacienda in Michoacán, first effectively settled by tenants and squatters in the late eighteenth century, was finally partitioned during the 1860s to form 36 separate farms. By 1912 through sale and testamentary division, the number of these holdings had risen to 167.[4] In both cases, however, the decisive elements of change were the indebtedness of the landlords and the prior existence of a relatively prosperous class of farmers with sufficient means for the purchase of land. Similarly, the avowed ethnic status of the first settlers in these districts was preponderantly Spanish rather than mestizo.

On the plains of the Bajío, however, the story was quite different.

For here, as we have seen above, the rancho took its start in the *vecindades* granted by town councils. True, François Chevalier averred that the great landlords or their agents soon invaded the limits of the municipal endowment conceded by the foundation charter.[5] But the evidence advanced to support this case derived mainly from San Felipe, an impoverished *villa* on the northern borders of the region. Elsewhere, in the jurisdiction of Celaya, the establishment of a new town at Salvatierra as late as 1644, with at least four large sitios assigned for distribution among its citizens, suggests that the day of the small property was not yet past.[6] Then again, at León there was no sign of any concerted drive by landowners to monopolise the ejidos of the town. Indeed, it was only in the last decades of the seventeenth century that the zone known as El Monte or Tepetates was finally apportioned in a new series of vecindades. Finally, at much the same time two large sitios in Rincón were partitioned through testamentary division and henceforth became the nucleus of an entire group of small properties.

At this point, for the sake of clarity, it is convenient to rehearse our previous observations. In 1700 the distinctive feature in the pattern of land tenure at León was the survival of the small proprietary farm. Despite marginal encroachments by haciendas such as Duarte, Otates and Santa Rosa, the bulk of the original endowment, which, together with tracts of unclaimed lands between the estancia grants, comprised over fourteen large sitios, was still divided among a numerous, variegated range of small properties. From the outset, however, the standard vecindades of $3\frac{1}{2}$ cab. or 370 acres had been combined to form small estates or large farms called *labores* which extended from 500 to 1,400 acres. By 1710 there were about thirty of these holdings. Then, beneath this level, we encounter at least another fifty ranchos with between 100 and 370 acres. Needless to say, this distinction, made on the basis of acreage, tells us little about the internal organisation of the enterprises. No doubt most *labores* hired peons to drive their plough teams; but there is little evidence as to whether the ordinary rancho operated as a simple family concern or whether the owners also employed outside help. On vecindades of long standing, it was already common practice for families to divide the farm into sections without recourse to the notary for formal partition. By contrast, in the grants issued since 1680 only a small part of the ground had yet been cleared for cultivation. Finally, in at least one case a rancho was described as being 'settled with tenants'.[7]

It was this complex, variegated pattern of land tenure which in certain measure determined the subsequent history of the rancho in León. Some properties survived the hazards of the inheritance laws and emerged as miniature haciendas. By 1828 there were still at least twelve small estates which in the previous epoch would have been called *labores*.[8] In two instances the same family retained possession throughout our period, but as a general rule the turnover in ownership was as frequent as on haciendas. Indeed, Patiña, a prosperous farm of over 1,000 acres, was sold six times in a period of eighty years. By contrast, at the other end of the scale the progressive subdivision of ranchos led to a multiplication of small-holdings. By 1828 at least twelve former vecindades had become small villages or rancherías where fields were now measured in yards rather than by the caballería. Here, too, the market in land was volatile, with farms enlarged or divided across the generations according to individual energy or skill. In effect, therefore, the term rancho, as it was employed from the late eighteenth century onwards, encompassed two distinct types of enterprise. A ranchero could be either a prosperous, commercial farmer aided by several peons, or alternatively, he could be a small-holder eking out a bare subsistence on three or four acres of land. In English terms, it was as if yeomen and cottage farmers were included within the same broad class.

But no discussion of the ranchero in León can omit consideration of the changes wrought by the expansion in the area occupied by the great estate. For an entire range of small properties, ranchos and *labores* alike, were amalgamated through purchase either to enlarge or to create new haciendas. In consequence a significant nucleus of peasant proprietors was eliminated. Men who once had farmed their own lands became tenants or sharecroppers. True, in mitigation it can be argued that by the close of the eighteenth century, the difference in wealth or in social position between a tenant farmer and a small-holder with a few acres was not very great. But we must always remember that the absence of any system of contractual lease-hold, other than for the largest units or whole estates, meant that the ordinary tenant, and still more the sharecropper, was entirely dependent on the whim or will of the landlord for the maintenance of his livelihood. In the exercises which follow, we trace the varying fortunes of ranchero families. The method is descriptive, but the sample generous. The nature of the documents precludes discussion of anything other than the bare facts of economic life.

## II

The sequence by which a standard vecindad served as the basis for
an entire village is nowhere better illustrated than by the case of
Los Castillos, situated just north of León. In 1635 Pedro de Castilla
Calvo, an immigrant from the Peninsula, bequeathed a rancho of
370 acres to be shared between his four children, all described as
illegitimate mulattoes. A certain prosperity was attained by a grandson, Agustín de Castilla, who first succeeded in buying out his uncles
and then paid 162 pesos in *composición* to the Crown in order to
obtain rights over a further six caballerías which lay further up the
valley. In his will – signed by proxy because he was illiterate –
Agustín declared that at the time of his marriage he only had 105
acres and hence 'I supported myself by my own personal labour,
renting oxen for sowing.' By his death in 1733, he owned nearly
1,000 acres which, together with a herd of 24 cows and a small
maguey plantation, was worth 3,460 pesos. His four sons all lived on
the farm and after his death each took a caballería for cultivation,
leaving about 365 acres undivided to serve for common pasture.
Their father had already built a small chapel so that the settlement
already wore some of the aspect of a village.[9] In passing, we may
note that Agustín had reared an Indian 'nephew' from childhood,
giving him the task of managing the livestock, in return for which
he obtained about 50 acres for his own farm.

The ethnic composition of the family was decidedly complex,
since, although Agustín was described in all legal documents as a
free mulatto, his mother was an Indian, and his two successive wives
were mestizas. His children quietly appropriated the maternal status
and hence escaped the ignominy of tribute. It is a comment both on
the ethnic mixture and the type of family labour that characterised
the settlement that the mestiza widow of a grandson should marry
an Indian who dwelt and worked for her father-in-law, Juan de Dios
de Castilla, for sixteen years. This arrangement was all the more
necessary since the drought of 1750 had carried off the herd of sixty
cattle owned by Juan de Dios so that he had little to bequeath his
six children other than their share of 105 acres of arable and their
rights to pasture.[10]

In the last third of the eighteenth century, however, the surviving
Castilla descendants sold a great part of their best land. A neighbour,
the creole ranchero Domingo Echeveste purchased about 200 acres
to add to his growing estate and Gregorio Falcón, a mulatto who

possibly married into the family, acquired 315 acres in a series of transactions notarised during the 1780s. The going rate varied from 350 to 400 pesos a caballería. In their turn, the heirs of Falcón divided his farm and in subsequent years the usual unit of sale was a *fanega de sembradura*, or 15 acres, which by the 1850s sold for about a hundred pesos each.[11] It was during this decade that the settlement was officially recognised as a civil *congregación*.

One surprising feature of the lower stratum of rancheros was the number of Indians who figured as small landowners. Already well-advanced on the road to cultural assimilation, these Indian rancheros were usually described as *indios ladinos*, whose native tongue was Castilian. For example, in 1711 we find that the three Alfaro brothers, whom this rubric covered, owned a herd of 34 brood mares and 9½ caballerías situated in the hill valley still called Cañada de Alfaro. The imminent absorption of the family into the *casta* community is demonstrated by the marriage of one brother to an illegitimate mulatto woman, probably the daughter of a slave, since she was reared in the household of a Spanish landowner.[12] Whatever the case, within a generation the Alfaros sold most of their inheritance to neighbouring estates, and we encounter no further references to them in the notary register until the decade 1847–57 when their last descendants sold several narrow strips of land to an hacienda ironically called Alfaro.[13]

Further evidence of the diffusion of prosperity among the Indian community at the start of our period is provided by the will filed in 1713 by a Tarascan Indian, Nicolás Hernández, who declared that whereas at marriage he only possessed a yoke of oxen and five sheep, he now owned no less than six yoke of oxen, 43 sheep, 20 mares, 9 cows with calves and 60 fanegas of maize, assets which were appraised at a total value of 318 pesos.[14] Since he made no mention of land, we must presume that either he farmed in the area held collectively by the villages of Coecillo and San Miguel or that alternatively he rented land from local haciendas.

That this range of property was then not uncommon can be shown by the rise to fortune of Lorenzo Ramírez, an Otomí Indian described as a fluent speaker of Castilian, who for 550 pesos, cash down, purchased 8½ caballerías or nearly 900 acres from the Martínez Solano brothers. Although he later claimed that at marriage he owned no goods worth listing, in 1705 when a local merchant obtained an embargo order for debt collection, the magistrates found that he possessed six yoke of oxen, 30 cows, and 12 mules fitted out for

freight. Apparently in later years his affairs failed to prosper, since by
his death in 1733 he only maintained four yoke of oxen, an indication
that he may have employed his eight children to cultivate the land.
Subsequently, the eldest son, Nicolás Ramírez, succeeded in pre-
venting his fellow heirs from effecting any formal partition of the
estate.[15] But in 1756, after his death, his children sold 3½ caballerías
to an Indian from Silao, who paid the 300 pesos demanded by
putting up a third in cash, a third in maize and by writing a
promissory note for the remainder. The next year, other members of
the family sold 4 caballerías for 750 pesos, of which 200 pesos was
deducted in favour of the endowment funds of the town council.
The purchasers in this case were the Almaguer brothers, shrewd
creole rancheros. It is striking that the reason advanced to justify
these sales was that 'there was no easy way of dividing' the land
between the various heirs.[16] At all levels of colonial society, the
testamentary system operated to dissipate accumulated capital.
A few fields were apparently retained by the family, since in 1786
Juan Andrés Ramírez, described as governor of the village of San
Miguel, sold three strips of land which in all measured 384 by 600
yards.[17]

Where rancheros succeeded in retaining possession of their farms,
the natural increase in the rural population eventually led to the
creation of minifundia. For example, the vecindad of Los Hernández, situated alongside the village of Coecillo, was acquired by an
Indian called Pedro Hernández in the middle years of the seventeenth century. Thereafter the property was divided among his
descendants to such an extent that by the 1780s fields were measured
either by the yard or in *fanegas de sembradura*. To take one case,
in 1786 José Ventura Ramírez, who owned 60 acres in two separate
tracts purchased from several members of the Hernández family,
sold his property for 96 pesos to an Indian from Coecillo. The
volatility of the land market within these settlements can be illustrated by the sale in 1803 of 22 acres to two brothers appropriately
called Hernández by one José Peñaflor who in turn had bought the
land in 1786 from another individual of the same name.[18] In this
situation outsiders also bought their way into the zone and a Spanish
ranchero succeeded in piecing together a farm of almost 170 acres.
By the close of the century the area was so densely settled that in
1804 a group of Hernández petitioned the Crown for recognition of
their ranchería as an Indian village and hence entitled to the statu-
tory endowment of communal land. By this time, so they claimed,

some 200 persons or fifty families lived in the village which already possessed its own chapel.[19] Nothing came of this application, however, and it was only in the 1850s that San Pedro de los Hernández was elevated to the level of a civil congregación. By then sales of land dealt in garden plots, in one instance measuring 52 by 360 yards (worth 52 pesos) and in another, 92 by 111 yards (worth 161 ps).[20]

The economic implications of this continuous reduction in the size of holdings can be traced from a lawsuit initiated in the 1830s over the ownership of Los Olaéz, a standard rancho adjoining Los Hernández, which had been purchased in 1731 by two mestizo brothers-in-law, José de Olaéz and Juan Ruiz. Witnesses declared that the families who still occupied the area, the Olaéz, Ruiz, Pérez and Barrera, rarely owned more than a fanega de sembradura and that indeed the most common allotment was a quarter of a fanega, or just under four acres of land, an area which could be cultivated with a single yoke of oxen. To judge from the size of fields put up for sale, 301 by 48 yards in one case and 320 by 86 yards in another, the land was divided into long narrow strips suitable for ploughing.[21] However, these small-holdings yielded their owners little more than the barest necessities, and in consequence these impecunious rancheros sought other sources of income. Some men assisted in the harvest on neighbouring haciendas, or, more commonly, rented land on a share-cropping basis; others combed the hills for firewood or tuna fruit; and the remainder took employment as muleteers. Thus, within the course of a hundred years, if independence was still preserved, prosperity had become a distant prospect.

Only rarely do the documents cast light on the nature of life on these settlements. In Rincón in 1675, Nicolás de Torres purchased half a large sitio, i.e. about 2,160 acres, for 200 pesos. Somewhat later, the San Roque, as the sitio was called, was divided equally between his twelve children, each section cut in a long strip measuring 5,000 yards long and 200 yards across. By 1731 a rancho of $3\frac{1}{2}$ caballerías, the equivalent of two such strips, sold for 900 pesos. It is of some interest to note that at much the same time a descendant of Torres was described as a mestizo.[22] However, the case with which we are concerned dealt with two men who had the status of Spaniard. It began in 1771 when Antonio Puente, a poor ranchero on San Roque, accused his more prosperous neighbour, Leoncio Cacho Ramírez, of wounding cattle when they strayed on to his land. Other witnesses asserted that Ramírez was a petty tyrant who was also guilty of beating young boys who minded the cattle, and even of attacking women. Needless to say, Cacho Ramírez denied these charges, but his defence largely consisted of accusing his opponents of envy, since with a rancho of $3\frac{1}{2}$ caballerías on which, with eight yoke of oxen, he had sown eight cargas of wheat, he numbered among the most wealthy farmers in the vicinity. Whatever the truth of the case, the magistrate banished Ramírez from San Roque, ordering him to reside at a distance of at least 36 miles. Victory in the law courts was always an expensive business in New Spain, however, especially when a lay magistrate required the assistance of a legal advisor. Before judgement was pronounced, Puente fled in order to avoid paying the legal costs. The foreclosure of his possessions revealed that he owned $1\frac{1}{4}$ caballerías or 131 acres on which he had sown three small *milpas* comprising $1\frac{1}{2}$ fanegas de sembradura, i.e. about 23 acres. His house was built of adobe, with two rooms, a kitchen, and a small corral surrounded with cactus.[23] Here, then we glimpse at the manner of life of the prosperous peasantry.

Emphasis on the forces which pushed the lower stratum of the ranchero class towards the margins of subsistence should not obscure the role of individual enterprise which permitted some men of industry or initiative to escape the general fate. For example, in his will, Juan José Nuñez del Prado averred that at his marriage in 1732 his wife brought him a dowry of three cows, which he had to sell since 'I then owned nothing other than the cloak on my shoulders.' Nevertheless, hard work and the economy of his wife, exercised over a period of 22 years, at last enabled him to purchase a small farm situated close to town in the area known as Piscina. The price was 225 pesos for 184 acres ($1\frac{3}{4}$ cab.). To judge from the inventory drawn up in 1766 after his death, Nuñez del Prado was a soap-maker by profession, since in addition to his house in León, the land, four oxen and three donkeys, there were listed 1,537 pounds of liquid tallow. This touching story of honest toil meeting its just reward is only marred by the suit moved by his eight children of the first marriage against the widow, complaining that the bride of his old age had dissipated a good part of their expected inheritance. In the upshot, they each received 48 pesos out of an estate valued at 398 pesos. But to distribute these assets – a year's salary for a trusted peon – they first had to sell $1\frac{1}{4}$ caballerías for 190 pesos. The remaining 52 acres were then divided among them, since by 1819 we encounter sale of two strips of land, which measured 308 by 500 yards and 175 by 150 yards.[24]

A similar case of rags to riches and back again within two, rather than the customary three, generations can be found somewhat later in the century. In 1787 Cristóbal Baltierra, a native of Silao of un-specified ethnic origin, purchased the same 3½ caballerías in Tepe-tates which had been sold by the heirs of Nicolás Ramírez in 1756. In his will, signed by proxy since he was illiterate, Baltierra declared that at marriage the couple lacked all capital and that 'the few goods there are, which I shall name, we gained with our own bodily labour'. In fact, his assets in 1791 were considerable, since in addition to the rancho, they included 42 freight mules and 73 plough oxen, and were appraised at a total value of 4,270 pesos. His widow kept the property together for another two decades, selling only one caballería. In 1820, however, her nine children at last effected a partition of the remaining 262 acres, each receiving fields measuring 217,137 square yards. As elsewhere, further subdivision occurred and by 1859 we find one Baltierra selling a fanega de sembradura for 100 pesos.[25] The interest of this case is that it confirms that even late in the century it was still possible for some individuals to better their fortunes.

Finally, it is clear that ownership of land was not the only road to prosperity. The reduction in the number of the small proprietors should not be interpreted as effecting a universal decline in fortune, since in fact many former owners were able to rent lands. At times independent farmers also leased land from haciendas. For example, in his will drawn up in 1829, José María Fuentes, an illiterate mulatto whose family had owned a rancho next to Los Hernández since the beginning of the eighteenth century, declared that although at marriage he possessed only a few animals, he later inherited about 45 acres of land or three fanegas from his father. More important, however, he rented three separate tracts in the distant Gavia hacienda which together comprised about 135 acres. He also owned 24 plough oxen and had 27 donkeys fitted out for freight. Here, then, is an illustration of how small proprietors were able to profit from the growing trend within haciendas to lease considerable sections of their land.[26] In short, not all members of the lower stratum of rancheros were driven down to the level of small-holders eking out a livelihood close to the margins of subsistence. In at least some cases, they were able to maintain their position as prosperous farmers who hired labour to plough their fields.

## III

The reduction of once prosperous ranchero families to the condition of cottage farmers might well have been averted had not the
expansion of the great estate so sharply curtailed the supply of land
available for purchase. As Table 36 indicates, at least 300 caballerías
of the former municipal endowment were absorbed by the creation
or enlargement of some nine haciendas during the course of the
eighteenth century. This was the equivalent in area of 86 vecindades

TABLE 35    *The formation of San Nicolás hacienda: purchases 1742–51*

The following sales to Agustín de Septién y Montero are recorded in Notary
Register at León.

| | |
|---|---|
| 15 March 1742 | 5½ caballerías for 14,000 ps (including 5,000 ps capellanía) from Manuel Díaz Cacho who acquired it in 1718. The original title dated *c.* 1601. The price included 71 oxen and buildings. |
| 27 September 1742 | 1 caballería for 430 ps from heirs of Diego Aranda. |
| 29 July 1745 | 4½ caballerías for 4,500 ps (including 2,000 ps capellanía) from Isabel de Zuñiga who bought it in 1723. The original title dated 1601. |
| 8 November 1745 | 4½ caballerías for 350 ps from Juana de Ferrer who bought it in 1731. Original title 1694. |
| 28 October 1745 | ⅜ caballería for 225 ps from grand-children of Gabriel de la Cruz who acquired it in 1698. |
| 17 October 1750 | 1⅜ caballerías for 800 ps from heirs of Pedro de León Galván. Their grandfather bought it in 1628. |
| 26 October 1750 | 1½ caballería for 525 ps from heirs of Agustín Rico, Indians whose grandfather acquired it in 1669. Original title issued in 1661. |
| 9 November 1750 | 1 caballería for 300 ps from Santos Ramírez and others, Indians whose family occupied land since 1612. |
| 30 December 1750 | ⅖ and ¹⁄₂₀ caballería for 112½ ps from grand-children of Juan de Castañeda, a mestizo, who bought land in 1700. |
| 26 January 1751 | 2½ caballerías for 200 ps from heirs of Antonio de Mendoza, an Indian who bought it in 1737. In El Monte. |
| 6 February 1750 | 1 caballería for 225 ps from Cristina Ramírez and others, Indians who held the land since 1709. Original title 1667. |
| 6 March 1751 | 3½ caballerías for 800 ps from heirs of Juana de Ferrer, who bought it in 1745. Original title 1606. |
| 31 March 1751 | 3⅓ caballerías for 2,750 ps from Manuel de Herrera, whose father bought it in 1696. Original title 1628. |
| 19 May 1751 | 1 caballería for 325 ps from children of Pedro Manrique whose grandfather first acquired it. |
| 4 September 1751 | 1 caballería for 350 ps from Salvador Castañeda and others, mestizos whose father bought it in 1700. |
| ? 1751 | ¼ caballería for 200 ps from Juan de Escamilla. |

Total area was 31¾ caballerías purchased for 26,792½ ps (7,200 capellanias).

or 31,165 acres. Of course a considerable proportion of this land was already occupied by at least fifteen *labores* formed in the previous century. Indeed, by 1800, the hacienda of Ibarrilla represented the amalgamation of four prosperous small estates which ranged in size from 945 to 1,680 acres. However, in the case of both San Nicolás and San Pedro del Monte, an entire group of small farms were taken over. In this respect the years between 1740 and 1760 were decisive. An important nucleus of peasant proprietors lost control of their land and became tenants or sharecroppers or simply abandoned the district. It is noticeable that Indian, and to a lesser extent mulatto and mestizo, landowners were the most clearly affected by the changes of this period. For there was also a parallel movement within the ranchero sector whereby locally-born Spaniards bought out Indian and mestizo small-holders. In short, economic expansion served to strengthen the ethnic hierarchy of colonial society.

The formation of the San Nicolás hacienda immediately south of León led several Indian proprietors to relinquish their lands. During the drought years of 1750–51, two families, both called Ramírez, each sold a caballería to Agustín de Septién y Montero, although in one instance no less than four generations had cultivated the land since 1612 when it was first acquired. The going price here was 300 pesos. At much the same time, the grand-children of Antonio Mendoza sold 2½ caballerías of low quality land situated in El Monte for 200 pesos. It is of interest to note that Mendoza himself, an Indian, had rented a rancho called Marmol on the Gavia latifundium owned by José de Austri, and that by his death in 1738, he owned no less than 9 yoke of oxen, 65 brood mares, 30 mules and 22 cattle, all pastured in Gavia.[27]

The intricate sequence of inheritance and sale which lay behind these acquisitions by Septién can be best illustrated by the property owned by Hernando Galván de Rojas, which in the late seventeenth century comprised 2½ caballerías, or 527 acres, in part irrigated. Divided into four equal sections by his children, in 1696 two heirs sold their land – i.e. 263 acres – to Francisco Herrera Calderón. Then in 1714 a third heir ceded his share to Juan de Castañeda, a mestizo ranchero. All these divided sections eventually entered the San Nicolás. First, in 1750 the remaining Galván de Rojas, grand-children of Hernando, sold their 132 acres for 800 pesos. Then, after the partition of their property, the eleven children of Juan de Castañeda sold it in separate lots to Septién. In one case he paid 12½ pesos for some 4.7 acres, or one twentieth of a caballería. Finally, the son of Herrera Calderón, who also owned the prosperous labor called Herrera, relinquished his share, to which other lands had been added, for 2,750 pesos.[28]

In much the same area, on the borders between the haciendas of San Nicolás and Granjeno, in 1664 Gaspar Francisco Rico, whose descendants were described as Indian chiefs or caciques, bought three caballerías from the recipient of a council grant only issued three years before. This farm was first divided into two equal sections, and then in 1750 the grand-children on one side of the family sold their land to Septién for 575 pesos. By contrast, the other heirs retained control over their share of the farm, but then divided it into small plots, so that by 1813 Cristóbal Rico sold a field which measured 550 by 150 yards for only 48 pesos.[29] This sequence was exactly paralleled by a neighbouring family of mulattoes, the descendants of Marcos Pérez who had been given two caballerías at the beginning of the century by Miguel Gonzales del Pinal. The farm was later partitioned into some eight separate sections and in the years 1750–54 all but half a caballería – about 50 acres – was sold to Antonio de la Pompa, a merchant who had created the Pompa hacienda through the amalgamation of the small sitio called Granjeno with the *labor* of Concepción.[30] Thereafter, the lands which were left to the Pérez and Rico families formed a densely settled nucleus of small-holdings, within which property circulated with some rapidity. As late as the 1840s several persons called Pérez notarised sales of narrow fields within the area.[31]

Further south in the zone known as Tepetates, the same trends can be observed. In 1688 the Indian Juan Pablo Rico obtained a grant of a vecindad from the town council. His six children first divided the farm into equal sections and then in the years 1743–50 they or their children slowly sold the entire property to Francisco Sartuche, a creole ranchero from San Luis Potosí. In one case, half a caballería had been divided into five parts of about 10 acres each. The price in this case was 150 pesos for a caballería, and 12½ pesos for a tenth, which is to say, just over a peso for an acre.[32] It is significant that in at least one case a vendor explicitly chose to remain on the farm as a tenant.

It was not only lands owned by Indians that were absorbed by haciendas. In 1688 Pedro Urenda, a mestizo from Rincón, who had worked for many years on several estates in the district, obtained a standard vecindad from the council. But the owners of the neighbouring estate of Santa Rosa promptly ejected him, claiming that in fact he had already leased the same land from the hacienda for a nominal rent of two hens a year. Attempts to secure legal redress failed, since as a descendant later observed: 'the poor man who goes to court against the more powerful, far from winning his plea, often loses all he owns'.[33] However, in 1709, his son Simón was able to buy another rancho for a mere 60 pesos and by his death had cleared about 60 acres for maize. The farm supported eight yoke of oxen, 40 sheep and 35 mares. All this went to an illegitimate son, who in 1751 sold one caballería to the new hacienda of San Pedro del Monte, and in 1784–86 ceded the remainder now called San Antonio, to his son-in-law, a creole ranchero.[34]

In much the same area of Tepetates, Matías de Urquieta, the illegitimate mestizo son of an immigrant from the Peninsula, after serving as mayordomo on an hacienda, acquired a rancho called Santa Lucía by the simple expedient of accepting the 900 pesos mortgage charged on the property. His affairs prospered, since by his death in 1747 he owned 56 plough oxen, 33 transport mules and small herds of sheep, cattle and mares. In addition, he had assisted his two sons to acquire other tracts of land.[35] Despite this promising start, his heirs decided to sell 280 acres to the San Pedro del Monte hacienda and in 1767 his grand-children, by then unable to meet the annual 45 pesos interest on the Santa Lucía, relinquished possession without gaining any profit on the transaction. Nevertheless, some lands were apparently retained by the family, since as late as 1845 persons called Urquieta were recorded in the notary register as selling small fields.[36]

That service as a mayordomo offered considerable opportunity is further illustrated by the careers of two mestizo brothers, Esteban and Lázaro Gómez, who at one time were employed by the owners of the Cerrogordo hacienda. Their rise to fortune started in 1707 when they acquired a farm of 7½ caballerías or 785 acres, situated on the western outskirts of León, by accepting the 2,500 pesos mortgage imposed on the property by the hospital of San Juan de Dios. Another rancho of 3½ caballerías, close by, was bought for a mere 203 pesos.[37] Thereafter, the brothers each went their own way and the two farms were divided between them. By his death in 1730, Lázaro had accumulated a fortune worth 3,869 pesos, including nine yoke of oxen and fifty transport mules. A clue as to the social status of this prosperous ranchero is afforded by his marriage to the illegitimate daughter of a land-owner, the offspring of either a slave or an Indian woman. Equally interesting, the daugher of this

marriage, Melchora Gómez, married Gregorio Marmolejo, a nephew
of the parish priest, Bachiller Juan Antonio Marmolejo, whom we
encounter in 1771 acting as mayordomo of the Palote hacienda.
Although the widow of Lázaro Gómez sold much of his land, the
original 3¾ caballerías of the rancho now called Los Gómez remained
in the family until 1787 when the grand-children finally succeeded
in selling the property in order to obtain their inheritance. Unfortunately, since the mortgage of 1,250 pesos still remained charged on
the farm, all they received was 400 pesos.[38] It is of interest to note
that prior to the sale the land had been leased to some nine persons
for an annual rent of 65 pesos.

The second brother, Esteban Gómez, prospered yet more, and
with the acquisition of the small sitio called Laurel became a landowner of some standing. At his death in 1747 his assets, valued at
over 10,000 pesos, included 15 yoke of oxen, 170 mares and 42 mules
fitted for freight. His estate was equal in value to the Cerrogordo
hacienda owned by his former employers.[39] Since Gómez never
married, his possessions were divided among his four illegitimate
children who, in the years 1747–53 sold the Laurel in separate lots
to the Losa brothers, owners of the adjoining sitio of Lagunillas.
The overall price here was 1,480 pesos.[40] However, it was not until
1803 that a grandson, Lázaro Gómez, finally sold the original 3¾
caballerías of the rancho also called Los Gómez. The current owner
of Cerrogordo bought the property for 2,250 pesos, of which 1,250
pesos consisted of transferred charges. In the years prior to the sale,
Gómez had leased the farm for 120 pesos a year, reserving two
fanegas de sembradura or some 30 acres for his own use.[41]


## IV

The disappearance or progressive diminishment of the small property
makes for a dramatic story, especially when compared with the
expansion of the great estate. But it is not the whole story. For
a certain number of rancheros, for the most part creoles, benefited
from the general upsurge in economic activity which characterised the decades after 1770. In many cases the basis of their
prosperity was farms purchased from Indian or mestizo small-
holders. In consequence, although the number of *labores* dropped
from about thirty in 1710 to around twelve in 1828, several ranchos
of 370 acres had been transformed into thriving commercial enterprises. For example, once the various sections of the rancho called

Santa Rosalía had been purchased from the heirs of the Juan Pablo Rico, the property was converted into a small estate which in 1781 required 45 plough oxen. With total assets valued at nearly 3,000 pesos, the inventory included a herd of 70 cows and listed 91 pesos owed by an unspecified number of peons.[42] Much the same was true of Patiña, a *labor* of over 1,000 acres situated between the haciendas of Palote and Cerrogordo. By 1807 the estate was appraised at a value of nearly 12,000 pesos and forty years later was leased at an annual rent of 1,000 pesos. At one time held by Agustín de Septién y Montero, Patiña had six different owners in a period of eighty years, before its purchase in 1828 by the widow of Francisco de Arcocha, who occupied the adjoining hacienda of Cerrogordo.[43] In the next decade, the estate was inherited by a younger son, and hence remained a separate enterprise.

Most of the rancheros who managed these large, commercial farms belonged to a comparatively restricted group of Spanish families who formed a stratum in rural society best defined in English terms as yeomen. At times the descendants or close relatives of hacendados, in other cases they rose to fortune as mayordomos. Although they were usually in a position to hire labour for the plough-teams, nevertheless, most of them were practical agriculturists whose livelihood depended on a close, personal supervision of their farms. In this respect the natural bias of legal documents in favour of financial success should not obscure the precarious nature of their station. The laws of inheritance, and still more the remorseless fertility of their womenfolk, exerted strong downward pressures. For although a favoured few found security in the priesthood, many men were obliged to leave the district to seek employment as miners or muleteers; others took service as mayordomos of haciendas and not a few were driven to lease land from the great estates, and in effect became tenant farmers. In short, these families inhabited a narrow promontory in agrarian society on which the impoverished children of former hacendados mingled with ambitious men of enterprise. When we hear of upward social mobility in the Mexican countryside, it was generally from this thin stratum that the new men emerged. Needless to say, in the civil wars which followed the attainment of Independence it was these rancheros who were the most successful in utilising their family network for military or political purpose.

A typical family of prosperous rancheros were the De la Fuentes of Concepción, who were closely related to the owners of the adjoining hacienda of Sauces, the Pérez de León. The first notice of their existence dates from 1711 when the widows of Manuel and Andrés de la Fuente, two sisters called Juana and Andrea de Almaguer, exhibited their deed titles for an hacienda of 14 caballerías or 1,470 acres which comprised four vecindades, issued by the town council in the middle decades of the previous century. As much as their Indian counterparts, these Spaniards obeyed the same rules of testamentary partition, with the result that each woman first took half the estate and then divided it equally in lots of $2\frac{1}{3}$ caballerías or 245 acres between a total of six children.[44] In the next generation, Blas de la Fuente was described as *dueño de recua*, the owner of commercial freight-teams, who was responsible for the shipment of silver to Mexico City.

The extent of his operations is shown by an inventory taken in 1734 which lists 130 mules, with equipment for 80, and a herd of 176 brood mares reserved for mule-breeding. Apparently he managed the lands of his brother and sister, since some seven caballerías are listed of which four had been cleared for ploughing. The item of 600 pesos in unpaid rent suggests that a good proportion of the farm was under lease. Despite these considerable assets, which were valued at a total of 7,378 pesos, De la Fuente was threatened with foreclosure by a merchant to whom he owed a thousand pesos. At this point his total debts amounted to 2,400 pesos. Whatever the outcome of this case, the family retained possession of the farm by then called Concepción, and indeed, his widow succeeded in adding to its area. However, in 1762 her six children, together with their cousins, ceded the estate, which by then comprised $9\frac{2}{3}$ caballerías to their brother-in-law, Juan Antonio Velásquez. The price of 2,770 pesos was in part met by loans and since this legacy of debt was never shaken off, in 1771 his heirs sold the farm to a distant relative, José Manuel de Almaguer.[45]

Turning to the other branch of the family, we find much the same pattern. In 1752 Andrés de la Fuente bequeathed a farm of 370 acres on which he maintained 28 plough oxen, a mule-team of 45 head and a herd of 255 brood mares. It is of interest to note that he lived in town rather than on his farm where the house was described as in ruinous condition. Despite assets worth over 4,000 pesos, his heirs were obliged to sell all the stock, other than the plough oxen, to meet his debts. The accounts here show that in the last six months of 1752 the mule-team earned 167 pesos taking goods to Guanajuato, and that the wages of the farm peons for 1753 amounted to 156 pesos.

Here, then, is a clear case of a relatively small property serving as the base of operations for a mixed enterprise which engaged in both stockraising and commercial freight, as well as the production of maize.

Over a period of over forty years, between 1750 and 1791, all the De la Fuente lands on this side of the family were purchased by Pedro Sánchez, who in six separate transactions pieced together a small estate of $9\frac{1}{3}$ caballerías, or 980 acres at a total cost of 1,420 pesos.[46] It is a commentary on the vicissitudes of fortune that in 1786 a young grandson of Andrés de la Fuente sought legal permission to sell the caballería he had inherited from his mother for 150 pesos, since he suffered 'extreme hunger and nakedness'.[47] By contrast, the Sánchez, who were closely related to the Guerrero family of Talayote in Rincón, prospered, since 1795 Lorenzo Sánchez, the son and heir of Pedro, purchased the thriving labor of Patiña. By 1807 this creole ranchero, with Guadalupe, as the de la Fuente lands were called, and Patiña, possessed assets worth nearly 22,000 pesos, which, set off against mortgages of only 6,600 pesos, meant that he was more wealthy than many hacendados in the district. However, he was later obliged to dispose of Patiña in order to meet debts incurred on his wife's estate. Moreover, in the next generation, although his son, the priest Bachiller Urbano Sánchez Guzmán, succeeded in extending the area of Guadalupe to 16 caballerías or nearly 1,700 acres, the other heirs pressed for a division of the property. Once this was effected in 1828, the inevitable round of sales began. In 1841, the eldest son, Angel Sánchez still retained about 580 acres to form a rancho called Trinidad, but in other cases we find sales of 100 acres or less.[48]

Closely allied to the De la Fuente both by marriage and in social status, was the Almaguer family who for at least one generation were the personification of enterprising creole rancheros. Although they must have settled in León during the seventeenth century, the first specific mention in the male line occurs in 1755, when José Cayetano de Almaguer (whose mother was Mariana de la Fuente) drew up his will where he admitted that at the time of this marriage thirty years before, his entire capital amounted to 100 pesos.[49] In true patriarchal fashion his bride, as befitted a farmer's daughter, brought a dowry which included a horse, two oxen, a bull, six calves, twenty lambs and two mules fitted for freight. How he supported a growing family of ten children he does not inform us, but his sons were all taught to read and write and one became a priest with the title of Bachiller.

It was only in 1750 that he bought a farm of 262 acres, paying 350 pesos cash and charging another 750 pesos on the farm as mortgage. Within five years the mortgage was redeemed and by then his stock comprised 108 cattle, 40 mares, 19 mules and 60 sheep.

In his will, Almaguer paid tributes to the enterprise and industry of his two sons, Juan Manuel and Vicente Ferrer, who had delayed their marriages well past the age of 25 in order to devote their efforts to building up the farm. In 1757, shortly after the death of their father, the two brothers raised a loan of 1,000 pesos from the parish priest at León, a sum they employed to acquire 5¾ caballerías, or about 600 acres, most of which came from the heirs of the Indian Nicolás Ramírez. Seven years later they had paid off the loan and acquired another seven caballerías for 430 pesos, the low price here an indication of its low quality. All these properties were in the general area Tepetates, with council titles dating from the late seventeenth century. The round of acquisitions terminated in 1777 when José Manuel, acting on his own account, bought Concepción, the former property of the De la Fuente family, for 1,800 pesos, putting up a mere 300 pesos in cash, the remainder being charged on the farm until he was able to raise the money. In some degree, this transaction represented a transfer of property within the same family, since José Manuel's first wife was María Luz de la Fuente, a prolific mother who, after presenting her husband with five children in as many years, found refuge in the grave.[50] It is surely significant that the Almaguer consistently relied on credit to acquire farmlands, apparently confident that their industry or enterprise would yield sufficient immediate returns as to enable them to redeem the loans within a relatively short period of years.

The two brothers differed considerably in business acumen, since in the 1790s, when they eventually divided the lands worked in common, Vicente Ferrer only received 5¼ caballerías, which on sale only brought him 2,000 pesos. By contrast, when José Manuel filed his will in 1800, he listed three separate ranchos – Los Lorenzos, Los Aguileras, and Concepción – which together comprised 15⅔ caballerías or 1,644 acres. With total assets valued at 13,317 pesos, the inventory included 40 plough oxen, a mule-team of 33 head and 96 cattle. It is noticeable that he lived in town and, as against a mere 500 pesos mortgage, had lent over 3,000 pesos to a variety of individuals.[51] As so often was the case, his death entailed the disruption of this capital accumulation. Out of three successive marriages, there survived six children, one of whom had entered the priesthood. In order to distribute the inheritance, one rancho was sold and another broken up and Francisco de Almaguer, who retained Concepción, had to raise 1,700 pesos in mortgages to satisfy the outstanding claims of his fellow heirs. Soon after, the onset of the Insurgency brought in its wake a considerable loss of livestock and in later years his widow and children found it ever more difficult to meet the heavy interest charges accruing from the mortgages incurred during the inheritance settlement. In 1841 the property was leased for a mere 308 pesos rent.[52] It is a commentary on the close family connexions of this group of rancheros that a daughter of Francisco de Almaguer (whose mother was a De la Fuente) should have married Angel Sánchez, a grandson of the Pedro Sánchez who bought Guadalupe from the other branch of the De la Fuente.

With the expansion of the haciendas ambitious rancheros were often driven to exploit the resources of marginal territory. In the hills to the north of León, beyond the immediate circle of estancia grants, lay a group of ranchos with eighteenth-century titles which, as elsewhere, were broken down into small-holdings by successive generations. In the case of the Candelas, however, we encounter a striking example of upward social mobility. The first reference occurs in 1758 when Francisco Candelas, possibly a descendant of former owners of the hacienda of Sauces, purchased the rancho of San Jorge from Francisco Javier de Marmolejo for 400 pesos, of which no less than 350 pesos consisted of transferred charges. His affairs prospered, since in 1766 he noted that whereas at marriage he had only possessed a team of twelve mules, he now owned ten yoke of oxen, two herds of brood mares, thirty cattle and a mule-team of 25 head. In addition to San Jorge, he had obtained a council grant of $5\frac{1}{2}$ caballerías of adjacent land, described as 'barren, foggy and without water'.[53] After his death his two sons failed to effect a legal partition, a decision which eventually brought them to dispute and litigation. Whereas Francisco, the younger, wished to plough up the best land, Nicolás, who had a considerable range of livestock, wanted to keep most of the rancho for pasture. Eventually, in 1793, after a certain display of knife-waving by Nicolás and his son Gordiano, Francisco sold his share in the property for a thousand pesos. Thereafter, the Cain of this family quarrel, Nicolás Candelas, extended his holdings with the purchase of two more ranchos situated in much the same area. By 1799 he proudly declared that as the result of his efforts he now owned 45 plough oxen, 45 transport mules and herds of 30 mares, 50 cattle and 180 sheep.[54]

In the next generation, the two sons of Nicolás each took a rancho and despite the upsets of the Insurgency, succeeded in increasing their fortunes. In 1823, for example, Gordiano Candelas, purchased the two *labores* of Los Naranjos and Coecillo which had once formed the base of operations for Francisco Javier de Marmolejo. In all, he paid 7,300 pesos (of which 3,200 were transferred mortgages), for 17¾ caballerías or 1,860 acres. At his death in 1844 his total assets were valued at 16,000 pesos, a sure sign that the economic depression which wasted the export economy of Mexico during the first decades after Independence did not prevent all individual accumulation of wealth. Similarly, his brother, Juan Manuel Candelas, bequeathed his children an estate worth 7,700 pesos. By this time, much of the original rancho of San Jorge was leased to tenants, since in 1843 some 150 pesos were owed on rents as against 281 pesos already paid.[55] It is of interest to note that in addition to several plots of land, he had also acquired nine small houses in León, with a combined value of 2,280 pesos.

Emphasis on the financial success of a few families should not obscure the difficulties experienced by the majority of rancheros. As the constant turnover in the ownership of small properties indicates, the rise to a modest degree of prosperity was often a fitful business which rarely extended beyond one generation. For example, in the last decade of the seventeenth century Pedro de Aguilera, an immigrant from the Peninsula, bequeathed a range of assets, among them the hacienda of Santa Ana. One of his sons became a landowner in San Pedro Piedragorda and another, Bachiller Pedro Aguilera, a priest, took over Santa Ana, an estate which in 1718 was sold for 2,500 pesos.[56] But the other children failed to maintain such a level of prosperity. True, one branch of the family retained possession of a rancho of seven caballerías situated in Tepetates. But the land was of low quality and in 1753 they sold it for only 430 pesos. Another branch, the heirs of Josefa de Aguilera y Vera, developed the rancho left to her by her brother, Bachiller Pedro. Divided into two farms of 157 acres the grand-children attained a certain fortune, since during the 1750s inventories reveal that in one case the assets amounted to 997 pesos and in the other, to no less than 3,100 pesos. Stockraising was as important as cultivation of maize, and in the second instance the possession of a mule-team of 34 head indicates engagement in commercial freight.[57]

The other line of this family of which we have notice descended the social scale. In 1725 Juan de Aguilera was obliged to sell his rancho of three caballerías to José de Austri for 500 pesos. A generation later, in a will filed in 1762, his son José declared that at marriage he did not own any goods worthy of mention, and that during this first marriage, he worked for José de Austri without any capital gain. His second wife brought as her dowry three yoke of oxen and six cows, and with this assistance he contrived to increase his holdings until he finally possessed twelve yoke of oxen, six horses and 18 cattle. Since he failed to list any land, we must conclude that he remained a tenant farmer all his life.[58] It was his son, Santiago Aguilera, who staged what might be called a social comeback when, in 1779, for 600 pesos, he purchased a rancho of 370 acres situated in the same area of Tepetates. Nevertheless, in 1800 he was obliged to cede a part of the land to the children of his first marriage. Then, in 1805 he and his son Miguel sold 2½ caballerías for 1,300 pesos, of which 400 pesos formed a mortgage raised to meet the claims of other heirs.[59] At much he same time, the notary register records the presence of one Vicente Aguilera, first as the lease-holder of the entire San Nicolás hacienda and then during the 1790s as a substantial tenant on the Santa Rosa, paying 400 pesos rent.[60] Here, then, is a family which survived at the very margin of their class, with each generation driven to seek a livelihood without much other assistance than a few inherited oxen.

In the ranchero class one mistake could destroy the work of a lifetime. In 1781 Miguel Durán, a creole farmer, acquired one caballería from the Urquieta family. Then, in 1784–86, his mestizo father-in-law, Domingo de Urenda, ceded him a further 262 acres. This round of purchases was completed in 1791 with the Santa Lucía, a rancho of 3½ caballerías, once owned by the Urquieta family. The total cost of these lands was 1,220 pesos.[61] Duran greatly improved the farms and succeeded in irrigating 154 acres for wheat-growing. By his death in 1822, despite losses incurred during the Insurgency, his fortune was valued at 4,500 pesos. But this respectable accumulation was lost through a very human error. In 1809 Durán, along with Domingo Echeveste, agreed to act as guarantor for Bernardo Muñoz Ledo, who had obtained the leasehold of the San Pedro del Monte hacienda for a contractual period of nine years. But the Insurgency of 1810 damned all hopes of meeting the terms of the contract and the guarantors were called upon to pay the deficit. In 1820 Durán borrowed 3,781 pesos to pay the Count of Valenciana, the owner of the San Pedro. But after his death, his widow was obliged to cede possession of the Santa Lucía and the other rancho called San Antonio. All the family retained was one caballería, and even this was soon divided, since in the 1840s one heir sold a field measuring 116 by 110 yards and another raised a 150 pesos loan on a 24 acre farm.[62]

It was the same disastrous error of judgement which brought an untimely end to the career of yet another prosperous ranchero family. In 1772 Domingo Echeveste, mayordomo on the Ibarrilla, an hacienda which was managed by his father for Agustín de Septién, purchased a rancho of 3½ caballerías situated just to the north of León from the widow of Cristóbal de Marmolejo for 1,400 pesos. Thereafter, over the years Echeveste slowly built up an estate of 8 caballerías, buying tracts of land from various members of the Castilla and Gómez families. However, from the outset, he was hampered by a 3,000-peso mortgage charged on his property, possibly the result of an overly ambitious attempt to buy a small hacienda in Lagos. By 1807, the San José del Cerrito was a thriving *labor*, with 18 yoke of oxen. Moreover, its proximity to León in some measure protected it from the Insurgent raids, so that in 1815 it was still worth 5,620 pesos.[63] However, all this patient effort proved of no avail when the Count of Valenciana exacted payment for the guarantee offered by Domingo Echeveste for Bernardo Muñoz Ledo. In 1820 San José del Cerrito, then assessed at nearly 10 caballerías or over 1,000 acres, was sold to José Francisco Arcocha, the owner of the neighbouring hacienda of Cerrogordo, for 5,800 pesos. Thereafter, in 1829 we find Miguel Echeveste buying several small strips of land on the outskirts of the town.[64]

But not all family fortunes had to be rebuilt each generation. There were two *labores* which were retained by the same family throughout our period. In the case of the Medina, who owned San Cayetano, a certain addiction to the priesthood appears to have reduced the flow of competing heirs who otherwise might have urged partition. By contrast, the Muñoz Ledo divided their property on one occasion, but subsequently the most successful line bought up the separated sections. The story starts in 1672 when Cristóbal Muñoz Ledo, the owner of a refining mill at Guanajuato, and probably an immigrant from the Peninsula, acquired a small estate of 10½ caballerías, or 1,470 acres, called Laborcita alias San Miguel de los Otates. In the next generation his children first divided their inheritance and then engaged in litigation. In the upshot, by 1743 the youngest son, Martín, held 8½ caballerías on which he maintained 17 yoke of oxen, 32 cattle, 26 mares and 12 transport mules, assets with a total value of just over 4,000 pesos. Apparently he had employed the 1,000 pesos dowry of his wife to buy the share of a sister.[65] At this time, a brother still worked another two caballerías on his own account.

In the third generation, Antonio Muñoz Ledo proved to be a man of enterprise who succeeded in reuniting the family estate. In 1779 his mother, Martín's widow, sold him 6½ caballerías for 1,500 pesos cash down. Not content with minding his own farm, in 1791 we find him acting as the general manager of all the estates in León owned by the dowager Countess of Valenciana. Equally important, he invested in a refining mill at Comanja. In consequence by 1804 he reckoned his assets at no less than 33,413 pesos, of which a considerable part consisted of crude ore awaiting refining. By this time Laborcita was valued at 11,521 pesos, with an inventory which included 103 oxen, 81 mules fitted out for freight, 83 mares with offspring, and a herd of 218 cattle. But this handsome fortune soon fell victim to the Insurgency, which destroyed the mining investments and halved the value of the agricultural estate. In 1821, despite the enlargement of Laborcita to 9½ caballerías through purchase from a brother, there were only 21 oxen, 9 mares and 20 mules. Much given to matrimony, Muñoz Ledo left twelve children from the last two of his four marriages.[66] The importance of individual enterprise is illustrated by the fate of his brother, Tomás, who in 1786 returned to León after a long sojourn in Valle de Santiago with total assets of a horse and three donkeys.[67] Other members of the family survived by renting entire haciendas, as in the disastrous case of San Pedro del Monte discussed above. Similarly, in 1807 one José María Muñoz Ledo brought a part of the Santa Rosalía rancho for 1,800 pesos.[68] Finally, we may note that although at some point in the nineteenth century Laborcita was divided into relatively small farms, nevertheless the Catastral map of 1922 lists several persons called Muñoz Ledo as owners of various sections. By then one Manuel Muñoz Ledo had already served a term as Governor of the State of Guanajuato.

## V

Viewed in retrospect, the sixty or more years between the 1680s and 1740s must have appeared like a golden age to the rancheros of León. For in this period the mounting curve of silver production at Guanajuato and Comanja was matched by a sustained growth in rural population which enabled the area of land under plough to be enlarged without driving up either the price of maize or the value of uncleared land. Indeed, with land and livestock in abundant supply, labour remained relatively scarce and hence comparatively expensive. Any trend towards the concentration of land in *labores* was offset by the issue of new vecindades in both the hills and in Tepetates. On many haciendas effective colonisation had yet to begin so that tenants were still welcomed at low or even nominal rents. In short, the structure of agricultural production still offered ample opportunity for all classes in the countryside to profit in varying degrees from the general renewal in economic activity.

But then, in the middle decades of the eighteenth century, especially in the three decades between 1740 and 1770, the pattern of land tenure in León was sharply modified by the incursions of mercantile capital. The creation of new haciendas and the enlargement of existing estates drastically reduced the area of land available for ranchero exploitation. At least 31,000 acres were absorbed by the expansion of the great estate. At the same time the pace of natural increase within the rural population now intensified the pressure on the remaining stock of land so that by the close of the century a number of former vecindades formed dense concentrations of small-holdings. Only a few ranchero families, for the most part Spaniards in status, succeeded in profiting from the urban boom which followed the discovery of the Valenciana mine at Guanajuato.

At no point, however, was there any danger of the disappearance of the small landowner. In 1828 the municipal authorities compiled a list of 56 ranchos. Included under this heading were three distinct types of property. First, there were twelve *labores*, which on average comprised ten caballerías or 1,055 acres. Next, we encounter about the same number of rancherías which, as their names suggest, were simply groups of small-holders, occupying areas which certainly did not exceed the limits of the original vecindad and indeed which may well have occupied much less. Finally, the remaining 32 ranchos

TABLE 36    *Estimated area of ranchero sector: León 1828*

|  | Average area | | Total area | |
|---|---|---|---|---|
|  | Caballerías | Acres | Caballerías | Acres |
| 12 Labores | 10 | 1,057 | 120 | 12,691 |
| 12 Rancherías | 3½ | 370 | 42 | 4,442 |
| 32 Ranchos | 3½ | 370 | 112 | 11,845 |
| Total: 56 | – | – | 274 | 28,978 |

*Source:* AHML, 1828 (3)–45.

consisted of small commercial farms and a number of properties for which we lack inventories or indication of size. The evidence here suggests that few of these farms exceeded 3½ caballerías or 370 acres. If these calculations prove acceptable, then we are left with the scheme of land tenure shown in Table 36.

In effect, the expansion of the great estate halved the supply of land open to the ranchero sector. Two observations of a comparative nature may provide a perspective on these calculations. The two adjacent haciendas of Duarte and Otates occupied a territory about equal in area to the entire holdings of the ranchos in León. But only about 6,500 acres of their land were cultivated since the remainder was composed of hill-side pasture. However, on the open plains of the Bajío the two haciendas of Sandía and Santa Ana, at this time owned by the Count of Valenciana, comprised some 35,000 acres, most of which was fertile and a considerable part irrigated. It was thus the primordial concessions of land in estancias as much as the subsequent engrossment of municipal lands which offered a barrier to the rise of small landowners in León.

Finally, we must emphasise that changes in the pattern of land tenure did not necessarily reduce rancheros to the level of peons. The practice of leasing land to a wide range of tenants ensured that farmers who possessed at least a yoke of oxen could always earn a livelihood without engaging in wage labour. It was not so much the loss of land as the later transition from cash tenancy to sharecropping which probably undermined the prosperity of the lower stratum of ranchero. Then again, the development of haciendas created a certain, if limited, range of employment as mayordomos. Similarly, the growing practice of leasing entire estates for a period of years offered opportunities for profit to the more enterprising rancheros. Moreover, by the early nineteenth century several haciendas were already on the point of disintegration. In short, although the structure of agricultural production in León was always determined by clear long-term influences, the pattern of land tenure and of employment was always complex and variegated.

## CHAPTER 8

# Agricultural prices and the demographic crises

## I

At present our knowledge of Bourbon Mexico is partial and inconsistent. Although progressive increments of quantitative data have effaced the traditional image of this epoch, the new lines of research have yet to be framed within a general perspective. Since the salient opened by our work on León may prove difficult to capture, it behoves us to examine its implications for the current debate. In any case, the history of a particular locality rarely makes much sense without some consideration of its place within the overall context.

The conventional view of Bourbon Mexico as the golden age of the colonial regime was first propounded in the last century by the conservative historian, Lucas Alamán, who painted a bitter contrast between the economic retrogression and political disorder which followed the attainment of Independence and the enlightened government and diffusion of prosperity which characterised the last decades of the previous century.[1] The burden of proof here rested on the array of statistics presented in the *Essai Politique* of Alexander von Humboldt. These figures showed that it was in the years after the general Inspection of José de Gálvez (1765–71) that silver output leapt forward from about 11 million pesos to a peak in 1805 of 25 million pesos. At much the same time overseas trade and government revenue registered substantial increases. Equally important, the Church tithe levied on agricultural production in the six leading dioceses rose by 60% from 1.19 million pesos in 1771 to 1.91 million in 1789. Moreover, behind this economic expansion lay the growth in population from an estimated $2\frac{1}{2}$ million in 1742 to a probable 6 million persons in 1810.[2] Here, then, was an epoch in which an enlightened administration proved remarkably successful in its promotion of economic progress.

Modern corroboration for this rosy picture came from a detailed examination of the silver-mining industry. True, the prerequisites for the increase in mintage consisted of a quadrupling of production at the royal mercury mines of Almadén in Spain and the natural growth of the Mexican population which provided an abundant supply of mine-labour. But the dramatic breakthrough of the 1770s sprang from the close collaboration of government and entrepreneurs. The price of mercury, the indispensable ingredient in silver refining, was halved and tax exemptions were conceded to enterprises of great risk or cost. In return, as mining profits rose, first mining entrepreneurs and then the great merchant houses invested in the construction of deep shafts and drainage adits designed to throw open further strata of ore.[3] The spectacular profits which rewarded these endeavours resulted from a singular union of a technology skilfully adapted to local circumstances, extensive fiscal concessions, and a wide range of capital investment.

The history of Guanajuato is especially instructive. For, whereas at the start of the eighteenth century the local industry depended for its credit on the silver banks operated by trading firms in Mexico City, by the 1750s local merchants such as Agustín and Martín de Septién y Montero had come to provide the main financial backing for new ventures. Then during the 1770s, as the discovery of the Valenciana transformed the structure of production, leading miners such as Antonio de Obregón and Manuel de Otero became the dominant figures.[4] In certain measure Guanajuato was thus liberated from the financial control of Mexico City capital.

The same study, however, revealed that the rate of growth within the mining industry slowed considerably by the close of the century. Whether the decisive agent here was resource depletion accompanied by rising costs, or whether the decline in mercury supplies caused by the British naval blockades of this period were more important, still remains an open question. In any case, the decisive fall in output occurred after 1810 as a direct result of the depredations of the Insurgents. More important for our purpose, was the discovery that the resurgence in silver production in part depended on a reduction in the real earnings of the work-force. During the 1790s, the owners of the Valenciana took steps to eliminate the customary system whereby all pick and blast men received a share of the ore cut each day. In Zacatecas a similar measure was enforced by the owners of the Quebradilla mine.[5]

The chief challenge to the optimistic, nostalgic view of Bourbon Mexico, came from research in the domestic economy. For here a series of studies depicted a desperate world living close to the margins of subsistence, still afflicted by the twin scourges of epidemic disease and famine. In his pioneering review of the movement of maize price in Mexico City, Enrique Florescano argued that, apart from seasonal fluctuations which pushed prices one or two reales beyond the annual level, there was an identifiable cycle of harvest prices marked by crises of approximately decennial incidence. These agricultural crises – defined by dramatic upward surges in maize prices – provoked extensive dislocation in the economic life of town and country alike, leading to famine, internal migration, banditry and, in the worst cases, the death of thousands. The great epidemics of this period, so Florescano averred, were all 'closely associated' with this cycle.[6] Equally important, although for most of the century prices fluctuated from decade to decade without any apparent long-term trend, during the 1790s a permanent upward movement occurred. By contrast, wages remained at their previous level. Moreover, in the same years, so Florescano asserted, the great estates extended their control over agricultural production. The result was an explosive situation in which recurrent epidemics and famine united with a pervasive downward drift in the levels of subsistence to provoke widespread popular discontent. This radical reassessment of the late eighteenth century had the obvious merit of accounting for the enthusiastic violence with which the Mexican masses greeted the Insurgency led by Hidalgo and Morelos.

Further challenge to the former emphasis on economic growth came from several demographic studies. For the Mixteca Alta in southern Mexico Sherburne F. Cook and Woodrow Borah calculated that from the middle decades of the seventeenth century the population began to grow in number so that, by the period 1720–60, the coefficient of population movement registered positive annual values of over one per cent, only thereafter to decline steadily to reach a nadir of 0.16 in the decade 1790–1800. Although the curve later moved upwards, it was not until 1860 that the previous level of over one per cent was regained.[7] These computations suggest that the rapid economic increase of the last Bourbon decades in certain measure rested on the prior demographic growth of the years before 1760. Moreover, in grim fashion they indicate the underlying unity of the century 1760–1860.

The trends in Mixteca Alta, identified by the method of graphic interpolation between fixed census points, was confirmed by no less than three separate district surveys, all based on parish records. Claude Morin on Santa Inés Zacatelco, Tomás Calvo on Acatzingo and Cecilia Rabell Romero on San Luis de la Paz, all found that these communities experienced an unexpectedly rapid period of population growth in the years between 1660 and the 1720s. Leaving to one side the unresolved question of persistent under-registration of infant burials, the recorded series of burials and baptisms yield an average annual rate of increase of about 2.5%. But then after 1727–36, this sharp upward curve fell steadily to about 1% until 1760, and then flattened towards a horizontal during the years which followed.[8] In all three parishes the last two decades of the eighteenth century were characterised by a secular arrest in demographic growth. It is significant that Morin and Calvo both fix upon the matlazahuatl epidemic of 1737 – a form of typhus or typhoid fever – as the turning point in the history of the two southern parishes. In each case about a quarter of the population died, and with a heavy proportion of adults among the deceased, the reproductive capacity of these communities was permanently impaired. If we note that Donald B. Cooper described an entire series of epidemics in which yellow fever, smallpox and typhus carried off thousands of victims in Mexico City during the years 1761–62, 1779, 1784–87, 1797–98 and 1813–14, then the fatal impact of disease cannot be over-estimated.[9] But the relation between agricultural crisis and epidemic remains less certain. For although in some instances the malnutrition that resulted from poor harvests and high prices preceded and intensified the incidence of disease, in general, as Morin argues, the geographical incursions of the great epidemics extended far beyond the limits of local droughts or frosts.[10] Whatever the causes, all three studies agree that the late eighteenth century witnessed an acceleration in the rhythm of disease and famine. For the indigenous population of these parishes, the Indian summer of the colonial regime proved but a bitter winter.

The place occupied by León in this debate is ambiguous. By reason of its frontier position the district experienced a remarkable growth in both agricultural production and population during the course of the eighteenth century. Moreover, the distribution of landownership faithfully reflected the prevailing balance of financial power at Guanajuato. For here also the early predominance of Mexico City capital, embodied in the vast possessions of González del Pinal and the Mariscal de Castilla, made way for the rise of local merchants such as José de Austri and Agustín de Septién. Similarly, during the 1780s the Count of Valenciana became the chief territorial magnate in the district. Unfortunately, the loss of tithe returns after 1769 prevents any comparison of the curve of agricultural and silver production, but if the example of Silao be applied then the 1770s opened a decade of expansion which was only terminated by the great famine of 1785–86. Moreover, the investments in dams and irrigation channels promoted by the Count of Valenciana and his associates indicated an intensification of land use, a trend certainly reflected in the rising value of land.

It is the evidence on population movement already presented in Chapter 3 that questions the notion of a general demographic crisis in the last years of the eighteenth century. True, the annual rate of increase, measured in terms of recorded baptisms and burials, declined sharply from an improbable 4.1% in the quinquennium 1756–60 to 0.85% in the tragic decade 1784–93. But in subsequent years the absolute number of baptisms rose markedly and by 1828, as a result of internal migration and natural increase, the overall population stood at an estimated 50,000 souls, a total almost double the number of 1793. By then the rate of annual increase was 1.26%. In short, although León fully participated in the roster of epidemic, famine and war which afflicted all Mexico, the persistent excess of registered baptisms over burials suggests that the population continued to grow in number throughout the period.

That León was not alone in its resilience in the face of adversity was demonstrated by Sherburne F. Cook and Woodrow Borah in their study of New Galicia, a zone enlarged to include the adjoining sections of Michoacán and Zacatecas.[11] With the assistance of graphic interpolation, they calculated that the annual rate of population increase remained at the remarkably high level of 2.18–2.64% throughout the entire eighteenth century. Moreover, if during the decade 1800–10 this value dropped precipitously to 0.69%, in subsequent years it averaged just over one per cent, a figure more than sufficient to assure continued growth.

In these calculations we encounter evidence of a remarkable divergence in the demographic history of the different regions of Mexico. But it is a divergence which is as much ethnic as regional. For it was the predominantly Indian districts of Mixteca Alta, Zacatelco, Acatzingo and San Luis de la Paz which experienced a reversal of their previously high rates of natural increase. It was the predominantly *casta* and Spanish districts of New Galicia and León which witnessed a continuous growth in the overall number of their inhabitants. The contrast is strengthened still further if we recall that Morin and Calvo observed that the small group of mestizo and Spanish families in their districts were less susceptible to the effects of epidemic and came to represent a larger proportion of the local population. Similarly, at León the Indian share of total baptisms dwindled from nearly 60% at the start of the century to under 30% by 1800. Further confirmation of this distinction was provided by the intendant of Michoacán who reported that although the population of his province had doubled in the forty years between 1750–90, the Indian villages had not participated in this increase, and indeed in some cases had declined in number.[12] Needless to say, since the greatest concentration of Indian communities was to be found in central and Southern Mexico, the divergence in demographic fortunes of the Indians as against the *casta* and creoles entailed a decisive shift in the balance of agricultural settlement. Viewed from the long perspective of colonial history, Meso-America had entered a phase of secular stagnation, whereas the frontier zones north of the river Lerma, the Bajío and New Galicia, were on the march. The growth and prosperity of Bourbon Mexico was apparently quite localised.

## II

But what of the crises which afflicted the population of León during this period? Some answers to these questions can be obtained from a comparison of the curve of annual maize prices with the series of recorded burials. For although the burial rate is the least faithful of the life statistics recorded at this time, it is also the most interesting. It is the barometer of social disaster. Its astonishing oscillations register with remarkable fidelity the incidence and impact of both epidemic and harvest failure. It forms the best commentary on the work of Florescano and his school.

Before opening the discussion, however, two premises must be accepted: (a) During the years 1700–1830, the burial register understates by an unknown quantum the actual number of deaths. This rate of under-registration probably declined in the course of the century; it is least apparent after 1830. (b) During months of 'social crisis', the degree of under-registration did not decline relative to the 'normal' years preceding or following them; if anything, a greater proportion of deaths went unnoted. These assumptions are our minimum demands for the subsequent debate. They undermine the possibility of any exact comparison of the effects of two social disasters widely distant in time. They admit, however, the comparison of two crises in the same decade, and with the 'normal' years preceding them.

To start with, we must first ascertain the curve of maize prices and the volume of annual production. Table 37 provides prices and volume for León and Silao; Figure 1 describes the conflated León–Silao price curve. The physical similarity and proximity of these adjacent parishes precludes any marked variation in their weather or production. Calculated on the basis of the tithe-collectors' reports, the prices represent annual averages, an admittedly unsatisfactory figure, since it excludes seasonal variations. The collectors were paid on commission, so it is probable that they sold the tithe maize in the summer months when supplies were most scarce. Their prices, therefore, may be somewhat higher than the overall market price for any given year.

TABLE 37    *Annual prices and production of maize: tithe returns in the parishes of Leon and Silao 1660–1789*

| Years | Average annual prices, reales per fanega | | Volume in fanegas (one tenth of production) | |
|---|---|---|---|---|
| | León | Silao | León | Silao |
| 1660 | – | – | 2,493 | 1,243* |
| 1661 | 10 | 10 | 822 | 589* |
| 1662 | 28 | 20 | 2,450 | 1,316 |
| 1663 | 11 | 12 | 4,541 | 1,114* |
| 1664 | 6.5 | 8.1 | 4,388 | 2,102* |
| 1665 | 4 | 5 | 1,192 | 731* |
| 1666 | 8 | 8 | 3,611 | 1,866 |
| 1667 | 7 | 7.3 | 1,381 | 718 |
| 1668 | 14.4 | – | 1,906 | 1,641 |
| 1669 | 12 | 12 | 3,741 | 2,982 |
| 1670 | 4.8 | – | 4,836 | 2,783 |
| 1671 | 2.5 | 3 | 2,573 | 1,829 |
| 1672 | 4 | 4 | 4,213 | 2,719 |
| 1673 | 8 | 8 | 3,462 | 2,401 |
| 1674 | 12 | 12 | 4,042 | 2,359 |
| 1675 | 5.2 | 4.3 | 5,394 | 3,102 |
| 1676 | 4 | 3.8 | 3,823 | 2,324 |
| 1677 | 3.2 | 3.7 | 2,258 | 1,701 |
| 1678 | 8.5 | 8 | – | – |
| 1679 | – | – | 2,984 | 1,803 |
| 1680 | 11 | 10.7 | – | – |
| 1681 | – | – | 1,036 | 1,129 |
| 1682 | – | 11.4 | 2,604 | 2,517 |
| 1683 | 8 | 8 | 3,324 | 2,649 |
| 1684 | 4.8 | 5 | – | – |
| 1685 | – | – | 1,716 | 2,234 |
| 1686 | – | – | 1,039 | 1,084 |
| 1687 | 16 | 16 | 4,105 | 2,909 |
| 1688 | – | – | – | – |
| 1689 | – | – | 3,049 | 2,558 |

| Years | Average annual prices, reales per fanega | | Volume in fanegas (one tenth of production) | |
|---|---|---|---|---|
| | León | Silao | León | Silao |
| 1690 | 3.5 | 3.2 | 3,471 | 2,781 |
| 1691 | 4.5 | 4.5 | 5,545 | 4,386 |
| 1692 | 10.4 | 9.7 | – | 2,004 |
| 1693 | – | 14 | 5,311 | 4,259 |
| 1694 | 6 | 6 | 3,138 | – |
| 1695 | 8.6 | – | 2,842 | 2,293 |
| 1696 | 24.9 | 22.1 | 703 | 915 |
| 1697 | 32 | 30.5 | 2,630 | 2,998 |
| 1698 | 8 | 8 | 4,177 | 2,868 |
| 1699 | 6 | 7.7 | – | 4,630 |
| 1700 | 5 | 6 | 6,704 | 2,928 |
| 1701 | 11 | 10 | 6,063 | – |
| 1702 | 6.4 | – | 2,100 | 2,447 |
| 1703 | 7.1 | 8 | 4,601 | 4,334* |
| 1704 | 8 | 8 | 5,691 | – |
| 1705 | 5 | – | 4,400 | – |
| 1706 | 4.7 | – | 4,342 | – |
| 1707 | 5.9 | – | – | – |
| 1708–12 | missing | – | – | – |
| 1713 | – | – | 5,586 | – |
| 1714 | 30.5 | – | 5,122 | – |
| 1715 | 4.3 | – | 6,151 | 8,391 |
| 1716 | 3.1 | 1.9 | 4,682 | 5,781 |
| 1717 | 2.3 | 1.9 | 3,000 | – |
| 1718 | 7.9 | – | – | – |
| 1719–22 | missing | – | – | – |
| 1723 | – | – | 5,057 | 7,317* |
| 1724 | 3.1 | – | 3,742 | 4,840* |
| 1725 | 3.5 | 4 | 4,883 | 5,672* |
| 1726 | 7 | 7.5 | 2,449 | 3,784* |
| 1727 | 11.6 | 14.5 | – | 8,653* |
| 1728 | – | 3 | 4,972 | 5,576 |
| 1729 | 4.2 | 4 | 3,725 | 2,631 |
| 1730 | 11.9 | 12 | 5,842 | 6,430 |
| 1731 | 8.9 | 8 | 5,061 | 3,493 |
| 1732 | 8.8 | 8.5 | 4,355 | 6,786 |
| 1733 | 5 | 4 | 5,641 | – |
| 1734 | 9 | – | 4,274 | – |
| 1735 | 9 | – | 6,029 | – |
| 1736 | 6 | – | 7,482 | – |
| 1737 | 3 | – | 6,720 | – |
| 1738 | 4.6 | – | 4,063 | 5,346 |
| 1739 | 8.9 | 10.6 | 5,582 | 5,233 |
| 1740 | 8.7 | – | 4,499 | 4,228 |
| 1741 | 11.5 | 13 | 6,331 | 5,321 |
| 1742 | 11 | 14 | 7,708 | 6,480 |
| 1743 | 4.6 | 5.8 | 6,596 | 5,212 |
| 1744 | 4.3 | 6 | 8,334 | 6,452 |
| 1745 | 4.3 | 6 | 7,531 | 5,969 |
| 1746 | 7.9 | 10 | 4,948 | 4,781 |

TABLE 37—*continued*

| Years | Average annual prices, reales per fanega | | Volume in fanegas (one tenth of production) | |
|---|---|---|---|---|
| | León | Silao | León | Silao |
| 1747 | 9.8 | 12 | 7,057 | 7,292 |
| 1748 | 5.2 | – | 4,951 | 5,313 |
| 1749 | – | 12 | 974 | 1,008 |
| 1750 | 36.3 | 34.5 | 4,528 | 3,732 |
| 1751 | 16 | 14 | 11,041 | 12,506 |
| 1752 | 3 | 5 | 8,543 | 9,344 |
| 1753 | 2 | 3.5 | 5,865 | 8,217 |
| 1754 | 3 | 3.9 | 6,854 | 6,912 |
| 1755 | 5 | 6 | 4,935 | 8,172 |
| 1756 | 7 | 8.6 | 8,089 | – |
| 1757 | 3.5 | – | 10,555 | 12,578 |
| 1758 | 4 | 5 | 9,212 | 10,549 |
| 1759 | 4.4 | 5.7 | 5,833 | 5,674 |
| 1760 | 7.6 | 8.6 | 5,773 | 6,699 |
| 1761 | 11.4 | 13.1 | 3,280 | 4,297 |
| 1762 | 13.5 | 11.3 | 9,130 | 10,276 |
| 1763 | 3.1 | 4.2 | 9,649 | 7,363 |
| 1764 | 3.4 | – | 5,579 | 7,905 |
| 1765 | 6.3 | 6 | 2,400 | 3,624 |
| 1766 | 8.2 | 7.8 | 10,679 | 6,803 |
| 1767 | 2.9 | 4.2 | 5,319 | – |
| 1768 | 4.6 | – | – | 6,591 |
| 1769 | – | 6.8 | – | 7,071 |
| 1770 | – | 10.2 | – | 8,434 |
| 1771 | – | 10.3 | – | 6,689 |
| 1772 | – | 14.2 | – | 2,731 |
| 1773 | – | 12.2 | – | 8,236 |
| 1774 | – | 12.6 | – | 19,293 |
| 1775 | – | 6.7 | – | 8,456 |
| 1776 | – | 8.5 | – | 22,684 |
| 1777 | – | 4.8 | – | 15,126 |
| 1778 | – | 5.5 | – | 17,838 |
| 1779 | – | 8.1 | – | 10,378 |
| 1780 | – | 10.9 | – | 17,179 |
| 1781 | – | 12.5 | – | 18,855 |
| 1782 | – | 7.4 | – | 22,709 |
| 1783 | – | 4.4 | – | 11,954 |
| 1784 | – | 14 | – | 5,123 |
| 1785 | – | 21.2 | – | 1,825 |
| 1786 | – | 48 | – | 10,343 |
| 1787 | – | 12.9 | – | 20,081 |
| 1788 | – | 6.5 | – | 8,155 |
| 1789 | – | 13.8 | – | – |

* Two-ninths of tithe already deducted.

*Note:* Since the maize harvest occurred in late autumn, it was consumed the following calendar year, so that the prices of any year were determined by the harvest of the preceding calendar year.

*Sources:* ACM 846, 848, 854, 857, tithe collectors' reports.

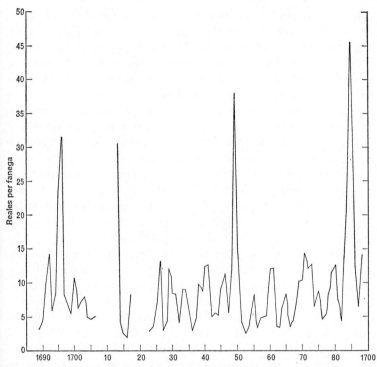

Figure 1    Maize prices: León and Silao 1690–1788

To judge from Table 37, the curve of maize prices in León and
Silao followed no fixed pattern. Instead, annual prices continually
oscillated between troughs of 2–4 reales and crests of 12–15 reales.
Within each year seasonal fluctuations tipped summer prices one or
two reales beyond the annual average. During a period of 92
recorded years, the median annual price at León was 6 reales a
fanega, and in three quarters of these occasions, the average level
never surpassed 8 reales. Prior to 1769 the long-term trend was
downward, since whereas before 1717 in only 28% of listed years
were annual averages pitched at 4 reales or below, after 1723 some
41% failed to rise above this low level. Moreover, the years between
1752 and 1768 were remarkable for their persistently low prices,
with an overall median of only 4.5 reales a fanega. At Silao, perhaps
by reason of its proximity to Guanajuato, prices were usually,
although by no means invariably, about two reales higher than in
León. Equally important, after 1769 the Silao series manifests an
upward movement, with the median close to 10 reales.

But the minor fluctuations are not the whole story. Thrusting through these ranges were the four great peaks of 1695–96, 1713, 1749–50 and 1785–86, when prices vaulted to 30, 36 and even 48 reales a fanega. An examination of the volume of production confirms this impression. The minor price rises were caused by poor or mediocre harvests. The continuous variations in both the incidence and quantity of rainfall on the Mexican altiplanicie alone precluded any annual constancy in crop yield. Both prices and volume of production could double or halve from year to year, although generally the variation was rarely so precipitous. The surplus of the bumper crop was consumed in the poor year. Standing in marked contrast to this continual oscillation, were the four great harvest failures of 1696, 1713, 1749 and 1784–85, when production plummeted to a fifth and even a tenth of normal yield, being in each case preceded or followed by an 'ordinary' poor harvest.

A radical distinction must be drawn between times of hardship and catastrophe. Poor harvests tightened belts, nearly total crop failure drove thousands to an early grave. Corroboration for this distinction can be obtained from some estimates of food consumption provided by Charles Gibson.[13] He calculated that an average Indian family ate 10–20 fanegas of maize a year. In an 'ordinary' year of high prices, i.e. when maize cost 14 reales a fanega, their staple food thus cost them $17\frac{1}{2}$ to 35 pesos a year. This, of course, represents an overstatement. Most of Mexico's rural population, certainly in León, had access, either personally or by family connection, to a milpa plot, however small in dimension. Many received rations of maize as part of their salary. In general, as Florescano correctly argues, the effect of mediocre or poor harvests was to increase the profits of those landowners with dry, ample storage for the surplus yield of good years.[14] The poorer classes had then to spend more of their income on food, and probably many went hungry in the months preceding the next harvest. It is doubtful, however, whether many actually died of starvation. In conclusion, therefore, it seems best to restrict the term 'crisis' to the great catastrophes of harvest failure and famine. Death is its best measure.

Corroboration for this argument can be obtained from an examination of the burial rates presented in Figures 2–4. The dramatic consequences of the two great crises of 1749–50 and 1785–86 require no emphasis. Moreover, our starting premise – that possible variations in under-registration precludes comparisons of points widely separate in time – clearly applies here. It is obvious, however, that

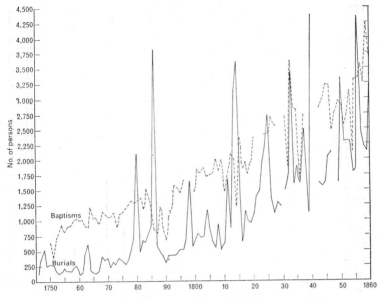

Figure 2   Baptisms and burials: León 1750–1850

the very poor harvest of 1784 followed by near failure in 1785 killed thousands in what was probably the greatest social catastrophe to occur in Mexico since the sixteenth century.

  What the burial curve does not register are the minor fluctuations in prices. Instead, it indicates the severe and periodic impact of the epidemic disease of matlazahuatl in 1737–38 and 1762–63; of small-pox in 1779–80, 1798 and 1804. But can the incidence of these epidemics be associated with previous or simultaneous poor harvests, and hence with malnutrition? The question admits no easy response. In the first place, if the phenomena are simultaneous then either could provoke the other, i.e. it is quite possible that epidemics pre-vented complete harvesting of the year's crops. Moreover, on several occasions, prices crested without any effect on the burial rate. Neither the epidemics of 1737–38 nor 1779–80 were preceded by poor harvests: they occurred in the same year, in the latter case the epidemic was well established before the harvest was collected. For the attack of 1762–63, however, a case can be made. It was preceded by mediocre harvests in 1760–61, in which summer prices pushed as high as 16 reales. Admittedly, more deaths occurred in 1763, after the good autumn harvest of 1762, but malnutrition may well have assisted the initial assault of matlazahuatl. In general,

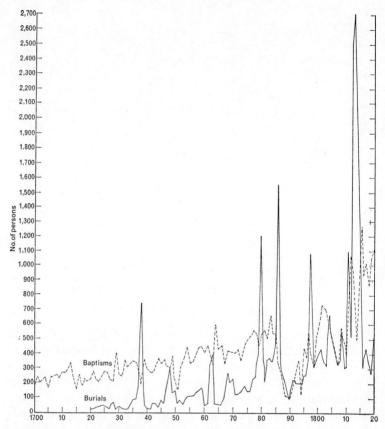

Figure 3    Baptisms and burials of Indians: León 1720–1820

our evidence does not justify the assertion of causality. Minor rises in prices rarely provoked epidemics; indeed, at times they were possibly their result.

The impact of disease extends far beyond its relation to the oscillation of maize prices. For Mexico City, Cooper has demonstrated a rising incidence of epidemics during the period 1762–1813. The burial register of León faithfully reflects each of these visitations. What attacked the capital, attacked the Bajío. The mysterious epidemic of 1813–14, variously described as typhus, yellow fever, smallpox, or matlazahuatl, proved peculiarly virulent. Nor did Independence witness any abatement of these ravages. Despite the introduction of vaccination, in 1840 thousands died of smallpox. Cholera, the nineteenth-century newcomer, made its appearance in

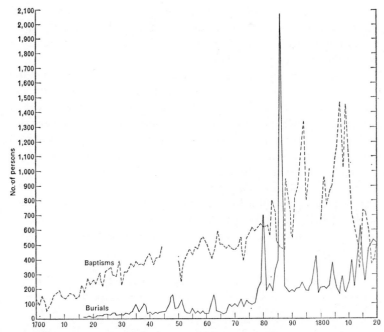

Figure 4   Baptisms and burials of *castas*: León 1720–1820

1833 and 1850. In León two further, unexplained sudden increases in deaths occurred in 1825 and 1856, the former possibly in part due to measles.[15] Lacking any curve of maize prices, we cannot assess the effects of harvest failure during this period.

Some notion of the dimension of these social disasters can be obtained from an inspection of Figures 2–4. Burials suddenly increased by multiples of three, five, and seven. Moreover, during these times of stress many deaths undoubtedly went unrecorded. At the same time, exaggeration should be avoided. Here are no plagues of Black Death violence. In 1780, for example, at the height of the smallpox epidemics, 2,049 deaths were registered in León. Even if Romero's figure of 18,500 inhabitants be accepted, then the proportion of deaths amounted to about a ninth of the population. Admittedly, as we shall see below, this value rose to a possible fifth during the great famine of 1785–86.

The danger of exaggeration can be further illustrated from the cholera attack of 1833. The parish priest kept special note of the victims of this disease, which afflicted the town during the three months from 2 August to 1 November. In all it killed 1,645 persons.

Since the ordinary death rate at this time was c. 1,680, the effect of cholera was to double the number of deaths for that year. A similar pattern occurred in 1850 when the same disease accounted for 1,403 deaths out of 3,344 recorded burials.

In general, epidemics carried off the least resistant members of the community, that is to say, Indians and children. The traditional notion that matlazahuatl – possibly a form of typhus – was a peculiarly Indian illness receives confirmation in the burial register of León. But in fact, expressed in absolute numbers, Indians always contributed more epidemic victims than the castas and Spaniards. Certainly this generalisation applied to the three smallpox epidemics of 1779–80, 1798 and 1804. A comparison of the years 1771–75 with 1779–80 shows that the Indian share of burials rose from 48.2% to 57.8%. During the 1798 attack, at a time when the Indian share of baptisms had fallen to under 30%, their proportion of total deaths leapt to 66%.

TABLE 38    *Infant mortality during smallpox epidemics and famine 1779–1804*

|  | Smallpox | | | Famine |
|---|---|---|---|---|
|  | 1779–80 | 1798 | 1804 | 1786 |
| Spaniards |  |  |  |  |
| TT. | 249 | 141 | 111 | 152 |
| Child | 123 | 66 | 20 | 27 |
| % | 49.3 | 46.8 | 18.0 | 17.8 |
| Castas |  |  |  |  |
| TT. | 914 | 413 | 372 | 2,075 |
| Child | 533 | 281 | 175 | 808 |
| % | 58.3 | 68.0 | 47.0 | 41.8 |
| Indians |  |  |  |  |
| TT | 1,601 | 1,077 | 659 | 1,553 |
| Child | 1,182 | 755 | 399 | 597 |
| % | 73.8 | 70.1 | 60.5 | 38.5 |
| Total |  |  |  |  |
| TT. | 2,764 | 1,631 | 1,142 | 3,780 |
| Child | 1,838 | 1,102 | 594 | 1,432 |
| % | 66.5 | 67.5 | 52.0 | 37.8 |

*Note:* TT equals total deaths; child equals total párvulo deaths.
*Source:* Registro de entierros. Archivo Parroquial de León.

In the second place, epidemics struck sharply at the children of all ethnic categories. During the smallpox attacks of 1779–80 and 1798 párvulos accounted for two thirds of all deaths. For Spaniards, the proportion of infants among their recorded burials more than doubled. The castas experienced a similar increase. Among the

Indians, the proportion of children leapt from the usual 51% to over 70%. The introduction of vaccination in 1804 somewhat lowered infant mortality for all groups, but fully succeeded only with the Spaniards.[16] In these statistics of mortality, further explanation can be found for the discrepancy in the Indian share of baptisms and burials. At the same time, however, the very preponderance of children in deaths caused by epidemic suggests that these attacks affected the population's capacity for growth far less than might have been expected. In the years immediately after each epidemic baptisms at once increased.

## III

The harvest failure of 1785 has been described by Charles Gibson as 'the most disastrous single event in the whole history of colonial maize agriculture'. Enrique Florescano has devoted several elequent pages depicting its tragic effect on the population. Donald Cooper has defined the various diseases which afflicted the underfed masses. Alexander von Humboldt, reporting contemporary opinion, estimated that no less than 300,000 persons died of this combination of hunger and disease.[17] Since León did not escape the common fate, it may prove helpful to examine in detail the stages and effects of this great crisis.

The tithe records for Silao demonstrate that it was not just one harvest failure which caused so much human suffering. The bumper crop of 1782 was followed first by a mediocre year, and then, in 1784, by a decidedly poor harvest in which production fell to about a third of previous average yields. At this stage prices from a very low level of 4.4 reales a fanega in 1782, rose to 21.2 reales in 1784, their highest point since 1749. Tragedy began when, in August 1785, sudden early frosts destroyed the grain. The autumn harvest yielded perhaps a sixth or seventh of previous years; it amounted to under a tenth of the 1782 crop. At once prices leapt to the unparalleled level of 48 reales. It was at this stage, in the last months of 1785, and for most of 1786, that hundreds died of starvation or the numerous infirmities to which malnutrition exposed them.

Although the tithe records for León are lost, the accounts of the municipal granary throw light on the local sequence of events. The cabildo appointed a special commissioner to buy and sell maize to the public. This active intervention in the market at least ensured a minimum supply of grain even if it did not force down prices.[18]

In 1784, the pósito sold 6,466 fanegas at prices ranging from 7 to 14 reales. In the following year, with stocks clearly exhausted, it sold no more than 3,700 fanegas at 30–32 reales. At this point in December 1785 the cabildo borrowed 20,000 pesos from the diocesan court at Valladolid.[19] In 1786, cash in hand, the granary bought and sold 7,694 fanegas of maize, just over half of which it sold at the prevailing rate of 48 reales. Perhaps its most significant achievement was to obtain 3,547 fanegas at an unspecified low price and to sell the entire consignment at 20–21 reales. These accounts further demonstrate that the mediocre harvest of 1786 itself, no doubt in part caused by lack of grain to sow, kept prices still high. From March to September 1787 the granary bought various quantities of maize at prices varying from 17 to 21 reales.[20] It was only in September with a bumper crop, that prices at last fell to 3–4 reales a fanega.

Despite the strenuous efforts of public authorities, both ecclesiastical and civil, the prolonged agricultural crisis provoked a major social tragedy. Thousands died an early death. Its strictly economic effects, however, were less severe. Silver production, for example, dropped by less than a fifth in 1785–87, and regained its former level as early as 1788. Similarly overseas trade followed its own rhythm. But the most striking commentary on the crisis is not to be found in such indices of production and exchange, but rather in the parochial registers scattered throughout the colony. It is only there that its local incidence and respective severity can be measured.

All three vital series presented in Table 39 demand separate

TABLE 39   *Maize prices and burials: León and Silao 1782–88*

|  | Silao | | León | | |
|---|---|---|---|---|---|
| Year | Maize tithes (in fanegas) | Average prices (in reales) | Baptisms | Burials | Marriages |
| 1782 | 22,709 | 7.4 | 1,225 | 679 | 317 |
| 1783 | 11,954 | 4.4 | 1,533 | 612 | 295 |
| 1784 | 5,123 | 14.0 | 1,341 | 760 | 251 |
| 1785 | 1,825 | 21.2 | 1,101 | 917 | 159 |
| 1786 | 10,343 | 48.0 | 861 | 3,780 | 79 |
| 1787 | 20,081 | 12.9 | 814 | 580 | 250 |
| 1788 | 8,155 | 6.5 | 1,211 | 465 | 363 |
| 1789 | – | 13.8 | 900 | 394 | 202 |

*Note:* The harvest was taken during the late autumn, so that current prices were determined by the previous year's harvest.
*Sources:* ACM, 857 tithe collector's reports; APL, registers.

discussion, especially since, when broken down by ethnic category, they reveal their usual perplexing trends. To take burials first, it must be emphasised that it is greatly married by omissions. In February 1787 the Bishop of Valladolid requested estimates from his parish priests of the number of deaths in the last year. Most replied that during the famine hundreds of unrecorded deaths had occurred in the fields and streets. The cura of San Miguel el Grande, for example, counted 3,356 burials but reckoned unregistered deaths at another 1,000.[21] Obviously, such high rates of deficiency render all analysis suspect. Nevertheless, comparison of the available figures with their equivalents of the 1779–80 smallpox epidemics yields instructive results, sufficient to justify the attempt.

In the first place, the 1786 disaster was the only occasion in the eighteenth century when, in absolute numbers, castas provided more corpses than the Indians. In both the smallpox attacks of 1779–80 and 1798, despite their preponderant share in baptisms, they were easily outnumbered by Indians. In 1786, however, their total of burials increased by a multiple of six to eight, depending on the year selected for comparison – a ratio similar to that of the Indians. By contrast, little more than double the average number of Spaniards died that year. Secondly, as Table 38 indicates, there was a striking difference in the age composition of recorded deaths during the epidemics and the great famine.

In contrast to smallpox which especially attacked children, the great famine carried off both infants and adults alike. Indeed, for the Spaniards and Indians, the proportion, as distinct to the number, was nearly identical to that of normal years. The castas diverged somewhat from this pattern; even so, about three fifths of their recorded deaths were adults. The relative immunity of the Spaniards, as befitted the most prosperous section, is indicated by their low infant mortality. Far fewer of their children died of famine than of smallpox. An obvious conclusion to be drawn from this comparison is that it was the 1786 crisis, far more than the epidemics, which impaired the population's capacity for demographic growth.

The baptismal register also reflected the impact of crisis. In 1786–87 recorded births fell by about 40% compared to previous averages, and, despite a brief rally in 1788, did not permanently regain the former level until 1792. Broken down by ethnic category, the story becomes more complex. Indian baptisms followed a descending curve in which the lowest points occurred in 1789–90 when their number barely equalled a fifth of their former average.

Spanish baptisms maintained their own rhythm with a major decline which spanned the entire decade 1783–94. By contrast *casta* baptisms moved in a contrary fashion. As early as 1788 their numbers reached a new high point and thereafter continued to exceed pre-crisis levels. In part this resilience of course sprang from intermarriage. Indian women bore *casta* children. But it is doubtful whether this explanation fully accounts for the rapidity of the recovery.

The matrimonial register completes the story of popular reaction to crisis. In 1786 the number of marriages fell by about two thirds. But as soon as 1787 the former rate was regained, and in 1788 surpassed. This activity, however, cannot be construed as a mere return to 'normality'. As the marriage testimonies demonstrate, much of it sprang from a rapid remarriage. Whereas in 1784 only 13% of male informants and 8.2% of the females declared themselves widowers and widows, in 1787 no less than 37.7% of the men and 28.1% of the women admitted previous marriage. For 1788 these proportions remained at a high level – 21.6% and 20.7% respectively. By 1792 – we lack samples for the intervening years – the number of remarriages had fallen to a proportion below that of 1784. In passing, it may be noted that among Indian informants the share of informants in 1787 seeking remarriage rose to three fifths. Clearly, few Mexicans favoured single life.

One further change in marriage patterns may be noticed. In the urgent quest for new partners, ethnic barriers tended to crumble. In 1787, about a half of all Indian and mulatto men about to marry chose women outside their own category. For the latter this proved a temporary trend; their intermarriage rate soon returned to its usual rate of about a third of the total. But for the Indians, 1786–87 marked a turning point. Henceforth more than half their men continued to marry non-Indians. The strange decline in Indian baptisms in 1789–90, compared to the contrasting rise in *casta* baptisms thus derived from this sudden upsurge in intermarriage. As a homogeneous social group the Indians of León had entered the road towards extinction.

## IV

A great famine or epidemic affects society in ways analogous to war. In some sectors the crisis is sharp but transient. For example, the Mexican mining industry certainly experienced a setback as silver production fell from a peak of 23.7 million pesos in 1783 to a mere 16.1 million by 1787. But the next year the mint coined 20.1 million pesos, and in the ensuing decade output easily surpassed previous records.[22] By contrast, the Indian community suffered a permanent loss, since the series of epidemics impaired its reproductive capacity. Similarly, in León a major shift in the pattern of land-ownership occurred in the years 1750–51, when the maize harvest of 1749 dropped to a seventh of the previous average, causing prices to soar to 36 reales a fanega. As a result, an entire group of Indian and mestizo rancheros sold their land to the entrepreneurs already engaged in the creation of the haciendas of San Nicolás, San Pedro del Monte, Pompa and Lagunillas. One vendor explained his motives for selling in these terms: 'Because of this year's drought [1750], I now not only lack oxen for sowing corn, but also I and my family are suffering grievously from the want of maize, which is at such a high price that I and my children are in danger of perishing'.[23] Nevertheless, although this crisis undoubtedly marked a watershed in the history of the ranchero community in León, its chief effect was simply to accelerate a trend already in operation. The famine was the occasion rather than the formal cause of this transfer in landownership; the active agent was mercantile capital.

No matter how dramatic the periodic inroads of famine or disease, it is only during the 1780s that we encounter evidence of a per-manent, long-term trend in the value of commodities. On the external account, the terms of trade moved in favour of Mexico, since with the lifting of the British naval blockade the colonial market was swamped by a veritable flood of merchandise, both Spanish and foreign. Import prices soon tumbled and commercial profits declined. It was this delayed effect of the 1778 edict of *Comercio libre* which drove many established merchant houses to abandon overseas trade and invest their capital in mining and haciendas. This type of productive investment had become all the more attractive after the Crown raised mining profits by its policy of tax exemptions and the reduction in the cost of mercury. It is noticeable that at much the same time the price of silver in the mining camps rose by about two reales a mark.[24] By contrast, internal costs in commerce increased appreciably, since as early as 1781 a leading official commented on the shortage of mule-teams to handle the growing volume of imports entering Veracruz, despite the rise of a third in freight charges. By the close of the decade, the Consulado, the merchant guild of Mexico City, reckoned that in the last few years – they gave no specific dates – freight costs had increased by about a half.[25]

As import prices declined, the value of goods in the domestic economy rose. In the same report, the Consulado averred that whereas three-year-old mules had once cost 9–10 pesos, now in 1788 they sold for 20–22 pesos.[26] Similarly, the value of a horse had risen from 4–5 pesos to 8–10 pesos. These claims certainly tally with the evidence of the inventories of estate in León, where, during the 1780s, as we observed in Chapter 4, the value of all types of livestock attained new levels, at which they were to remain until the Insurgency. Equally important, the Consulado observed that whereas since 1674 the city slaughterhouse had always sold 6½ pounds of beef for one real, after 1781 it only supplied 5 pounds for the same one real. Similiarly, the cost of tallow rose from 20 to 29 reales for an arroba of 25 pounds. Once again, these figures can be confirmed from records in León. For here, the contractors to the municipal slaughterhouse, who during the 1760s had offered 8–9 pounds of beef for one real, after 1786 only supplied 5–6 pounds. Similarly, the ounces of mutton which could be purchased for a real fell from 48–50 in the 1760s to 24–28 after 1784. Then again, the value of hides rose from 8–10 to 12–16 reales, and an arroba of tallow sold for 24–32 reales in place of the former 16–18 reales.[27] If the 1760s were years of exceptional cheapness, the 1780s found prices surging forward to unprecedented heights and, equally important, remaining at this new level until 1810 when the Insurgency brought a fresh round of inflation.

A decade later, in the 1790s, there is evidence that maize prices also moved permanently upwards. In the Mexico City grain market, Florescano discovered that if the average price in the years 1762–69 was 9.7 reales a fanega, thereafter values increased markedly, since although prices certainly dropped once the famine of 1785–86 was past, nevertheless, from 1794–95 onwards a new plateau was attained. Even if the crisis years of 1809–11 be discounted, the average price was about 19–20 reales a fanega as compared with the range of 11.6 to 15.5 reales prevailing across the period 1720–83.[28] On this score, evidence from León is not forthcoming. But at Silao the median price rose to 10 reales during the 1770s. A straw in the wind comes from a report of the intendant of Guanajuato who, in September 1809, commented that the scarce rainfall of that summer had driven up the cost of maize to 20 reales a fanega, a level about double the usual price.[29]

There can be no doubt that at some point during these years prices in León followed the general trend. By 1826 the city authorities assumed that maize normally cost between 8 and 12 reales.[30] Confirmation for this upward movement can be obtained from the voluntary tithe returns for the years 1833–63, presented in Table 41. It is at once noticeable that in this new series prices were both higher and more stable than in the previous century. The median was 10 reales a fanega, and in 14 out of 23 years the range only varied between 8 and 11 reales. If it be recalled that across the period 1660–1769 the median price was 6 reales, then we find an increase in value of about two thirds.

TABLE 40   *Prices of meat, hides and tallow in municipal slaughter-house:*
*León 1616–1808*

| Auction date (for 2–3 years) | Beef for one real (pounds) | Mutton for one real (ounces) | One sheep (reales) | One hide (reales) | 25 pounds of tallow (reales) |
|---|---|---|---|---|---|
| 28 February 1616 AHML 1615/17–20 | 9 | – | – | 10–12 | – |
| 3 March 1643 AHML 1642/43–29 | 12½ | – | – | 7–8 | 16 |
| 28 January 1662 AHML 1761/63–10 | 9 | – | – | 8–10 | 20 |
| 6 March 1670 AHML 1664/72–30 | 12 | – | – | 10 | 20 |
| 25 March 1676 AHML 1673/77–23 | 12 | – | – | 8–9 | 17 |
| 25 March 1680 AHML 1677/80–18 | 12 | – | – | 8–9 | 18 |
| 20 May 1701 AHML 1701/02–1 | 4 | – | – | 12 | 24 |
| 21 May 1702 AHML 1702/05–6 | 5 | – | – | 12 | 16 |
| 6 April 1706 AHML 1705/08–9 | 5½ | – | 13 | 12 | – |
| 3 April 1707 (ANL) | 6 | – | 16 | 12 | 18 |
| 16 March 1714 AHML 1712/15–3 | 6 | – | 16 | 12 | – |
| 30 March 1716 AHML 1716/18–1 | 7 | – | 11–14 | 8 | 12 |
| ?? 1734 (reduction to 7½ pounds sought in 1735) | 9¼ | – | – | – | – |
| 6 April 1754 AHML 1754/55–8 | 7 | 36 | – | 10 | 18–20 |
| 20 March 1759 ANL, 30 April 1759 | 8¼ | 40 | 14–20 | 10 | 18 |

TABLE 40—*continued*

| Auction date (for 2–3 years) | Beef for one real (pounds) | Mutton for one real (ounces) | One sheep (reales) | One hide (reales) | 25 pounds of tallow (reales) |
|---|---|---|---|---|---|
| 5 March 1762 (ANL) | 8½ | 44 | 12–14 | 8–9 | 16–18 |
| 17 November 1762 (ANL) | 9 | 50 | 12–14 | 8–9 | 16–18 |
| 18 October 1764 (ANL) | 9½ | 48 | 14–17 | 8–9 | 20–22 |
| 30 October 1767 | 8¾ | 36 | 12–16 | 7 | – |
| ANL, 19 December 1768 | | | | | |
| 22 February 1776 | 8 | 36 | 14–16 | 6–8 | 20–24 |
| ANL, 11 April 1776 | | | | | |
| 11 April 1778 | 7½ | 32 | 14–16 | 8–10 | 20–24 |
| AHML 1776/78–21 | | | | | |
| 11 February 1780 | 7½ | 34 | 14–18 | 10 | 22–24 |
| AHML 1779/80–18 | | | | | |
| 27 February 1782 (ANL) | 7¾ | 36 | – | – | – |
| 28 February 1784 | 8½ | 28 | – | 12 | 24–30 |
| ANL, 12 March 1784 | | | | | |
| 18 March 1786 (ANL) | 6 | 24 | – | 8–10 | 20–32 |
| 1 March 1790 (ANL) | 5 | 24 | – | 10–12 | 20–24 |
| 24 February 1792 | 5 | 28 | 20–24 | 12–14 | 24–32 |
| ANL, 6 March 1792 | | | | | |
| 31 January 1801 | 5½ | 28 | 20–24 | 14–16 | 24–32 |
| ANL, 20 February 1801 | | | | | |
| 7 February 1803 | 6 | 30 | 20–24 | 14–16 | 24–28 |
| AHML 1803(2)–15 | | | | | |
| 14 November 1806 | 5½ | 28 | – | 14–16 | 28–32 |
| ANL, 30 December 1806 | | | | | |
| 8 October 1808 | 5 | 24 | – | 14–16 | 28–32 |
| AHML 1810(1)–36 | | | | | |

*Note:* The range in sheep prices derives from sales of animals *en canal* or *en pie*, dressed or not. Hide prices varied according to whether they came from cows, oxen or bulls. The lower price for tallow was for *sebo en oja* or *en greña*, tallow in slices; the higher price was for *sebo en pan frito*, soap cakes.

Needless to say, changes in the monetary value of commodities cannot be interpreted realistically without comparison with the corresponding changes in the level of earning or in the range of profit. Unfortunately, in this respect we tread uncertain ground, since as yet we quite lack any consistent series of wages. To judge from a scatter of heterogeneous data, however, there is a strong presumption that the money wages of agricultural labourers remained fixed at 1½ to 2 reales a day from the mid seventeenth century until the 1880s.[31] But since most resident peons received maize rations free of charge, they were insulated in part from the inflation of corn prices. Similarly, with a considerable proportion of the rural population engaged in production, either as small-holders or as tenants, any rise

TABLE 41     *Maize prices at León and Comanja: voluntary tithe returns 1833–56*

| Year | Volume (fanegas) | Average annual price (reales per fanega) | Total income (pesos) |
|------|------|------|------|
| 1833 | 1,424 | 13.5 | 2,347 |
| 1834 | 1,555 | 18.7 | 3,636 |
| 1836 | 2,977 | 10.5 | 3,914 |
| 1837 | 3,204 | 8.7 | 3,482 |
| 1838 | 2,136 | 8 | 2,149 |
| 1839 | 2,378 | 8.1 | 2,418 |
| 1841 | 407 | 13.6 | 695 |
| 1842 | 3,849 | 10.2 | 4,897 |
| 1843 | 5,893 | 5 | 3,697 |
| 1844 | 2,718 | 8.4 | 2,879 |
| 1845 | 2,722 | 13 | 4,425 |
| 1846 | 1,722 | 14.8 | 3,188 |
| 1847 | 2,530 | 9 | 2,846 |
| 1848 | 3,437 | 9 | 3,905 |
| 1851 | 4,716 | 11 | 6,496 |
| 1852 | 4,698 | 9.4 | 5,437 |
| 1853 | 3,878 | 10.3 | 5,006 |
| 1854 | 3,624 | 10.6 | 4,837 |
| 1855 | 2,187 | 10.3 | 2,827 |
| 1857 | 600 | 7 | 525 |
| 1861 | 722 | 23.4 | 2,111 |
| 1862 | 2,801 | 8.4 | 2,957 |
| 1863 | 4,128 | 22 | 11,351 |

*Source:* ACM 908, tithe collector's reports

in the price of maize brought as much benefit as loss. In short, although there are good reasons to suppose that the labouring classes in Mexico suffered a decisive fall in their standard of living at the close of the eighteenth century, for most countrydwellers the case cannot rest simply on the long-term immobility of wage rates.

There is another strand of evidence, however, which also points towards a deterioration in real earnings. In the years about 1800 – the data is too sparse for greater precision – inventories of estate in León register a substantial rise in the appraised value of land. A caballería of unirrigated arable worth 300 pesos for most of the century was now appraised at 400 pesos and 500 pesos according to its quality.[32] Since this increase coincided with a growing surplus of agricultural manpower, landowners accordingly raised rents by an equivalent amount. In addition, they sought to restrict the rights to firewood and free pasture hitherto enjoyed by many tenants. Evidence of this trend comes from across the Bajío. For example, in 1804 at León the tenants of Santa Rosa complained that Baltazar

Muciño, a future insurgent who had leased the entire hacienda for 3,200 pesos a year, was steadily raising their rents, in one case from 25 pesos to 60 pesos, and in another instance from 333 pesos to 400 pesos. Furthermore, he demanded that they should assist him at harvest or else send a peon, an obligation, so they claimed, hitherto unknown on the Santa Rosa.[33] Finally, he forbade them to set up lime furnaces on their farms – a customary supplement to their income – on the pretext that they injured hacienda land.

Similarly, at Querétaro on an hacienda called Atongo a group of Indian tenants complained that in the 1790s a new administrator had increased their rents from 6 to 10 pesos for a fanega de sembradura. In addition, he forbade them to touch the magueys or to cut firewood, and to compound the injury, summoned them to work for the hacienda most days of the week, paying them the old rate of one real a day. In response to these accusations, the owner asserted that in fact labour services were only required during the harvest. The charges for pasture, which hitherto had been free, were low, and firewood for personal use was still free. But he did not deny that rents had been increased or that wages remained pitched at the same low rate. In the upshot, the tenants proved restless and the owner quelled the disturbance by expelling the four leaders from the hacienda.[34] In the absence of written contracts, all tenancy agreements expired each year with no guarantee of renewal other than the goodwill of the landlord.

Then again, in 1807, José Mora, the father of the Liberal theorist, leased the hacienda of Los Morales in Chamacuero, a subordinate district of Celaya.[35] He found that the standard rent of 10 pesos a fanega de sembradura was satisfied by the tenants providing a yoke of oxen and a peon two days a week when needed, a service which was credited to their account at the rate of 2 reales a day. Pasture for their oxen and, by customary extension, for all their livestock was free, but for firewood and tuna they supplied another six days work each year. Similarly, the arrimados, or squatters, who dwelt on their farms were expected to work for the landlord 12 days a year. In addition, the hacienda also housed several gangs of gañanes, peons paid eight reales for a six day week, who had their own gardens and free pasture for their animals. Dissatisfied with this complicated system, Mora proposed to pay all workers, tenants and peons alike, 1½ reales a day. Tenants were no longer obliged to provide plough teams, but they could still pay their rent in labour services. In addition, Mora now charged them for pasture and commuted the work requirement for firewood and tuna into a cash payment of 12 reales. So also, the arrimados were obliged to pay two pesos a year in lieu of seasonal assistance. Presumably, he also exacted more rigorous service from the gañanes, since he complained that some acted as if they owned the estate, rarely working more than one or two days a week. His reforms provoked such unrest that he called upon the local magistrates to aid him expel several protestors from the hacienda.

All our evidence points in the same direction. In the years before 1810, the labouring classes in Mexico experienced a decline in their standard of living. The eloquent testimony of the burial register requires no further emphasis. The cycle of harvest failures and high maize prices brought widespread distress. The series of epidemics apparently halted further growth of the Indian population. But we must take care not to paint too black a picture, since not all regions were affected in equal measure, or in the same manner. In the Bajío, the reproductive capacity of the *castas* and creoles proved more than sufficient to maintain an abundant supply of manpower. There are no signs of any labour shortage when agriculture rapidly expanded production to meet the growing demand of the urban economy. Indeed, the first element to show the impact of the sharp expansion in economic activity was livestock, since by the 1780s the price of virtually all animals and of meat registered a marked increase. If we discount the violent distortions induced by the great famine of 1785–86, it was not until the mid 1790s that maize prices in Mexico City finally moved upwards to a new level from which they rarely descended. Then, about the close of the century, the value of all types of land recorded a commensurate increase. It was this long-term inflationary sequence which effected a fall in real earnings. With money wages apparently constant, as the price of land and of livestock rose so the value of labour declined.

That it was the surplus of manpower which was largely responsible for this fundamental change in the relation of labour and capital can be demonstrated by the parallel trends in mining and agriculture. When León was still a frontier society, landowners welcomed tenants on to their estates, charging low rents and granting free pasture and firewood. But with labour no longer a scarce resource, rents were raised and traditional privileges curtailed. Similarly, in mining the customary bait to lure workers into an arduous and dangerous occupation was the *partido*, a share of the ore produced. But in the 1790s the mine-owners terminated the system and their pick and blast men were henceforward paid a daily wage of 8–10 reales.

If there can be little doubt that it was the play of the market which determined the ultimate level of both maize prices and agricultural wages, at the same time the role of the State should not be overlooked. For if mine-owners and landlords had the confidence to enforce a reduction in the real income of workers and tenants, it was in part because they could rely upon the assistance of magistrates and militia to quell any riots or protests. The system of militia regiments, backed by a small regular army, undoubtedly strengthened the effective authority of the Bourbon State. In the long term, however, the fall in real earnings stemmed from the prior allocation of lands by the viceregal regime. The consolidation of the hacienda as the predominant form of landownership obviously prevented the peasantry from acquiring their own farms, and when the rural population increased, the economic advantage of the landlords, either as producers or as rentiers, grew in equal measure. Nevertheless, in the last resort, even if most land had been distributed in small farms, the dramatic growth of population would have acted to depress the standard of living hitherto enjoyed by the peasantry of the Bajío. Viewed from this Malthusian perspective, the role of epidemic disease and famine was to provide periodic relief from the pressure on natural resources exerted by the multiplication of mouths to be fed.

## V

With the outbreak of the Insurgency in 1810 the Bajío experienced all the horrors of civil war. In the first phase of the rebellion the parish priest of Dolores, Miguel Hidalgo y Costilla, succeeded in uniting both creoles and Indians, rancheros and mine-workers in a common front against the colonial State. The property and indeed the very persons of the hated gachupines – the peninsular Spaniards – was offered as popular booty. But in the years after his defeat the surviving patriot forces, now at times more close to bandits than guerillas, ravaged haciendas without distinction and threatened the safety of the towns. The leadership of these marauding bands devolved on former 'field labourers, majordomos and muleteers. . .' so that the lines of conflict soon came to reflect the class and ethnic divisions of colonial society.[36] When the heroic expedition organised by Javier Mina fought its way south into the Bajío in 1817, the insurgent chieftains, illiterate and envious, offered little welcome to the Spanish general's plans for a liberal revolution.

All sectors of the local economy suffered from the weary prolongation of hostilities. Many haciendas were virtually abandoned, their casco buildings burnt or left in ruins, the dams broken, and their livestock either slaughtered or stolen. Estates such as Duarte and Otates situated along the highway between León and Silao sharply curtailed their operations. Most landlords were eventually obliged to suspend the payment of interest on their Church mortgages. In the towns the situation was no better. After the capture of Guanajuato by Hidalgo's forces, the great mines slowly flooded, since the indiscriminate massacre of the peninsular merchants cut off the flow of credit necessary to maintain the costly system of underground drainage. Somewhat later the surface installations of the Valenciana were burnt to the ground during an insurgent raid. After Independence foreign travellers commented on the ruinous aspect of the numerous refining mills which lined the entrance to the city.[37] Much the same was true at Querétaro where the interruption of the northern wool trade soon brought the obrajes to a standstill. In this case the attainment of Independence only heightened the crisis, since with the opening of the Mexican ports to foreign shipping cheap British textiles – the manufactures of the Industrial Revolution – swamped the market undercutting national produce.[38] In the Bajío, if not throughout all Mexico, the Insurgency and its aftermath effected a massive destruction of capital both in agriculture and in industry.

Evidence as to the scale of the economic crisis is provided by Charles Harris in his study of the Sánchez Navarro estates situated in the northern frontier province of Coahuila. Whereas before 1810 these haciendas despatched great quantities of sheep for slaughter in Mexico City and of wool for manufacture at Querétaro and San Miguel el Grande, the onset of hostilities sharply reduced the volume and value of sales with the nearby towns of Saltillo and San Luis Potosí emerging as the chief outlets. In effect, the Insurgency dislocated the entire circle of commercial exchange within the national economy. So prolonged was this crisis that it was only during the late 1830s that the meat contracts for the Capital were renewed.[39] Then, in the next decade, the demand for wool revived and the area under cultivation for cotton was rapidly extended.

It is the tardy and incomplete nature of the return to prosperity which requires emphasis. By any score the Mexican economy experienced a severe depression which in varying degrees endured for at least a quarter of a century. Silver production, which after 1810 plunged to less than half the previous peak of 27 million pesos, only slowly in the 1830s regained an annual mintage rate of 16–18 million pesos, a level not permanently surpassed until the 1870s. At Guanajuato the investment of British capital in the local mines met with but qualified success, so that it was not until the discovery of a rich lode at La Luz in the hills behind the town that the industry experienced a remarkable bonanza with mintage in the years 1848–54 soaring to the record figure of nine million pesos.[40] Much the same rhythm of recovery characterised the textile industry. In response to the challenge from Great Britain, the conservative government of Lucas Alamán established a state finance bank and a protective tariff to promote a modern, mechanised industry. By the late 1830s the new mills were providing a new range of employment and offered a growing market for the wool and cotton of the northern provinces.[41] It is in this recovery in both mining and textiles, together with the commercial opportunities presented by the westward expansion of the United States, that we must seek an explanation of the marked increase in the value of haciendas observed after 1840 both in León and in San Luis Potosí.[42]

The impact of the depression on the condition of life of the labouring classes is difficult to estimate. With the decline of employment in urban industry, many former townsmen no doubt sought a livelihood in the countryside. A contemporary chronicler recorded a march of workless artisans across the Bajío from Querétaro to Guanajuato. But at the same time urban demand for rural produce obviously diminished. Generally, such an imbalance between an increased supply of labour and a reduction in purchasing power would have led to a fall in real earnings. And certainly in 1822 a pamphleteer accused landlords in Querétaro of taking advantage of the surplus labour in the locality to cut the wages of peons from $1\frac{1}{2}$ to 1 real a day.[43] But this policy probably as much reflected the cash shortage of the owners as much as their abuse of any new-found political power. For the Insurgency had so disrupted agricultural production as to drive many hacendados either to lease the greater part of their lands or else to turn to sharecropping in order to avoid the outlay of cash consequent upon direct cultivation. Whether it is to the prolonged economic crisis of these years that we must attribute the rise of *aparcería* – the system of sharecropping which was to prevail in the Bajío by the close of the century – is a question which only future research will resolve.

One effect of the depression, however, can be established beyond debate. Both François Chevalier and Jan Bazant found that in the vast zone of the near north several haciendas were broken up into a series of small farms.[44] In effect, landlords, who by reason of the inherited weight of Church mortgages were unable to raise credit to renovate their estates after the depredations of the Insurgents, chose either to partition their haciendas between heirs or, more commonly, to sell the land outright to former tenants or neighbouring farmers. In some states this process was forwarded by the political authorities, as in the case of Zacatecas where the liberal governor Francisco García purchased no less than six haciendas for distribution among small-holders and rancheros. At León we have already observed that both Gavia and San Nicolás de Arriba were partitioned among various heirs to form what was in effect a group of prosperous ranchos. Further south in Pénjamo during the 1840s the Obregón family sold over 77 plots of land in the casco of the former hacienda of Cuitzeo de los Naranjos.[45] Equally important, in the uplands districts in Jalisco bordering San Pedro Piedragorda, the owners of the great latifundium of Jalpa sold at least 379 caballerías – nearly 40,000 acres – in 23 separate transactions, employing the receipts to repair and extend the dams which irrigated the remainder of the property.[46] The case is significant since, with the sales occurring over a period of years between 1827 and 1851, it demonstrates that the Reform Laws of 1857–59, which cancelled the accumulated Church mortgages at a remarkably low rate of redemption cost, more accelerated than initiated the movement to break up the great estate.

It was in these years that the district now known as Los Altos, famous in the twentieth century as the centre of the Cristero rebellion, emerged as a nucleus of rancheros, devout peasant proprietors. Already in the early 1850s the latifundium called Santa Ana Pacueco which stretched from Pénjamo deep into Las Arandas, was finally broken up and sold to a numerous group of local farmers. Further west, in the neighbouring uplands of Michoacán, the hacienda of Cojumatlán was partitioned among over fifty purchasers, many of them former tenants. In Pénjamo itself Cueramaro was expropriated from the Camilian fathers and divided into a series of ranchos.[47] Needless to say, this trend towards the dissolution of the great estate was sporadic and more pronounced in the hills bordering the Bajío than on the fertile plains situated close to urban markets. In all cases, the greater the degree of previous investment in irrigation, the less the likelihood of partition.

If most estates remained intact, they often changed hands. In

León about half of all haciendas in the district were sold during the middle years of the nineteenth century. The revival of the economy – admittedly somewhat undercut by the political and military events of the period – came too late to rescue many families who had risen to fortune during the heady expansion of the Bourbon era. In particular, the Obregón heirs – the chief beneficiaries of the mining bonanzas at both Valenciana and Catorce – proved unable to maintain their vast patrimony. As creditors pressed for redemption of outstanding debts, one by one the entire chain of haciendas once owned by the Count of Valenciana and Ignacio Obregón entered the land market. Their cycle of dominion had lasted for little more than sixty years. Of the men who purchased these haciendas we know little. For sure, Manuel Doblado, who took over Losa, was the Liberal governor of Guanajuato, and Lucas Guerrero was a ranchero who previously leased Sandía before buying the estate. But as to the sources of their wealth the documents are silent: the nineteenth century in Mexico has yet to find its historian.

## CHAPTER 9

# Epilogue: agrarian reform 1919–40

## I

Whatever occurred elsewhere in Mexico, in the Bajío there is no evidence to suggest that the period known as the Porfiriato (1876–1910) witnessed any concentration of landownership. Indeed, since the census recorded that the number of haciendas and ranchos in the State of Guanajuato respectively increased from 442 and 2,716 in 1882 to 534 and 3,999 in 1910 the average size of these units obviously diminished.[1] Certainly in León, although the largest haciendas such as Otates, Santa Rosa and Sandía continued without partition, other estates like Palote, Sauces, Pompa, Losa, and Hoya were divided and sections sold. By far the most striking example in this latter group is afforded by San Nicolás which in 1894 was broken up into ten separate farms or ranchos by the widow and children of Miguel Urteaga Septién. Moreover, since these properties only comprised $1\frac{3}{4}$ caballerías or 75 acres, it is clear that the outlying rancho called Noria de Septién already had been sold. In this fashion the estate so patiently pieced together by Agustín de Septién y Montero in the 1740s, after four generations of subsequent possession by the same family, finally disappeared from the map. It is a commentary on the value of lands situated close to the expanding limits of the city that in 1922 just one caballería of the former San Nicolás sold for 19,000 pesos.[2]

If the dissolution of haciendas occurred without much comment, it was in part because landlords had often abandoned direct cultivation of their estates in favour of leasing their land to tenant farmers and sharecroppers. Indeed, most observers agreed that by the start of the twentieth century most haciendas in Central Mexico only cultivated the 'irrigated or humid lands', leaving the remainder of the estate to peasant enterprise. Even in the Valley of Toluca the great latifundium of Gavia was let to over 2,000 'renters and croppers'.[3] As yet, however, the origins, development and final extension of sharecropping remain an unexplored theme which awaits its historian. Sufficient here to note that so prevalent had the practice become by 1910, that one student of agriculture foresaw a natural evolution whereby, with the price of corn falling owing to world trends, peons on haciendas would first turn to sharecropping and then become farmers in their own right. Many landlords, so he claimed, 'have started to sub-divide their lands and hand them over to sharecroppers and tenants'.[4] Moreover, other sources testify that even in provinces where this process had yet to be initiated, land-owners already anticipated the eventual fragmentation of their estates. In their eyes, the chief obstacle to such an operation was the indolent and improvident nature of the Mexican peon.[5]

In León oral testimony avers that by 1910 virtually all maize grown on haciendas was produced by sharecroppers. Rents varied from a third to a half of the harvest according to whether the tenants possessed their own plough-teams or leased them from the landlord. In addition, many estates still possessed extensive tracts of land under irrigation, directly managed by the landlord, which were devoted to the cultivation of wheat. The sharecroppers in maize worked as wage-earners during the wheat harvest.[6] Written confirmation of this evidence is preserved in the municipal archive where a typed list dating from 1925 records the presence of only 135 *peones acasillados* on over forty haciendas. To take the largest estates, Santa Rosa employed only 49 peons as against 460 aparceros or sharecroppers and Sandía maintained but 15 peons compared with 150 share-croppers.[7] Admittedly, these figures may reflect the disruption caused by the Revolution. In a subsequent application for an ejido land grant, the labourers resident on Duarte claimed that the casco was in ruins and that they were all sharecroppers who owned enough plough-teams and implements to maintain production. This evidence of a certain diffusion of prosperity is confirmed by a similar petition from Losa where the residents asserted that they regularly obtained half of the annual harvest of wheat, maize and chili.[8] Clearly, no discussion of changes in the real earnings of agricultural workers can ignore the extension in the area let to sharecroppers.

Any remote chance of a natural evolution in which the play of market forces would induce the dissolution of the great estate disappeared forever with the outbreak of the Mexican Revolution. For both the villagers of central Mexico and the ambitious caudillos from the north sought the partition of the traditional hacienda. These dual aspirations – the restitution or extension of communal lands and the promotion of capitalist agriculture – found expression in the national Constitution promulgated in 1917. The famous agrarian article, no. 27, first defined the nation itself as the primordial owner of all territory within the Republic, and hence empowered to license or abrogate all individual rights in respect to landed property. It explicitly demanded the dissolution of latifundia in order (a) to foster the development of the small property, later defined as any farm not exceeding 240 acres of irrigated and 480 acres of unirrigated arable land and (b) the endowment of all 'centres of population' with lands sufficient to cover their necessities, a grant which where reckoned advisable could be held in communal tenure.[9] From the outset, therefore, agrarian reform in Mexico entertained the twofold aim of encouraging commercial agriculture and satisfying the claims of the traditional peasantry.

Implementation of the Constitution, however, was delayed by the fear that any immediate or drastic expropriation would endanger the production of foodstuffs and the flow of exports. Moreover, once the villages, usually of Indian background, had received their lands, debate was soon joined as to the precise legal nature of the ejido, as the communal grants were now called. After all, mestizo Mexico had little experience of this type of ownership. It was not until 1925–27 that regulatory laws were issued which defined ejido lands as unalienable, with the ownership titles vested in the community, but with the usufruct exercised through individual or family parcels ranging in area from 7 to 18 acres. In the Agrarian Code of March 1934 any rural settlement of 25 households, no matter what their past status or occupation, could apply for the grant of an ejido.[10]

Although in later years the ejido came to be viewed as a collectivist not to say socialist, institution, during the 1920s President Calles defended communal tenure simply as a legal device introduced to safeguard the small peasant plot from absorption by neighbouring properties. Moreover, he clearly distinguished the stratum of poor peasants who required such protection from what he called the men of 'greater energy and initiative', usually former tenants or sharecroppers, who should become small proprietors. As late as 1929 an official party statement envisaged three classes in the Mexican countryside, consisting of the poor peasantry of the ejidos, the middle peasants with their own small-holding, and the 'agricultural entrepreneurs of more considerable means and initiative'.[11] Then again, although President Lázaro Cárdenas (1935–40) undoubtedly favoured the ejido as the chief instrument of agrarian reform, his government also began the practice of issuing to small proprietors *títulos de inafectabilidad*, title deeds which certified that the land in question was a genuine small property and hence un-expropriable for ejido grants. During the 1930s the expansion of the area under communal tenure to encompass almost half the arable land of Mexico was matched by an equally significant increase in the number of small properties. After all, many of the leaders of the Revolution were rancheros who, as much as the villagers of Morelos, desired to advance the interests of their class and family.

## II

To trace the stages of the dissolution of the great estate in León, it is necessary first to consult the public register of property which recorded all sales of land during this period, and then to inspect the files of the Department of Agrarian Affairs for information about the ejidos. Needless to say, these official sources simply register legal effects without reference to political causes or individual motives. That León was a Cristero stronghold firmly opposed to the anti-clerical regime of President Calles, probably affected the course of agrarian reform in the district; but it is not an issue which finds echo in this sort of document.[12] Despite such obvious deficiencies, the sequence of transactions and distribution in León forms a case-study of some interest, especially in regard to the timing and extent of land reform in the Bajío.

The main emphasis at León during the early 1920s was on the creation of small properties. For with Coecillo and San Miguel long since absorbed within the city, there were no villages with a communal tradition to act as a focus of popular demands. Until 1927 only the congregación of Sauces, the former casco village of a divided hacienda, both solicited and obtained the grant of an ejido.[13] The dominant approach was clearly expressed in 1921 when the *Bulletin* of the local chamber of agriculture printed this message from the State authorities: 'It does not seem likely that owners of lands will refuse to partition their estates, considering how little they produce and their lack of credit to renovate them.' The same journal also praised *Corcuera Hermanos*, a company which had purchased the hacienda of Otates for 182,000 pesos with the purpose of effecting a *fraccionamiento*. Already, so it was claimed, some 1,480 acres had been sold to small-holders from neighbouring villages.[14] That this was no passing phase can be shown from the property register which records separate sales to some twenty persons over the years 1923–30, the total area sold amounting to over 4,310 acres, an average of 214 acres a head.[15]

Several landlords also broke up their estates at this period. At Rincón Sauz de Armenta, an hacienda which had always leased a considerable part of its territory, was divided into its component farms by the current owner, Hilario Torres, an industrialist from León. Between 1921–24 he sold 2,580 acres to 26 individuals for a total 75,193 pesos, an average of 2,892 pesos for just under 100 acres. In addition, two remaining sections, which included the casco fabric, dams and 1,996 acres went for 69,000 pesos.[16] Another case of the partition of an entire hacienda was the Sitio de San Ignacio, situated in the hills, which was distributed in relatively large sections in the years 1921–26.[17] However, it is necessary to insist that although most landlords now attempted to sell tracts of land or to distribute various fractions of haciendas among their families, the overall movement was slow and irregular, and in some cases nominal. Moreover, there is no sign that the most prosperous latifundia, Santa Rosa and Sandía, had reached the point of dissolution.

The first real challenge to the interests of the landlords came in May 1927, when a group of sharecroppers on Duarte petitioned for the grant of an ejido. The response of the owner was to divide the hacienda into ten parts between different members of his family, the distribution all notarised as sales with the term of payment extended over a period of ten years. But in 1929 President Emilio Portes Gil chose to recognise the sharecroppers' petition and gave them an ejido of 2,708 acres, which amounted to about a fifth of the entire area of Duarte.[18] Moreover, since the grant included a high proportion of irrigated and arable land, the owners lost far more in value than the actual acreage might suggest.

At much the same time four other applications for land grants were submitted and by 1931 three new ejidos were carved out of haciendas. These decrees proved to be the signal for a veritable flurry of petitions, since in the years 1930–34 no less than 16 *solicitudes* for ejidos were published in the state gazette of Guanajuato. By then it was clear to all landlords that the penalty for inertia was expropriation. In consequence, the owners of haciendas now desperately sought to dispose of their land. The race was all the more pressing, since once a petition for an ejido was published all further sales were deemed invalid. For example, on Otates purchases involving no less than 4,183 acres in the years 1931–32 were disallowed because the

Agrarian Commission recognised the legal standing of a petition signed in September 1930, even though in this case it had not been published until 1932.[19] Clearly, a great deal depended on personal influence, with the rules varying according to the particular case. For instance, on 11 November 1933 the children of the former owner of San Juan de Abajo divided this small hacienda into nine separate properties. A week later, 21 November 1933, a petition for an ejido was published. After a prolonged review of these events the Agrarian Commission, in 1937, found in favour of the applicants, granting them an ejido which absorbed 761 of the 2,075 acres on the original estate.[20] In justification of this decision the Commission stated that the heirs had taken no practical steps to manage the lands separately, so that the partition should be regarded as a mere legal device to forestall expropriation.

Since an ejido originated in the *solicitud* presented to the state authorities by a group of labourers or sharecroppers, it was at times possible for landlords to organise an internal distribution of land without recourse to communal tenure. Many peasants welcomed the chance of becoming small-holders. An example of what might be called private agrarian reform is afforded by San Pedro del Monte, an hacienda of 5,869 acres formed from the purchase of small ranchos in the eighteenth century. First, in the years 1919–23, the owners sold 2,449 acres in three sections. In their turn the purchasers of these lots sold about 120 acres in small-holdings and distributed another 100 acres among relatives.[21] Then, in December 1933, the remainder of the hacienda – some 3,414 acres – was sold in five separate sections, that is to say, in tracts which approached the legal definition of a small property. Finally, in May 1940, three of the new owners divided no less than 2,100 acres into 137 individual plots, each of about 14 acres. Payment for these small-holdings was spread over an indefinite number of years and consisted of one third of the value of the annual harvest.[22] In this fashion San Pedro del Monte escaped the operations of agrarian reform, since a petition for an ejido presented in 1936 was denied recognition and it was only in 1959 that some 761 acres were expropriated to establish an ejido for 74 households. It is not clear whether all this land came from within the area of the former hacienda.

The most striking example of an hacienda avoiding the intrusion of an ejido is provided by Jalpa, situated just outside the district of León, in Manuel Doblado, the former San Pedro Piedragorda. This great estate, the property of the wealthy Braniff family, became

| Ejidos | No. of ejidatarios | Date of Presidential decree | Date of petition | Land assigned (hectares) | | | | Estates providing lands |
|---|---|---|---|---|---|---|---|---|
| | | | | Irrigated | Arable | Pasture | Total | |
| PRESIDENT PLUTARCO ELIAS CALLES | | | | | | | | |
| Los Sauces | 143 | 14 Oct. 1926 | (1 Nov. 1921) | – | 858 | – | 858 | Losa, Sauces, Otates |
| PRESIDENT EMILIO PORTES GIL | | | | | | | | |
| Duarte | 239 | 18 Aug. 1929 | (13 May 1927) | 99 | 726 | 271 | 1,096 | Duarte |
| PRESIDENT PASCUAL ORTIZ RUBIO | | | | | | | | |
| Losa | 125 | 6 March 1931 | (10 Sept. 1928) | 94 | 343 | 231 | 670 | Losa |
| Laborcita | 80 | 9 April 1931 | (9 Feb. 1927) | – | 401 | 218 | 620 | Duarte, Otates |
| Los López | 50 | 9 April 1931 | (17 Nov. 1926) | – | 254 | – | 254 | Concepción, Trinidad, etc. |
| Los Romeros | 22 | 7 July 1933 | (11 Oct. 1929) | 50 | 72 | 88 | 216 | Los Romeros, Albarradones, etc. |
| PRESIDENT LAZARO CARDENAS | | | | | | | | |
| S. Isidro de los Sauces | 27 | 11 March 1935 | (29 June 1931) | 112 | – | 100 | 212 | Sauces, Santa Ana |
| Sandía | 163 | 13 Aug. 1935 | (11 Feb. 1930) | 400 | 512 | 328 | 1,240 | Sandía |
| Barretos | 122 | 13 Aug. 1935 | (11 Sept. 1932) | 400 | 184 | 200 | 784 | Santa Ana |
| La Estancia | 24 | 20 Aug. 1935 | (30 Aug. 1934) | 38 | 124 | 100 | 262 | Sandía |
| El Panal | 33 | 27 Aug. 1935 | (17 Feb. 1934) | 68 | 136 | 150 | 354 | Sandía |
| San Rafael | 20 | 12 Nov. 1935 | (28 June 1934) | 84 | – | 120 | 204 | Sandía |
| Albarradones | 22 | 22 April 1936 | (24 May 1930) | 18 | 100 | 167 | 285 | Albarradones, Duarte |
| Sandía (amp.) | 275 | 8 July 1936 | (10 March 1936) | 601 | 998 | 106 | 1,705 | Sandía |
| El Tomate | 35 | 8 July 1936 | (7 Dec. 1935) | 93 | 195 | 449 | 644 | Sandía |
| La Estancia (amp) | 24 | 8 July 1936 | (21 March 1936) | – | 200 | – | 200 | Sandía |
| La Arcina | 46 | 8 July 1936 | (12 Jan. 1933) | 133 | 107 | – | 240 | Gavia |
| El Escopio | 74 | 8 July 1936 | (20 July 1932) | 300 | – | 300 | 600 | Santa Ana |
| Jagüey | 70 | 8 July 1936 | (16 June 1932) | 97 | 374 | 607 | 1,078 | Santa Ana |

TABLE 42—*continued*

| Ejidos | No. of ejidatarios | Date of Presidential decree | Date of petition | Irrigated | Arable | Pasture | Total | Estates providing lands |
|---|---|---|---|---|---|---|---|---|
| | | | | Land assigned (hectares) | | | | |
| Otates | 186 | 26 Aug. 1936 | (5 Sept. 1931) | — | 1,126 | 300 | 1,426 | Otates, Losa, San Nicolás |
| Plan de Ayala | 214 | 2 Sept. 1936 | (12 Feb. 1933) | 535 | 648 | 722 | 1,906 | Santa Rosa |
| La Joya | 60 | 31 March 1937 | (15 April 1932) | 25 | 458 | 300 | 787 | La Joya |
| Puerta de San Germán | 114 | 21 July 1937 | (20 Nov. 1936) | 32 | 856 | 200 | 1,104 | Santa Rosa |
| San Juan Abajo | 42 | 4 Aug. 1937 | (21 Nov. 1933) | 36 | 272 | 41 | 349 | San Juan Abajo, Noria de Septién |
| La Arcina (amp) | 27 | 8 Sept. 1937 | (21 March 1936) | 44 | 128 | 100 | 272 | Santa Ana |
| Providencia | 31 | 8 Sept. 1937 | (16 Dec. 1933) | 20 | 236 | 88 | 344 | Purísima, Noria, etc. |
| Santa Ana | 180 | 29 Sept. 1937 | (10 Aug. 1936) | 272 | 904 | 848 | 2,024 | Santa Ana |
| Zaragosa | 32 | 20 Oct. 1937 | (21 Nov. 1935) | 18 | 58 | 251 | 327 | Albarradones |
| Rancho Nuevo | 38 | 22 June 1938 | (16 Aug. 1936) | — | 311 | 228 | 539 | Santa Ana |
| Ibarrilla | 92 | ? | (17 Aug. 1938) | — | 106 | 893 | 999 | Ibarrilla, Naranjos |
| Los Arcos | 46 | 6 Sept. 1939 | (14 Jan. 1938) | 113 | 245 | 16 | 379 | Los Arcos |
| Capellanía | 60 | 27 Sept. 1939 | (22 Feb. 1938) | — | 348 | 216 | 566 | Capellanía |
| Los Ramírez | 67 | 21 Feb. 1940 | (11 Sept. 1936) | 90 | 454 | 350 | 894 | Los Ramírez, Mirasol |
| Nuevo Valle de Moreno | 96 | 13 Nov. 1940 | (23 Aug. 1921) | 40 | 462 | 1,663 | 2,165 | Otates, San Martín |
| PRESIDENT MANUEL AVILA CAMACHO | | | | | | | | |
| Durán y El Resplandor | 38 | 27 Aug. 1941 | (27 Sept. 1937) | — | 312 | 148 | 460 | El Resplandor, Duran |
| S. José Resplandor | 48 | 27 Aug. 1941 | (29 July 1938) | 48 | 296 | 44 | 388 | El Resplandor, Los Ramírez |
| San Pedro de Los | 25 | 12 Aug. 1942 | (15 June 1931) | — | 208 | 483 | 691 | Medina, etc. |

| | | | | | | | | |
|---|---|---|---|---|---|---|---|---|
| Los Arcos (amp) | – | 22 Oct. 1947 | (19 Aug. 1942) | 80 | 180 | – | 260 | Pompa, Noria |
| Sauz Seco | 34 | 3 Dec. 1947 | (8 July 1945) | – | 35 | 432 | 465 | Otates |
| Corral de Piedra | 32 | 10 Aug. 1949 | (23 Sept. 1936) | – | – | 82 | 96 | Corral de Piedra |
| Cuesta Blanca | 49 | 7 Sept. 1949 | (9 April 1945) | – | 35 | – | 35 | Duarte |
| Estancia de Otates | 24 | 21 Dec. 1949 | (27 May 1945) | – | – | 1,090 | 1,090 | Otates (mountains) |
| Mirasol | 27 | 26 Nov. 1952 | (30 Aug. 1944) | 53 | 53 | – | 53 | Santa Ana |
| PRESIDENT ADOLFO RUIZ CORTINES | | | | | | | | |
| San Nicolás González | 53 | 30 June 1954 | (29 Jan. 1933) | – | 424 | 112 | 536 | Otates, S. Nicolás |
| Santa Ana (amp) | 60 | 11 Nov. 1954 | (6 Oct. 1940) | 80 | 33 | 58 | 91 | Santa Ana |
| El Escopio (amp) | 28 | 18 Jan. 1956 | (22 Feb. 1949) | – | 33 | 76 | 109 | Santa Ana |
| PRESIDENT ADOLFO LOPEZ MATEOS | | | | | | | | |
| Alfaro | ? | 9 June 1959 | (22 May 1953) | – | 39 | – | 39 | Alfaro |
| San Pedro del Monte | 74 | 9 June 1959 | (14 Jan. 1951) | – | 308 | – | 308 | San Pedro (sections) |
| San Judas | 89 | 20 Dec. 1962 | (14 Sept. 1941) | – | 220 | – | 220 | S. José Resplandor |
| Barranca del Venadero | 32 | 7 June 1964 | (19 April 1959) | – | 280 | – | 280 | Barranca |

*Note:* At times total of lands is somewhat greater than combined entries because lands for housing are not included.

*Source:* DAG, ejido files

a Cristero stronghold in the late 1920s and hence bitterly opposed to the agraristas.[23] First, the hacienda was partitioned into some forty farms which varied in size according to the nature of the terrain. But then towards the close of the 1930s the new owners combined to sub-divide the entire latifundium into over 500 plots ranging in size from 8 to 17 acres. A few large farms of about 100 acres were preserved or were formed later through the purchase of small lots.[24] One practical advantage of this internal distribution of land was that it ensured the maintenance of the great dams which supplied the entire area with water for irrigation. It must be emphasised that the approval of the state Agrarian Commission was obtained for this scheme and that in 1943–44 most of the newly created small properties received *títulos de inafectabilidad*. In recent years, despite the periodic rumblings of the local peasant league, the association of proprietory farmers of Jalpa have successfully defended their lands from the threat of communal tenure.

In León itself, however, the most prosperous and fertile haciendas were converted into ejidos. That in both cases the owners were foreign citizens, French and Spanish, may well have influenced the course of events. In 1913 the Santa Rosa passed by inheritance to Carlos Markassusa Bernal, apparently a French citizen, whose widow, Guadalupe Alcocer, later married an Italian whose nationality she then assumed. As early as 1928, so it was alleged, she obtained permission from the state authorities to partition her estate, and in June 1932 she sold some 2,989 acres of the best land to eleven individuals, most of whom like herself, resided in Mexico City. In August of the same year another 3,352 acres were divided among the twelve French heirs of her first husband. A month later another 453 acres were sold to twelve local farmers. No further transactions occurred until 12 February 1933 when a petition for an ejido was signed, although not published. At once a round of sales began, most of which were inserted in the municipal property register on 28 February, with a few more in March. On this occasion about 3,017 acres went in relatively large sections to twelve individuals and another 899 acres to 37 men in plots of about 24 acres. With few exceptions, the terms of payment were spread over periods of five to ten years.[25] Thereafter, with the publication of the *solicitud* no further transactions were recorded until the creation of two large ejidos in 1937–37, when some 7,437 acres were allocated to 328 applicants. In this instance the ejido plots were generous, comprising 23 acres of which about 15 consisted of irrigated or arable land.

Nevertheless, with a total area of 17,600 acres, the ejido grants only amounted to 42% of the original estate.[26]

As the case of Santa Rosa indicates, pressure for the dissolution of the great estate increased dramatically in the early 1930s as an entire series of petitions for ejidos were presented to the state authorities. It was, of course, the presidency of Lázaro Cárdenas (1935–40) which was responsible for the full application of agrarian reform. During his period of office no less than 23 ejidos were established in León, as compared with a mere six in the years since 1917. Moreover, of the 15 ejidos created after he relinquished office, at least 7 were based on claims published before 1940. However, it must be emphasised that over half of the ejidos he formed derived from petitions presented before he became President. In other words, the achievement of Cárdenas in this respect was to deal swiftly with the log-jam of applications awaiting resolution. At the same time the rapidity with which the reform was introduced prevented any systematic allocation of land. The endowment of an ejido was largely determined by the number of heads of household who signed the original petition as compared with the amount of land available in the locality. In consequence, the individual plots varied in size from 10 to 22 acres of arable or irrigated land, and the total area of ejidos ranged from 500 to 5,000 acres. Similarly, if on estates such as Duarte only one collective was established, on other haciendas several ejidos were created. Then again, the proportion of any estate set aside for communal tenure varied greatly. It was this highly particular, *ad hoc* mode of distribution which gave such scope for the intervention of personal or political interests.

By far the largest number of ejidos were carved out of the extensive, fertile lands of the haciendas called Santa Ana del Conde and Sandía. These estates, once the property of the Count of Valenciana, had been united anew under a common management by Juan Velasco y Palacios, a Basque immigrant, who acquired Sandía from his marriage to María Guerrero and Santa Ana by purchase for the sum of 220,000 pesos. After his death in 1908 the latifundia, which by then encompassed over 35,000 acres, passed to distant heirs resident in the Peninsula at Bilbao.[27] Petitions for ejidos were presented as early as 1930 but apart from a section awarded to the congregación of Sauces it was not until 1935–37 that any significant land grants were distributed. This lack of State action permitted the owners to utilise the period between October 1933 and April 1935 to sell no less than 10,400 acres to some 78 individuals. The size of the purchases varied greatly, with the average on Sandía being little more than 26 acres. Moreover, the persons who acquired large sections soon proceeded to divide their holdings among different members of their family. In this context it is surely significant that at least ten Spaniards figured among the recipients of lots ranging from 200 to 440 acres. The possibility of simulated transfer in respect to such sales cannot be discounted.[28] Whatever the nature of these transactions, in the years which followed some 24,774 acres or 70% of the original estates were allocated to twelve separate ejidos. Most of these communities enjoyed access to irrigated lands and indeed, in the case of the ejido called Santa Ana del Conde, an entire dam covering 265 acres was appropriated for collective use.[29] To judge from the distribution of all types of land, there are no grounds for the argument that ejidos only received poor quality soils. On the other hand, it is highly unlikely that the elaborate system of dams and irrigation channels survived the fragmentation of the estate.

## III

The application of agrarian reform in Mexico was in large measure determined by the nature of the regional economy. If today the proportion of land in the State of Guanajuato occupied by ejidos only amounts to 38% of the total area, as compared with 51% in Puebla and 82% in Morelos, this difference springs from the divergent paths of agricultural production pursued in the course of the preceding century.[30] By 1910 the great estate in the Bajío had become a mere unit of ownership rather than a centrally administered enterprise. Both tenants and sharecroppers operated their own farms. At the same time the survival, not to say expansion in number of ranchos and small-holdings meant that once the great estate was threatened by expropriation, an extensive class of farmers stood ready to purchase tracts of land. It was these men who stood to benefit the most from the extraordinary activity in the market for land which characterised the years after the Revolution.

The advantage of communal tenure as against free-hold plots is by no means obvious. At best it was an institutional device to prevent wealthy farmers from acquiring the land of their impoverished brethren. At worst it led to the disruption of existing systems of irrigation and the eventual deterioration of the soil. In the long run the growing demands of Mexico City for all kinds of rural produce raised the value of privately-owned land to the point where it became profitable to sink artesian wells in order to extend the area under irrigation. The legal defence against expropriation provided by the *títulos de inafectabilidad* encouraged small proprietors to invest their capital in new techniques and crops. By contrast the essential role of the ejido was to act as convenient reservoirs of seasonal labour. In the last resort, it was the prosperous farmer, the independent ranchero, together with the heirs of former hacendados, who profited the most from the immense increase in urban demand for foodstuffs. It is possible that even without agrarian reform, the intensification of agricultural production and the subsequent rise in land values would have promoted the slow dissolution of the great estate. Whether the decision to distribute some 83,000 acres among 48 ejidos was either necessary or wise only time will tell. Whatever the verdict, it is surely significant that the State, in the persons of both Viceroys and Presidents, was responsible for the allocation of land both at the outset and at the close of our period. The pattern of landownership reflected the balance of political power within society. But that is a theme which demands another book.

# APPENDIX I

## Select genealogy of Marmolejo family

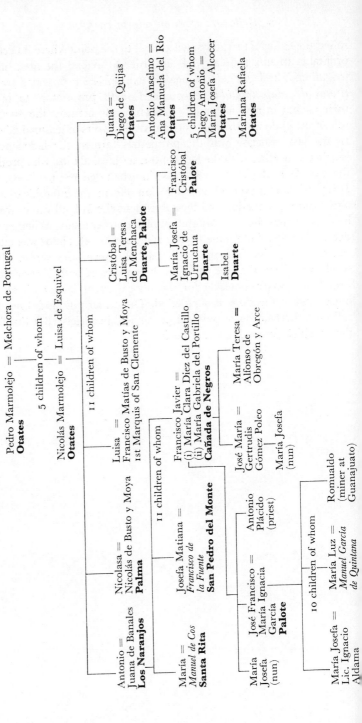

APPENDIX 2A

Select genealogy of the Austri, Septién and Obregón families

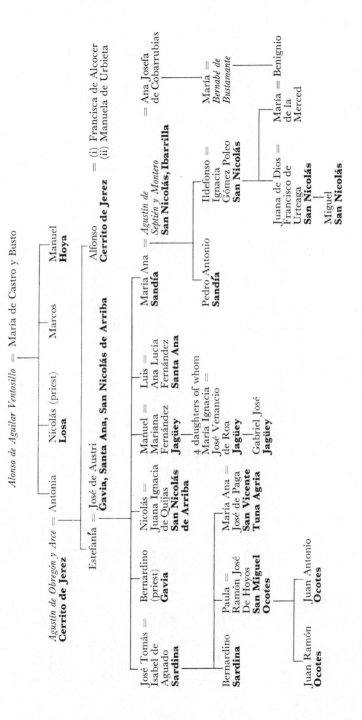

# APPENDIX 2B

## Select genealogy of the Austri, Septién and Obregón families

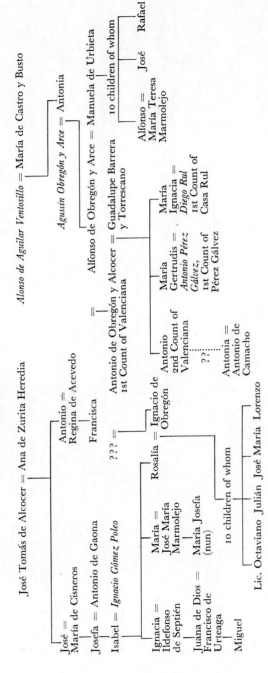

*Archival references of inventories of estate and sales*

The purpose of this appendix is to provide a guide to the location of all accessible inventories of estate for haciendas and ranchos in León and Rincón. In addition references for sales are inserted. From these joint sources it is possible to reconstruct the history of most estates.

## León

| Haciendas | Inventories | Sales |
|---|---|---|
| Cerrito de Jerez | AHML 1695/99–28; 1712/15–5; 1785/86–15 | ANL, 13 May 1729; 4 May 1751; 6 February 1771; 3 March 1786; 31 May 1790; 30 September 1839 |
| Cerrogordo | ANL, 4 March 1738; AHML 1787/1788–7; 1825(3)–4; 1833(2)–11 | ANL, 1 September 1713; 2 December 1863 |
| Duarte | AHML 1758/59–31; AHG, Bienes Difuntos 1843/45 | ANL, 4 December 1716; 26 June 1737; August 1832 |
| Gavia | AHML 1748/50–13 | ANL, 3 March 1728; 14 May 1729; AHGP, 23 February 1790 |
| Ibarrilla | AHML 1757/58–4; 1764/65–14 | AHML 1767–7; ANL, 23 September 1783; 22 November 1793; 23 February 1828; AHGP, 7 March 1851; ANL, 28 February 1860 |
| Jagüey | AHML 1748/50–13; 1787/88–8 | ANL, 25 October 1849 |
| Lagunillas | AHML 1746/47–4; 1776/78–2; ANL, 15 May 1784 | ANL, 13 January 1753, 12 January 1746 |
| Losa and Hoya | AHML 1743/44–1 (for 1730); 1809(1)–6 | ANL, 16 May 1729; 24 May 1730; 16 May 1838; 28 October 1847; AHGP, 23 May 1863 |
| Ocotes | AHML 1806–10 (for 1798); 1831(1)–3 | ANL, 18 June 1841 |
| Otates | AHML 1660/63–16; 1708/10–18 (for 1688 and 1706); AGN, Civil 283–3 (for 1787); AHML 1837(1)–6 | ANL, 24 June 1710 (in vol. 1704–11); 24 March 1832; 8 November 1854; 7 January 1859 |

| Haciendas | Inventories | Sales |
|---|---|---|
| Palote and Palma | AHML 1726/29–10; 1758/59–1; 1774–1, 4; 1795/96–21 (for 1786 and 1793); 1804/05–14 (for 1798) | ANL, 21 July 1759; 11 July 1810; 12 January 1849; 24 August 1859 |
| Pompa | AHML 1742/43–3; 1808–13 | ANL, 11 May 1729; 8 February 1742; 4 August 1750; AHML 1848(3)–6 |
| Potrero | AHML 1776/78–19; 1819(4)–21 (for 1810) | ANL, 3 December 1742; AHML 1769–10; ANL, 5 June 1778; 30 January 1783; 26 May 1829; 26 November 1840; 18 August 1845; AHML 1861–70 |
| Sauces | AHML 1741/42–1 (for 1714); 1769/70–15 (for 1763) | ANL, 8 February 1749; 16 May 1749; 29 August 1752 |
| Sandía | —— | AHGP, 23 August 1788; 7 December 1853; ANL, 22 December 1860 |
| San Nicolás | AHML 1793/94–20 (stock); 1842(2)–3 (partial) | ANL, 11 April 1836 |
| San Nicolás Arriba y Abajo | AHML 1748/50–13 | ANL, 6 March 1782, 16 October 1786; AHGP, 23 October 1806; ANL, 23 October 1806; 18 October 1859 |
| San Pedro del Monte | AHML 1734/36–1; 1772/73–22 | ANL, 28 June 1781 |
| Santa Rosa | AHML 1752–17 (for 1733); 1739/40–6 for Santa Rita | AHML 1734–14; ANL, 2 August 1852 |

| Ranchos | Inventories |
|---|---|
| Arroyohondo | AHML 1789/90–5 |
| Los Castillos | AHML 1764/65–24 (for 1734) |
| Concepción | AHML 1734–17; 1801–11; 1842(1)–8 |
| Echeveste | AHML 1815(2)–27 |
| Los Hinojas | AHML 1736/38–23 |
| Los Gómez | AHML 1729/31–8; 1748/50–7; 1833(2)–1; 1838(1)–1 |
| Guadalupe | AHML 1757/58–7; 1807–2; 1842(1)–8 |
| Guarachita | AHML 1759/60–2 |
| Laborcita | AHML 1754/55–24 (for 1743); 1804–3; 1821(4)16 |
| Los Naranjos | AHML 1736/38–2; 1776–14; 1776/78–2; 1823(2) |
| Patiña | AHML 1750/52–17; 1807–2 |
| Pedraza | AHML 1808–14; 1835(1)–14 |
| San Cayetano | AHML 1716/18–21 |
| San Isidro | AHML 1757/58–15 |
| San Jorge | AHML 1843(1)–7 |
| San Juan Zitaquaro | AHML 1741/42–2; 1849(2)–5 |
| Santa Ana | AHML 1756/57–3, 8 |
| Santa Rosalía | AHML 1781/82–12; 1806–2 |
| Sardaneta | AHML 1726/29–25 |
| Saucillo | AHML 1759/60–1; 1836(1)–6 |

*Rincón*

| Haciendas | Inventories | Sales |
|---|---|---|
| Cañada de Negros | AHML 1776–14 (stock); ANL, 7 March 1771 (land) | ANL, 24 March 1763; 23 July 1790; AHGP, 17 October 1856 |
| Fuentes de Medina | AHML 1711/12–17; 1759/60–22; 1793/94–25; 1824(3)–6 | ANL, 23 May 1704; 8 January 1772; 16 September 1789; 26 January 1793 |
| Pedregal | AHML 1756/57–23; 1769/70–14 | ANL, 5 May 1728; 30 October 1795; AHGP, 17 October 1856 |
| Peñuelas | | ANL, 7 May 1799 |
| Sauz de Armenta | | ANL, 7 April 1708 |
| San Cristóbal | AHML 1827(3)–26 (for 1823) ANL, 8 April 1826 | ANL, 6 February 1734; 11 August 1752; 13 December 1770; 4 February 1782; AGHP, 28 December 1850; 5 April 1854 |
| San Isidro | ANL, 19 October 1799 | ANL, 19 November 1781; 4 January 1836 |
| San Lorenzo | AGN, Tierras 619–14 (for 1749) | ANL, 30 October 1742; 26 May 1849 |
| Los Sapos | AGN, Tierras 1206–2 (for 1786) | ANL, 22 October 1745; 31 December 1774; 1 October 1796; 7 October 1836; 23 October 1855; 31 May 1864 |
| Sarteneja | AHML 1708/10–6; 1743/54–13; 1765/66–18 (for 1759); 1791/92–13 | ANL, 16 April 1728; 1 February 1751; 22 January 1781; 6 October 1842 |
| Talayote | AHML 1793/94–25; 1803(2)–36; 1824(2)–36 | ANL, 17 May 1729 |
| Los Tanques | AHML 1779/80–5 (for 1774); 1815(1)–4 (for 1812) | ANL, 14 December 1713; 22 March 1741; 16 January 1780; 24 January 1791 |
| Terrero | | AHGP, 5 January 1782; 19 August 1852 |

| Ranchos | Inventories | |
|---|---|---|
| Guadalupe | AHML 1754/55–22 (for 1728); 1766/67–11 (for 1762) | |
| San Bernardo | AHML 1746/47–1 | |
| Talayote | AHML 1803(2)–26 | |

# Archival abbreviations

| | |
|---|---|
| ACM | Archivo Casa Morelos (Morelia) |
| AGI | Archivo General de Indias (Seville) |
| AGN | Archivo General de la Nación (Mexico City) |
| AHG | Archivo Histórico de Guanajuato |
| AHGP | Archivo Histórico de Guanajuato, Protocolos de Cabildo |
| AHML | Archivo Histórico Municipal de León |
| AMM | Archivo Municipal de Morelia |
| ANL | Archivo Notarial de León |
| APL | Archivo Parroquial de León |
| BN | Biblioteca Nacional (Mexico City) |
| DAG | Delegación Agraria de Guanajuato |
| RPPL | Registro Publico de Propiedad de León |

# Notes

## CHAPTER 1: INTRODUCTION: THE MEXICAN HACIENDA

1  François Chevalier, *La formación de los grandes latifundios en México* (Mexico, 1956), p. 3.
2  Fray Agustín de Morfi, *Viaje de Indias y diario de Nuevo México* (ed. Vito Alessio Robles, Mexico, 1935) pp. 44–49.
3  H. G. Ward, *Mexico in 1827* (2 vols., London, 1828) II, 474.
4  Gaspar Melchor de Jovellanos, *Informe...de ley agraria* (Madrid, 1820) *passim*.
5  T. G. Powell, *El liberalismo y el campesinado en el centro de México 1850 a 1876* (Mexico, 1974) pp. 74–92, 154–56.
6  Luis de la Rosa, *Observaciones sobre...Zacatecas* (Mexico, 1851) p. 38.
7  Francisco Zarco, *Historia del congreso constituyente 1856–67* (Mexico, 1956) pp. 387–404.
9  Andrés Molina Enríquez, *Los grandes problemas nacionales* (Mexico, 1909) pp. 81–104.
10 G. M. McBride, *The Land Systems of Mexico* (New York, 1923) pp. 43–51.
11 S. A. Zavala, 'De encomiendas y propriedad territorial en algunas regiones de la América Española', in his *Estudios Indianos* (Mexico, 1948) pp. 205–307.
12 Chevalier, *Los grandes latifundios*, pp. 226–33.
13 Charles Gibson, *The Aztecs under Spanish Rule* (Stanford, 1964) pp. 272–98, 322–34.
14 William B. Taylor, *Landlord and Peasant in Colonial Oaxaca* (Stanford, 1972) pp. 65, 77–84, 142–52.
15 Jan Bazant, *Cinco haciendas mexicanas* (Mexico, 1975) pp. 89, 103–11, 161–75.
16 For a comparison see Cristóbal Kay, 'Comparative Development of European Manorial System and the Latin American Hacienda System', *The Journal of Peasant Studies* 2 (1974) pp. 69–98.
17 Luis González, *Pueblo en vilo* (Mexico, 1968) 93–97, 138–43; see also Paul S. Taylor, *A Spanish–Mexican Peasant Community. Arandas in Jalisco* (Berkeley and Los Angeles, 1933) pp. 13, 26–29.
18 Andre Gunder Frank, *Capitalism and Underdevelopment in Latin America* (New York, 1967) *passim*.
19 A. V. Chayanov, *On the Theory of Peasant Economy* (ed. Daniel Thorner, Homewood, Illinois, 1966), pp. 28, 88–89, 115.
20 Witold Kula, *Théorie Economique du Systeme Féodal* (Paris, 1970) pp. 17–31; see also Juan Martínez Alier, 'Estudio teórico del campesinado', in his *Los huacchilleros del Perú* (Lima, 1973) pp. 51–52, 58–59.
21 Marcello Carmagnani, *Les Mecanismes de la Vie Economique dans une Société Coloniale. Le Chilé 1680–1830* (Paris, 1973) pp. 221–37.
22 Gibson, *The Aztecs*, pp. 78–80, 224–36.

23  See Karl Marx, *Pre-Capitalist Economic Formations* (ed. Eric J. Hobsbawm, New York, 1966) pp. 34, 70.
24  Brian Hammett, *Politics and Trade in Southern Mexico 1750–1821* (Cambridge, 1971) pp. 11–23.
25  P. J. Bakewell, *Silver Mining and Society in Colonial Mexico: Zacatecas 1546–1700* (Cambridge, 1971) pp. 115–21.
26  Gibson, *The Aztecs*, pp. 233–36, 249–56.
27  Jerome Blum, *Landlord and Peasant in Russia* (Princeton, 1961) pp. 259–76, 376–85.
28  D. A. Brading, 'La estructura de la producción agrícola en el Bajío 1700 a 1850', in *Haciendas, latifundios y plantaciones en América Latina* (ed. Enrique Florescano, Mexico, 1975) pp. 112–13.
29  Murdo J. Macleod, *Spanish Central America. A social and economic history 1520–1720* (Berkeley and Los Angeles, 1973) pp. 282–302, 389.
30  Taylor, *Landlord and Peasant*, pp. 148–52.
31  Enrique Florescano, *Precios de maíz y crisis agrícolas en México 1708–1810* (Mexico, 1969) pp. 183–89; also his *Estructuras agrarias de México 1500–1821* (Mexico, 1971) pp. 125–48.
32  For evidence on this theme see Chapter 5.
33  Frederick Katz, 'Labour Conditions on Haciendas in Porfirian Mexico: Some Trends and Tendencies', *Hispanic American Historical Review* 54 (1974) pp. 1–47.
34  Martínez, Alier, *Los huacchilleros* pp. 48–50.

## CHAPTER 2: THE BAJIO

1   AGI, Mexico, 1570, Branciforte to Gardoqui, 31 April 1795.
2   Alexander von Humboldt, *Ensayo político sobre el reino de la Nueva España* (ed. Juan A. Ortega y Medina, Mexico, 1966) p. 238.
3   J. R. Poinsett, *Notes on Mexico* (London, 1825) p. 143.
4   Ward, *Mexico in 1827*, II, 421.
5   Robert C. West, 'Surface Configuration and Associated Geology of Middle America', in *Handbook of Middle American Indians. I.* (ed. Robert Wauchope, Austin, Texas, 1964) pp. 44–49.
6   Jorge L. Tamayo, *El problema fundamental de la agricultura mexicana* (Mexico, 1964) p. 30; Carlos Manuel Castillo, 'Le economía agrícola en la región de el Bajío', *Problemas agrícolas é industriales de México* VIII (1965) pp. 8–13.
7   Philip L. Wagner, 'Natural Vegetation of Middle America', in *Handbook of Middle American Indians*, I, 222, 255–57.
8   Bakewell, *Silver and Society*, pp. 126–28.
9   P. W. Powell, *Soldiers, Indians and Silver* (Berkeley and Los Angeles, 1969) pp. 194–97.
10  Pedro Rojas, *Acámbaro colonial* (Mexico, 1967) pp. 143–50.
11  Powell, *Soldiers, Indians and Silver*, pp. 157–71; Bazant, *Cinco haciendas*, pp. 19–23.
12  AGN, Templos 10–2, Tapía founded convent in 1604; Luisa died in 1663.
13  Wigberto Jiménez Moreno, *Estudios de historia colonial* (Mexico, 1958) pp. 57, 81–82, 89.
14  J. C. Super, *Querétaro: Society and Economy in Early Provincial Mexico* (doctoral dissertation, University of California, Los Angeles, 1973) pp. 3–7, 21, 39.

15 Chevalier, *Los grandes latifundios* pp. 46–50; Melchor Vera, *Salvatierra* (Guanajuato, 1944) pp. 16–17.
16 For these measures see, Orozco, *Legislación*, II, 756–58.
17 Chevalier, *Los grandes latifundios* pp. 212–18.
18 Bakewell, *Silver and Society*, pp. 60–63; Super, *Querétaro*, p. 279.
19 Eric R. Wolf, 'The Mexican Bajío in the 18th century: an analysis of cultural integration', *Synoptic Studies of Mexican Culture* (ed. Munro S. Edmundson, New Orleans, 1957) *passim*.
20 D. A. Brading, *Miners and Merchants in Bourbon Mexico 1763–1810* (Cambridge, 1971) pp. 247–302.
21 José Mariá Zelaa e Hidalgo, *Glorias de Querétaro* (Mexico, 1803) pp. 2–3; John C. Super, 'Querétaro Obrajes: Industry and Society in Provincial Mexico 1600–1810', *Hispanic American Historical Review* 56 (1976) pp. 197–216.
22 AGI, Mexico 1887, intendant of Michoacán to viceroy, 4 October 1794; Miguel Ramos Arizpe, *Memoria sobre el estado de las provincias internas de oriente* (Mexico, 1932) pp. 85, 89–90.
23 José Miranda, 'La población indígena de México en el siglo XVII', *Historia mexicana* 12 (1963) pp. 182–89.
24 Claude Morin, *Croissance et disparite sociales dans une economie coloniale: le Centre-Ouest Mexican au XVIII^e siecle* (Thèse du doctorat de troisième cycle, Paris, 1974) pp. 37–82.
25 Cecilia Andrea Rabel Romero, *San Luis de la Paz: estudio de economía y demografía históricas 1645–1810* (dissertation, INAH Mexico, 1975) p. 57.
26 AGN, Historia 523, f. 88.
27 AGI, Mexico 1454, intendant to viceroy, 25 September 1797.
28 Wolf, *The Mexican Bajío*, p. 191; Brading, *Miners and Merchants* pp. 227–29.
29 AGN, Historia 523, f. 76, 90.
30 Peter Hall (ed.) *Von Thünen's Isolated State* (London, 1966).
31 ACM 854, 857, tithe collector's reports.
32 ACM 851, tithe reports.
33 Silvia Galicia Morales, *Precios y producción en San Miguel el Grande* (Dissertation, UNAM, Mexico, 1975) p. 115.
34 Rabel Romero, *San Luis de la Paz*, pp. 88–89.
35 AGN, Historia 523, f. 76; AGN, Historia 72, f. 169. The actual total for 1792 was 421 haciendas and 889 ranchos; there are added 14 haciendas and 29 ranchos for the omitted district of Rincón.
36 Rabel Romero, *San Luis de la Paz*, pp. 105–18.
37 AGN, Padrones 41, introduction.
38 Taylor, *Arandas in Jalisco*, pp. 13, 26–7; J. Ignacio Rubio Mañé, *Gente de España en la ciudad de México. Año de 1689* (Mexico, 1966) pp. 258–61.
39 AHML 1767, inventory 15 February 1767.
40 AHML 1773/74, 20 August 1773.
41 AGN, Vínculos 263–3, Inventory 25 January 1707.
42 AHML 1726/29–20, inventory 26 July 1728; ACM 858, tithe reports for 1779.
43 AHML 1711/12–2, inventory 19 June 1711.
44 AHML 1741/42–3, inventory 22 October 1721. The new owner was Nicolás Genera; he was backed by the Guanajuato merchant Juan de Hervas.
45 AGN, Vínculos 22–2, inventory February 1751. Pedro de Clavería had

bought the estate from Manuel de la Canal, the son-in-law of Juan de Hervas.

46 AGN, Vínculos 23, auction 24 April 1762; Jan Bazant, 'The Division of Some Mexican Haciendas during the Liberal Revolution 1856–1862', *Journal of Latin American Studies* 3 (1971) pp. 25–37.

47 AHML 1708/10–20, inventory 19 November 1707. The Alcocer family owned it.

48 ANL, 14 July 1791.

49 ACM 858, tithe report for 1779.

50 I wish to thank Professor Jan Bazant for suggesting, and Señora Beatriz Braniff for permitting me to examine the manuscript volumes of Jalpa deed titles. Unless otherwise stated, all material in this section is taken from this source.

51 Taylor, *Arandas in Jalisco*, pp. 26–27.

52 Leopoldo Martínez Cosío, *Los caballeros de las órdenes militares en México* (Mexico, 1946) pp. 62–65.

53 AGN, Bienes nacionales 85–37, 26 April 1749; ANL, 10 March 1758.

54 AGN, Vínculos 221–3. He borrowed this sum from the estate of the defunct marchioness of Colima; see also Ricardo Ortega y Pérez Gallardo, *Historia genealógica de las familias mas antiguas de México* (3 vols, Mexico 1908–10) II, 'Condado de la Presa de Jalpa'.

55 RPPL, Anotaciones de hipoteca, libro de becerro I, 25 May 1798.

56 Miguel J. Malo Zozaya, *La casa y mayorazgo de la Canal de la villa de San Miguel el Grande* (Mexico, 1962) pp. 106, 132–36.

57 For these estates see the introductory lists in AGN, Padrones 24, 30, 41, 42; the names are printed in D. A. Brading, 'La estructura de la producción agrícola en el Bajío de 1700 a 1850', *Historia mexicana* 90 (1973) pp. 197–237.

58 AGN, Vínculos 118–3, all the material in this section is taken from this calendar of titles of 127 folios.

59 See J. I. Israel, *Race, Class and Politics in Colonial Mexico 1600–1670* (Oxford, 1975) p. 35.

60 Martínez Cosío, *Los caballeros*, pp. 135–36; he is called a minor in the Jalpa papers.

61 Ortega y Pérez Gallardo, *Historia genealógica*, III, 'Mariscales de Castilla'.

62 ANL, 24 September 1703. One recipient was a shepherd and another ceded his lands to the Jesuits before the *merced* was actually granted.

63 RPPL, Anotaciones de hipoteca, libro de becerro, I, 8 November 1800.

64 AGN, Vínculos 117, entire volume.

65 AGN, Padrones 24. In Dolores only La Erre had a large number of tenants.

66 The clearest inventory is in AGN, Tierras 2646, 7 September 1753.

67 All material on Juchitlán is taken from three volumes AGN, Tierras 826–28.

68 AGN, Bienes nacionales 1864–65, 1 September 1806.

69 AGN, Subdelegados 5, Domínguez to viceroy, 31 October 1802.

70 González, *Pueblo en vilo*, *passim*.

## CHAPTER 3: POPULATION

1 Peter Gerhard, *A Guide to the Historical Geography of New Spain* (Cambridge, 1972) pp. 166–68.

2   Eduardo Salceda López, 'La fundación de San Miguel de la Corona', *Boletín* v (AHML, 1969) no. 54, 20 June 1969.

3   AGN, Tierras 1124–1, Purísima was granted a square league of land, 26 October 1648.

4   Ramón López Lara (ed.) *El obispado de Michoacán en el siglo XVII* (Morelia, 1973) pp. 69, 175–78.

5   AHML 1685/90–7, report on tributaries, undated.

6   Jesús Silva Herzog, *Relaciones estadísticas de Nueva España de principios del siglo XIX* (Mexico, 1944) p. 84.

7   Biblioteca del Real Palacio (Madrid) mss. 2824, miscelánea de Ayala x–25, ff. 232–33, Lic. Diego Peredo to Arriaga, 3 April 1761.

8   Sherburne F. Cook and Woodrow Borah, *Essays in Population History: Mexico and the Caribbean* (Berkeley and Los Angeles, 2 vols., 1971–74) I, 255–63.

9   Jean Pierre Berthe, 'La peste de 1643 en Michoacán: exámen crítico de una tradición', in *Historia y sociedad en el mundo de habla española. Homenaje a José Miranda* (ed. Bernardo García Martínez, Mexico, 1970) pp. 247–62.

10  AGN, Historia 523, f. 88.

11  Dr Morin cites ACM 685 as the source reference for this census.

12  Dr Morin cites ACM 707 for this parish census. See also Luis Manrique, *Brevísima relación histórica...de León* (León, 1854) p. 28. This was reprinted in *Biblioteca del Archivo Histórico Municipal* (León, 1969). Also Manuel Muñoz Ledo, *Memoria del estado libre y soberano de Guanajuato* (Guanajuato, 1882) section *censo*.

13  No individual citation is made in the pages which follow. The register is arranged by years. The numbers affixed to them are arbitrary later additions.

14  Brading, *Miners and Merchants*, pp. 249–50.

15  Poinsett, *Notes on Mexico*, pp. 208–20.

16  Garcilaso de la Vega, *La Florida del Inca* (Mexico, 1956) p. 76.

17  D. A. Brading, 'Grupos étnicos; clases y estructura ocupacional en Guanajuato (1792)'; and Marcelo Carmagnani, 'Demografía y sociedad: la estructura social de los centros mineros del norte de México 1600–1720', both in *Historia mexicana* 83 (1972) pp. 419–80.

18  J. Haynal, 'European Marriage Patterns in Perspective' in *Population in History* (ed. D. V. Glass and D. E. C. Eversley, London, 1956) pp. 101–45.

19  For a similar calculation see D. E. C. Eversley, 'A Survey of Population in an Area of Worcestershire from 1600 to 1850 on the Basis of Parish Registers', in *Population in History*, pp. 403–04.

20  El Colegio de México, *Dinámica de la población de México* (Mexico, 1970) p. 47.

21  The small number of *coyotes*, *lobos* and *moriscos* are included with the mulattoes and the *castizos* with the mestizos. See Magnus Mörner, *Race Mixture in the History of Latin America* (New York, 1967) pp. 58–9.

22  AHML 1771–28, 9 October 1772.

23  Humboldt, *Ensayo político*, pp. 571–72.

24  Rabel Romero, *San Luis de la Paz*, pp. 56–57.

25  *Dinámica de la población*, p. 7.

26  This is confirmed by Cook and Borah, *Essays in Population History*, II, 295, 319.

## CHAPTER 4:
# THE STRUCTURE OF AGRICULTURAL PRODUCTION

1  *Merced*, 2 May 1591, to Alvaro Sánchez in *Libro de títulos, radical y de successiones de la hacienda de labor y cría de ganados nombrada San José de los Sapos* in possession of Lic. José Luis Leal.

2  These documents are located in AHG, Tierras 1711–16. I am indebted to Señor Jesús Rodríguez Frausto for informing me of their existence.

3  See Chapter 6 for the history of many of these estates.

4  AHG, Tierras 1711, 13 January 1711, alcaldes of the two villages. San Miguel later lost its lands through sales made by its governors: see AGN, Tierras 1361–5, appeal for lands to viceroy, August 1803.

5  ANL, 13 May 1729, 2 June 1730; AHML 1748/50–13, will of José de Austri.

6  AHML 1828(3)–45. Some 29 properties are listed as haciendas, but one was a hill-side estancia and two more subordinate parts of other estates.

7  AHML 1828(3)–45. There were 64 entries, but 10 were later crossed off the list.

8  ANL, 8 April 1741; AGN, Tierras 671–5. The lawsuits lasted some thirty years and cost 5,000 ps. The lawyer, Lic. Juan del Barrio Lorenzot, took the haciendas of San Isidro and Terreros as payment.

9  Edmundo Leal, *Carta catastral del distrito de León, año de 1920* (Mexico, 1921).

10  Humboldt, *Ensayo político*, pp. 250–51.

11  José Antonio del Raso, *Notas estadísticas del departamento de Querétaro* (Mexico, 1848) pp. 37–39, 50–51.

12  AHML 1757/58–8, 21 February 1757.

13  Pedro González, *Estudio sobre estadística agrícola del estado de Guanajuato* (Guanajuato, 1903) p. 5.

14  For example, see Gibson, *The Aztecs*, pp. 309–10, 551–52.

15  AHML, file called *Datos agrícolas de León*.

16  AGN, Ayuntamientos 196, Pedro de Obregón, 21 February 1758.

17  AHG, Bienes difuntos 1843–45, Duarte inventory, February 1844.

18  Humboldt, *Ensayo político*, pp. 257–58; AHML 1757/58–8, February 1757.

19  González, *Estadística agrícola*, p. 6; Raso, *Notas estadísticas*, p. 51.

20  AHML 1757/58–8, February 1757.

21  AHML 1758/59–31, Duarte inventory, 26 January 1758; AHML 1807–2, Patiña inventory, 11 July 1807.

22  For León tithes see ACM 846, 848, 908; for Silao ACM 854, 857, 931. Unless otherwise stated, all subsequent discussion in this section is based on these documents.

23  Rabel Romero, *San Luis de la Paz*, pp. 88–98; Galicia Morales, *San Miguel el Grande* p. 115.

24  AHML 1826(4)–11, report 19 October 1826.

25  AHML 1757/58–8.

26  In addition to San Nicolás, he owned Ibarrilla (in which was included Herrera) and Patiña alias Asunción.

27  AHML 1752–17, Santa Rosa inventory, 29 August 1733. For Sarteneja see ANL, 19 November 1731. For Los Gómez ANL, 28 September 1730; AHML 1799/1800–9, inventory, 10 February 1783.

28  AGN, Tierras 1296–1; AHG, Tierras 1846–51; AHML 1839(1)–4; ANL, 25 October 1858.

29   For Jagüey ANL, 25 August 1796. In 1805 the entire estate was let for
     2,200 ps: ANL, 11 February 1805. For Gavia inventory, AHG, Tierras
     1846–51. For Losa AHML 1809(1)–6, inventory of Losa and Hoya. The
     latter hacienda had 48 tenants paying total 1,159 ps in rent. For San
     Cristóbal AHML 1839(1)–4, will 23 October 1838. Los Sapos: ANL,
     25 October 1858.
30   AHML 1842/(2)–3, 20 August 1844.
31   AHML 1759/60–2. The mayordomo of Sauces bought a rancho of
     3½ caballerías: AHML 1805/06–10; 1839(1)–4, will 23 October 1838.
32   ANL, 6 August 1750, Juan Cayetano Rico.
33   AHML 1756/57–23, Pedregal inventory, February 1757; AHML 1776–
     14, January 1767. For Palote see AHML 1774/(2)–2, 4, inventory
     18 December 1770; AHML, 1804/05–14, inventory, 25 February 1798.
34   AGN, Civil 286–3, Otates inventory February 1787. For Losa inventory
     AHML 1809(1)–6.
35   For freight charges see AGN, Ayuntamientos 245. The charge from San
     Pedro Piedragorda was 2½ reales. Duarte also sent 3,000 fanegas to
     Sierra de Pinos: AHML 1795/96–3. For citation AGN, Civil 279–1.
36   AHML 1758/59–31, Palote inventory.
37   AHML 1734–17, Blas de la Fuente, 15 April 1734.
38   AHML 1758/59–31, Palote inventory.
39   AHML 1764/65–15, 21 February 1764.
40   ANL, 26 October 1745. Luis de Fagoaga ordered 640 mules in 1753 and
     another 604 in 1755 from Cañada de Negros: ANL, 20 October 1757.
41   AHML 1748/50–13, Gavia inventory February 1750; AHML 1787/
     88–8, Jagüey inventory, July 1787.
42   ANL, 26 October 1745, 7 March 1771, 23 July 1790.
43   AHML 1774(2)–2; 1795/96–2; 1804/05–14.
44   For Cerrogordo AHML 1787/88–7; 1833(2)–11. For Otates AGN, Civil
     272–5. For San Cristóbal ANL, 4 and 27 February 1782.
45   ANL, 30 January 1806, 10 December 1807; RPPL 50–638, 14 February
     1938.
46   AHML 1708/10–6. The owner claimed he invested 1,600 ps in Sar-
     teneja. Also AHML 1791/92–13, inventory July 1792. For Talayote
     AGN, Tierras 1081–1, sale 17 May 1729; AHML 1793/95–25, inven-
     tory.
47   ANL, 4 March 1738; AHML 1825(3)–4; 2 December 1863.
48   ANL, 20 June 1836. But see ANL, 11 April 1836 where estate valued at
     32,000 ps.
49   ANL, 3 December 1742, 30 January 1783, 18 August 1845.
50   For original value AHML 1748/49–13. For Jagüey AHML 1787/88–8;
     ANL, 25 October 1849. For Sandía AHGP, 23 August 1788; ANL, 22
     December 1860.
51   AHML 1708/10–18; AGN, Civil 286–3; AHML 1837(1)–6.
52   AHML 1758/59–31; 1804/05–14.
53   Sarteneja inventories in AHML 1708/10–6; 1765/66–18; 1791/92–13.
54   ANL, 11 April 1836; AHML 1842(2)–3; ANL, 10 June 1836; AHML
     1793/94–20.
55   AHML 1806–9.
56   ANL, 31 December 1852, 8 November 1854, 7 January 1859.
57   For Sandía AHML 1785/86–13; AHGP, 23 August 1788; ANL, 8
     March 1856, 22 December 1860. For Santa Ana, AHGP, 18 December
     1839, 15 September 1840; ANL, 19 November 1861.
58   ANL, 5 April 1834. The tenant, José Tomás Pompa, owned 960 cattle

and 103 brood mares. In ANL, 28 September 1857, the tenant Luis Manrique was said to own livestock worth 5,629 ps.

59 For Sandía tenant ANL, 17 March 1819. For San Pedro del Monte, ANL, 11 March 1820.

60 For San Cristóbal ANL, 13 December 1770, 4 February 1782. For Peñuelas ANL, 7 May 1799, 27 November 1824. The funds were assigned as follows: 12,000 ps in two capellanías; 5,000 ps for six hospital beds in León; 16,000 ps for poor widows in León; 1,000 ps for altar lamp in Apaseo; 5,333 ps for poor of Apaseo; 5,333 ps for poor in Silao; 2,666 ps for poor in León; 2,666 ps for poor in Rincón; 2,000 ps for masses for soul of donor, Bachiller José Manuel de Ibarra.

61 ANL, 22 March 1848, 12 January 1849, 8 July 1850.

62 Taylor, *Landlord and Peasant*, pp. 250–51.

## CHAPTER 5:
### PROFITS AND RENTS: THREE HACIENDAS

1 AHG, Tierras 1710–11, 22 February 1711.
2 AHML 1757/58–8, 21 February 1757.
3 ACM 846, tithe reports.
4 AHML 1758/59–31.
5 The trustee was Julián de Obregón, the owner Isabel de Urruchua. For the sources of the subsequent discussion see Table 25.
6 AHG, Bienes difuntos 1843–45, inventory 1 February 1844.
7 AHG, Tierras 1710–11, 14 January 1710.
8 For inventories AHML 1708/10–18; AGN, Civil 286–3.
9 ACM 846, tithe reports.
10 ANL, 7 May 1804.
11 AHML 1815(1)–1, 26 June 1810.
12 These papers are located in AHML 1828(4)–2.
13 ANL, 21 February 1820. The new tenant agreed to pay for the 'maintenance of the troops who garrison the property'.
14 I here paraphrase Georges Duby, *Rural Economy and Country Life in the Medieval West* (London, 1968) p. 171. 'The destiny of every manor was individual and its structure unique.'
15 ANL, 31 December 1852, 8 November 1854.
16 ANL, 7 April 1708.
17 ACM 851, tithe reports for Rincón. AHML 1793/94–4.
18 Inventory in AHML 1827(3)–26. For sources of subsequent discussion see Table 28.
19 AHML 1822(3)–2.

## CHAPTER 6: LANDLORDS

1 ANL, 11 April 1749.
2 The names, ranks and interests of these councillors were as follows: Pedro de Obregón, *fiel ejecutor*, peninsular, merchant, owner of Los Sapos hacienda; José Tomás de Austri, *alférez real*, creole, owner of Sardina hacienda; Blas de Escudia, *alguacil mayor*, peninsular, merchant; Francisco Javier de Marmolejo, *alcalde provincial*, creole, merchant, owner of Cañada de Negros; Ignacio Gómez Poleo, *regidor* peninsular, merchant, later owner of Palote; José Santiago de Herrera, *procurador general*, creole, owner of Cerrogordo.

3 This account is based on José María Ots de Capdequí, *Historia de América: Instituciones* (Barcelona and Madrid, 1959) pp. 311–12, 320–24. The relevant laws are found in *Novísima recopilación de las leyes de España* (6 vols., Madrid, 1805–06) lib. x, tit, 4, 6, 20.

4 Brading, *Miners and Merchants*, pp. 102–03, 264–65, 274.

5 For the history and dimensions of these estates see AHG, Tierras 1710–11.

6 For parents AHML 1695/99–28; 1712/15–5. For purchases ANL, 13 May 1729, 8 January 1720; mortgage ANL, 30 May 1720, last will, 9, 14 June 1742.

7 AHML 1769/70–10. For Rafael AHML 1781/82–1. For José at Comanja AHML 1804/05–12; for Alfonso AHML 1800–30.

8 For Laurel sales ANL, 31 January 1748, 22 May, 1 October 1749, 19 August 1751, 13 January 1753. For Lagunillas ANL, 12 January 1746. For Losa AGN, Civil 272–5, 279–1; ANL, 27 September 1755, 4 July 1771. Luis de Carmona bought the hacienda for 9,700 ps.

9 For Losa AHML 1702/03–3; ANL, 2 October 1701, 16 May 1729, 24 May 1730.

10 ANL, 18 April 1731. See also Francisco Javier Alegre, *Historia de la provincia de la compañia de Jesús de Nueva España* (ed. Ernest J. Burrus and Félix Zubillaga, 4 vols., Rome, 1956–60) IV, 347.

11 ANL, 1 May 1729. For Austri's will AHML 1748/49–13. His wife never learnt to sign her name: ANL, 23 August 1763.

12 The *labor* was called Ojeda: ANL, 13 November 1780. For purchases ANL, 26 April 1711, 5 February 1712, 23 December 1711, 3 September 1722, 26 January 1729, 23 June 1731; AHML 1712/15–25.

13 For Gavia ANL, 3 March 1728; for Santa Ana ANL, 20 January 1727, 14 May 1729.

14 The inventory is in AHML 1748/49–13.

15 Granjeno sale ANL, 4 April 1750; inventory AHML 1742/43–3. Concepción titles and sales ANL, 20 December 1733, 8 February 1742. For later mortgages ANL, 19 November 1801; AHML 1808–13.

16 ANL, 3–7 December 1742; AHML 1769–10; 1776/78–19; ANL, 9 July, 13 August 1757.

17 ANL, 5 June, 16 December 1778, 30 January 1783; for later history ANL, 26 November 1840, 26 November 1845.

18 For Septién see Brading, *Miners and Merchants* pp. 312–14.

19 For sales ANL, 15 March 1742, 31 March 1751; AHML 1744/45–15. See Table 35.

20 ANL, 19 October 1761. For Herrera, AHML 1767–7; inventory 1757/58–4. For subsequent history ANL, 22 November 1793.

21 ANL, 22 July 1762. For history ANL, 7 August 1807.

22 The purchases are in ANL, 14 June 1728, 26 September 1738, 11 August 1744, 2 September 1744, 11 December 1751, 27 March 1752. *Composición* in AHML 1746/47–18.

23 For a list see AHML 1756/57–23.

24 AHML 1757/58–8; she first let the estate; ANL, 22 March 1762. For sale to Valenciana ANL, 28 June 1781.

25 ANL, 28 February 1782, 6 May 1782, 18 January 1783.

26 Estefanía de Obregón only died in 1770. For division of estate ANL, 6 November 1777. For division of Sardina ANL, 19 September 1778.

27 The contract was notarised in ANL, 3 October 1772, 5 March 1773. The Santa Ana was first embargoed in 1776. For auction see AHML 1776–17; ANL, 29 August 1781, 7 January, 6 March 1782.

28  ANL, 16 October 1786. Here is a history of the estate.
29  AHML 1787/88–8; ANL, 26 April 1773, 8 January 1780, 9 August 1787.
30  AHGP, 23 February 1790; AGI, Mexico 1779, appeal 5 September 1794.
31  AHML 1791/92–18; ANL, 6 June 1796.
32  ANL, 24 March 1859.
33  Brading, *Miners and Merchants*, p. 313; ANL, 23 September 1783 Ibarrilla sold. For Sandía AHGP, 23 August 1788. Both estates were previously let.
34  He married Ignacia Gómez Poleo, daughter of the Andalusian owner of Palote. The grandson was Miguel Urteaga Septién. See ANL, 25 August 1831, 11 April 1836, 9 July 1894, 11 January 1904.
35  AHML 1660/63–16; 1708/10–18.
36  ANL, 24 June 1710, in volume marked 1704–11.
37  ANL, 10 June 1759, 1 October 1783, 7 May 1804; AHML 1804/05–13.
38  Brading, *Miners and Merchants*, pp. 304, 349.
39  ANL, 22 December 1742.
40  AHML 1736/38–2.
41  ANL, 7 February 1728. His previous oath was a period of four years.
42  ANL, 29 August 1713. The Palote sale included 101 oxen and other stock; AML, 30 October 1720. For Duarte purchase ANL, 26 June 1737.
43  AHML 1758/59–32.
44  AHML 1774(2)–1–4; ANL, 21 July 1758, 6 September, 2 October 1764, 15 October 1766.
45  ANL, 1 August 1771, 23 December 1782, 28 January 1790.
46  Her will is inserted in ANL, August 1832. She had purchased the adjoining hacienda of Comanjillas.
47  AHML 1776–14; ANL, 3 February 1745, 4 February 1748.
48  ANL, 15 May 1756, 5 June 1763, 27 June 1763.
49  AHML 1776–14; ANL, 24 March, 28 May 1763, 1 February 1772.
50  ANL, 7 April, 30 December 1777; AHML 1781/82–6; sale of Cañada de Negros ANL, 23 July 1790.
51  AHML 1804/05–14; 1802/03–11; ANL, 11 July 1810.
52  AHML 1774(2)–4.
53  Brading, *Miners and Merchants*, p. 265; ANL, 20 January 1727, 26 June 1737.
54  For Sauz de Armenta ANL, 7 April 1708, 16 April 1765, 24 April 1789. For Sardaneta ANL, 4 August 1710, 30 June 1750, 22 September 1798.
55  Titles in AHML 1734–14. Sale AHML 1752–17. The capellanías were 6,200 ps.
56  AHML 1739/40–6; ANL, 15 June 1734, 3 October 1742.
57  ANL, 1 March 1779. For Hinojosa ANL, 1 July 1772, 18 April 1775. For Arroyohondo ANL, 11 December 1775.
58  The Marquis owed 154,000 ps to the *consolidación* junta: AMM 153, 2 May 1807. For Santa Rosa, sale price unspecified, ANL, 2 August 1852.
59  Brading, *Miners and Merchants*, pp. 278–79, 291–93, 307–09. For Austri's will AHML 1748/50–13.
60  ANL, 30 January 1806, 10 December 1807.
61  Francisco Antúnez Echagaray, *Monografía histórica y minera sobre el distrito de Guanajuato* (Mexico, 1964) pp. 464–66, 480–81, 527–29.
62  AHGP, 18 December 1839, 15 September 1840.
63  For Santa Rosa, ANL, 2 August 1852. San Cristóbal was sold to Ignacio Alcocer for 75,000 ps: AHGP, 21 January 1852.

64 Sandía was first sold to José Guadalupe Ibargüengoitia in 1852 for an unspecified price. He then sold it to Guerrero in 1860: AHGP, 7 December 1853; ANL, 22 December 1860.

65 AHML 1787/88–8; ANL, 25 October 1849.

66 Brading, *Miners and Merchants*, pp. 196, 310. Through his marriage he became brother-in-law of José Ildefonso de Septién: AHML 1804–6; ANL, 13 February 1810.

67 For Cañada de Negros, ANL, 23 July 1790. For Pedregal ANL, 30 October 1795.

68 AGN, Tierras 1206–2, sale 26 April 1792.

69 RPPL, anotaciones de hipoteca, libro de becerro, 1, 26 January 1790; AGN, Vínculos 216–10.

70 RPPL, anotaciones de hipoteca, libro de becerro II, 26 January 1804, 14 December 1809, 3 February 1814. In this misappropriation Obregón was the associate of the Marquis de San Juan de Rayas, the Administrator-general; AGI, Mexico 2254, Fausto de Elhuyar to Lizana, 17 December 1809.

71 Ward, *Mexico in 1827*, II, 501–06; Octaviano Cabrera Ipiña, *El Real de Catorce* (Mexico, 1970) pp. 91–92; for debts, ANL, 30 August 1846.

72 ANL, 4 April 1835. The last owners, Teresa and Josefa Gaona y Alcocer were his great-aunts.

73 ANL, August 1832. She left only 9,000 ps in charitable bequests, but all her jewels and silver went to the church of La Soledad where she had already paid for the construction of the high altar.

74 AHML 1828(4)–4; ANL, 24 March 1832.

75 ANL, 23 February 1846, 4 May 1853; AHG, Bienes difuntos 1843–45 for auction of Duarte. For Cuitzeo there are multiple entries in ANL register between February 1844 and December 1846.

76 AHGP, 17 October 1856. The purchaser, José Guadalupe Ibargüengoitia, borrowed 80,000 ps from Juan Antonio de Béistegui: AHML 1857(1)–17.

77 ANL, 22 November 1793, 23 December 1810. Sardaneta sale ANL, 22 September, 1 October 1798. For debts AHML 1825(3)–3.

78 ANL, 23 February 1828. In 1851 the price was 38,000 ps: AHGP, 7 March 1851; ANL, 28 February 1860.

79 AHML 1809(1)–6; RPPL, anotaciones de hipoteca, libro de becerro I, 12 October 1793; Brading, *Miners and Merchants*, p. 288; ANL, 10 March 1810.

80 ANL, 11 July 1810, the nephew, Antonio Bernardino de Quiros, left his fortune to his young Quijano cousins. For division ANL, 24 October 1836, 19 April 1837.

81 ANL, 30 September 1835, 9 October 1844, 6 July 1850.

82 ANL, 12 January 1849. For Oratory see Luis Manrique, *Brevísima relación histórica...de León* (León, 1854) pp. 20–21.

83 ANL, 16 May 1838. Losa was first sold to Bachiller José Hilario Ibargüengoitia. For sale to Doblado AHGP, 23 May 1863. The price was 60,000 ps of which 44,000 ps was charged in deposit on the hacienda.

84 ANL, 23 December 1857. The lease-holder claimed the right to ownership.

85 ANL, 6 November 1807; AHGP, 23 October 1806; AMM 145–20.

86 For division ANL, 21 August, 6 September 1820. For San Juan de Abajo ANL, 11 October 1859.

87 1798 inventory in AHML 1806–10. José Ramón de Hoyos, grandson of

*regidor* José Tomás de Austri acted as Subdelegate for Hidalgo: AHML 1810(1)–10. For division AHML 1831(1)–3.

88　ANL, 10 January 1791, 28 April 1807; AHML 1801/02–21. For auction ANL, 18 October 1826.
89　The hacienda had been already once divided by the Castros: ANL, 20 June 1834, 12 June 1844; AHML 1849(2)–2.
90　AMM 157–17; AHML 1822(2)–7. For Liceaga family Brading, *Miners and Merchants*, p. 318; AHG, Tierras 1846–51.
91　ANL, 20 June 1861, 10 February 1863, 21 April 1869; ANL, Torres, 21 August 1926.
92　ANL, 1 September 1713, 4 March 1738, 19 November 1796, 25 August 1808; AHML 1787/88–7; 1803(1)–6.
93　For inventory AHML 1825(3)–4. For purchases 2 May 1803, 23 July 1819, Los Gómez; 16 May 1820 Cerrito; 14 August 1828 Patiña.
94　For division ANL, 19 April 1837; final sale ANL 2 December 1863.
95　ANL, 17 May 1729; AHML 1756/57–23.
96　All the material in this section on Talayote comes from AGN, Tierras 1081–1.
97　AHML 1781/82–22; 1787/88–2; 1788/89–17.
98　ANL, 16 September 1789, 26 January 1793. The hacienda was worth 11,505 ps with 6,550 ps mortgages.
99　Inventory in AHML 1793/94–25. Rancho inventory in AHML 1803(3)–2.
100　The residuary heir was José Angel Guerrero. ANL, 16 September 1805, 3 December 1805, 12 June 1806, 5 February 1810.
101　AHML 1824(2)–36; 1823(3)–37.
102　ANL, 8 March 1856, 22 December 1860; RPPL, 34–236, 22 February 1918; 37–138, 23 April 1922. She married Juan Velasco y Palacios.

## CHAPTER 7: RANCHEROS

1　For example, Carl Sartorious, *Mexico about 1850* (reprint, Stuttgart, 1961) pp. 93, 167, 179–80, 185; Luis G. Inclán, *Astucia* (3 vols., Mexico, 1946) I, 12–13.
2　McBride, *Land Systems of Mexico*, pp. 82–102; Molina Enríquez, *Los grandes problemas nacionales*, pp. 81–104; Orozco, *Legislación*, I, 42; II, 937–59.
3　González, *Pueblo en vilo*, pp. 93–97, 138–43.
4　Taylor, *Arandas in Jalisco*, pp. 13, 26–29.
5　Chevalier, *Los grandes latifundios*, pp. 175–78.
6　Vera, *Salvatierra*, pp. 16–17.
7　ANL, 28 September 1730.
8　For 1828 list see AHML 1828(3)–45.
9　AHML 1646–1; 1702/05–7; AHG, Tierras 1711; ANL, 26 October, 6 November, 31 December 1731, 9 December 1733.
10　AHML, 1764/65–24; 1756–19; ANL, 27 March 1764.
11　Sales to Echeveste ANL, 3 October 1775, 19 July 1777, 28 February 1791; for Falcón ANL, 18 August 1791, 18 February 1797. 1¼ *fanegas de sembradura* sold for 150 ps: ANL, 23 February 1856.
12　AHG, Tierras 1711; ANL, 2 April 1719, 18 February 1712.
13　ANL, 22 July 1726, 20 May 1845, 2 March 1857.
14　AHML 1716/18–3.
15　AHG, Tierras 1711; AHML 1705/08–2; ANL, 8 April 1707, 31 December 1731.

16  AHML 1756/57–17, 23; ANL, 20 July 1746, 26 February 1756, 5 February 1759. It is noteworthy that Nicolás Ramírez could sign his name and owned a house in town.
17  ANL, 1 July 1786.
18  For origins AHG, Tierras, 1711; ANL, 10 June 1746. The descent is intricate: AHML 1781/82–14. For sales ANL, 14 August 1786, 23 May 1803.
19  AGN, Tierras 1361–6.
20  ANL, 13 July 1822, 17 February 1849.
21  The lawsuit is in AHML 1838(1)–17. For sales ANL, 7 January 1826, 10 February 1859.
22  ANL, 5 March 1731; AHML 1754/55–21.
23  AGN, Tierras 963–2.
24  AHML 1769–1; ANL, 30 April 1756. For sales AHML 1788/89–20; ANL, 11 March 1807, 16 June 1819.
25  ANL, 18 January 1787; AHML 1819/20–13; ANL, 18 December 1820, 18 September 1821, 5 October 1857, 1 October 1859, 16 February 1861.
26  ANL, 15 December 1806, 25 February 1830.
27  ANL, 9 November 1750, 6 February 1751; ANL, 30 March 1748, 26 January 1751.
28  ANL, 17 October 1750, 20 November, 30 December 1750, 4 September, 31 March 1751.
29  ANL, 26 October, 6 November 1750, 19 October 1813, 29 December 1815.
30  ANL, 7 October, 9 December 1750, 17 September 1751; AHML 1773/74–28; 1731/32–3.
31  ANL, 16 November 1847, 25 May 1835.
32  ANL, 12 September 1743, 19 September 1745, 18 April, 21 May, 4 August 1746, 6 March, 6 August 1750.
33  AGN, Tierras 956–4; AHML 1798/99–28.
34  ANL, 11 November 1709, 18 November 1745; sales ANL, 11 December 1751, 31 July 1784, 3 January 1786, 16 February 1787.
35  ANL, 7 November 1725, 17 May 1727, 13 April 1747.
36  Sales ANL, 29 May 1751; Santa Lucía sale ANL, 14 May 1767; one caballería 27 March 1781. Last sale 24 December 1845.
37  AHG, Tierras 1711; ANL, 5 October 1705.
38  AHML 1711/12–9; 1729/31–8; 1736/38–1; 1781/82–13; ANL, 30 May 1725, 23 February 1787.
39  AHML 1748/50–7; ANL, 9 April 1744.
40  For Laurel sales ANL, 31 January 1748, 22 May, 1 October 1749, 19 April 1751, 11 May 1753.
41  For Los Gómez sale ANL, 2 May 1803; for renting ANL, 7 September 1755, 7 September 1799.
42  AHML 1781/82–12.
43  ANL, 7 August 1802, 14 August 1828, 25 October 1849; AHML 1807–2.
44  AHG, Tierras 1711; ANL, 3 April 1762.
45  AHML 1734–17; ANL, 23 April 1733, 2 May 1747, 3 April 1762, 4 June 1763, 7 June 1764, 31 December 1777.
46  AHML 1767/68–7. For a list of these purchases ANL, 1 June 1795.
47  AHML 1785/86–28.
48  AHML 1807–2; 1821(4)–3; ANL, 16 January 1828, 7 February 1831, 22 April 1841.
49  ANL, 3 April 1750, 23 April 1755; AHML 1756/57–23.

50  AHML 1756/57-33; ANL, 5 June 1761, 9 June, 9 September 1763, 31 December 1777, 18 August 1800.
51  For Vicente ANL, 4 February 1799; for José Manuel AHML 1801-11; for division of estates ANL, 25 April 1798.
52  AHML 1801/02-21; 1842(1)-8; ANL, 24 July 1833.
53  ANL, 3 August 1741, 22 May 1758, 9 August 1766; AHML 1759/60-24.
54  For quarrel AHML 1793-4. For Nicolás ANL, 28 July 1786, 26 May 1786, 12 January 1789; AHML 1798/99-20; 1801/02-21.
55  For Gordiano AHML 1823(2)-14; ANL, 21 August 1833, 27 March, 10 April 1844. For Juan Manuel AHML 1843(1)-7.
56  AHML 1701/02-10; 1718/20-1; ANL, 26 January 1709, 28 January 1718.
57  ANL, 5 June 1761. The owners were Vicente and Julián Buso: AHML 1756/57-3, 18.
58  ANL, 27 November 1725, 8 March 1762.
59  ANL, 30 September 1779, 26 April 1800, 11 January 1805.
60  ANL, 6 April 1786. For San Nicolás ANL, 22 May 1779. For Santa Rosa AHML 1798/99-1.
61  ANL, 27 March 1781, 31 July 1784, 3 January 1786, 16 February 1787.
62  For inventory AHML 1824(1)-1; ANL, 16 May 1820, 28 July 1823, 6 September 1825. For later transactions ANL, 22 February 1845, 12 January 1847.
63  AHML 1773/74-12; ANL, 21 March 1772, 4 February 1773, 8-11 January 1781, 3 November 1807, 26 February 1813; AHML 1815(2)-27.
64  ANL, 16 May 1820. The estate passed to a younger son and was managed as a separate enterprise. For Miguel Echeveste ANL, 11 August, 19-24 December 1829.
65  AHML 1754/55-2; 1759/60-4; ANL, 26 September 1743, 18 December 1787.
66  ANL, 18 February 1779, 16 July 1791, 9 February 1801; inventories in AHML 1804-3; 1821(4)-16.
67  ANL, 11 March 1800.
68  ANL, 27 June 1807.

## CHAPTER 8: AGRICULTURAL
## PRICES AND THE DEMOGRAPHIC CRISIS

1  Lucas Alamán, *Historia de Méjico* (5 vols., Mexico, 1968-69) I, 63-85; V, 547-98.
2  Humboldt, *Ensayo político*, pp. 385-89, 495-502; Peter Gerhard, *México en 1742* (Mexico, 1962) *passim*; Fernando Navarro y Noriega, *Memoria sobre la población del reino de la Nueva España* (Mexico, 1954) foldpaper; Florescano, *Estructuras y problemas agrarios*, p. 100.
3  Brading, *Miners and Merchants*, pp. 129-58.
4  *Ibid.*, pp. 261-302.
5  *Ibid.*, pp. 146-49, 276-78, 289-91.
6  Florescano, *Precios del maíz*, pp. 111-35, 160.
7  Cook and Borah, *Essays in Population History*, I, 107-17.
8  Claude Morin, 'Population et épidémies dans une paroise mexicaine: Santa Inés Zecatelco xviii^e^-xix^e^ siecles' and Thomas Calvo, 'Demographie historique d'une paroisse mexicaine: Acatzingo 1606-1810', both in *Cahiers des Ameriques Latines* 6 (1972) pp. 1-73. Both articles

were later published (INAH, Mexico, 1973) with titles *Santa Inés
Zacatelco* and *Acatzingo*. Also see Rabel Romero, *San Luis de la Paz*.

9  Donald B. Cooper, *Epidemic Disease in Mexico City, 1761–1813* (Austin,
   Texas, 1965) *passim*.
10  Morin, *Zacatelco*, pp. 45–50.
11  Cook and Borah, *Essays in Population History*, I, 310–21, 355.
12  British Museum, Egerton Mss. 1801, f. 269.
13  Gibson, *Aztecs under Spanish Rule*, p. 311.
14  Florescano, *Estructuras y problemas agrarios*, pp. 125–28.
15  A list of these epidemics is printed in *Boletín* (AHML) III (1967) no. 35,
   pp. 3–4.
16  Francisco Fernández del Castillo, *Los viajes de don Francisco Javier de
   Balmis* (Mexico, 1960) pp. 147–67.
17  Gibson, *Aztecs under Spanish Rule*, p. 316; Florescano, *Precios del maíz*
   pp. 17–77; Cooper, *Epidemic Disease*, pp. 70–85; Humboldt, *Ensayo
   político*, p. 47.
18  AHML 1788/89–30.
19  AHML 1785/86–17. The loan, made 6 December 1785, was repaid
   31 October 1787.
20  AGN, Ayuntamientos 245, purchases of León alhóndiga, 10 April
   1786–31 December 1787.
21  ACM 598, cura to bishop, 14 February 1787.
22  Humboldt, *Ensayo político*, pp. 385–89.
23  ANL, 6 March 1750; the vendor was Cristóbal Manuel Rico, an *indio
   ladino*.
24  Brading, *Miners and Merchants*, pp. 114–19, 126–28, 141–43, 151.
25  AGI, Mexico, 1511, Cossío to Mayorga, 22 August 1781.
26  BN (Mexico) mss. 1304, Consulado report c. 1789.
27  ANL, 5 March, 17 November 1762, 18 October 1764, 19 December
   1768; AHML 1776/78–21; ANL, 27 February 1782, 12 March 1784,
   18 March 1786, 6 March 1792.
28  Florescano, *Precios del maíz*, pp. 114–18.
29  AGN, Intendencias 73, Riaño to viceroy 25 April, 11 September 1809.
30  AHML 1826(4)–11.
31  Compare Gibson, *Aztecs under Spanish rule*, pp. 250–52 with Bazant,
   *Cinco haciendas*, pp. 29, 89–90, 105–09, 163–64, 175.
32  See chapter 4, section iv.
33  AHML 1798/99–1; 1807–27, tenants' complaint, 8 March 1804.
34  AGN, Vínculos 5–3, Indian protest, 9 March 1802.
35  For this case AGN, Tierras 1383–3. Expulsion of leaders March 1808.
   Also José María Luis Mora, *Obras sueltas* (Mexico, 1963) p. 169.
36  William Davis Robinson, *Memoirs of the Mexican Revolution: including
   a narrative of the expedition of General Xavier Mina* (Philadelphia,
   1820) p. 218.
37  Poinsett, *Notes on Mexico*, pp. 143–48.
38  Ward, *Mexico in 1827*, II, 418–19; Carlos María de Bustamante,
   *Continuación del cuadro histórico de la revolución mexicana* (4 vols.,
   Mexico, 1953–63) III, 221–24.
39  Charles H. Harris III, *A Mexican Family Empire. The latifundio of the
   Sánchez Navarro Family 1765–1867* (Austin, Texas, 1975) pp. 82–93,
   113–21, 231–41, 152–57.
40  Lucio Marmolejo *Efemérides guanajuatenses* (4 vols., Guanajuato, 1884)
   III, 278, 287–89; IV, 10, 23, 87; M. P. Laur, 'De la métalurgie de
   l'argent au Mexique', *Annales des Mines* 6th series, 20 (1871) pp. 38–

317; Robert W. Randell, *Real del Monte. A British Mining Venture in Mexico* (Austin, Texas, 1972) pp. 73–85, 201–09.

41 Robert A. Potash, *El banco de avío de México* (Mexico, 1959) *passim*.

42 Bazant, *Cinco haciendas* pp. 67, 93–95.

43 Bustamante, *Continuación del cuadro histórico*, III, 221–24; Pedro Telmo Primo, *Querétaro en 1822* (Mexico, 1944) p. 25.

44 Francois Chevalier, 'Survivances Seigneuriales et Presages de la Revolution Agraire', *Revue Historique* CCXXII (1959) pp. 1–18; Jan Bazant, 'The Division of Some Mexican Haciendas during the Liberal Revolution 1856–1862', *Journal of Latin American Studies* 3 (1971) pp. 25–37.

45 Multiple entries in ANL, February–October 1844, February–December 1846, 17–18 January 1847, 11 February 1848.

46 Brading, 'La estructura de la producción agrícola en el Bajío de 1700 a 1850', *Historia mexicana* XXIII (1975) pp. 217–20.

47 Taylor, *Arandas in Jalisco*, pp. 26–27; González, *Pueblo en vilo*, pp. 96–98, 108.

## CHAPTER 9: EPILOGUE: AGRARIAN REFORM 1919–40

1 Manuel Muñoz Ledo, *Memoria del estado de Guanajuato* (Guanajuato, 1882) no. 46; McBride, *Land Systems of Mexico*, pp. 78, 98.

2 ANL, 9 July 1894, 11 January 1904; ANL, Torres, 25 January, 19 July 1922.

3 Frank Tannenbaum, *The Mexican Agrarian Revolution* (Washington, 1930) pp. 121–24; Frederick Katz, 'Labour Conditions on Haciendas in Porfirian Mexico: Some Trends and Tendencies', *Hispanic American Historical Review* 54 (1974) pp. 1–47.

4 O. Preust, *Estadística agrícola* (Mexico, 1910) pp. 14–17.

5 Bazant, *Cinco haciendas*, pp. 149–50.

6 I am indebted to Señor Jorge Obregón for this description.

7 AHML in file *Datos agrícolas de León*.

8 RPPL, 41–179, 27 August 1929 for Duarte; RPPL, 43–95, 6 October 1931 for Losa. In both cases the owners claimed that the *aparceros* were in fact *peones acasillados*.

9 For the text of article 27 see Felipe Tena Ramírez, *Leyes fundamentales de México 1808–1967* (Mexico, 1967) pp. 825–33.

10 Jesús Silva Herzog, *El agrarismo mexicano y la reforma agraria* (Mexico, 1959) pp. 325–26.

11 *Ibid.*, pp. 336–37, 372–74.

12 Jean Meyer, *The Cristero Rebellion. The Mexican People between Church and State 1926–31* (Cambridge, 1976) pp. 51, 93–4.

13 DAG, ejido files, petition 1 November 1921, presidential decree 14 October 1926.

14 *Boletín de la camara agrícola nacional de León* VIII (October, 1921) pp. 114–15. There is a copy in AHML, file *Datos agrícolas de León*.

15 For a list of these sales see RPPL, 49–51, 15 October 1936.

16 ANL, Torres, multiple entries, 16–21 October 1921, 23 February 1922, 9 May 1923, 6 April–9 October 1925, 15 June 1929.

17 ANL, Torres, multiple entries, years 1922–26.

18 RPPL, 40–10, 31 October 1927; presidential decree in RPPL, 41–179, 7 August 1929.

19 RPPL, 49–51, 15 October 1936.

20 RPPL, 43–125, 11 November 1931; 50–59, 13 October 1937.

21 RPPL, 37–215, 19 February 1923.

22 RPPL, 53: 86–191, 14–23 May 1940; 269–92, 21–23 September 1940; 303–11, 22 October–8 November 1940.

23 Meyer, *The Cristero Rebellion*, p. 91: ANL, Enrique Mendoza, 11 January, 17–18 August 1931. Guadalupe Cánovas, whose father married into the Monterde family, took Tomás Braniff as husband.

24 DAG, dotación de tierras, expediente 2509.

25 RPPL, 34, 21 May 1913. Markussa inherited the estate from Antonia del Moral y Otero. For transactions see RPPL 44, multiple entries 22 June–14 September 1932; 45, multiple entries 12 February–19 April 1933.

26 DAG, ejido files; RPPL, 50–69, 22 October 1937.

27 RPPL, 8, 23 September 1889; for inheritance RPPL, 37–138, 23 August 1922; 34–236, 12 February 1918. The value of the three haciendas of Sandía, Santa Ana and Sopeña in Silao was estimated at 792,832 ps in 1918.

28 RPPL, 46–47, multiple entries, October 1933–April 1933.

29 DAG, ejido files on León; RPPL, 50–638, 14 February 1938.

30 Leopoldo Solís, *La realidad económica mexicana: retrovisión y perspectivas* (Mexico, 1970) p. 201.

# Bibliography

A. Primary sources
(Mss. cited in notes)

ACM – *Archivo Casa Morelos* (Morelia)
Legajos 598, 846, 851, 854, 857, 908, 931.

AGI – *Archivo General de Indias* (Seville)
Audiencia de México, legajos 1454, 1511, 1570, 1779, 1887, 2254.

AGN – *Archivo General de la Nación* (Mexico City)
Ayuntamientos, volumes 196, 245.
Bienes nacionales, volume 85.
Civil, volumes 272, 279, 286.
Historia, volumes 72, 523.
Intendencias, volume 73.
Padrones, volumes 24, 30, 41, 42.
Subdelegados, volume 5.
Templos, volume 10.
Tierras, volumes 671, 826–28, 956, 963, 1081, 1124, 1206, 1296, 1361, 1383, 1246.
Vínculos, volumes 5, 22, 23, 117–18, 216, 221, 263.

AHG – *Archivo Histórico de Guanajuato*
Bienes difuntos, legajo, 1843–45.
Protocolos de cabildo, yearly volumes 1788, 1790, 1839, 1851–53, 1856, 1863.
Tierras, legajos 1710; 1711; 1711–16.

AHML – *Archivo Histórico Municipal de León*
92 cajas for years 1691–1810.
Cajas for years 1815(2), 1819/20, 1821(4), 1822(3), 1823(2), 1825(3), 1826(4), 1827(3), 1828(4), 1831(1), 1833(2), 1837(1), 1838(1), 1839(1), 1842(2), 1843(1), 1849(2), 1857(1).

AMM – *Archivo Municipal de Morelia*
legajos 145, 153, 157.

ANL – *Archivo Notarial de León*
Yearly volumes 1695–1862.

APL – *Archivo Parroquial de León*
Baptisms, burials and marriages 1689–1863.
Marriage testimonies 1782–93, 1858–60.

BM – *British Museum* (London)
Egerton Mss. 1801.

BN – *Biblioteca Nacional* (Mexico City)
Mss. 1304.

BRP – *Biblioteca del Real Palacio* (Madrid)
Mss. 2824.

DAG – *Delegación Agraria de Guanajuato*
Ejido files for León.
Tierras, expediente 2509.

RPPL – *Registro Público de Propiedad de León*
Anotaciones de hipotecas, libros de becerro, for years 1791–1804.
Registro público, volumes 34–53, for years 1918–40.

B. Printed materials and secondary works
(cited in notes)

Alamán, Lucas, *Historia de Méjico* (5 vols., Mexico, 1942)
Alegre, Francisco Javier, *Historia de la provincia de la compañía de Jesús de Nueva España* (ed. Ernest J. Burrus and Félix Zubillaga, 4 vols., Rome, 1956–60)
Antúnez Echagaray, Francisco, *Monografía histórica y minera sobre el distrito de Guanajuato* (Mexico, 1964)
Bakewell, P. J., *Silver Mining and Society in Colonial Mexico: Zacatecas 1546–1700* (Cambridge, 1971)
Bazant, Jan, *Cinco haciendas mexicanas: tres siglos de vida rural en San Luis Potosí 1600–1910* (Mexico, 1975)
'The Division of Some Mexican Haciendas during the Liberal Revolution 1856–1862', *Journal of Latin American Studies* 3 (1971) pp. 25–37
Berthe, Jean Pierre, 'La peste de 1643 en Michoacán: exámen crítico de una tradición', in *Historia y sociedad en el mundo de habla española: Homenaje a José Miranda* (ed. Bernardo García Martínez, Mexico, 1970)
Blum, Jerome, *Landlord and Peasant in Russia* (Princeton, 1961)
Brading, D. A., 'Creole Nationalism and Mexican Liberalism', *Journal of Interamerican Studies and World Affairs* 15 (1973) pp. 139–90
'Government and Elite in Late Colonial Mexico', *Hispanic American Historical Review* 53 (1973) pp. 389–414
'Hacienda Profits and Tenant Farming in the Mexican Bajío 1700–1860' in *Land and Labour in Latin America* (ed. K. Duncan and I. Rutledge, Cambridge, 1977)

'La estructura de producción agrícola en el Bajío de 1700 a 1850', *Historia mexicana* XXIII (1973) pp. 197–237

*Los orígenes del nacionalismo mexicano* (Sep-Setentas, Mexico, 1973)

*Miners and Merchants in Bourbon Mexico 1763–1810* (Cambridge, 1971)

'Relación sobre la economía de Querétaro y de su Corregidor Don Miguel Domínguez 1802–1811', edited in *Boletín* (AGN, Mexico City) 2nd series XI (1970) pp. 275–318

'The Capital Structure of Mexican Haciendas: León 1700–1850', *Ibero-Amerikanisches Archiv* I (1975) pp. 151–82

D. A. Brading and Harry E. Cross, 'Colonial Silver Mining: Mexico and Peru', *Hispanic American Historical Review* 52 (1972) pp. 545–79

D. A. Brading and Celia Wu, 'Population Growth and Crisis: León 1720–1860', *Journal of Latin American Studies* 5 (1973) pp. 1–36

Bustamante, Carlos María, *Continuación del cuadro histórico de la revolución mexicana* (4 vols., Mexico, 1953–63)

Cabrera, Ipiña, Octaviano, *El Real de Catorce* (Mexico, 1970)

Calvo, Thomas, *Acatzingo: demografía de una parroquia mexicana* (Mexico, 1973)

'Demographie historique d'une paroisse mexicaine: Acatzingo 1606–1810,' *Cahiers des Ameriques Latines* 6 (1972)

Carmagnani, Marcello, *Les Mecanismes de la Vie Economique dans une Societé Coloniale. Le Chilé 1680–1830* (Paris, 1973)

Castillo, Carlos Manuel, 'La economía agrícola en la region de el Bajío', *Problemas agrícolas é industriales de México* VIII (Mexico, 1965).

Chayanov, A. V., *On the Theory of Peasant Economy* (ed. Daniel Thorner, Homewood, Illinois, 1966)

Chevalier, François, *La formación de los grandes latifundios en México* (Mexico, 1956)

Colegio de México, *Dinámica de la población de México* (Mexico, 1970)

Cook, Sherburne F. and Woodrow Borah, *Essays in Population History: Mexico and the Caribbean* (2 vols., Berkeley and Los Angeles, 1971–74)

Cooper, Donald B., *Epidemic Disease in Mexico City 1761–1813* (Austin, Texas, 1965)

Eversley, D. E. C., 'A Survey of Population in an Area of Worcestershire from 1600 to 1850 on the basis of Parish Registers', in *Population in History* (ed. D. V. Glass and D. E. C. Eversley, London, 1965)

Fernández del Castillo, Francisco, *Los viajes de don Francisco Javier de Balmis* (Mexico, 1960)

Florescano, Enrique, *Estructuras agrarias de México 1500–1821* (Sep-Setentas, Mexico, 1971)

Florescano, Enrique (ed.) *Haciendas, latifundios y plantaciones en América Latina* (Mexico, 1975)

*Precios de maíz y crisis agrícolas en México 1708–1810* (Mexico, 1969)

Frank, Andre Gunder, *Capitalism and Underdevelopment in Latin America* (New York, 1967)

Garcilaso de la Vega, El Inca, *La Florida del Inca* (Mexico, 1956)

Galicia Morales, Silvia, *Precios y producción en San Miguel el Grande* (Dissertation, UNAM, Mexico, 1975)

Gerhard, Peter, *A Guide to the Historical Geography of New Spain* (Cambridge, 1972)

Gibson, Charles, *The Aztecs under Spanish Rule* (Stanford, 1964)

González, Luis, *Pueblo en vilo* (Mexico, 1968)

González, Pedro, *Estudio sobre estadística agrícola del estado de Guanajuato* (Guanajuato, 1903)

Hall, Peter (ed.) *Von Thünen's Isolated State* (London, 1966)

Hamnett, Brian, *Politics and Trade in Southern Mexico 1750–1821* (Cambridge, 1971)

Harris, Charles H. III, *A Mexican Family. The Latifundio of the Sánchez Navarro Family 1765–1867* (Austin, Texas, 1975)

Haynal, J., 'European Marriage Patterns in Perspective' in *Population in History* (ed. D. V. Glass and D. E. C. Eversley, London, 1965)

Humboldt, Alexander von, *Ensayo político sobre el reino de la Nueva España* (ed. Juan A. Ortega y Medina, Mexico, 1966)

Inclán, Luis G., *Astucia* (3 vols., Mexico, 1946)

Israel, J. I., *Race, Class and Politics in Colonial Mexico 1600–1670* (Oxford, 1975)

Jiménez Moreno, Wigberto, *Estudios de historia colonial* (Mexico, 1958)

Jovellanos, Gaspar Melchor de, *Informe...de ley agraria* (Madrid, 1820)

Katz, Frederick, 'Labour Conditions on Haciendas in Porfirian Mexico: Some Trends and Tendencies', *Hispanic American Historical Review* 54 (1974) pp. 1–47

Kay, Cristóbal, 'Comparative Development of European Manorial System and the Latin American Hacienda System', *The Journal of Peasant Studies* 2 (1974) pp. 69–98.

Kula, Witold, *Théorie Economique du Systeme Féodal* (Paris, 1970)

Laur, M. P., 'De la métalurgie de l'argent au Mexique', *Annales des Mines*, 6th series, 20 (1871) pp. 38–317

Leal, Edmundo, *Carta catastral del distrito de León, año de 1920* (Mexico, 1921)

López Lara, Ramón (ed.), *El obispado de Michoacán en el siglo XVII* (Morelia, 1973)

McBride, G. M., *The Land Systems of Mexico* (New York, 1923)

Macleod, Murdo J., *Spanish Central America. A social and economic history 1520–1720* (Berkeley and Los Angeles, 1973)

Malo Zozaya, Miguel J., *La casa y mayorazgo de la Canal de la villa de San Miguel el Grande* (Mexico, 1962)

Manrique, Luis, *Brevísima relación histórica...de León* (León, 1854)

Marmolejo, Lucio, *Efemérides guanajuatenses* (4 vols., Guanajuato, 1884)

Martínez Alier, Juan, *Los huacchilleros del Perú* (Lima, 1973)

Martínez Cosío, Leopoldo, *Las caballeros de las órdenes militares en México* (Mexico, 1946)

Marx, Karl, *Pre-Capitalist Economic Formations* (ed. Eric J. Hobsbawm, New York, 1966)

Meyer, Jean, *The Cristero Rebellion* (Cambridge, 1976)

Miranda, José, 'La población indígena de México en el siglo XVII', *Historia mexicana* 12 (1963) pp. 182–89.

Molina Enríquez, Andrés, *Los grandes problemas nacionales* (Mexico, 1909)

Morfi, Fray Agustín de, *Viaje de Indias y diario de Nuevo México* (ed., Vito Alessio Robles, Mexico, 1935)

Morin, Claude, *Croissance et disparite sociales dans une economie coloniale: Le centre-ouest mexicain au XVIIIᵉ siècle* (Thèse du doctorat de troisième cycle, Paris, 1974)

   'Population et épidémies dans une paroise mexicaine: Santa Inés Zacatelco xviiiᵉ–xixᵉ siècles', *Cahiers des Ameriques Latines* 6 (1972) pp. 43–73.

   *Santa Inés Zacatelco 1646–1812* (Mexico, 1973)

   'Sens et portée du xviiiᵉ siècle en Amérique latine: le cas du Centre-Ouest mexicain', *Historical Papers* (Canadian Historical Association, Ottawa, 1976)

Muñoz Ledo, Manuel, *Memoria del estado de Guanajuato* (Guanajuato, 1882)

Navarro y Noriega, Fernando, *Memoria sobre la población del reino de la Nueva España* (Mexico, 1954)

Orozco, Wistano Luis, *Legislación y jurisprudencia sobre terrenos baldíos* (2 vols., Mexico, 1895)

Ortega y Pérez Gallardo, Ricardo, *Historia genealógica de las familias más antiguas de México* (3 vols., Mexico, 1908–10)

Ots de Capdequí, José María, *Historia de América: Instituciones* (Barcelona and Madrid, 1959)

Poinsett, Joel, *Notes on Mexico* (London, 1825)

Potash, Robert A., *El banco de avío de México* (Mexico, 1959)

Powell, P. W., *Soldiers, Indians and Silver* (Berkeley and Los Angeles, 1969)

Powell, T. G., *El liberalismo y el campesinado en el centro de México 1850 a 1876* (Sep-Setentas, Mexico, 1974)

Preust, O., *Estadística agrícola* (Mexico, 1910)

Rabel Romero, Cecilia Andrea, *San Luis de la Paz: estudio de economía y demografía históricas 1645–1810* (Dissertation, INAH, Mexico, 1975)

Ramos Arizpe, Miguel, *Memoria sobre el estado de las provincias internas de oriente* (Mexico, 1932)

Randell, Robert W., *Real del Monte. A British Mining Venture in Mexico* (Austin, Texas, 1972)

Raso, José Antonio del, *Notas estadísticas del departamento de Querétaro* (Mexico, 1848)

Rojas, Pedro, *Acámbaro colonial* (Mexico, 1967)

Rosa, Luis de la, *Observaciones sobre. . .Zacatecas* (Mexico, 1851)

Rubio Mañé, J. Ignacio, *Gente de España en la ciudad de México. Año de 1689* (Mexico, 1966)

Salceda López, Eduardo, 'La fundación de San Miguel de la Corona', *Boletín* v (AHM, León, 1969) no. 54.

Sartorious, Carl, *Mexico about 1850* (reprint, Stuttgart, 1961)

Silva Herzog, Jesus, *El agrarismo mexicano y la reforma agraria* (Mexico, 1959)

*Relaciones estadísticas de Nueva España de principios del siglo XIX* (Mexico, 1944)

Solís Leopoldo, *La realidad económica mexicana: retrovisión y perspectivas* (Mexico, 1970)

Super, John C., 'Querétaro Obrajes: Industry and Society in Provincial Mexico 1600–1810', *Hispanic American Historical Review* 56 (1976) pp. 197–216

  *Querétaro: Society and Economy in Early Provincial Mexico* (doctoral dissertation, University of California, Los Angeles, 1973)

Tamayo, Jorge L., *El problema fundamental de la agricultura mexicana* (Mexico, 1964)

Tannenbaum, Frank, *The Mexican Agrarian Revolution* (Washington, 1930)

Taylor, Paul S., *A Spanish–Mexican Peasant Community. Arandas in Jalisco* (Berkeley and Los Angeles, 1933)

Taylor, William B., *Landlord and Peasant in Colonial Oaxaca* (Stanford, 1972)

Tena Ramírez, Felipe, *Leyes fundamentales de México 1808–1967* (Mexico, 1967)

Vera, Melchor, *Salvatierra* (Guanajuato, 1944)

Wagner, Philip L., 'Natural Vegetation of Middle America', in *Handbook of Middle American Indians* (ed. Robert Wauchope, Texas, 1964) vol. 1.

Ward, H. G., *Mexico in 1827* (2 vols., London, 1828)

West, Robert C., 'Surface Configuration and Associated Geology of Middle America', in *Handbook of Middle American Indians. I.* (ed., Robert Wauchope, Austin, Texas, 1964)

Wolf, Eric R., 'The Mexican Bajío in the 18th century: an analysis of cultural integration', in *Synoptic Studies of Mexican Culture* (ed., Munro S. Edmundson, New Orleans, 1957)

Zavala, Silvio A., *Estudios indianos* (Mexico, 1948)

Zarco, Francisco, *Historia del congreso constituyente 1856–57* (Mexico, 1956)

Zelaa e Hidalgo, José María, *Glorias de Querétaro* (Mexico, 1803)

# Index

Acámbaro, 15
Acatzingo, 176–8
Aguilar Ventosillo family, 122–3
Aguilera family, 168–9
Alamán, Lucas, 172, 202
Alcocer family, 24,135; Guadalupe, 214
Alfaro family, 153
Almaguer family, 154, 164–7
Altamira, Marquis of, 23
Altos, Los, 203; see Jalpa and Las
  Arandas
Amortisation, see consolidation
Anglo-Mexican Mining Company,
  136, 140
Apaseo, 13, 16, 37
Arandas, Las, 23, 149, 203
Arcocha, Francisco de, 170; see
  Herrera Arcocha family
Arrendatarios, 5; in Chile, 7; in
  Mexico, 9–12; in Pénjamo, 25–7,
  33; in Querétaro, 36–8; in León,
  73–4; on haciendas, 102–3, 107–
  10, 138; as a class, 151, 157, 168–
  9, 173; their rents, 197–8; buying
  land, 203, 205–6
Arriaga, Ponciano, 2
Arroyo, Simón Eugenio de, 134
Atongo, 198
Austri family, as estate owners, 116–
  17; origins, 123–5; partition of
  estates, 127–8, 143–4; genealogy,
  219–20
Austri, José de, 121, 123–5, 135, 143,
  168–9, 177

Bajío, landscape and climate, 13–14;
  early settlement, 15–17; population, 18–19; agriculture, 20–1;
  estates, 21–2; mercedes, 17, 27,
  29, 31; structure of production,
  37–8; fall in earnings, 197–9;
  Insurgency, 200–3; in Porfiriato,
  205; land reform, 205, 216; 44,

58, 65, 67, 76–7, 124, 144, 149,
  173, 179, 186
Baltierra, Cristóbal, 157
Basques, 148, 215
Bazant, Jan, 5, 37, 203
Borah, Woodrow, 41, 176, 179
Bourbon Mexico, interpretations,
  174–9; State, 202
Braniff family, 210
Busto y Moya, Nicolás, 134

Cabrera, Inés de, 27
Cacho Ramírez, Leonicio, 156–7
Caciques, 5, 160
Cadereyta, 34
Calles, Plutarco Elías, 208, 211
Calvo, Tomás, 176–8
Camargo, 126
Camilian Fathers, 22–5, 203
Cañada de Alfaro, 153
Cañada de Negros hacienda, 76, 79,
  80–1, 92; owners, 117, 132–3;
  values, 138–40
Canal, Tomás Manuel de la, 29, 121
Candelas family, 167–8
Capitalism, 6–7
Cárdenas, Lázaro, 207, 211–12, 215
Carmagnani, Marcello, 7
Carrillo Altamirano, Hernán, 30
Castañeda, Juan de, 159
Castas, 41, 43; intermarriage, 44–7;
  baptisms and burials, 52–8, 178–9;
  188, 191–2, 199
Castilla, Agustín de, 152; Luis de,
  27, 30; Pedro Lorenzo de, 30
Castilla Calvo, Pedro de, 152
Castillos, Los, 64, 152–3, 170
Catorce, 115, 138–40, 204
Celaya, 14–19, 22, 67, 128, 150, 198
Cerrito de Jerez hacienda, 61–3, 80,
  92, 116–17, 121–2, 135
Cerrogordo hacienda, 61, 80–2, 92,
  116, 144–5, 161–3, 170

Chamacuero, 198
Chayanov, A. V., 6–7, 10
Chevalier, François, 1, 4, 150, 203
Chichimecas, 14–15, 27, 39
Chile, 7, 16
Cholera, 186–8
Church, mortmain, 1–2; mortgages, 5, 28, 30, 34, 37; mortgages in León, 91–4, 108, 113, 118, 123–5, 128, 133, 140; estate ownership, 123; estate embargo, 127, 132; *see* Jesuits, Oratory, Santa Clara and Valladolid
Coahuila, 15, 18, 20, 201
Coecillo village, 39–40, 62, 130, 153–4, 208
Comanja, 122–3, 142, 171
Comanjillas, 140
*Composición*, 17, 28, 61, 95, 104, 121, 126, 152
Concepción rancho, 164, 166–7; convent, 28
Consolidation, 135, 139, 143
Consulado, 193–4
Contreras, José Francisco de, 136–8
Cook, Sherburne F., 41, 176, 178
Cooper, Donald B., 177, 186, 189
Corcuera *hermanos*, 208
Corralejo hacienda, 22–6, 55, 203
Creoles, 115, 122, 142; spendthrift, 127–8, 131; as merchants, 131; as landowners, 133, 146; as rancheros, 162–4; *see* Spaniards
Cristeros, 208, 214
Cuerámaro hacienda, 22–6, 203
Cuitzeo hacienda, 23, 25–6, 140, 203

Dams, 25, 28–9, 67; in León, 81, 88–9, 214, 216
Debt peonage, 4–5; weakness, 9; in reverse, 24–6, 36; in León, 76–7, 97, 102, 110
Díaz, Porfirio, 148, 205
Diez de Bracamonte, Juan, 28
Diez Quijano family, 141–2; José Manuel de, 142
Doblado, Manuel, 142, 204
Dolores Hidalgo, 1, 17, 29–31, 33, 69
Domínguez, Miguel, 38; Pedro Antonio, 141
Duarte hacienda, 61–2; maize yields, 65–7, 71, 78; land clearance, 80; mortgage, 92; inventory, 96; production, 97–100; workers and tenants, 102; profits, 102–4; owners, 116, 130–2; sharecroppers, 206; partition, 209; 136, 140, 150, 173, 201
Durán, Miguel, 169–70
Durango, 15, 146

Echeveste, Domingo, 152, 169, 170
Ejidos, 16, 150, 207–17
encomiendas, 3, 7–8, 16, 27
Erre, La, 1, 29, 31–3
Estancias, 12, 17, 62–3

Fagoaga, José Mariá de, 140
Falcón, Gregorio, 152–3
Fanega de sembradura, 66–7; rents, 74–5, 102–3, 107; sales, 153, 157
Florescano, Enrique, 10, 176, 179, 184, 189, 194
Frank, A. G., 6
Fuente, Francisco de la, 126; Blas de la, 164; Andrés de la, 164–5; family, 164–7
Fuentes, José María, 157
Fuentes de Medina hacienda, 80, 92, 116–17, 146–7

Galván de Rojas, Hernando, 159
Gálvez, José de, 54–5, 174
Garciá, Francisco, 203
Garza, Genaro de la, 141
Gavia hacienda, 41, 61–4; tenants, 74, 157–9; land values, 79–84; owners, 116–17; formation, 121–4; partition, 127–8, 143–4; 92, 203
Gibson, Charles, 4, 184, 189
Gómez, Los, 74, 161–2, 145, 170; Esteban and Lázaro, 161–2
Gómez Poleo, Ignacio, 133
González, Luis, 6, 38, 149; Pedro, 66–7; 143
González del Pinal, Miguel, 64, 121–4, 145, 160, 177
Granjeno, 61–2, 121, 124, 160
Guadalajara, 140
Guadalupe rancho, 165–7
Guanajuato, 13–14, 16, 18, 30–1, 39–41, 44, 47, 58, 64, 77, 93, 101, 115, 123, 125, 135–7, 141, 164, 170–1, 175, 177, 183, 201, 202; intendency, 19, 41, 194; state, 66, 149, 171, 205, 208–9, 216
Guerrero, Diego Francisco, 146–7; Lucas, 148, 204; María, 215; family, 117, 145–8

Haciendas, general character, 1–12; in Bajío, 17, 21–2; in Pénjamo, 22–7; of Mariscal de Castilla, 29–34; Jalpa, 27–9; Juchitlán, 34–7; origins in León, 61–5; production, 72–6; organisation, 76–9; land values, 79–85, 89; leases, 89–91; church mortgages, 91–4; Duarte, 95–104; Otates, 104–8; Sauz de Armenta, 108–14; turnover in ownership, 115–19; sales, 120–2; merchant owners, 123–8; Marmolejo family estates, 129–34; Guanajuato miners, 134–41; Church ownership, 142–3; partition of estates, 143–4; rancheros, 145–8; absorption of ranchos, 158–61; increase in rents, 197–9; partition after Independence, 202–4; in Porfiriato, 204; sharecropping, 206; partition into ejidos, 208–17
Harris, Charles, 201
Hernández, Los, 64, 154–5, 157; Nicolás, 153
Herrera Arcocha family, 116, 144–5, 163, 170
Herrera Calderón, Francisco, 160–1
Hidalgo y Costilla, Cristóbal, 24
Hidalgo Rebellion, 44, 57, 176, 200–1
Hinojosa family, 134
Hoya hacienda, 61, 92–3, 116–17, 123, 141–3, 205
Hoyos, José Ramon, 143
Huango, 16, 27
Humboldt, Alexander von, 13, 15, 58, 65, 174, 819

Ibarrilla hacienda, 61, 63, 116–17, 126–8, 141, 159, 170
Independence, 42–3, 51–2, 58, 82, 89–90, 93–4, 107, 139, 144, 163, 168, 201
Indians, 3–5, 7–10; settlements in Bajío, 14–17, 19, 33; as tenants, 36, 38; in León, 39, 41; intermarriages, 44–7; age of marriage, 47–50; baptisms, and burials, 52–8; 125, 146; as rancheros, 152–5; sale of lands, 159–60, 166; demographic crisis, 178–9; maize rations, 184; epidemics, 189–9, 191–2; 199, 207
Insurgency, 88–9, 91–2, 95, 97, 101, 106, 134, 136, 141–4, 167–71, 175–6, 200–2

Irapuato, 23, 30–1
Istla, 37

Jagüey hacienda, 79, 83, 116–7, 177, 138
Jalisco, 5, 17, 23, 27, 31, 144, 149, 178, 203
Jalpa hacienda, 27–9, 132, 203, 210–11
Jaral, 1
Jerez, 2
Jesuits, 93, 123, 141, 143
Jovellanos, Gaspar Melchor de, 1, 3
Juchitlán el Grande, 34–7

Kula, Wittold, 7

Laborcita, 73, 170–1
*Labores*, 16, 62–4, 123, 129–30, 132, 134, 145, 150–1, 159, 162, 168, 170–2
Lagos, Santa María de, 27, 44, 120, 129, 132–3, 139–40, 170
Lagunillas hacienda, 61–2, 80–1, 90, 92, 121–2, 136–8, 162, 193
Land values, 79–85, 126, 137–8, 197–8
Laurel, 61, 162
León, foundations, 39–41; occupations in town, 40; census, 41–2; parish registers, 43–4; marriages, 44–50; baptisms and burials, 50–8; population increase, 58–60; estates, 61–5; agriculture, 66–74; *arrendatarios*, 74–6; debt peonage, 76; livestock, 77–9; land clearance, 79–81; estate values, 82–9; Church mortgages, 91–4; three haciendas, 95–114; estate owners, 115–20; merchants and miners, 123–41; partition of estates, 143–4; rancheros, 149; Indians, mestizos and mulattoes as rancheros, 152–7; absorption of ranchos, 158–62; Creole rancheros, 162–71; maize prices and epidemics, 180–9; the 1785–86 crisis, 189–92; price movements, 194–7; fall in real earnings, 197–200; partition of haciendas, 203, 205; sharecropping, 206, 209–10; formation of ejidos, 208–17
León, river, 62, 65, 67, 73, 81, 134
Lerma, river, 14, 16, 179
Liceaga family, 144

Llerana, 122, 125
López de Lara, Andrés, 120; Rafael, 122
Losa, Gerónimo and Gaspar, 122, 162
Losa hacienda, 61, 63; tenants, 75; oxen, 77, 80, 92–3, 121; formation, 122–3; owners, 116–17, 141–3; sharecroppers, 205–6
Luna y Arellano, Carlos, 30

McBride, G. M., 3, 149
Macleod, M., 9
Magueyes, 34, 37, 67, 96, 101
Maize, rations, 9; prices, 10; sharecropping, 12; climate, 14; production in Bajío, 20–1; harvests, 22; in Jalpa, 29; in Juchitlán, 35; yields in León, 65–7; production in León-Silao, 180–5; 1785 harvest failure, 189–92; rising prices, 194–7; sharecropping in, 206
Malthusian, 60, 200
Mariscal de Castilla, 22–3, 29–34, 64, 116–17, 119, 177
Markassusa Bernal, Carlos, 214
Marmolejo, Francisco Cristóbal, 131–2; Francisco Javier, 132–3; Cristóbal, 130–2, 170; Pedro, 129; Gregorio, 162; family, 116–17, 129–34, 218
Marx, Karl, 8
Matlazahuatl, 56, 176–7, 185–9
Mayorazgo, 29
Mayordomos, 23–4, 40, 75, 134, 145, 161, 163, 170, 173, 200
Medina family, 170
Mejía Altamirano, Rodrigo, 30; Juana, 30
Menchaca, Teresa de, 130
Mercedes, 17, 27; in Bajío, 29–31; of haciendas, 61, 95, 120–1, 134
Merchants, of Mexico City, 8, 28–9; of silver, 23, 25; in León, 115, 122; as hacendados, 123–7, 142; creoles, 130–2; 172, 175, 193
Meso-America, 14–15, 179
Mestizos, 19; marriages, 44–7; 55, 125; as rancheros, 126, 155–6, 160–2, 169, 207; increase, 178–9
Mexico City, 17, 23, 27–9, 31, 61, 78, 121–3, 131, 139, 164, 175–7, 186, 193–4, 199, 201, 214, 216
Michoacán, 5–6, 17–18, 68, 149, 178–9, 203

Mina, Javier, 97, 103, 200
Miners, 28, 115, 122–3, 127, 130; from Guanajuato, 134–41; from Comanja, 122–3, 170–1; 141, 146, 204
Mining Industry, 4, 10, 14–15; production at Guanajuato, 18, 135–8; at Comanja, 122–3; at Catorce, 138–41; in Mexico, 175, 192–3; crisis, 201–2
Mixteca Alta, 176, 178
Molina Enríquez, Andrés, 2–4, 6, 10–11, 47, 149
Monte, El, 62, 150
Monterde y Antillón, Jerónimo de, 28; José Luis de, 28–9; Rafael de, 55; family, 121
Mora, José, 198
Morelia, 20; see Valladolid
Morelos, 208, 216
Morfi, Juan Agustín de, 1
Morin, Claude, 19, 42, 176–8
Muciño, Baltazar, 197–8
Mulattoes, 19, 24, 33; as rancheros, 126, 152, 157, 160, 192; in León: designation, 44; marriages, 44–50; burials and baptisms, 52–8
Mules, breeding, 71, 79; values, 86–8; teams, 77–8, 101, 131–3, 164; prices, 194
Muñoz Ledo, Bernardo, 169–70; Antonio, 171; family, 170–1

Naranjos, Los, 130, 132, 168
New Galicia, 178–9; see Jalisco
New León, 18, 20, 28–9
Nuñez del Prado, Juan José, 156

Oaxaca, 5, 93
Obregón family, estates, 116–17; origins, 122; wealth, 135–41, 203–4; genealogy, 203–4
Obregón y Alcocer, Antonio de, 135; Lorenzo, 139–40; María Antonia, 136–8
Obregón y Alcocer, Antonio de 135; see Valenciana
Obregón y Arce, Alfonso de, 122–3, 175; Estefanía, 123
Olaéz, Los, 155
Oratory, 93, 123, 142–3
Orozco, Wistano Luis, 2–3, 149
Ortiz Saavedra, Diego, 27

Otates hacienda, 61–2, 73; oxen, 77; dams, 80–1; values, 82, 84–5, 88; rents, 90, 92; tithes, 104; inventory, 105; accounts, 106; workers and tenants, 107; owners, 116, 129, 140, 150, 173, 201, 205; partition, 208–9
Otero, Concepción de, 138; Manuel de, 175
Otomies, 15, 39, 153
Oxen, breeding, 71; prices, 77; values, 85–6; on haciendas, 101, 104–5, 108–10; 24–8

Palacios, Francisco Aniceto, 43
Palma, 61, 76, 81, 93, 131
Palote hacienda, 71; mayordomo, 75; peon debts, 76–7; mules, 78; land clearance, 80–1; land values, 84–5, 88; church mortgages, 92–3; owners, 116–17, 130–1, 133, 142–3, 162, 205
Partido, 175, 199–200
Párvulos, 56–8, 188–9
Patiña rancho, 67, 126, 145, 151, 163, 165
Pedregal, San Angel, 76, 80, 93, 117, 121, 138–40
Peninsulars, 115, 123–6, 128, 131, 133, 141–2, 170, 200
Pénjamo, 15, 17, 22–6, 29, 31, 39, 41, 77, 135, 140, 144, 203
Peñuelas, 91, 93, 117
Peons, 3–4, 9–10; in Pénjamo, 25–6; on haciendas, 35–8; debts, 76–7; on haciendas, 97–100, 102, 107, 110, 113; wages, 196–7, 202; work, 198–9, 206
Pérez de Bocanegra, Hernán, 16
Pérez family, 160
Piscina, 156
Poinsett, Joel, 13, 15
Pompa, Antonio de la, 124, 160; Pablo, 104–5
Pompa hacienda, 63, 81, 88, 92, 116–17, 124, 136, 160, 193, 205
Porfiriato, 205
Portes Gil, Emilio, 209, 211
Positivists, 3, 6
Potrero hacienda, 61, 82, 92, 117, 124
Presa de Jalpa, Count of, 28–9
Puebla, 79, 216
Puente, Antonio, 155–6

Querétaro, 10, 13, 15–19, 34, 38, 65, 69, 125, 128, 198, 201–2
Quijas, Diego Clemente de, 129; family, 104

Rabel Romero, Cecilia, 22, 58, 176–7
Ramírez family, 153–4, 157, 158, 166
Rancheros, 1–3, 6, 10; in Bajío, 38; 72–3, 125–6; as a class, 149–51; in León, 149–73; mulattoes, 152, 157, 160; Indians, 152–5; mestizos, 155–6, 162; creoles, 162–73; loss of lands, 158–62, 193; in Los Altos, 203; in Revolution, 208, 217
Ranchos, in Bajío, 16–18, 21–2; in Pénjamo, 22–8, 38; in León, 62–4, 73–6, 122–5, 145–7; number in Mexico, 149; origins in Bajío, 149–50; in León, 149–73, 205, 216
Rayas mine, 28, 134
Reforma, 21, 25, 93–4, 118, 125, 143, 149, 203
Repartimientos, 3, 8
Rico family, 160, 163
Rincón, 39, 41–2, 44, 64, 69, 74–5, 79–82, 91–33, 120, 127, 132, 135–6, 139, 145–7, 155–6, 160, 165, 209
Río Turbio, 30–1, 61
Romero, José Guadalupe, 41–2, 59, 189
Romita, 124

Salamanca, 13, 16, 18
Salvatierra, 16–17, 150
San Cayetano, 170
Sánchez Navarro estates, 201
Sánchez, Pedro, 165, 167
Sánchez de Tagle family, 23
San Clemente, Marquis of, 123, 130, 134
San Cristóbal hacienda, 74–5, 80–1, 91, 93, 138–9
Sandía hacienda, tenants, 75; dam, 81; value, 83, 90; mortgages, 92; owners, 116–17, 128, 136–8, 148, 173; sharecropping, 204–6; partition, 215–16
San Felipe, 16, 129
San Jorge, 167–8
San José del Cerrito, 145, 170
San Juan de Abajo, 143, 210
San Luis de la Paz, 19–20, 22, 58, 69, 176–8

San Luis Potosí, 5, 15, 37, 135, 139, 160, 201–2

San Miguel village, 39–40, 62, 153–4, 208

San Miguel el Grande, 16, 18, 20, 29, 33, 69, 121, 130, 191, 201

San Nicolás hacienda, 63; its wheat, 73; tenants, 75; leasing of estate, 90, 92, 169; owners, 116–17; formation, 125, 128, 158–60, 193; partition, 205

San Nicolás de Arriba y Abajo hacienda, 92; owners, 116–17; formation, 123–4, 127; partition, 143, 203

San Pedro del Monte hacienda, 63; maize yields, 65; mortgages, 92; owners, 116–17; formation, 126, 136–8, 159, 161; leases, 169–71, 193; partition, 210

San Pedro Piedragorda, 20, 23, 27, 39, 41, 69, 127, 168, 203, 210

San Roque, 155–6

Santa Ana hacienda, 41, 61; land clearance, 79–81; value, 90; Church mortgages, 92; owners, 116–17; formation, 123–4, 127; values, 136–8; 168, 173; partition, 215–16

Santa Ana Pacueco, 22–4, 26, 203

Santa Clara convent, 16, 30, 91, 93, 125, 133

Santa Lucía, 161, 169

Santander, 122, 125–6, 141, 144

Santa Rosa hacienda, 61–3, 74, 81; tenants, 74, 90, 91; owners, 116–17, 134–8; 150, 160, 169; rents, 197–8, 205; sharecropping, 206; partition, 214–15

Santa Rosalía, 163, 171

Sapos, Los, 61, 74, 78, 93, 121

Sardaneta *labor*, 141

Sardaneta, Pedro de, 134; José Mariano de, 135; family, 134–5, 147

Sardina, 148

Sarteneja hacienda, 74, 80–1, 93, 117

Sartuche, Francisco, 160

Sauces hacienda, 61, 75, 92, 164, 167, 205, 208

Sauz de Armenta hacienda, Church mortgages, 93; area, 108; inventory, 109; tenants, 110; accounts, 111–13; owners, 117, 134, 147; partition, 209

Septién family, 124–6; partial genealogy, 219–20

Septién y Montero, Agustín de, 73, 116–17, 125–6, 145, 158–9, 163, 170, 175, 177; José Ildefonso, 128; Manuel de, 124–5; Martín de, 132, 175; Pedro de, 128

Seville, 133

Sharecroppers, 12, 38; in León, 74–5; on haciendas, 103, 151, 173; prevalence, 202, 205–6; on ejidos, 209–10

Sierra de Pinos, 78, 129

Silao, 13, 31, 41, 44, 61–2, 68, 121, 124, 131, 154, 157, 201; maize harvests, 20, 69–71, 178, 180–3, 189–90, 194

Smallpox, 56, 176–7, 185–9, 191

Solís sisters, 64

Somera, José Cristóbal, 142; José Manuel, 142

Spaniards, as settlers, 15–17; in León, 41; marriages, 44–50; baptisms and burials, 52–8; as landowners, 115–48; as rancheros, 162–73; in epidemics, 191, 199; *see* Creoles and Peninsulars

Talayote hacienda, 81, 93, 121, 117, 145–8, 165

Tanques, Los, 121

Tapia, Diego de, 16

Tarascans, 14–15, 39, 153

Taylor, William B., 5

Tepetates, 62, 126, 150, 160–1, 166, 168–9, 171

Terrero, 137–8

Thünen, J. H. von, 20

Tithes, 26, 32, 68–70; collectors, 127–8, 174; annual payments, 180–3

Toluca, 205

Torres, Hilario, 209

Tuna Agria, San Vicente, 143

United States, 202

Urenda, Pedro, 160–1; Domingo, 169

Urquieta, Matías de, 161, 169

Urruchúa, Isabel de, 132, 140

Urteaga Septién, Miguel, 205

Valenciana, first count of, 83, 126, 135–6, 144, 177–8, 215; second count of, 81, 90, 136–7, 143, 169–70, 173, 204; dowager countess of, 123, 139, 141, 171

Valenciana mine, 135–6, 141, 171, 201, 204

Valladolid, 20, 68, 91, 125, 127, 190; bishop of, 41, 191

Vallecarriedo, 141

Valle de Santiago, 171

Velasco y Palacios, Juan de, 215

Veracruz, 193

Villamor, Francisco de, 128, 139, 144

Villaseñor, Juan de, 15, 27

Ward, H. G., 1, 13

Wheat, 11, 14, 20, 24–5, 29; seed yields, 67; production in León, 70–1, 73

Yuriria, 22

Zacatecas, 15–18, 78, 129, 135, 175, 178, 203

Zacatelco, Santa Inés, 176–8

Zavala, Silvio, 3

# CAMBRIDGE LATIN AMERICAN STUDIES

1   Simon Collier. *Ideas and Politics of Chilean Independence, 1808–1833*
2   Michael P. Costeloe. *Church Wealth in Mexico: A study of the Juzgado de Capellanías in the Archbishopric of Mexico, 1800–1856*
3   Peter Calvert. *The Mexican Revolution, 1910–1914: The Diplomacy of Anglo-American Conflict*
4   Richard Graham. *Britain and the Onset of Modernization in Brazil, 1850–1914*
5   Herbert S. Klein. *Parties and Political Change in Bolivia, 1880–1952*
6   Leslie Bethell. *The Abolition of the Brazilian Slave Trade: Britain, Brazil and the Slave Trade Question, 1807–1869*
7   David Barkin and Timothy King. *Regional Economic Development: The River Basin Approach in Mexico*
8   Celso Furtado. *Economic Development of Latin America: Historical Background and Contemporary Problems* (second edition)
9   William Paul McGreevey. *An Economic History of Colombia, 1845–1930*
10  D. A. Brading. *Miners and Merchants in Bourbon Mexico, 1763–1810*
11  Jan Bazant. *Alienation of Church Wealth in Mexico: Social and Economic Aspects of the Liberal Revolution, 1856–1875*
12  Brian R. Hamnett. *Politics and Trade in Southern Mexico, 1750–1821*
13  J. Valerie Fifer. *Bolivia: Land, Location, and Politics since 1825*
14  Peter Gerhard. *A Guide to the Historical Geography of New Spain*
15  P. J. Bakewell. *Silver Mining and Society in Colonial Mexico, Zacatecas 1564–1700*
16  Kenneth R. Maxwell. *Conflicts and Conspiracies: Brazil and Portugal, 1750–1808*
17  Verena Martinez-Alier. *Marriage, Class and Colour in Nineteenth-Century Cuba: A Study of Racial Attitudes and Sexual Values in a Slave Society*
18  Tulio Halperin-Donghi. *Politics, Economics and Society in Argentina in the Revolutionary Period*
19  David Rock. *Politics in Argentina 1890–1930: The Rise and Fall of Radicalism*
20  Mario Gongora. *Studies in the Colonial History of Spanish America*
21  Arnold J. Bauer. *Chilean Rural Society from the Spanish Conquest to 1930*
22  James Lockhart and Enrique Otte. *Letters and People of the Spanish Indies: The Sixteenth Century*
23  Leslie B. Rout Jr, *The History of the African in Spanish America from 1502 to the Present Day*
24  Jean A. Meyer. *The Cristero Rebellion: The Mexican People between Church and State, 1926–1929*
25  Stefan de Vylder. *Allende's Chile: The Political economy of the Rise and Fall of the Unidad Popular*
26  Kenneth Duncan and Ian Rutledge with the collaboration of Colin Harding. *Land and Labour in Latin America: Essays on the development of agrarian capitalism in the nineteenth and twentieth centuries*

27 Guillermo Lora, edited by Laurence Whitehead. *A History of the Bolivian Labour Movement, 1848–1971*

28 Victor Nunes Leal. *Coronelismo: The Municipality and Representative Government in Brazil*

29 Anthony Hall. *Drought and Irrigation in North-east Brazil*

30 S. M. Socolow. *The Merchants of Buenos Aires 1778–1810: Family and Commerce*

31 Charles F. Nunn. *Foreign Immigrants in Early Bourbon Mexico, 1700–1760*

32 D. A. Brading. *Haciendas and Ranchos in the Mexican Bajío: León 1700–1860*

33 Billie R. DeWalt. *Modernization in a Mexican Ejido: A Study in Economic Adaptation*